Fawn McKay Brodie

Fawn Brodie in the late 1940s, probably in New Haven/Bethany, where she and her family lived from 1945 to 1950. Courtesy Bruce and Janet Brodie.

Fawn McKay Brodie

A BIOGRAPHER'S LIFE

NEWELL G. BRINGHURST

University of Oklahoma Press : Norman

Also by Newell G. Bringhurst

Saints, Slaves, and Blacks: The Changing Place of Black People within Mormonism (Westport, Conn., 1981)
Brigham Young and the Expanding American Frontier (Boston, 1986)
(ed.) *Reconsidering "No Man Knows My History": Fawn Brodie and Joseph Smith in Retrospect* (Logan, Utah, 1996)

This book is published with the generous assistance of Edith Gaylord Harper.

Library of Congress Cataloging-in-Publication Data

Bringhurst, Newell G.
    Fawn McKay Brodie: a biographer's life / Newell G. Bringhurst.
        p.   cm.
    "Works by Fawn McKay Brodie": p.
    Includes bibliographical references and index.
    ISBN 0-8061-3181-0 (alk. paper)
    1. Brodie, Fawn McKay, 1915–1981.   2. Biographers—United States
Biography.   I. Title.
CT275.B7447B75   1999
920.073—dc21   99-34845
                                                                          CIP

Text design by Gail Carter.

To my two brothers,

Steven Cooper Bringhurst

and

Scott John Bringhurst,

with fraternal fondness

and admiration for the diverse

abilities of each

To write a book is an act of arrogance, and to write a biography is an exaggerated act of arrogance, especially if the biography attempts to do what psychiatrists do—illuminate the inner conflicts, and try to explain patterns of behavior that are established in childhood and persist into adulthood.

FAWN M. BRODIE,
"The Childhood of Richard Nixon"
(unpublished manuscript, n.d.)

Contents

List of Illustrations   xi

Preface   xiii

Acknowledgments   xvii

Introduction   3

1. "An Idyllic Childhood": 1915–1932   7

2. "A Quiet Kind of Moving Out": 1932–1938   45

3. "A Compelling Piece of Detective Work": 1938–1946   71

4. "An Enormously Fulfilling Role": 1946–1959   116

5. "A Fun Book to Write": 1960–1967   155

6. "An Elaborate Psychological Exploration": 1967–1974   185

7. "The Hardest Book": 1974–1981   223

Epilogue: Controversy and Legacy   259

Notes   271

Works by Fawn McKay Brodie   321

Selected Bibliography   325

Index   341

Illustrations

Fawn McKay Brodie in the late 1940s   frontispiece

Fawn McKay as an infant, 1916   9

George H. Brimhall   14

Sketch of the McKay family home, Huntsville, Utah   20

Fawn McKay in 1931 at age 15   38

Fawn McKay in 1935 at age 19   55

Fawn McKay Brodie, August 1936   59

Wedding photograph of Fawn and Bernard Brodie, August 1936   64

Thomas E. and Fawn Brimhall McKay   76

Fawn Brodie with infant son Richard McKay, ca. 1943   79

Fawn Brodie in 1945 at age 30   97

David O. McKay   109

Three generations of the Thomas McKay family, 1953   142

Fawn Brodie, 1955   150

Bernard Brodie, ca. 1974   204

Dale L. Morgan, ca. 1950s   209

Fawn Brodie in 1974 at age 59   216

"Visit the Ruins with Fawn Brodie," a political cartoon, 1981   262

Preface

metaphor

For some thirteen years I was involved in an intense intimate relationship with a woman other than my wife—a relationship that was most stimulating but that generated controversy both within my own family and within the family of the "other woman," as such affairs are prone to do. Actually, I was familiar with the other woman, Fawn McKay Brodie, long before I met my wife. Having been born of Mormon parents and having grown up in Utah during the 1950s, I developed an initially negative, albeit superficial, impression of Fawn Brodie during my youth, seeing her as "that heretic" excommunicated from the Mormon Church for having written *No Man Knows My History*—the controversial biography that presented Joseph Smith, Mormonism's founder, in a somewhat less-than-flattering light.

Why was I motivated to research and write about the life of Fawn Brodie? In searching for an answer to this question, I find insight in the observations of Brodie herself, who noted that "there is always a deep personal commitment in the writing of a biography," including "compelling inner reasons." The subject chosen, she continued, can "tell a lot about [the] biographer." Similar observations have been made by two other writers familiar with the art of biographical writing. Leon Edel, who spent twenty years writing his five-volume life of Henry James, stated that "biographers are invariably drawn to the writing of biography out of some deep personal motive." James Atlas went one step further, suggesting that "the biographer's subject enacts the main themes of the biographer's own life."[1]

These observations, I confess, characterize my literary affair with Fawn M. Brodie. There are clear parallels between my own life and hers. She was born of stalwart Mormon pioneer stock, her ancestors having migrated to Utah during the mid-nineteenth century. Similarly, my own Mormon ancestors migrated west under Brigham Young's direction. Also like Fawn, who grew up in Huntsville, a rural Mormon hamlet ten miles east of Ogden, I was reared in a small Utah town twelve miles south of Salt Lake City. As teenagers, both Fawn McKay and I questioned basic Mormon beliefs. Both of us married outside the Mormon faith. Our basic disbelief was reinforced as a result of careful research into certain disturbing aspects of Mormonism's historical past. In Brodie's case, this involved meticulous research over a period of some seven years into the life of Joseph Smith, which caused her to conclude that Mormonism's founder was a "conscious imposter," a fraud.[2] In my own case, the process involved careful research into the origins and evolution of Mormon practices relative to black people. Like Brodie, I developed a sense of moral outrage at what I saw as the contradictions and tortured reasoning used to justify Mormonism's now-defunct policy of denying priesthood to blacks.[3] In my later historical research I followed Brodie in developing an intense fascination with biography, examining the lives and activities of several noteworthy personalities, including Brigham Young, Samuel Brannan, and Fawn Brodie herself.

As I became more deeply involved in research, I detected one other important element of identification. I was hauntingly reminded of my own late mother in examining certain aspects of Brodie's personality and behavior. Like my mother, Fawn was a caring, empathic individual who considered the welfare and needs of her immediate family first, despite her active quest for knowledge and her strong desire to express herself through writing. Putting her husband and children first, as was expected of all married women in post–World War II America, Fawn, like my own mother, deferred a career in teaching and full-time research and writing until her three children (the same number as in my own birth family) were fully grown. Both Fawn and my mother enjoyed people, eagerly interacting with a wide variety of individuals. Also, both women graduated from the University of Utah with degrees in English, and both with honors. Both were teachers who related well with their students. Finally, and most unfortunately, both died while relatively young; Fawn was sixty-five and my own mother a youthful forty-nine.

My long-term affair with Fawn has affected my own life in a manner not unlike the way Brodie's life was altered as a consequence of her interactions with Joseph Smith, Thaddeus Stevens, Richard F. Burton, Thomas Jefferson, and Richard Nixon—the subjects of her five book-length biographies, written over the course of some forty years. As Frank Vandiver, himself a biographer, has stated, "Biographers lucky enough to live for some time in the company of a character sense a change in their own lives."[4]

Despite my close, intense relationship with Fawn Brodie, I have sought to deal with her life in a comprehensive and objective, yet sensitive, manner. Consistent with the approach of many modern biographies, I have tried to present the whole individual, emphasizing not only her varied accomplishments and contributions as a preeminent biographer but also assessing her frailties, frustrations, and failures—all reflective of the complex, compelling individual she was. I have also tried to deal with one other important recurring question: Why did Fawn Brodie find herself embroiled in controversy throughout her life?

In examining these and other varied aspects of Fawn Brodie's life and career, I have made use of a variety of sources. Brodie's various writings, both published and unpublished—always interesting, often provocative, and sometimes controversial—have been most illuminating and useful. Providing further insights into the inner individual have been unpublished letters and other correspondence between Brodie and family members and close friends. In these Brodie sometimes bared her soul, disclosing deeply held feelings and emotions, including hopes, fears, and anxieties. Also of great value has been information gained through oral interviews of fifty to sixty people, including various members of Brodie's family, her friends, and her acquaintances. In using these materials to weave together the intriguing events of Brodie's life, I have looked to the renowned English biographer Paul Murray Kendall, who stated that the ultimate mission of biography is to "perpetuate" the individual as that individual was in the days he or she lived—to "elicit, from the coldness of paper, the warmth of a life being lived."[5]

Acknowledgments

I am extremely grateful to a number of individuals and institutions who provided significant help and encouragement over the thirteen-year period it took me to research and write this biography. Dr. Gregory Thompson and his staff in the University of Utah's Special Collections were especially helpful as I made use of crucial information in the Brodie papers contained in that library. Equally important, this same staff transcribed some fifty to sixty oral interviews that I conducted with Fawn Brodie's family, friends, and colleagues and in turn made the transcribed information available to me. Also providing critical manuscript information were the following: the Bancroft Library at the University of California, Berkeley; the library of the Utah State Historical Society; the University of California at Los Angeles library; the University of Texas at Austin library; the W. W. Norton library in New York City; the archives at the Brigham Young University library; and the Library-Archives of the Church of Jesus Christ of Latter-day Saints. Also making available to me personal copies of Fawn Brodie's correspondence were the following individuals: Alexander and Juliette George, Charles Hitch, Norris Hundley, Patricia Jensen, Peter Loewenberg, Jan Shipps, Barbara McKay Smith, the late Wallace Stegner, and Sam Weller.

I am especially grateful to the many individuals who knew Fawn McKay Brodie over the course of her life and who allowed me to interview them, thereby providing valuable information and insights unavailable elsewhere. The names of these individuals are noted in the text and/or end-notes throughout this work. Of particular value was the transcript of Shirley E. Stephenson's extensive interview of Fawn Brodie conducted in November 1975. I deeply appreciate Ms. Stephenson's making this important document available to me, along with a copy of an interview she conducted with Flora McKay Jensen Crawford, Fawn Brodie's older sister.

As I started to write up the results of my research in 1988, I received encouragement from the editors of a number of scholarly journals who published my preliminary findings, each allowing me a forum to test my ideas and conclusions. These journals include *Dialogue: A Journal of Mormon Thought, Journal of Mormon History, Utah Historical Quarterly, John Whitmer Historical Association Journal, Pacific Historical Review,* and *California History.*

Also most helpful were the following individuals who read all or part of my manuscript, critiqued it, and offered useful, often insightful sugges-tions for improvement: Lois Cooper Allen, Elaine Andrew, Joseph Barba, Jackson Benson, M. Guy Bishop, George S. Bringhurst, Mary Ann Bringhurst, Steven C. Bringhurst, Pamela Brodie, Ida June Brunner, Craig Foster, Klaus Hansen, Daniel Howe, Peter Loewenberg, Michael Magliari, Jerry Pelovsky, Glen Robertson, Barbara McKay Smith, and Gary Topping.

I am extremely grateful to the University of Oklahoma Press, in particular to John Drayton, Randolph Lewis, and Ursula Smith, whose sagacious editorial skills enabled me to improve significantly the manuscript.

Last but not least, I deeply appreciate the aid and encouragement of my wife, Mary Ann, who patiently tolerated my obsessive affair with Fawn M. Brodie and is now relieved to see the controversial psychobiographer "depart from our midst" after a long, sometimes difficult thirteen years.

Fawn McKay Brodie

Introduction

        During the course of Fawn McKay Brodie's eventful life,
modern biography came of age. Lytton Strachey, the acknowledged
father of modern biography, brought forth his *Eminent Victorians* (1918)
and *Queen Victoria* (1921) shortly after Brodie's birth in 1915. Strachey's
works represented a bold departure from traditional Victorian biography.
Thomas Carlyle, most identified with the traditional form, characterized
the craft of biography as the rendering of "the history [of] great men: to
find these, clean the dirt from them, and place them on their proper
pedestals." Carlyle and his cohorts made biography "the domain of the
unique and exemplary citizen."[1]

By contrast, Lytton Strachey cast a wider net, considering a variety of
biographical subjects and examining their lives in a critical, comprehensive manner. He applied the principles of psychology, combining them
with a "joyous iconoclasm" and "evocative literary form." Through his
"ironic detachment from his material, his lacquered style, his delicacy of
selection and his dramatic touch," Strachey anticipated later biographers,
including Fawn Brodie.[2]

Exerting more direct influence were Sigmund Freud and Erik Erikson.
Inspired by Freud, the father of modern psychiatry, Brodie proclaimed
her best-known biography, *Thomas Jefferson: An Intimate History*, "similar in
spirit to Freud's classic study of the psychosexuality of Leonardo da
Vinci." According to Brodie, Freud admonished biographers to consider

four basic factors. The first was the importance of the subject's childhood and the role of the subject's parents. The second was the subject's sexuality, broadly interpreted to include not just one's sex life but also the capacity for love and hate. A third important factor was the individual's fantasy life; the fourth, behavior emanating from one's unconscious mind.[3]

Brodie was also influenced by the great psychobiographer Erik Erikson, author of the definitive, highly influential *Young Man Luther: A Study in Psychoanalysis and History* (1958). Brodie proclaimed Erikson an "authentic genius" and one of her mentors. In her own biographies, however, she avoided what she dubbed the "clinical language" employed by Erikson and Freud. She was not comfortable with such language, believing it "better left with the clinicians." A large portion of the audience was alienated by the use of clinical language, she asserted, concluding that English itself was so rich as to make any substitute unnecessary.[4]

Brodie's life also encompassed the years in which biography enjoyed ever-increasing popularity. During her formative years, from 1916 to 1930, some 4,800 biographies were published in the United States, an average of more than 300 a year. In 1929 alone, 667 such works were published, marking the height of the era's "biographical boom." Such popularity has increased down to the present. In the 1980s, the number of biographies published each year was double the number published annually in the 1960s. "We read biography the way we used to read novels," biographer Stephen B. Oates noted in 1986. Writing in 1994, psychobiographer Alan C. Elms proclaimed biography as "one of the most popular genres in publishing, with psychobiography being particularly popular.[5]

This popularity continues, even though biography has been scorned in certain intellectual circles as lacking academic legitimacy.[6] Brodie encountered such prejudice when her own work was discounted by certain of her UCLA colleagues. This occurred as her *Thomas Jefferson: An Intimate History* was enjoying immense popularity, appearing on the *New York Times* best-seller list for a total of some thirteen weeks following its publication in 1974.

Such success, completely unexpected, affected and altered the course of Brodie's life. *Thomas Jefferson* secured for its author recognition as a preeminent American biographer. The work encompassed the problems of race, class, and gender—all of particular concern during the late 1960s and early 1970s—but the book's great popularity resulted largely from Brodie's controversial assertion that Jefferson had carried on a long-term sexual relationship with one of his black slaves, Sally Hemings, by whom he fathered seven children. The author refuted the popular view that Thomas Jefferson was incapable of such a relationship, given his avowed antimiscegenation views, or of being intimately involved with any woman other than his wife, Martha Wayles Skelton, who was deceased by the time of his involvement with Hemings. A pathbreaking study, Brodie's *Thomas Jefferson* affected the way subsequent scholars have come to view the American Revolutionary leader and third president. Recent DNA evidence, in fact, proves nearly conclusively that Jefferson fathered at least one child by Hemings, thus vindicating Brodie's earlier assertions.

Even before the appearance of *Thomas Jefferson,* Brodie's three previous biographies had altered prevailing perceptions of their subjects while affecting the course of the author's own life. Her first, *No Man Knows My History: The Life of Joseph Smith,* published in 1945, was a frank portrait of the founder of Mormonism—the childhood faith in which she was raised. In proclaiming Smith a "conscious fraud" rather than a divinely inspired prophet as asserted by devout Latter-day Saints, Brodie was influenced by the climate of iconoclastic skepticism prevalent during the 1930s and 1940s. Her work generated a firestorm of controversy and led to her highly publicized excommunication from the Mormon Church in May 1946. But *No Man Knows My History* inexorably altered the way subsequent scholars viewed the Mormon leader.

Brodie's second biography, *Thaddeus Stevens: Scourge of the South,* published in 1959, was concerned with the most important congressional leader of Radical Reconstruction. This work reflected contemporary concern with the issues of race and the fledgling civil rights movement of the late 1940s and 1950s. Brodie's generally sympathetic portrait of Thaddeus Stevens promoted the revisionist view of American Reconstruction history while refuting the traditionalist, or "Dunning school." The latter, heretofore dominant, had presented Stevens as a vindictive man and the Reconstruction era that he personified as a time of revenge and corruption. Brodie's biography broke new ground in another way in that it was an important piece of psychohistory, reflecting the author's deepening interest in the fields of psychohistory and psychobiography.[7]

Brodie's third biography, *The Devil Drives: A Life of Richard F. Burton,* chronicled the life of the flamboyant, nonconformist, individualistic English explorer-author. Burton manifested often outrageous behavior, including unconventional sexual experimentation. In this work, completed in 1967, Brodie suggested that certain patterns of behavior evident in Burton's life paralleled behaviors of the 1960s, a decade characterized by rebellion. This biography also reflected—and facilitated—Brodie's efforts to come to terms with her own sexuality, a persistent problem since adolescence.

Brodie's final biography, *Richard Nixon: The Shaping of His Character,* published in 1981, was a highly critical presentation in which the author probed the origins of what she saw as the ex-president's deeply flawed personality. Her negative portrait echoed the prevailing climate of opinion in the late 1970s wherein the recently resigned president was held in low esteem, not just by liberal Democrats, including Brodie, but by virtually all Americans. *Richard Nixon,* the most negative of Brodie's biographies, projected the mood of melancholy that dominated the author's final years as she dealt first with her husband's protracted illness and death from cancer and then her own battle with the disease and her struggle to complete the biography before her death.

Each of Brodie's five biographies dealt with an engaging personality. Each presented its subject from a highly provocative perspective. And each, in succession, used an increasingly elaborate psychoanalytical framework in probing what Brodie characterized as the subject's private, or inner, life. By the time of her death in 1981, Brodie was a biographer of international stature.

ONE

"An Idyllic Childhood"

1915–1932

Fawn McKay Brodie fondly recalled her hometown—Huntsville, Utah, fifty miles northeast of Salt Lake City—as a small Mormon village of great beauty situated in a high valley. She remembered the spectacular mountain peaks encircling the larger valley, with majestic pine trees sweeping down from the snowline "in a blue-green carpet to the foothills." The houses were set in neat checkerboard squares, and the streets were lined with Lombardy poplars. Fawn's childhood home, a "wonderful old white house" with fourteen rooms set on a large lot and surrounded by a white picket fence, was "a great place to grow up," she said in later life.[1]

Brodie often characterized her formative years in Huntsville as "idyllic," providing "freedom and . . . affection and [a] sense of belonging to a community." Her son Bruce could not remember his mother saying "a single negative thing" about this childhood she saw as a sort of "Paradise Lost."[2]

FAMILY AND EARLY CHILDHOOD

Such recollections of an idyllic childhood environment are overstated and somewhat misleading. Fawn McKay, the second child of Thomas E. and Fawn Brimhall McKay, was born on 15 September 1915. She grew up in an extremely protected environment, in part because of problems in her physical development. "Fawn was an adorable chubby baby," one old-time family acquaintance recalled, but because of her excessive weight, she was not able to walk until she was fourteen months old. She also suffered from hay fever, which was particularly severe in the spring and summer. Fawn's condition was further complicated by chronic allergies, the probable cause of her frequent sore throats. All this meant trips to the family doctor, Joseph R. Morrell—Fawn's uncle, the husband of her Aunt Jeanette. But her medical treatments were limited because Morrell's practice was located in Ogden, ten miles down the steep, narrow canyon. Huntsville itself lacked a resident physician, and responding to Fawn's varied maladies, the McKay family often resorted to faith healings, whereby Thomas E. McKay and other Mormon brethren would lay their hands on her head and pray that she be made well. "She got the hands on her head a lot more than I did," recalled Fawn's older sister, Flora.[3]

As the subject of these faith healings, Fawn quite naturally became a religious child, but her religiosity also sprang from her stalwart Mormon background. Her paternal great-grandfather, William McKay, along with his immediate family, natives of Scotland, had embraced Mormonism as preached by visiting missionaries, converting to the recently formed American religion in 1850. Shortly thereafter, William and his family left Scotland, migrating to the United States to join their coreligionists in Utah. There the William McKays settled first in Ogden, fifty miles north of Salt Lake City, later moving to Huntsville, where McKay maintained large herds of cattle and sheep for his meat market in Ogden.[4]

Meanwhile, William's son, David, the future author's grandfather, reached adulthood, becoming somewhat of a martinet, having been raised in a highly structured family environment where discipline and motivation were essential virtues. These attributes were, in turn, passed down to subsequent generations of McKays and were clearly manifest within Fawn McKay Brodie's own immediate family.[5]

In time, David McKay fell in love with Jennette Evans, marrying her on 9 April 1867. Jennette Evans was considered one of the most beautiful and popular young women in Ogden. Her physical beauty was matched with an engaging personality: though high spirited and strong willed, she was also even-tempered and self-possessed. With dark brown eyes that

Earliest known photograph of Fawn McKay, less than one year old, taken in May 1916 on the front porch of the old Huntsville home. She is the baby to the left held by her paternal grandfather, David McKay. Reprinted by permission, Utah State Historical Society, all rights reserved.

expressed any rising emotion, Jennette exercised a disciplined demeanor that held such feelings under perfect control. These attributes were later to be found in her granddaughter Fawn.[6]

Following their marriage, David and Jennette McKay moved to Huntsville, where the young couple faced the difficulties of life in a rude frontier environment. The newlyweds initially lived in a log cabin on the family property, but shortly after the arrival of their first two children, Margaret and Ellena—born in January 1869 and May 1870, respectively—David and Jennette moved into a much more comfortable dwelling, a five-room, two-story rock house. This would later be incorporated into the fourteen-room structure in which Fawn grew up. Here eight other children were born, including David Oman McKay, a future president of the Mormon Church, on 8 September 1873, and Thomas Evans McKay, the future author's father, on 29 October 1875.[7]

During the 1870s the family prospered economically, thanks to diversified landholdings and good yields during a time of general agricultural prosperity for Utah and the nation. But they also encountered hardship. In 1880, tragedy struck twice with the sickness and sudden deaths of their two oldest children, eleven-year-old Margaret and nine-year-old Ellena. One year later, David was called by church officials to do missionary work in his native Scotland. This call came just as Jennette was about to give birth to another child, Annie, who arrived within a month of David's departure. During David's two years in Scotland, Jennette demonstrated both strong will and initiative in caring for her family and in managing the farm: She supervised the planting, cultivation, and harvesting of the hay and grain, and she oversaw the building of a large addition to the family residence.[8]

Immediately after returning from his mission, David McKay was called, in November 1883, to be the bishop of the Mormon ward, or congregation, in Eden—a small Ogden Valley agricultural community four and a half miles northwest of Huntsville. Then, in March 1885, he was appointed bishop of the larger Huntsville Ward, a position he held over the next twenty years. Also active in community affairs, McKay at various times served as a justice of the peace, as a trustee of the Huntsville school district, as a Weber County commissioner, as a member of the Weber Stake Academy Board of Education, and as a state legislator. He was also commissioned a major in the Utah militia (the National Guard) and placed in charge of both the Huntsville and the Eden companies.[9]

Despite serving as longtime bishop of the Huntsville Ward, David McKay never entered into the controversial Mormon practice of plural marriage. When asked why he never practiced polygamy, McKay reportedly replied, "You don't know my Jennette!" According to granddaughter Fawn Brodie's own vivid account, this handsome, strong-willed woman "bore the distinction of being the only Mormon bishop's wife who did not have to share her husband with another woman." Jennette's "extraordinary capacity to maintain the Victorian amenities [of monogamy] in so alien an atmosphere," Brodie asserted, was testament to her extraordinary ability to get her own way.[10]

Their personal rejection of polygamy notwithstanding, the McKays did offer their home as a refuge for local polygamists—some twenty couples—fleeing federal prosecution for this outlawed practice during the late nineteenth century. They were thus part of the so-called Mormon underground.[11]

In the meantime, Thomas E. McKay came of age. Like his mother, Thomas was striking in his physical appearance. Handsome, with a thin mustache, he was always impeccably dressed. He stood an imposing six feet two inches. (He would pass his height on to daughter Fawn, who grew to an impressive five feet ten). But Thomas, in contrast to his parents, was not overly assertive, either in personality or behavior. He was soft-spoken, with a friendly, approachable manner. He was most comfortable in the role of conciliator, manifesting what one descendant labeled a "quiet assertiveness." He never raised his voice or showed anger, and he gained the allegiance of everyone in his charge. All of these attributes served Thomas well in the realms of business, politics, and church but, unfortunately, served him less well in confronting problems within his own family.[12]

McKay attended the University of Utah, graduating in 1899. He then became principal of the Pingree School in Ogden, an appointment that lasted just one year. The following year he was called by the Mormon Church officials to serve in the Swiss-Austrian mission in Frankfurt. In attending the University of Utah and fulfilling a church mission abroad, Thomas followed in the footsteps of his brother David O., two years his senior. Throughout his life, the younger McKay would maintain an extremely close, mutually supportive relationship with his more famous older brother.[13]

In January 1905, Thomas and David O. faced a common sorrow in their mother's untimely death at the relatively young age of fifty-four. The two brothers were now compelled to look after their aging father while helping care for the younger McKay children, in particular William and Morgan, both of whom were adolescents. In these and other household tasks the two were aided by their four sisters—Jeanette, Annie, Elizabeth, and Katherine. All four young women were as assertive and strong-willed as their late mother, and the four emerged as the dominant force in running the so-called McKay Family Corporation, a legal entity set up to oversee management of the large family home. This organization was established in response to the wishes of their late mother, who "could not bear the idea of the family disintegration" her children's marriages would inevitably bring.[14]

By the time of Jennette's death, her oldest son, David O., had married Emma Ray Riggs, moved to Ogden, and begun his own family. To forestall such disintegration, at least in part, Jennette had decreed that no one of her children should be heir to the ancestral home but that all eight should share in it permanently. Although the eight McKay children were assigned an equal vote in the McKay Family Corporation, the sisters dominated discussions and decisions. As characterized by Fawn Brodie, they were "a formidable quartet of big, handsome women who marched through the family problems in an unbreakable phalanx."[15]

Thomas McKay, meanwhile, after returning from his mission pursued his own career, teaching first at Weber Academy, where he stayed for two years, 1903 to 1905, then at Utah Agricultural College in Logan. In 1907 he returned to Ogden as superintendent of Weber County schools. Then, two years later, McKay, thirty-six years old and still unmarried, was called by Mormon Church officials to serve as president of the Swiss-Austrian mission. He took up his duties at the mission headquarters in Zurich, Switzerland.[16]

While presiding over this mission, McKay met his future wife, Fawn Brimhall, who was in Zurich on vacation. They were introduced by her older brother, Dean Brimhall, then a missionary under McKay. Fawn Brimhall stood five feet seven inches; she was brown-eyed, gracious, beautiful, articulate, and well read. The couple courted in the breathtaking beauty of the Swiss Alps, and on 11 September 1912, upon their return to Utah, McKay, a month away from his thirty-seventh birthday, and twenty-three-old Fawn Brimhall, were married in the Salt Lake City temple.[17]

The new Mrs. McKay was the daughter of George H. Brimhall, then president of Brigham Young University. The Brimhalls, like the McKays, were descended from Mormon pioneer stock. George Washington Brimhall, the future author's great-grandfather had joined the church in 1844 after hearing Mormonism's message and had migrated to the Mormon headquarters, then at Nauvoo, Illinois. The following year, he met and married Lucretia Metcalfe, and the union bore him two children. But Lucretia refused to join her husband in the Mormon migration west to Utah, causing George W. to abandon both her and the children. In January 1852, he wed a second time, marrying Rachel Ann Myers (or Mayer)—a union that took place even though George had not formally divorced his first wife. The couple settled first along the Muddy River in present-day Nevada and then in Spanish Fork, Utah, some sixty miles south of Salt Lake City. Meanwhile, Brimhall formally embraced plural marriage, taking on four more wives during the ten years after 1852 and ultimately fathering a total of fourteen children, including George H., the author's maternal grandfather. In later years Brimhall recounted his varied experiences in *The Workers of Utah*, a vivid, straightforward account that anticipated the frank literary style of great-granddaughter Fawn.[18]

George Washington Brimhall's qualities of literary expression and native intellect, however, were first passed on to his oldest son and name-sake, George H. Brimhall. After graduating from Brigham Young Academy (later Brigham Young University) at Provo, George H. Brimhall served as principal of Spanish Fork schools, then as district superintendent of Utah County schools. He eventually returned to Brigham Young Academy, owned and operated by the Mormon Church, where he served in various administrative offices before becoming its president in 1900. George H. married Alsina Elizabeth Wilkins in 1874, a union that produced six children. Alsina, however, following the birth of her sixth child, suffered "brain fever" and was committed to the Utah State Hospital at Provo for the remainder of her life.[19]

Shortly after Alsina's confinement, Brimhall took a second wife, Flora Robertson—Fawn Brodie's maternal grandmother. Within the household, Flora assumed the role of stepmother to the six children left by Brimhall's first wife. In time she bore her husband an additional nine children, including Fawn, the future author's mother, born in 1889. Flora's task of raising and looking after fifteen children became more difficult because of increased antipolygamous prosecution by federal officials during the 1880s, which compelled her to flee into the Mormon underground.[20]

George H. Brimhall's domestic situation became somewhat more settled after 1890 when church president Wilford Woodruff issued a manifesto by which the Mormons publicly agreed to suspend any further sanctioning of plural marriages. This, in turn, paved the way for Utah statehood in 1896 and brought an end to federal prosecution of Mormon polygamists.[21]

Through these years, Brimhall focused his major energies on building up Brigham Young Academy—which he succeeded in elevating to the status of a university in 1903. Brimhall was characterized by his grand-

George H. Brimhall, Fawn Brodie's maternal grandfather. An important Utah educator, Brimhall was a onetime president of Brigham Young University who encouraged free and open inquiry within his own family and in the institution over which he presided. Reprinted by permission, Utah State Historical Society, all rights reserved.

daughter Fawn Brodie as an open-minded educator who was only "nominally devout" in the Mormon faith. Similarly, another family member dubbed him "a free spirit" with a "fine mind" who was independent in his attitudes, thinking, and dress. Many of these qualities would emerge in his granddaughter. Indeed, the future author would come to consider herself more a Brimhall than a McKay.[22]

Within his family, Brimhall encouraged open intellectual inquiry and inspired the same quality in his children—particularly in daughter Fawn and son Dean. Such openness was also evident in the strong-willed demeanor of his wife Flora, whose most admirable characteristic, according to George H., was her "self-assertion." Flora was also a woman constantly on the go, her heavy family responsibilities notwithstanding. An outspoken advocate of equal rights for women, she was active in the suffrage movement. She did not hesitate to disagree with her husband over polygamy, particularly what she saw as its negative effects within the Brimhall household.[23]

In turn, Fawn Brimhall was profoundly affected by all such influences while growing up. Like her mother, she did not approve of polygamy, knowing as she did the tensions of growing up within a polygamous household. As she reached young adulthood, she pursued her education at Brigham Young University, majoring in art. This reflected her sensitivity to the aesthetic beauty around her—in particular, the picturesque Utah valley where she had grown up. After graduation, Fawn taught art in various schools in Provo, eventually becoming art supervisor for all the city's schools. At the same time, she developed her own artistic talents, becoming an accomplished watercolorist of minor renown. Such creative instincts were ultimately passed on to her daughter and namesake, albeit in the form of literary rather than artistic talent.[24]

Fawn Brimhall took her varied experiences into her 1912 marriage to Thomas Evans McKay and a vastly different family environment—one much less tolerant of intellectual inquiry; expressions of frank opinions; and/or displays of anger, frustration, or anxiety. Following a short honeymoon, the newlyweds established their first home in Ogden. Shortly thereafter, they moved to the farm at Huntsville. As Thomas E. McKay himself frankly recalled years later, it was quite a change for his new wife, and he worried as to how she would respond. Fawn was clearly misplaced in the role of small-village homemaker and farmer's wife, which called for attributes sharply at variance with her natural tendencies as a scholar and artist. However, she was "long-suffering" and worked hard at running the big house, which for years lacked the basic amenities of running water, indoor plumbing, and electricity.[25]

Thomas and Fawn McKay confronted other difficulties as they struggled to provide for their growing family. Their first daughter, Flora, was born in 1913; Fawn's birth' followed two years later. Two years after that Thomas Brimhall was born and Barbara came along in 1920. The McKays' problems stemmed from well-meaning efforts by the aging family patriarch, David McKay, to divide his farmland among his four sons prior to his death in 1917. As Fawn Brodie later wrote, her grandfather, being "an indulgent and kindly man [wanted] to give his four sons their patrimony when they needed it the most." His sons had married or were about to marry, and the eldest already had young families. Because the McKay family farm was not large enough to support all the sons, the

four cast lots to determine which one would buy out the other three. The
choice, or rather burden, fell upon Thomas, who paid his brothers "a
stiff price" for their shares and mortgaged the whole farm to settle
outstanding debts.[26]

The burden of the mortgage on Thomas McKay was further increased
by the four brothers' decision to borrow money on the land and invest
it. They speculated variously in Arizona cotton and Canadian wheat,
hoping to make a fortune that would liquidate the mortgage. But the
investments were disastrous. Everything was lost, and the mortgage debt
grew to thirty-five thousand dollars, an astronomical sum for the time.
This overwhelming financial burden remained "immutable, fixed as the
polestar, the absolute" around which Fawn's family revolved, with Thomas
McKay bearing this huge debt over the next thirty years "like Atlas,
without hope and without lament."[27]

To make matters worse, the farmland itself, for various reasons, failed
to support sufficiently even the Thomas McKay family. Her parents
sought to supplement their meager income by raising what Fawn Brodie
characterized as "an astonishing variety of domestic animals in successive,
desperate attempts to lessen the mortgage load. . . . From cattle to pigs,
from pigs to dairy cows, from dairy cows to chickens, from chickens to
turkeys, from turkeys to sheep—the list encompassed all the livestock of
the West," she recalled.[28]

None of this sufficed to keep the family solvent, compelling Thomas
McKay to seek supplemental employment away from Huntsville. All
through Fawn's growing-up years, her father held a variety of jobs, each
better than the last but none adequate to ease the family's financial
burden. Among Fawn's earliest memories are those of her father "doing
the work of two men." This was dramatized in his daily routine. He
would rise each morning at four to milk the family's twenty-four cows.
He then hitched up the buggy, Fawn recalled, "to drive the twelve miles
to his job. When he returned, it was usually after dark. He would light
the lantern and walk down to the pasture gate, calling, 'Sic, Boss, sic,
Boss' in a strong, even voice that never betrayed his increasing weariness." Living in a state of "genteel poverty," young Fawn took financial
insecurity so much for granted that "it never occurred to [her] that
God had intended the good land of the valley to mean sustenance as
well as sacrifice."[29]

The Thomas McKays endured other difficulties. The family was not the master of the fourteen-room house in which it lived. Ownership of the house, lot, and barnyard belonged not to Thomas E. McKay but rather to the McKay Family Corporation. Every decision affecting the ancestral home was made by the eight McKay heirs in joint deliberation. No spouse was permitted to attend a McKay Family Corporation meeting, thus completely excluding Fawn Brimhall. She was no more eligible to vote on the hanging of a family portrait in the parlor than her four non-McKay brothers-in-law were able to vote on installing a new roof.[30]

Theoretically, each of the eight McKays had an equal voice. In fact, the corporation was dominated by the four McKay sisters, with significant influence exerted by oldest brother, David O. The power of the sisters stemmed largely from their strong, assertive personalities, clearly inherited from their mother. Each was intelligent and well educated, all having attended and, in most instances, graduated from college. All four had married into families of wealth and/or prominence.

The wealth and material comforts of the sisters stood in sharp contrast to the modest resources of the Thomas McKay family. As vividly recalled by Fawn, each of her four aunts had a fine city house with two bathrooms, hired help, the best automobiles—Lincolns, Packards, or Cadillacs—and collections of Dresden and Spode china and antique furniture.[31]

David O. McKay's influence within the McKay Family Corporation came not from his own economic resources—more substantial than those of Thomas E. but considerably less than those of his four sisters. Rather, David O. affected decisions through quiet assertiveness and through his stature as an important church leader. He had been appointed to the Mormon Church's ruling elite—the Council of the Twelve—in April 1906 at age thirty-two. He had also gained a reputation as a spellbinding public speaker. Dubbed "the Golden Tongue," he was compared with the nationally renowned orator, William Jennings Bryan.[32]

David O. McKay's status within the church provided prestige for the extended McKay family. Accordingly, the four McKay sisters deferred to his wishes on important family issues. "They were really in awe of him," explained one family member. Or, as Fawn Brodie, recalled, David O. McKay "dominated all of the McKay family, to an extraordinary degree, just like an old Chinese patriarch."[33] Indeed, male dominance through

patriarchy was an integral part of Mormon culture—a fact that in David
O.'s case allowed him to prevail ultimately in family matters.

By contrast, the two youngest McKay brothers, William and Morgan,
played a minimal role in the affairs of the McKay Family Corporation,
deferring to David O. and the four sisters. William McKay, a respected
Salt Lake City physician and one-time president of the Utah Public
Health Association, and Morgan, an agricultural agent and plant patholo-
gist based for a time in southern Utah and later in Idaho, were both
primarily concerned with their own professional activities and the responsibilities of their own immediate families .[34]

At the same time, Fawn's father was temperamentally unsuited and
unwilling to assert himself in family matters, particularly if it meant going
against his older brother and four sisters. Overly deferential to his five
strong siblings, Thomas sought to avoid confrontation within the McKay
clan, even to the detriment of his own immediate family. He "was most
happy when he could be compliant, gallant, and generous," daughter
Fawn recalled. Or, put more bluntly, "It was always his way to run away
from trouble rather than facing up to it," she said.[35]

For Fawn's mother, the situation was even worse. She was an in-law and
therefore not a voting member of the McKay Family Corporation. Even
within her own home, she was constantly treated as an outsider by the
four McKay sisters, who resented her and were critical of her management of the "old home," which they still considered theirs. They constantly made her aware of her subordinate status as a mere in-law and not
a "true McKay."[36]

The minimal influence of the Thomas McKays within their own home
was graphically evident in the limited living space allowed the family, the
only permanent residents of the house. Of the nine bedrooms, only two
were allotted to the Thomas McKay family, even though it grew to include
five children with the birth of a fourth daughter, Louise, in 1925. The
other bedrooms remained vacant during the winter, but throughout the
summer months these extra bedrooms were utilized by the four McKay
sisters and David O. McKay, who would come to Huntsville with their
multiple progeny to escape the valley heat, staying for weeks on end. "It
was one big party all summer long," Barbara, Brodie's sister remembered.
"I don't know how my parents put up with [it]."[37]

Yet neither Thomas nor his wife expressed any dissatisfaction, at least openly, about the annual summer intrusion or about the limited family living space allotted them or about their chronic economic difficulties. This silence was in keeping with a strongly held McKay family creed of "avoiding discussion of all matters deemed unpleasant." This was particularly evident in the behavior of the four McKay sisters, who according to Fawn Brodie, "worked with religious intensity at preserving an atmosphere of tranquility. They not only effectively silenced criticism of any McKay, adolescent or mature, but also managed by a combination of innuendo and affectionate firmness to stifle frank negative opinion on any topic whatever. Tact and discretion for these women were the supreme virtues; candor smelled of rebellion, sulphur, and brimstone."[38]

All family tensions were held in check through what Brodie later characterized with supreme irony as "the seemingly invincible discipline of Love." Discussion and dialogue were severely restricted; conversation among the McKay adults "consisted chiefly of praising each other's virtues and accomplishments, and extolling the somewhat insipid merits of the McKay children." When by accident discussion wandered outside the subject of family, there were only two legitimate targets of derogatory comment, the Democratic Party and the Catholic Church. Even upon these topics "the critical tone had an edge of sorrow rather than malice or contempt." All the McKays fled in consternation from anything that threatened to become a genuine argument.[39] Such a carefully controlled, constricted family environment profoundly affected Fawn Brodie's own developing attitudes and behavior.

Also important was the Mormon Church, which affected the future author's basic values and beliefs in various ways—both intended and unintended. Sundays were given over to church meetings held in the Huntsville Ward meetinghouse. These included Priesthood Meeting for all male members over twelve years of age; Sunday school for all members of the ward, usually held in the morning; and a general Sunday evening worship service known as Sacrament Meeting. For a special worship service held monthly and known as Fast and Testimony Meeting, church members fasted for a twenty-four-hour period, abstaining from all foods and beverages. The meeting itself was like a revival service in which attendees would spontaneously "bear their testimonies," that is verbally

The old Huntsville home where Fawn McKay grew up, as drawn by her mother, Fawn Brimhall McKay, a trained artist and Utah watercolorist of minor renown. This charcoal sketch was used on a customized Christmas card sent to family and friends of Thomas and Fawn Brimhall McKay sometime in the 1950s. Courtesy Barbara McKay Smith.

express their faith before the rest of the congregation. There were additional church functions throughout the week: Primary, a service for all children under twelve; Mutual, for teenagers and young adults; and Relief Society, for adult women. The meetinghouse was located across the street from the Huntsville town square, two blocks west of the McKay family home. It was the most impressive and prominent structure in the community, originally built in 1879 and enlarged and remodeled over the following four decades.

In addition to formalized practice and ritual within the local Mormon congregation, Fawn Brodie's developing religious attitudes were affected as much, if not more, by the contrasting beliefs and practices of her mother and father. Although Brodie later described both parents as devout Mormons, she pointed out some significant differences, characterizing her father as a "very devout . . . Mormon preacher of considerable talent," while labeling her mother "a quiet heretic."[40]

Thomas E. McKay's strong religious beliefs, rooted in deep conviction, were evident to all who knew him. While his pulpit style was not as charismatic as that of his brother David O., he nonetheless projected an intense spirituality, bore his testimony in front of the Mormon congregation, and affirmed his fundamental belief in the truth of Mormon doctrine. Such strong religious beliefs were consistent with his status as president of the Ogden Stake, or diocese, a position to which he was called in 1918 and held for two decades.[41]

McKay also manifested his strong religious convictions through ritual within his own home. The family routine included "a blessing at every meal and an evening prayer on our knees," Brodie's sister Flora recalled. On Sundays there was strict observance of the Sabbath; the McKay children were not allowed to play either outside or inside the house. Even the sewing of doll clothes was forbidden. And, according to the Mormon "Word of Wisdom," the consumption of all alcoholic beverages, as well as coffee and tea, was prohibited within the family.[42]

By contrast, Thomas's wife, Fawn Brimhall, was a "social Mormon," who allegedly asserted that "it didn't really matter whether you . . . were active in the Church or not. . . . The Lord would bless you anyway." She saw the Mormon Church as "a wonderful social order" but questioned its basic dogma, rejecting among other things, the Mormon view of eternity, asserting instead that "eternity is one generation to another." She allegedly had little use for formal ritual. She "hated the temple ceremonies so bad that it was just ghastly," her daughter Flora recalled, and she wondered aloud "how [Mormon Temple] garments could be sacred when they're worn next to a dirty body."[43]

Although Fawn Brodie would be profoundly affected by her parents' differing attitudes, particularly her mother's beliefs (or lack thereof), she continued to manifest the attributes and behavior of a devout, believing Latter-day Saint throughout her formative years. In addition to her spirituality, Fawn gave evidence of an extraordinary intelligence from a very early age. She was outspoken, inherently inquisitive, always asking questions, always curious, always wanting to learn. She was memorizing and reciting lengthy pieces of poetry by the time she was three; in this, she showed up her older sister Flora, two years her senior. "I remember mother trying to teach me to repeat the poem 'Little Orphan Annie,' Flora recalled. "I was struggling just to learn the first verse. One morning [when] mother and dad were in bed and we were playing at the foot of the bed . . . mother asked me to say the poem. I just barely got past the first verse and stopped. Fawn piped up, 'Let me say it, mother,' and she went through all three verses without one mistake."[44]

One year later, in 1919, when Flora was six and due to begin first grade, an epidemic of whooping cough hit Huntsville, running rampant through the local school. Since the disease was almost always fatal to infants and small children, Flora's mother would not allow her daughter to begin school, opting to teach the child at home. In looking for the most effective way of teaching the basic skills of reading, writing, and math, she consulted with her older brother, Dean Brimhall, recently graduated from Columbia University. With his help she utilized a new teaching method, sight reading, which involved a process whereby various objects around the house were carefully labeled with large letters on pieces of paper. The child associated the printed name with that object, be it a chair, light, or stove. Joining in this process was four-year-old Fawn, eager to participate with her older sister. Together, Fawn and Flora spent hours learning words, and in very little time both sisters were reading, writing, and doing simple arithmetic. Fawn's progress was exceptionally rapid. By that spring the precocious youngster was reading fourth-grade-level books.[45]

Young Fawn's early education continued during the McKay family's temporary residence in Salt Lake City beginning early in 1921. This move was the result of Thomas E. McKay's legislative duties. Being Republican majority leader in the Utah state senate required him to be in the capital during the months the legislature was in session. Further impetus for the family move was Thomas and Fawn McKay's desire to protect their children from various epidemics of diphtheria, whooping cough, measles, and pneumonia, all rampant in Huntsville. The McKays rented a large room normally used for merchandise display in the Hotel Utah, a Mormon Church-owned enterprise located in central Salt Lake City. "Mom took her trusty hotplate and a few dishes and set up housekeeping in this one room," recalled Flora. The family found particularly welcome the great luxury of indoor plumbing and hot water, both conspicuously lacking in the Huntsville home.[46]

Young Fawn and her older sister continued their education at home, learning supplemented by books borrowed from the Salt Lake City Public Library. Fawn devoured these volumes, and by the time the McKay family returned to Huntsville in the summer of 1921, books had become a dominant part of the bright youngster's life. "I was . . . a bookworm," Fawn recalled, but "my parents looked upon my being buried in books with indulgence."[47]

HUNTSVILLE SCHOOL DAYS

In September 1921, six-year-old Fawn and eight-year-old Flora finally were enrolled in public school. Initially both girls were placed in the third grade, though Fawn was reading sixth-grade-level books. Their mother had a compelling personal reason for keeping the two sisters in the same grade. She seemingly, almost inadvertently, made her daughters twins, seeking to replicate the circumstances of her own childhood as an identical twin. Fawn Brimhall was very close to her twin sister, Fay, a relationship that continued throughout their adult years.[48]

The Huntsville school was located two blocks west of the McKay family home and across the town square, next to the village church. From the beginning, young Fawn quickly stood out from her classmates. After two weeks in the third grade, the bright six-year-old and Flora were advanced to the fourth grade. This was the conventional way of giving gifted children a bit of an advantage. At the same time, Fawn achieved the top score in an IQ test. She also distinguished herself in a schoolwide spelling bee, defeating first her fourth-grade classmates, then all of the children in the fifth grade and most of the children in the sixth grade. She was defeated finally by a twelve-year-old sixth-grader. Fawn despaired over that loss. "She cried and cried," recalled Flora, "that this bright boy, twice her age, had spelled her down."[49]

Such behavior revealed Fawn's strongly competitive instincts as well as her extreme sensitivity. But young Fawn also had a stubborn, inflexible side. "Once she got an idea in her head, she would hang onto it," her cousin Edward McKay recalled. On one occasion the two children made a bet concerning the origin of cobwebs. Fawn maintained they were strictly from dust, whereas Edward asserted they were made by spiders. The bet involved a root beer. To settle the issue, the cousins looked in the dictionary, only to find that cobwebs were indeed made by spiders. Fawn, however, continued to maintain that cobwebs came strictly from dust and refused to pay off.[50] Such stubbornness would manifest itself later as a methodological weakness in Brodie's research and writing.

Stubborn, sensitive, competitive, intelligent, young Fawn, as well as her siblings, enjoyed the advantages of growing up in a family that was accorded special status within Huntsville. The Thomas McKays and Edward Jespersons—the latter family owned the local merchandise store—had the two largest, most prominent houses in town. Thomas McKay's position as Mormon Stake president and his political role as a state senator prompted the McKays to consider themselves a cut above other townspeople. In the eyes of many local Latter-day Saints, they were seen as "the Lord's anointed." Such status, however, demanded adequate monetary resources to validate their claims to membership in the village elite, and that the Thomas McKay family lacked. Their income from crops and livestock was insufficient to meet their expenses, especially during the early 1920s, a time of deepening agricultural depression. The McKay's financial difficulties were further complicated by the ever-present mortgage of thirty-five thousand dollars. "The farm . . . was in perpetual need of rescue," Fawn recalled.[51]

To supplement the family's meager income, Fawn Brimhall took in boarders for two years, from 1922 to 1924. Six teachers working at the local Huntsville school lived with the family, each paying thirty dollars a month for room and board. With the income, Fawn Brimhall was able to feed her own children properly "for the first time," but she incurred the wrath of the four McKay sisters who thought it terrible that she was taking in boarders—gross violation of the McKay family's image as local gentry.[52]

THREE YEARS IN SALT LAKE CITY

In 1924 the family's financial fortunes improved with Thomas McKay's appointment to a salaried position on the three-member Utah State Public Utilities Commission. This commission was established in 1917 as part of a Progressive reform to regulate the state's powerful if varied public utilities: eighteen telephone companies, seventeen railroads, and ten electric power companies. The largest included Mountain States Telephone and Telegraph, Union Pacific Railroad, and Utah Power and Light. Utilities alone constituted 33 percent of the state's total assessed valuation.[53]

Thomas McKay's appointment significantly increased the family's income, making it possible for him to purchase a house in Salt Lake City and move his family out of Huntsville. The Salt Lake City home was located on the East Bench overlooking the city and near the University of Utah. At Douglas Elementary School, nine-year-old Fawn and eleven-year-old Flora completed the sixth grade in the spring of 1925. The following September the girls were scheduled to begin seventh grade at Bryant Junior High School, an eight- to ten-block walk from their home. The McKays, however, did not want their daughters to make the long daily walk and enrolled them at the Stewart School, a training facility for student teachers on the campus of the University of Utah, just four blocks away. Flora characterized their schooling there as "the best two years of training" available to them on the junior-high level. Their course of study included algebra, science, and home economics, subjects generally not taught until high school.[54]

Fawn demonstrated her extraordinary precocity in many ways. She was constantly shown off by her proud mother, who would have her recite a poem or give a reading for visitors. Both her mother and father came to believe that if anybody was to excel in the Thomas E. McKay family it would be young Fawn.[55] The affection between mother and daughter was especially deep, as evidenced in Fawn's first published work, a poem entitled, "Just a Minute, Mother," which she wrote at age ten, and which appeared in the Mormon children's periodical, *The Juvenile Instructor*, in 1925:

> "Just a minute, mother,"
> Is heard in all childs' homes,
> From the cottage of the peasants,
> to the castles with great domes.
>
> If mother tried to count,
> The "just a minutes" of each day,
> We'd find that hours and hours
> Slip uselessly away.
>
> Let's drop our "just a minutes,"
> And make our mothers smile,
> And in this time we've wasted
> Do something that's worthwhile.[56]

Fawn later recalled the "unspeakable thrill" of seeing her name in print for the first time, which prompted "fantasies about writing great short stories and fine novels."[57]

In addition to her *Juvenile Instructor* verse, Fawn apparently produced a second poem, published in the national children's periodical *Child Life.* The poem won a contest, and Fawn received a check for five dollars. In 1925, she made her broadcast debut, giving a speech over KSL—a Salt Lake City radio station owned by the Mormon Church. The precocious ten-year-old was already making a name for herself. "Mother was so proud of her," recalled Flora, "because our family was the 'low one' of the McKay clan." It became "a habit . . . to *expect* Fawn to be superior in everything," Flora added, "and she certainly did not disappoint any of us."[58]

As a family, however, the McKays continued to experience disappointment. Thomas had health problems, developing tuberculosis of the bone in his neck and nearly dying of a related abscess. He recovered, but the McKay family then faced financial difficulties that forced them to give up their Salt Lake residence and move back to Huntsville. They simply lacked sufficient income to maintain both residences.[59]

ADOLESCENCE AND HIGH SCHOOL YEARS

Returning to Huntsville brought about a number of significant changes for twelve-year-old Fawn and her family. Her father was forced to spend much more time away from his home and family because of his work with the utilities commission, which necessitated a daily commute to Salt Lake City of fifty miles each way. Early each morning he would drive to the Ogden railroad depot where he boarded the Bamberger, an interurban line that transported him to Salt Lake. Usually he would not return to Huntsville until late evening. Commission hearings in various parts of the state often took him away from home and family for days at a time. Thus his wife assumed the primary role in domestic affairs, overseeing the farm and looking after the children. "In raising the children, mother was the one that had the strong hand," recalled Fawn's younger sister, Barbara.[60]

In addition to spending less time with his family, Thomas McKay had only a limited amount of time to work the Huntsville farm. Two years earlier, while still living in Salt Lake, he had started giving Flora, then just twelve years old, a major share of responsibility for working the farm during the summer months. Thus his oldest daughter learned at an early age to drive a team of horses and supervise the men hired to do the heavy work. Flora did not mind the responsibility at all. She, in fact, enjoyed working outdoors, taking naturally to the tasks of planting, cultivating, and harvesting, and her warm, outgoing personality enabled her to supervise effectively the workers hired during the planting and harvesting season. By 1927, with the family's return to Huntsville, McKay relied on his daughter's help more than ever. She was "the best hired hand I ever had on the farm," Thomas McKay said, and father and daughter developed an extremely close relationship.[61]

Young Fawn, by contrast, because of her hay fever, spent very little time out-of-doors. This was just as well, since Fawn, unlike Flora, was uncomfortable around farm animals, having once fallen off a horse and broken a bone. Now she stayed in the house with her mother, which strengthened that already close bond. Also, by staying inside, Fawn had much less work to do than her older sister; quickly completing her household chores, she had ample time to pursue her favorite pastime, reading. The family's modest library contained a few volumes, most notably a set of encyclopedias her father had purchased from an itinerant salesman, which Fawn used in writing school papers. Despite the set's usefulness to her, she characterized it as "the dullest encyclopedia ever written." Much more interesting were the few novels in the family library through which the precocious youngster was exposed to "deceit, treachery, [and] illicit love"—topics about which she would otherwise have known nothing because of her extremely sheltered environment. Fawn later vividly recalled one particular novel, *The Dear Pretender,* "about a man who loved his wife despite or because of the fact that she pretended to a happiness she did not always feel." Such recollections were a clear allusion to her mother's difficult situation, which increasingly concerned the sensitive daughter.[62]

One negative effect of remaining indoors was Fawn's failure to develop a close relationship with her father. Even so, she was ever anxious to please him. Thomas, however, was not as sweet to Fawn as he was to Flora. As Flora recalled, "He was everything to me, and I was everything to him. I was his very, very favorite." Fawn's correspondingly close relationship with her mother helped compensate for the lack of a close relationship with her father, but not completely. The two relationships were unequal from Fawn's perspective. In the patriarch-centered Mormon environment, young Fawn was encouraged to please her father first and foremost.[63]

Then came the uncomfortable changes of puberty. Fawn grew taller and taller, surpassing Flora's five feet six inches. Extremely anxious about her height, she would have someone measure her every week or so, and make a mark on her bedroom door. As the mark "kept going higher [Fawn's] tears . . . would flow." Ultimately she reached five feet ten, much taller than any of the girls at or near her age. "Being . . . tall at puberty was a real hardship on [Fawn]," Flora recalled, especially as the two sisters were beginning to take an interest in boys. Fawn was bothered that almost all the boys in her group of friends were shorter than she. When she started slumping to make herself shorter, her father would reprove her: "Stand up!" he would say. "You're beautiful."[64]

Fawn's height, combined with her extreme intelligence, made her shy and reticent. "Mixing with others was not her long suit," her brother Thomas B. remembered. Her shyness caused some to think she was stuck-up, especially in comparison to her outgoing older sister. Fawn lamented on one occasion, "I can't make a friend until Flora makes it first." She grew to depend on her older sister for her social involvement. Her anxieties made her think of herself, according to that old nursery rhyme, in relation to the day of her birth: "Wednesday's child is full of woe!"[65]

Fawn continued her precocious ways throughout her high school years. Not quite twelve years old, she along with Flora, entered Weber High—the county high school—in September 1927. This meant a daily commute to Ogden. The two sisters and their fellow high school students from Huntsville boarded an interurban streetcar—known as the Toonerville trolley—for the trip through the Ogden canyon to school. Weber High School, located near downtown Ogden, was a relatively new institution, having graduated its first class of 570 students the previous spring.[66]

Fawn, unintimidated by her new academic environment, continued to excel. In her classes she often taught the teachers. On occasion, a teacher would actually turn class instruction over to her. In addition to academics, she excelled in public speaking and forensics throughout her high school years, winning two statewide oratorical contests, and was a member of the Weber High School debate team that took the state championship.[67]

Fawn also demonstrated talents as a writer, anticipating her major area of expertise. She wrote and had published several poems in the *Golden Spike*, the high school annual. She also assisted in editing the annual and was involved with a second publication, *The Broadcaster*, the school newspaper, on which she served as social editor. Fawn's command of English was sophisticated and her prose carefully measured, one classmate, Jarvis Thurston, remembered.[68]

Despite her basic reticence and despite being three years younger than most of her fellow students, Fawn was popular with her classmates, holding her own socially. She served as president of the girls' club and was an attendant to the school beauty queen. She was "very beautiful" Jarvis Thurston recalled, "thin and tall."[69]

Fawn was now socially active at home in Huntsville as well, becoming involved with the Builders Club, a youth group affiliated with the local Mormon ward. She was also involved with other church-sponsored activities: She was invited to speak in church and to give readings at missionary farewells, special Mormon meetings recognizing individuals "set apart," or appointed to perform missionary service for the church. She also spoke outside of Huntsville to Mormon congregations in Ogden and other nearby communities.[70]

Fawn appeared strong in her basic religious beliefs throughout her high school years. She taught a Sunday school class of younger children within the Huntsville Ward, and she expressed her faith at local ward meetings. In one particular Fast and Testimony Meeting, she "bore a beautiful testimony" in an event vividly recalled by her brother, asserting her strong belief in the restored gospel of Mormonism. On another occasion, Fawn gave a talk citing specific evidence supporting the divine origins of the *Book of Mormon*. According to one old-time Huntsville resident, Melvin Engstrom, "Many times, many times [in various church meetings] did I hear her bear testimony to the truthfulness of the gospel" of Mormonism. According to her sister Flora, Fawn was the most religious of all the McKay children. This is corroborated in Fawn's own recollection to her cousin Monroe McKay, to whom she described herself as "a goody-goody girl . . . the best child in the whole [McKay] family when it came to church."[71]

Fawn's religious beliefs are, however, recalled differently by high school friend Jarvis Thurston, who sensed that she was not really a devout believer. And Flora suggested that although both sisters affirmed basic Mormon doctrine in teaching their Sunday school classes, each, as a teenager, began questioning Mormon beliefs, although neither openly discussed her doubts. Another high school friend, Gay Doman, remembered Fawn as "a normal devoted Latter-day Saint girl," but noted that that was only what one would have expected given her family and Huntsville's Mormon environment.[72]

Whatever the case, Fawn was obsessed with perfection, be it in her own actions or in the behavior of others. Her quest for perfection caused sibling rivalry with her younger brother, Thomas B. According to Flora, Fawn gave him a bad time, constantly criticizing him for not doing things right: He did not read enough, Fawn would complain, or he did not do well enough in school. Fawn was also bothered by her brother's failure to do more work on the farm, particularly as he got older. Thomas, in fact, did very little farmwork. Like his father, he was not inclined toward hard physical labor; he preferred to remain indoors. In this way he and Fawn were much alike. By contrast, Flora continued to do most of the farmwork, and that bothered Fawn, who expressed her feelings directly to her brother and other family members. Thomas B. responded to such criticism, by teasing Fawn on a regular basis during their growing-up years.[73]

Fawn was also bothered by what she saw as more serious imperfections among members of the extended McKay family. She noted the behavior of her four aunts, who during the summer months stayed in the Huntsville house. They were solemn and sober in demeanor and always dressed in black. But such deportment did not conceal what Fawn felt to be their major vice: Every afternoon the women would go into one of the back bedrooms, lock the door, and play bridge, an activity that, like all card playing, was considered a vice by Fawn's father and absolutely prohibited within his immediate family.[74]

Indeed, the mere summertime presence of the four aunts, along with their families and other relatives, continued to bother Fawn as she grew older. This presence was a painful reminder of another of life's imperfections—the fact that the Huntsville farmhouse in which the Thomas McKays lived did not belong to them. With the arrival of the McKay kin came a loss of privacy, and more important, additional work for her own family, particularly her mother, who was constantly preparing meals and looking after the visitors' various needs. Even the neighbors noticed that this less-than-ideal situation was taking a toll. "It was too much together-ness [and] pretty hard on Mrs. McKay," one resident of Huntsville recalled. But Fawn Brimhall herself never complained—at least not openly—about the annual deluge of relatives and the attendant inconveniences.[75]

This lack of complaint was in keeping with the McKay family tradition of avoiding confrontation. Instead, Fawn Brimhall sought relief by leaving the big house for significant periods during the summer. She had a small cabin consisting of two rooms and a loft placed on their farmland a few miles east of Huntsville. The Thomas McKays preferred living in this primitive cabin, where water, as well as food, was hauled in daily from the valley, to staying in the cramped quarters of the big house with the extended McKay family.[76]

When not helping her mother with household chores, Fawn would entertain her two younger sisters, Barbara and Louise, by telling them stories. She soon developed a reputation throughout Huntsville, as well as in her own home, as a talented storyteller. Wherever she went, the small fry would trail her, begging for a story. In response, she would spin wonderful, exciting tales about marvelous witches and fairies. These skills anticipated Fawn's ability to weave together in prose a vivid, descriptive narrative—a distinguishing feature of her biographical writing.[77]

But neither by fact nor fiction was the Thomas E. McKay family able to escape their state of genteel poverty, a condition that bothered and perplexed young Fawn more and more as she grew older. She saw her father as a romantic who nurtured a "smoldering hope" that the family's financial fortunes might be miraculously reversed. As she vividly recalled, her father

> talked periodically about prospecting on our rangeland for gold. There was an odd-shaped barren knoll at the foot of the mountain which seemed to him the likeliest spot for digging. He called it, without irreverence, the Hill Cumorah, after the hill where the first Mormon prophet [Joseph Smith] had found his legendary golden plates. . . . Our Hill Cumorah was a favorite spot for the rainbows that appeared so often in the valley after summer showers. When we

saw the bow's end shining on the hill, we would rush to show it to my father, and he would gravely say, "There's where I'll find my pot of gold," We took it all very seriously.[78]

But the miraculous discovery was never made.

There were humiliating consequences connected with the state of genteel poverty. Older sister Flora recalled that at the beginning of each school year their mother would take the two sisters down to a department store in Ogden and buy each a couple of dresses on credit. It would then take all winter for the McKays to pay off the bill. A couple of times, the department store actually cut off their credit because of slowness in payment. This was a terrible blow, given the family's prominence in both the church and the community.[79]

An even more humiliating reminder of the family's limited resources was the absence of indoor plumbing at the Huntsville farmhouse. Throughout Fawn's childhood, water was hauled from a well into the kitchen, heated on an old Monarch stove, and poured into a tin tub for bathing purposes. An outdoor privy stood at the end of a flagstone walk fifty feet west of the white-pillared house. Known as "Mrs. Grundy," it continued in use long after most other residences in Huntsville had indoor plumbing. Fawn bitterly recalled that as she "grew older and became aware of the social implications of [the privy's] permanence [it] became . . . a scandalous anachronism. The coming of guests, whether our parents' friends or our own, always meant a moment of apologetic explanation, which was humiliating to make or even to overhear."[80]

Conditions were the worst during the winter. There was no central heating, and temperatures in the interior of the house routinely fell below freezing. The kitchen, thanks to the wood stove, was the only warm room in the whole house. Except for sleeping, the family basically lived in the kitchen all winter. Fawn and Flora would take turns each night washing the dinner dishes. The unlucky one—the one who did not get to wash the dishes (after all, a warm activity)— had to retire first and warm up the freezing bed with her body. In addition to "Mrs. Grundy," there was also a chamber pot. But during the winter months, the human wastes had to be thawed on the kitchen stove in the morning before they could be disposed of in the outhouse.[81]

The lack of basic amenities in the McKay home was at sharp variance with the family's presumed status as part of Huntsville's elite. The Thomas E. McKays had a front to maintain in the community, but they lacked the financial resources to pull it off. This paradox was publicly acknowledged when Thomas McKay's aged automobile broke down. The family, of course, lacked the means to repair or replace it. In response, the membership of the Huntsville ward contributed to the purchase of a brand-new Model T Ford, which they gave to the family as a surprise. Flora recalled the contrasting reactions of her parents: Her father was extremely grateful, genuinely touched by this show of community affection and generosity, while her mother was simply embarrassed.[82]

In general, the awkward situations created by the family's economic status seemed bitterly ironic to young Fawn, particularly given that her more affluent relatives offered no financial assistance, despite their intrusions every summer. To make matters worse, these same relatives brazenly blocked all efforts to install indoor plumbing in the Huntsville house, though the Thomas McKay family desperately wanted it and the McKay Family Corporation clearly could afford it.[83]

More significantly, young Fawn came to believe that the root cause of her family's genteel poverty was her uncle David O. McKay's speculative ventures many years earlier—specifically, his ill-advised investments in Arizona cotton and other commodities. Inquiring into these ventures as she grew older, she became convinced that the investments were made entirely at David O.'s urging, that her own father had merely gone along with the wishes of his stronger-willed older brother. Fawn saw these speculative ventures as hypocritical and inexcusable, given David O.'s high Mormon calling in the Council of the Twelve.[84]

Within her immediate family, Fawn was bothered by other perceived imperfections—ones that stemmed from problems between her father and mother. Efforts were made to keep these hidden, as both parents sought to project the image of a completely harmonious relationship for the sake of their children as well as of others outside the family. On the whole, they succeeded. "They never fought," Flora recalled. "They never quarrelled. The only time I ever say my mother go against my father . . . was when he brought home a paper . . . mortgaging the farm, again, and she had to sign it."[85]

But as Fawn reached puberty, she and Flora detected serious problems in their parents' relationship. Bluntly stated, Flora claimed her mother "hated sex," a condition apparent in the family's sleeping arrangements. Fawn and Flora slept in a small upstairs bedroom in the front of the house, while their parents and the three younger children, Thomas B., Barbara, and Louise, all slept in the larger bedroom next door. There, Thomas E. slept in one bed with his son, and Fawn Brimhall slept in the other bed with her two daughters. Having the three younger children all jammed into a single bedroom with their parents gave Fawn Brimhall escape from her husband, her oldest daughter conjectured.[86]

Such attitudes influenced Fawn, particularly as she reached puberty and became aware of her own sexuality. On one occasion, Fawn reportedly confessed to her mother that she "wanted to feel [her own] vagina." Shocked and angered, her mother warned her, "Never touch it. Never touch it!" Fawn was ever the dutiful daughter, and yet later in life she told Flora, "I'd wiggle my big toes so I'd keep my hands away from my privates." In general, young Fawn was profoundly affected by her mother's attitudes and behavior, as evidenced in her almost obsessive fascination with the sexual lives in her future biographical subjects.[87]

A more immediate consequence was that young Fawn acquired some of the same sexual inhibitions her mother had exhibited. Her older sister, by contrast, was much more comfortable with her sexuality, attributing her liberated attitudes to significant time spent caring for the farm animals, whereby she observed sexual activity as normal and natural. Fawn "was always a little jealous of me," Flora remembered, "because of my freedom, sexually." She "used to think I was a 'sexpot.' She'd laugh at me. She said she couldn't do all those things that [I did]."

Fawn's inhibitions, combined with her height and her intelligence, caused the teenager additional anxiety as she reached dating age. "She couldn't get a boyfriend because she was taller than all the boys in Huntsville," Flora said. By contrast, Flora, a cute blonde of average height and vivacious personality, had no shortage of boyfriends.[88]

At the beginning of her senior year, Fawn found a boyfriend, Dilworth Jensen. Just thirteen years old, she became acquainted with Dilworth, five years her senior, through their mutual involvement with the Builders Club. Dilworth had already graduated from high school and was in his second year at Weber Junior College. Of Danish immigrant stock, he had red hair and was five feet ten inches tall—the same height as Fawn. Like Fawn, he had grown up in rural Ogden Valley. The Jensen family farm was three miles southwest of Huntsville, across the south fork of the Ogden River.[89] Distance, however, did not deter Fawn and Dilworth.

The two were attracted to each other in a number of ways. Dilworth, like Fawn, was extremely intelligent and excelled in school. Like Fawn, he was well-read and loved school and books. Such attributes soon made the young couple conspicuous in their small rural community, a place plagued by what observers labeled a pervasive anti-intellectualism. But anti-intellectualism was not restricted to the little community; it was also evident among many rank-and-file Latter-day Saints and even among church leaders. Most important, it was evident in the McKay family itself.[90]

The censure of others only drew Fawn and Dilworth closer together, allowing the two to enjoy a stimulating relationship. Cleverly articulate, they bantered back and forth. When they attended a dance, they would often stand in one spot, so absorbed in conversation that many times they were not even aware the music had stopped. Dilworth called Fawn "Lady Aristotle" because of her intellect and dignified appearance. And Fawn found her high school sweetheart "tender, sweet, witty, gallant." "I adored being with him," she would later recall. Dilworth, in turn, was very much in love with Fawn, and there was talk of eventual marriage.[91]

Reenforcing the young couple's relationship was the fact that Fawn's older sister, Flora, and Dilworth's older brother, Leslie, were seriously dating at the same time. The two brothers and two sisters frequently double-dated. In fact, the two sisters appeared to take the initiative in seeking the attention of the two brothers, according to the Jensens' sister. Fawn and Flora would frequently ride on horseback over to the Jensen farm with cakes and lemonade for Dilworth and Leslie. Such forward behavior by the McKay sisters apparently appalled Mrs. Jensen, who thought their behavior exceeded the bounds of propriety.[92]

In turn, Fawn Brimhall had her own reservations concerning the relationship of her daughters with the Jensen brothers. On a fundamental level, she worried about transgressing accepted boundaries of ethnicity and social class. She felt her daughters' relationships with Dilworth and Leslie crossed both boundaries. The Jensens' Scandinavian background, which she felt imposed inferior social standing on the family, clashed with the McKays' own status as part of Huntsville's elite. As a Brimhall married to a McKay, she considered her family a rung above the Jensens, whom she saw as mere farmers, a curiously ironic attitude given that the Jensens were economically better off than the McKays.[93]

Fawn Brimhall had another concern. She strongly disapproved of Leslie Jensen on personal grounds. She was repulsed by his "uncouth" behavior and abrasive personality. Leslie, for his part, understandably could not relate to Mrs. McKay and deliberately antagonized her. While courting Flora, he would go "straight from the field to see her without cleaning up," his sister Elizabeth Jensen Shafter recalled. Undaunted, Flora would go off with him, which further infuriated Mrs. McKay.[94]

Further complicating the situation was the simple fact that Fawn Brimhall was basically opposed to Fawn's and Flora's dating at all. She could not bear the thought of either daughter growing up. "I always felt that my mother wanted to keep us [both perpetually at] home as [the] young girls that she adored," Flora recalled. "She just hated me dating. She didn't trust any boy." This attitude stemmed, in part, from Fawn Brimhall's natural maternal instincts but also from her revulsion concerning things sexual.[95]

Despite strong parental concern, and indeed opposition, Fawn's and Flora's relationships with Dilworth and Leslie continued to flourish as the two daughters completed their high school studies and graduated from Weber High in May 1930. Graduation ceremonies were a memorable occasion. Fawn was class salutatorian, and the girls' grandfather George H. Brimhall, onetime president of Brigham Young University, addressed the graduating class. "He spoke about loyalty, loyalty to one's family, to one's church, and to one's God," Fawn recalled. "He was eloquent [and] a little frightening." She would remember her grandfather's speech with such vividness because she ultimately "violated all his admonitions." At the time, however, Fawn was still the dutiful daughter and a believing Latter-day Saint. She was, after all, just fourteen years of age.[96]

TWO YEARS AT WEBER COLLEGE

That September of 1930, Fawn and Flora entered Weber College. Located near downtown Ogden, the two-year school was owned and operated by the Mormon Church. A small institution, it boasted an enrollment of just over four hundred when the girls enrolled as freshmen. Its modest physical plant consisted of just two buildings.[97]

Fawn began college at a time of great economic distress. The stock market crash of October 1929 had made universal the economic difficulties previously limited to agriculture and other so-called economic soft spots. By now, Utah, along with the rest of United States, was in the grip of the Great Depression. The hard times were especially felt by Fawn's own family. Her father's salary from the Utah Public Utilities Commission was abruptly halved, cutting into the family's already meager income. More serious was the threatened loss of the family farm to what Fawn labeled "the hated bankers, who already had foreclosed mortgages on two-thirds of our valley neighbors." Because it was impossible for the McKay family to come up with the fifty dollars needed for Fawn's and Flora's college tuition, Fawn Brimhall painted a watercolor of the McKay family home in Huntsville and presented it to college president Aaron Tracy in lieu of cash payment.[98]

Fawn's entry into college brought her into contact with new individuals and new courses of study. Although the majority of Fawn's colleagues hailed from Ogden area schools, there were also students from other Utah communities—and from Idaho, California, Arizona, Tennessee, Virginia, Texas, Hawaii, and the Philippines. Fawn took new and challenging courses, including zoology, botany, geology, and physics. She also enrolled in English composition and literature—anticipating what would be her eventual field of major study. In addition, she took a year of French.[99]

Fawn was also exposed to the courses in scriptural studies required of all students at Weber College. During her first year, she took a course on the *Book of Mormon*. The basis on which Mormonism was founded, the *Book of Mormon* is scripture, considered by Latter-day Saints sacred and on a par with the Old and New Testaments of the Bible. Believing Latter-day Saints affirm the *Book of Mormon* to have been translated by Mormonism's founder, Joseph Smith, from a set of golden plates divinely revealed to him in the 1820s. This work is considered the sacred writings of an ancient pre-Columbian American civilization, ancestors of the American Indians and members of one of the tribes of Israel.[100]

Everett Doman, a fellow student in Fawn's *Book or Mormon* class, recalled that a number of their classmates questioned the official Mormon

Fawn McKay in 1931 at age fifteen as a student at Weber College in Ogden, Utah. This photo was taken of the young collegian when she was selected as an attendant to the school's Acorn Queen. Courtesy Weber State University Archives.

version of Smith's discovery and translation of the golden plates, but that Fawn was not among those skeptics. She remained a "true believer." Her faithfulness stemmed, in large measure, from the high esteem in which she held her teacher, Leland Monson, himself a devout Mormon. Monson, in turn, adored his outstanding student.[101]

Fawn was drawn to Monson as mentor because he was an intellectual like herself. In a tribute written for the *Acorn*, the school's yearbook, Fawn extolled his "simplicity, friendliness, and sincerity," adding that "behind each of his lectures is a wealth of tried and true philosophy, humanized by illustrations drawn from real life." Her bonds to Monson were further strengthened in that he also taught the courses in British literature and English composition that she took—and he was in charge of debate, an activity in which Fawn was extensively involved during her two years at Weber.[102]

Fawn stood out as an accomplished public speaker. On one occasion, she presented a Christmas story at a student devotional. Entitled "The Great Rushing of Wings," Fawn's story described the hardships of an impoverished peasant woman whose infant babe had been born without the use of his limbs. The woman, despite being good and virtuous, suffered much misfortune, but because of her strong religious faith, her child was finally healed in a Christmas miracle. Fawn's telling of the story "seemed to have an effect on [everyone]," a student reporter covering the event noted. Even the college president, Aaron Tracy, voiced his satisfaction, predicting that "the student body of Weber College would see and hear more of Miss McKay."[103]

Fawn's most significant public speaking came in debate. In her first year she gained extensive experience thanks to a school-sponsored three-week trip that took her and her debate partner, Jetta Barker, throughout the Midwest. On this trip the fifteen-year-old freshman was exposed, for the first time, to society and culture outside the Mormon-dominated Great Basin. Fawn and Jetta departed Ogden on 13 February 1931. Their first stop was Laramie, Wyoming, where Fawn had her first encounter with local citizens in a non-Mormon environment—one starkly different from Huntsville. The two young collegians were sitting in the lobby of the Laramie hotel, "watching the cowboys streaming in and out," when suddenly "two big men in cowboy hats" approached their table and presented them with martinis. The gentlemen then went back to the bar, promising to return. But Fawn and Jetta, being "deliciously frightened," hastened off to their room and poured the forbidden liquor down the washbasin.[104]

After leaving Laramie, the young debaters proceeded eastward, first to Kansas and then on to Missouri, where they commenced an exhaustive schedule of debates at various local colleges. Fawn and her partner were prepared to debate two questions. The first, "Resolved that the several states should enact legislation providing for compulsory unemployment insurance," was a most timely issue in face of the extremely high unemployment rate, already well over 20 percent nationally. The second issue concerned American trade policy: "Should the United States move toward a policy of free trade or higher protective tariff as the most effective means of stimulating the economy?" This latter issue was both relevant and timely, given recent enactment of the Hawley-Smoot tariff. The most restrictive tariff in American history, this 1930 measure was coauthored by U.S. Senator Reed Smoot, who represented Utah and at the same time was a member of the Mormon Church's ruling elite—the Council of the Twelve. In debates at schools in Winfield, Pittsburg, Kansas, and in Liberty, Maryville, and Columbia, Missouri, the young women won once, lost once, and had three "no-decisions." In Lebanon and Carlinville, Illinois, they posted two more victories before reaching the easternmost point of their tour, East Lafayette, Indiana, where they won again, this time over the Purdue debaters.[105]

Starting their return trip west, Fawn and Jetta backtracked first to Illinois, where they had the opportunity to visit Carthage and Nauvoo, both important in the early history of the Mormon Church. Fawn "viewed with intense interest that historic church landmark, the Carthage jail together with relics so sacred to the [Latter-day Saints]." It was at the jail in Carthage that Joseph Smith and his older brother, Hyrum, were killed by an anti-Mormon mob in June of 1844. Fawn was moved by her visit to the site, where bloodstains could still be seen on the floor of the jail.[106]

The young women then drove along the Mississippi River to Nauvoo, where they viewed many sites associated with the early history of the Mormon Church. While visiting Nauvoo, Fawn was involved in a significant exchange with a pastor from the Reorganized Church of Jesus Christ of Latter Day Saints who was in charge of a museum there. The Reorganized Church, with its headquarters in Independence, Missouri, had been formed in the late 1850s following the martyrdom of Joseph Smith. Although the Reorganized Church recognized the prophetic claims of Smith, including the *Book of Mormon* and other basic beliefs, it established itself as separate and distinct from the Utah-based Church of Jesus Christ of Latter-day Saints. It refused to recognize the leadership claims of Brigham Young, who had migrated west with the largest group of Saints during the late 1840s. Instead, the Reorganized Church looked for leadership to the heirs of Joseph Smith, commencing with the martyred prophet's oldest son and namesake, Joseph Smith III. The Reorganized Church, moreover, condemned the Utah Mormon practice of polygamy, asserting that Joseph Smith, as leader of the early church, had never practiced or sanctioned what they considered an odious and improper practice.[107]

According to Fawn's recollections, the Reorganized Church pastor, upon finding out that Fawn was a Utah Mormon, asked her how many wives she thought Joseph Smith had. "I was forced to confess absolute ignorance" concerning Joseph Smith's involvement with polygamy, Brodie recalled, "and was dumfounded when [the pastor] told me" the Utah Mormons, in contrast to the RLDS Church, believed that Smith had a total of twenty-seven wives. The disclosure was significant because it represented the first time that Fawn had heard anything concerning Smith's plural marriages, even though she was aware that several of her own immediate family, most prominently her grandfather George H. Brimhall, had practiced polygamy.[108]

After a debate against the men of Carthage College—another victory for the Weber women—Fawn and Jetta traveled north to Chicago. Fawn had "a glorious time" seeing—here she paraphrased Carl Sandburg—"the city of the big shoulders." Among other activities, she and Jetta attended church services at the two local branches of the Mormon Church.[109]

Departing Chicago, the duo traveled westward to Yankton, South Dakota, where they participated in a nondecision debate at the local college, then on to Nebraska for their final two debates. By this time, both women were "homesick & sick of dormitories," Fawn wrote to Dilworth. She also confessed to being "somewhat tired of never ending plains and rolling hills." The young women were counting the hours and finally the minutes until they should glimpse the Wasatch Mountains.[110]

In general, Fawn's first excursion outside of Utah was a significant one. She had had the "pleasure of . . . debating, of meeting new people, and of seeing remarkable . . . historical things." She was exposed to, in her own words, the world beyond "the parochialism of the Mormon community." She was struck by the number of young people she met who knew practically nothing about the Mormons. Some of the most interesting conversations "centered around our religion and the type of school we [represented]," Jetta noted. Students at each campus "asked us just what makes our church different from other churches," and the girls found themselves frequently having to explain the long-abandoned practice of polygamy.[111]

Following her return, Fawn resumed her studies at Weber College. That spring she was chosen as attendant to the queen of the Acorn Ball. She also involved herself in campus politics, running for student body vice-president, albeit unsuccessfully. She served as associate editor of the *Acorn*, the college yearbook, assuming primary responsibility for writing, editing, and generally putting the publication together.[112]

Meanwhile, Fawn's relationship with Dilworth Jensen entered a new phase. They has been temporarily separated, when he left Utah in the fall of 1930 to serve a Mormon mission. Dilworth had been "set apart" for the Swiss-German mission by Fawn's uncle, David O. McKay. This assignment, based in Hamburg, kept Dilworth away for two and a half years, during which time he and Fawn corresponded faithfully. Dilworth's letters gave firsthand accounts of the dramatic events unfolding in the troubled German nation, where the Weimar Republic was collapsing and Adolf Hitler was rising to power.[113]

Fawn, meanwhile, completed her second year at Weber college, continuing to excel academically. Throughout her two years at the school, she received almost straight As; her only lower grades were two Bs—one in physics and the other, curiously enough, in her major subject, English. The sixteen-year-old Fawn along with older sister Flora graduated in May 1932. Both sisters were presented their diplomas by their father, acting in his capacity as president of the Weber College Board, a position Thomas McKay held by virtue of his appointment as president of the Weber Stake.[114]

• • •

Fawn's childhood and adolescent years appear idyllic in certain respects. She was comparatively well off in several important respects: Given the economic hard times prior to and during the Great Depression, Fawn and her immediate family experienced much less difficulty than the vast majority of their contemporaries. Thomas E. McKay was assured a steady income thanks to his continuing employment with the Utah State Utilities Commission. Fawn was further privileged in that her parents possessed the means, albeit limited, to send her and her sister to college immediately after high school. She was also accorded social status within her community as "a McKay" and thus a member of the local elite.

But when she was being frank, Fawn Brodie admitted that her situation in early life was less than idyllic. The "genteel poverty" in which her family lived roused feelings of jealousy and disdain within young Fawn for the affluent members of the extended McKay family. At the same time, the sensitive youngster acknowledged that her parents were extremely protective, attempting to spare her and her siblings "the anxiety of their poverty."[115]

While acknowledging both parents as affectionate and giving, Fawn came to see that such "enormous affection" spawned some less positive attributes. "Everything was implicit instead of explicit," she said. Their caring fostered a repressive environment. "I was taught to be a lady and say what was appropriate and not what I felt or thought." But during her youth, Fawn did not appear to be unduly bothered by what she later characterized as a repressive and parochial environment. In keeping with her behavior as a McKay, she carefully repressed her negative feelings. Her commitment to family, home, community, and especially basic religious beliefs remained strong well into her adolescent years.[116]

Indeed, Fawn described herself in later years as having been "a model child" who "never [even] indulged in a healthy amount of mischief." She carefully adhered to the strict rules within the McKay family household, as did her sisters and brother. Whatever doubts, concerns, or resentments Fawn had developed by this time were held in check, in keeping with her own obsession with perfection and the McKay family tradition of avoiding all unpleasant topics. She was a private person who "never, ever let anything out."[117]

All these influences left their mark. Such childhood experiences within an extremely protective, if repressive, environment would be followed by what Fawn would later describe as "a quiet kind of moving out into . . . the larger society" and away from her family, community, and especially church, all occurring over the course of the next half-dozen years.[118]

TWO

"A Quiet Kind of Moving Out"

1932–1938

"I was devout until I went to the University of Utah," Fawn Brodie once said. She attended the university from September 1932 to June 1934, and it was there that she completed her undergraduate studies. During this period she began to distance herself from what she characterized as the parochialism of the Mormon community: "There was nothing very spectacular about it," she said. "It was a quiet kind of moving out into . . . the larger society and learning that the center of the universe was not Salt Lake City as I had been taught as a child."[1]

TWO YEARS AT THE UNIVERSITY OF UTAH

Fawn McKay would not have attended the University of Utah if her grandfather George H. Brimhall had had his way. He expected her, along with Flora, to attend Brigham Young University, the Provo institution over which he had served as president. But his daughter, Fawn's mother, was insistent that they not go to BYU. First, she dreaded the idea of her daughters, particularly young Fawn, being so far away from home. Provo was a hundred miles to the south, then a good day's travel from Huntsville. Second, Fawn Brimhall feared that her daughters would marry as a direct consequence of attending the Mormon-run school. BYU already had a well-earned reputation as a meeting place for young,

marriageable Mormons. Third, Fawn Brimhall's own religious heterodoxy, her deep-seated doubts, precluded her sending her daughters to
BYU. But the family's limited financial resources, combined with Thomas
E. McKay's daily commute to Salt Lake City in conjunction with his
position on the Public Utilities Commission, also influenced this decision.
Sending their daughters to the University of Utah rather than to BYU
would make it easier for their mother to stay in close contact with them
while providing food and other needed provisions.[2]

There was yet another influence in Fawn Brimhall's decision. She
remained embittered toward BYU because of its treatment of her father.
George Brimhall had been asked to resign the presidency of the school
in 1921 because of failing health. Admittedly, his physical problems had
made him increasingly ineffective—the elder Brimhall had been afflicted
with intense chest and abdominal pain throughout his life and the
condition had only worsened with age—but Fawn Brimhall still believed
her father's release was unjustified. Resigning as president, Brimhall
stayed on at BYU as head of the Department of Theology and Religion.
Over the next decade, his health continued to deteriorate to the point
that the pain became unbearable, and on 29 July 1932 Brimhall took his
own life, "splatter[ing] his brains" with a self-inflicted gunshot wound.
The gruesome suicide affected all family members, but especially Fawn
Brimhall, who, like her father, was prone to dark moods of depression,
and the vulnerable, sensitive sixteen-year-old Fawn.[3]

The McKay family's decision to send the girls to the University of Utah
represented a significant turning point in Fawn's life. As a secular, open
institution, the University of Utah stood in sharp contrast to Brigham
Young University. Dubbed by Fawn herself "the seat of anticlericalism in
Utah," the school sheltered a faculty and staff who were at times openly
critical of the Mormon Church, its policies, and its leaders.[4]

Fawn found the University of Utah different from Weber College in
other respects. It enrolled some three thousand students—five times more
than the Ogden school. In this environment, Fawn experienced a certain
anonymity for the first time in her life. As she later recalled, "I was known
only for myself rather than for my family." While this anonymity was at
first "humbling," she later came to cherish the freedom that it brought.[5]

But Fawn did find some similarities between the university and Weber
college. In its physical plant, the University of Utah was fairly small. It

consisted of just six buildings, located on a foothill bench just east of downtown Salt Lake City. Like Weber, the university was adversely impacted by the continuing harsh effects of the Great Depression. Enrollment had declined as had state funding. Fawn considered herself lucky to be in college during "these . . . deadliest of the depression years."[6]

Fawn and Flora, along with two other girls, shared an apartment a half-mile below the campus. Once or twice a week, Thomas E. McKay would have lunch with his daughters. Inevitably he brought food, including turkeys roasted by their mother, home-baked pies, farm vegetables, and gallons of milk.[7]

The young collegians had other family close by. Two cousins were attending the university at the same time—Emma Ray McKay, a daughter of David O., and Jeanette Morrell, daughter of Fawn's aunt Jeanette McKay Morrell. Jeanette shared an apartment with Fawn and Flora during their second year at the university. Also living in Salt Lake City were Fawn's aunt Fay Cummings, her mother's twin sister, and husband, Julian. Fawn and Flora were frequent dinner guests in the Cummings's home. Fay always made the girls feel more than welcome, despite her own large family of seven children and despite the somewhat eccentric behavior of her husband. Julian, a high school teacher and successful businessman, operated a flourishing root beer stand in downtown Salt Lake City. And he espoused a number of unusual beliefs. A devout Latter-day Saint, he viewed the Great Depression and the increased international turmoil of the 1930s as signs that the end of the world was imminent, echoing in this the millennialistic expectations of his nineteenth-century Mormon forebears.[8]

Two other relatives—an uncle, Dean R. Brimhall, and his wife, Lila Eccles Brimhall, who likewise lived in Salt Lake City—exerted an even more profound influence, serving as strong role models for young Fawn. Dean Brimhall was well educated, having received his bachelor's degree in psychology from Brigham Young University in 1913 and later his master's and Ph.D. degrees from Columbia University. He then taught at BYU and later at Columbia. Eventually he left academia, working for the New York–based Psychological Corporation. In the late 1920s, he left the field of psychology and, intrigued by the potential of air travel, became a pioneer in Utah aviation. Brimhall's wife, Lila Eccles, was the daughter of prominent Utah businessman David Eccles. Like her husband, Lila was well educated, having received her bachelor's degree in theater at the University of Utah and a master's from the University of Southern California. By 1929 Lila had become a professor of speech and theater at the University of Utah. An accomplished actress, she was recognized as "first lady of the Utah theater."[9]

Young Fawn quickly developed a close relationship with Dean and Lila Brimhall, which allowed her to observe, firsthand, these two accomplished, talented individuals pursuing separate careers while maintaining a successful marriage. Fawn also noted how her aunt and uncle were able to raise two children—a daughter, Frances, and a son, McKeen, the latter to whom Fawn was particularly close. The dynamics within the Brimhall household, particularly Lila's independent pursuit of a career outside the traditional role of housewife, were exceptional for the time. Lila's situation stood in sharp contrast to the constricted life Fawn's mother led back in Huntsville. Her Aunt Lila's situation seemed ideal.[10]

Young Fawn was also deeply affected by her uncle Dean Brimhall. Like his sister, Fawn's mother, he was less than orthodox in his religious views, despite having served a Mormon Church mission to Germany. He became a religious skeptic who liked to quote, with no little irony, the biblical verse "Seek ye the truth and the truth will make you free." Young Fawn expressed initial shock when first exposed to Brimhall's religious heterodoxy. In a revealing diary entry, she characterized her uncle as "stimulating and intelligent . . . but [lacking] the strength that can come only from a belief in revealed religion." Despite this, and despite the fact that he came across to some as biased and prejudiced, Fawn was drawn to her uncle. Their close relationship was, to some extent, a carryover of the bonds forged between Brimhall and Fawn's mother. That young Fawn had her mother's first name and bore a striking physical resemblance to her mother, accentuated the relationship between uncle and niece.[11]

The young collegian was impressed by her uncle's extensive learning and clear thinking. That Brimhall had always been a rebel fascinated Fawn. She identified with his effervescent curiosity, finding "his judgements and analyses of human behavior . . . always interesting and frequently disturbingly penetrating." Fawn was also enamored of his wry sense of humor. Brimhall's political convictions—he was a staunch liberal and partisan Democrat—intrigued Fawn and, over time, influenced her.

Significantly, such attributes represented everything that Fawn's own father lacked.[12]

The young woman, however, continued to echo the conservative Republican beliefs of her father, though such beliefs were shaken by a fall 1932 visit to Salt Lake City of then-president Herbert Hoover. Attending a Republican campaign gathering in downtown Salt Lake City, Fawn waited outside of the Hotel Utah, with great anticipation, to catch a glimpse of the president, who was inside at a campaign reception. When Hoover finally appeared, Fawn was shocked to see not the proud president of the United States she had imagined, but "a little man with a blotched skin and a desperate look of failure" pushing his way through the crowd, anxious to escape into his waiting limousine.[13]

Besides undermining her stalwart Republican beliefs, the shock of seeing such an unflattering aspect of a man whom she had previously admired planted seeds of doubt concerning male authority figures in general, be they political or religious. Such skepticism, then just emerging, would later affect the tone and tenor of her biographical writings.

Fawn's experiences at the university itself were also effecting change. As a member of the school's debate team, she traveled to southern California during the spring of her junior year. "The smell of orange blossoms coming into the open windows of the [railroad] car after our descent from the gloomy Nevada desert vastness" was her seductive introduction to the Golden State. She attended an Easter sunrise service at the Hollywood Bowl, concluding that the "thousands who had gathered there to hear trumpeters sound the glad tiding at dawn were indeed a reverent people." This caused her to question her preconceived image of California as "the fleshpots of Egypt"—a view nurtured by the common Mormon caricature of the state as pleasant but decadent and therefore rejected by her pioneer forebears as Mormonism's primary gathering place. Now Fawn asked, "Could Brigham Young have been so wrong?"[14]

The journey to California turned out to be Fawn's last debate trip. Back home in Utah, she left the team, confessing to having developed "a revulsion to the debaters' practice of canvassing varied documents on the nation's suffering only for the purpose of finding arguments with which to win." For example, on the issue of whether there should be, or should not be, unemployment insurance, a debater could argue with equal conviction on both sides at a time when the nation was in the depths of the Great Depression, and 12 million Americans—one out of every four workers—were unemployed. The decision to quit debate represented a critical turning point in defining Fawn's long-range career goals. "Whatever fleeting fantasies I had about going into law and politics, never articulated to my parents," she said, "vanished at this point forever."[15]

Instead, Fawn decided to major in English literature, a decision apparently also prompted by her father. Concerned for his daughters' welfare, Thomas E. McKay encouraged Fawn and Flora to focus their education in a field that would enable each to secure gainful employment upon graduation—an overriding concern, given the Great Depression. He considered education that field. It had provided him with his first job three decades earlier, and his own carefully forged political and ecclesiastical connections in the Ogden-Huntsville area all but assured his daughters of securing teaching positions close to home.[16]

Fawn's decision to major in English was a natural, given her love of books. She described her readings at the university as "a Gargantuan feast." During one three-month period of study—"the most rewarding months . . . of my life"—she read almost all of Shakespeare, and "a fair sampling" of Aeschylus, Sophocles, Euripides, Corneille, and Racine. And she developed "a taste for Russian novels" to which she would later become addicted. In Prof. S. B. Neff's Shakespeare class she read *Hamlet* for the first time. But it was *King Lear* that captivated her—"Lear who mistreated the daughter who loved him best." "I memorized his mad scene," Fawn recalled, "and recited 'Blow winds and crack your cheeks!' when fighting the cold winter winds walking to class. . . . I wept not at Hamlet's dying but at Cordelia's." In another class, Fawn read John Milton's *Paradise Lost* and learned that "Satan, wrongheaded and vulnerable, had heroic qualities and was far more likable than the omnipotent Jehovah. The impact on my religious faith was subtle but indelible."[17]

Outside of English, the young collegian was influenced by other courses. Prof. E. E. Ericksen, through Socratic questioning in his ethics class, "gently shook the faith of [the] . . . devout." There was also a child psychology course taught by Dr. Dorothy Nyswander, a close personal friend of Dean and Lila Brimhall. "Give me a child until the age of six and I will make of him or her anything I will," Nyswander said. At first, the young college student thought the idea arrogant but eventually accepted the concept as "the beginning of freedom from the pervasive social ideas that genealogy and blood line were the crucial factors in determining a child's development, a theory that was then accepted almost without question by my parents."[18]

Fawn also confronted situations outside the classroom that raised questions about some fundamental tenets of her Mormon faith. What she characterized as her "earliest shock of the intellect" came from one of her roommates, a tiny, auburn-haired girl from Price, Utah, the first non-Mormon that she had known. It was she who told Fawn of the prevalent view among academic anthropologists that the American Indians were Mongoloid in origin, that scholars universally rejected the Mormon claim that Native Americans were "descended from migrants from ancient Palestine." Although still a true believer, Fawn was clearly affected by her arguments with this young woman. "The shock of her argument stimulated, as I remember it, not doubt in the validity of the Book of Mormon but a fantasy of rushing to the rescue," Fawn recalled. "Someone surely, I thought, would research the matter soon and vindicate 'the Prophet.'" The seeds of Fawn's doubts were subtly being planted, although the full flowering of her skepticism would burst forth only after research into American Indian origins years later.[19]

Fawn was also exposed to both non-Mormon and anti-Mormon books that presented the church and its history in a less-than-heroic light. This came through her employment in the university library during the spring quarter of 1934. Both Fawn and her older sister were given jobs rebinding old or damaged library books. The twenty dollars that each received for the entire quarter came through a New Deal–sponsored Works Progress Administration program. Fawn was absolutely fascinated by books disputing the claims of Joseph Smith and the origins of Mormonism. She recalled, years later, her profound shock on first reading Hoffman Birney's scurrilous *Wives of the Prophet Joseph Smith*. "The book made me wild. 'No, no, these things simply can't be true,' I said."[20]

Fawn also encountered an unpublished master's thesis on Joseph Smith written by her own cousin-in-law, Alice Smith McKay, wife of Llewelyn McKay and daughter-in-law of David O. McKay. Submitted for a degree in psychology at the University of Utah in May 1930, the work was entitled "A Psychological Examination of a Few Prophecies of the Early Founders of Mormonism." It focused on Joseph Smith's role as a prophet—in particular, his abilities to forecast future events—and sought to place the Mormon leader within a historical context. More to the point, it downplayed the role of the supernatural as an influence in Joseph Smith's prophecies. It noted, for example, that Smith's famous 1832 "Prophecy on War and Rebellion" was clearly based on facts known at the time, as was his later and equally famous prophecy anticipating the ultimate westward migration of the Later-day Saints to the Rocky Mountains following his death. McKay's thesis asserted that Joseph Smith, "in the absence of [tangible] information, . . . was not able to utter prophecies to his people. Such instances arose when the Mormons were in need of his command for their welfare and were desperate in being left alone without his assistance. Being removed from the facts tended to limit Joseph Smith's ability to predict correctly for the deliverance of his people from cruel persecutions."[21]

The author concluded that the evidence on the few prophecies presented in her work showed they were the result of known facts and not, as suggested by certain devout church spokesmen, "humanly impossible" or "beyond the human power to discern or to calculate." McKay's thesis caused quite a stir within the extended McKay family, and its author predictably got "into a little hot water with the church," one family member recalled. More significantly, the work intrigued Fawn and would ultimately set her off on a similar course of inquiry.[22]

But for the moment, Fawn had more immediate concerns. Her longtime boyfriend, Dilworth Jensen, had returned from his mission in Germany and had joined Fawn at the University of Utah, where he enrolled as a student in September 1933. But changes had occurred during their long separation that now affected the relationship. "I did a lot of growing up and began to be critical of the church," Fawn recalled years later, while Dilworth had become even more devout in his Mormon beliefs. As Fawn's developing interest in Mormon Church history caused her to question some basic beliefs, Dilworth became increasingly "frustrated and worried." According to Fawn, their differences became "a problem we couldn't discuss." Nevertheless, their relationship continued, and they even made plans to marry. For Fawn, the situation roused complex feelings of doubt, anxiety, and turmoil.[23]

The young collegian sought solace in her academic studies. As she later recalled, "I fled from personal problems into the fantasy world of literature." She also confessed to having "fantasies about writing great short stories and fine novels" of her own. In this pursuit, she wrote a short story and entered it in the "Gleam-Scribbler Contest," a literary competition sponsored by the Associated Students of the University of Utah. Entitled "Experiment," it was her first—and only—published work of fiction, appearing in the spring 1934 issue of *The University Pen*. The tale involves a story within a story, narrated by its chief protagonist, a medical doctor, to his close friend, an eminent scientist. The doctor claims an ability to achieve human perfectibility. This can be done, he asserts, by revolutionizing a human subject in terms of appearance, behavior, and personality. The scientist friend quickly dismisses the claim as impossible. To support his assertion, the doctor then describes an experiment he has recently completed wherein an "utterly commonplace girl" named Jane, who lived in a small rural community known as "Hilltown," was raised to the level of human perfection.[24]

The story has a predictable twist at the end and many autobiographical elements. It is not a notable piece of fiction, far from original in concept and structure and clearly influenced by certain writers, including O. Henry and George Bernard Shaw—specifically, Shaw's famous play *Pygmalion*. But "Experiment" is noteworthy because it represented Fawn's first serious effort at creative writing. Even more important are the story's autobiographical elements: the acute frustrations, tensions, longings, and fantasies stemming from Fawn's less-than-idyllic youth and her current situation.

"Experiment" did not win the Gleam-Scribbler Contest or even garner honorable mention. Instead, Fawn was informed by one of her English professors, a Dr. Quivey, that she had no talent for fiction, a criticism to which she reacted with "ineffable bitterness." Quivey underscored his negative evaluation by assigning Fawn a final course grade of C in his short-story writing course. For the fledgling writer, this was devastating; besides crushing her ego, it affected her grade-point average, being the first and only C Fawn received in her academic career. Nevertheless, she was elected to Phi Kappa Phi honor society and graduated in June 1934 with high honors.[25]

Fawn's two years at the University of Utah were critically important. As she recalled, they "marked the beginning of separation, first from the warmth of an affectionate and very possessive family, and second, from the parochial ambience of my adolescence." But this separation, she carefully noted, "was tentative and constantly subject to testing." More important, "There was . . . a smashing of icons within those walls, but I did not hear the noise until later. It all happened . . . very quietly."[26]

A RETURN TO WEBER COLLEGE

Following graduation, with her bachelor's degree in hand, Fawn returned to Ogden, where she secured a teaching position in English at her alma mater, Weber College, in September 1934. Her status as a McKay had assured Fawn of the position, which was most crucial because of continuing economic distress. Her salary was a modest but welcome sixty dollars a month.[27]

Though her appointment came through her family connections, Fawn quickly demonstrated skills as an outstanding teacher. Despite her youth—at nineteen she was younger than many of her students—she "did a beautiful job," recalled cousin Jeanette Morrell, herself a fellow faculty member. Fawn "taught rings around" many of the long-established teachers, according to Morrell, and everyone respected her, particularly Weber College president Aaron Tracy.[28]

Meanwhile, Flora secured a teaching position at Quincy Elementary School in Ogden, earning seventy dollars a month. Their combined income enabled the sisters to rent a small house in Ogden, one large enough, in fact, to accommodate the rest of the Thomas McKay family. Thus the entire family was able to live away from Huntsville during the winter months, thereby escaping the discomforts of the primitive farmhouse.[29]

Fawn's ongoing relationship with Dilworth Jensen, meanwhile, appeared to flourish. By this time, responding to advice given by Fawn's uncle, Dean Brimhall (who was Dilworth's cousin through marriage), Dilworth had decided to pursue specialized study in entomology. Because of Utah State's better program in zoology—the essential prerequisite for entomology—Dilworth transferred from the University of Utah to Utah State Agricultural College in Logan at the beginning of the 1934–35 academic year. Despite the distance now separating them, Dilworth traveled from Logan to Ogden to see Fawn on weekends and any other

Fawn McKay in 1935 at age nineteen as a member of the Weber State College faculty where she taught English, 1934–35. Courtesy Weber State University Archives.

time he could get away. He completed his bachelor's degree in June 1935 and, because of his outstanding undergraduate record, was awarded a graduate fellowship at the University of California at Berkeley, commencing in the fall of 1935. Coincidentally, Fawn received a similar fellowship from the same institution to pursue graduate studies in English. All who knew Fawn and Dilworth, especially close friends and family, anticipated marriage for the young, bright, Berkeley-bound couple.[30]

Meanwhile, Flora and Leslie Jensen had become serious in their courtship, and in the fall of 1934, shortly after Flora had begun teaching in Ogden, they approached her parents, asking for permission to marry. Thomas McKay and his wife not only refused their request but, in a rare public display of anger, they ran Leslie Jensen off their property. Ultimately, the McKays and the young couple reached a compromise whereby

Flora and Leslie agreed to wait for a year to marry. In exchange, her parents gave their approval, albeit with great reluctance.[31]

The compromise proved extremely difficult for Flora and Leslie, who were most anxious to marry. To make matters worse, the couple had to endure a long-term separation after Leslie's departure for Los Angeles that fall to attend diesel engineering school. Finally, in the spring of 1935, having completed her first year of teaching, Flora was able to travel to California to visit Leslie. At this point they decided to elope, traveling from Los Angeles to Yuma, Arizona, where they were married. But they kept their marriage secret from both family and friends, thus avoiding the immediate wrath of the McKays and preventing Flora from losing her teaching position, for she was subject to the "no marriage clause" that was a part of all contracts signed by female elementary schoolteachers.[32]

Inevitably, word of the couple's marriage leaked out, and there was an uproar within the McKay family. Flora's mother was particularly upset because the elopement caused so much gossip within Huntsville. Rumors—completely unfounded—that Flora was pregnant—and thus "had to get married"—damaged the McKay family's well-cultivated image. Just as important, Fawn Brimhall was upset by the reality of now having Leslie Jensen as a son-in-law.[33]

Flora and Leslie's elopement directly affected young Fawn, forcing her to make a critical decision concerning her own future plans. She had the choice either of attending Berkeley with Dilworth, as she had originally planned, or of going to the University of Chicago, a choice her parents favored. The McKays were influenced by several factors in presenting Fawn with the option of attending the University of Chicago. First, Thomas was personally acquainted with Robert M. Hutchins, that university's dynamic young president. McKay also saw the school as an ideal place to send his daughter, for it was the center of the so-called Mormon Chicago movement. A number of bright, promising Latter-day Saints were pursuing advanced degrees at Chicago's highly regarded Divinity School. Fawn, as an accomplished young scholar herself, would fit into this environment. Finally, the University of Chicago was an appealing option simply because it was not the University of California at Berkeley. The McKays feared that their daughter's departure for California, accompanied by Dilworth Jensen, would lead directly to her marriage.[34]

Fawn and her parents briefly considered one other option—that of Fawn and Dilworth marrying immediately and going off to Berkeley together. This possibility, apparently discussed by Fawn and her parents without Dilworth's knowledge, was, however, mutually rejected. Fawn was reluctant to marry Dilworth because of her growing doubts, and her parents were not ready to accept another Jensen into the family, even though Dilworth was much more to their liking than Leslie.[35]

Thus Fawn chose the University of Chicago, in large measure because it was what her parents wanted, and she was still controlled by her desire to please them. But she was also motivated by her changing relationship with Dilworth. Although still very fond of him, she had growing doubts about marrying him. She wanted freedom and a chance to be on her own. Dilworth himself apparently sensed this.

Dilworth was naturally unhappy with Fawn's decision to go to Chicago but took comfort in her promise to write to him every day. Moreover, the young couple continued to talk of marriage, and it seemed to those who knew them that their relationship would continue despite the separation.[36]

THE UNIVERSITY OF CHICAGO AND MARRIAGE

Fawn's arrival in Chicago in September 1935 marked a return to "the city of big shoulders," the high point of her memorable 1931 trip. And entering the University of Chicago brought her an "enormously exhilarating . . . sense of liberation."[37]

This was not surprising, given the school's reputation as one of the great institutions of higher learning in the world. Located on the south side of Chicago, the university was founded in 1892 as a private institution with money provided by John D. Rockefeller. Under the leadership of its first president, William Raine Harper, the university emerged as one of the best graduate schools in the country. This pursuit of academic excellence continued under the leadership of Robert Maynard Hutchins, who took over in 1929. At barely thirty years of age, Hutchins was charismatic, energetic, and idealistic. He sought to strengthen the university's curriculum, and logical analysis became an integral feature of all courses of study. Hutchins encouraged study from original texts and extensive discussions of the ideas involved. To facilitate this goal, he developed the world-famous Great Books program in collaboration with Mortimer Adler. Thus Chicago was a vibrant institution open to all types of ideas and discussion—to the extent that, in the words of one historian, it "always hovered on the edge of the absurd." Such an open atmosphere was not always to the liking of public officials: In 1935, the year Fawn McKay arrived on campus, the university was denounced by certain members of the Illinois state legislature as being "infiltrated by Communism."[38]

Here, in this open environment, Fawn met people with tremendous intellectual curiosity. As for the campus's impact on her Mormon faith, Fawn remarked, "the confining aspects of the Mormon religion dropped off within a few weeks. . . . It was like taking off a hot coat in the summertime." A Mormon acquaintance in Chicago remembered Fawn's rapid alienation from Mormonism. Such recollections, however—including Fawn's own—greatly oversimplify the nature and speed of her disaffection. It was acutally a quiet, gradual process, not immediately evident. She remained close to fellow students from Utah and involved herself in Mormon activities, at least for the first several months following her arrival. To facilitate such connections, her father had contacted local Latter-day Saint officials, to make sure his daughter was properly settled and assured a place in the local Mormon congregation.[39]

Fawn interacted with fellow students from Utah through activities of the Utah Club. A nondenominational organization, the club was made up of University of Chicago students from the Beehive State who occasionally got together socially. Fawn also involved herself with the local Latter-day Saint congregation, the "university branch." In January 1936 she gave a reading during a sacrament meeting, the main Sunday service. Two months later, on 21 March 1936, she was a major participant at a special dinner marking the tenth anniversary of the formation of the congregation, serving as toastmistress. Such church activity was undoubtedly encouraged by the presence in the congregation of two individuals whom Fawn knew well: Aaron Tracy, onetime president of Weber College, and Leland Monson, her former mentor at the same school.[40]

Meanwhile, Fawn pursued her university studies, taking graduate classes in English literature. She focused on various literary figures, including D. H. Lawrence, on whom she wrote a "master's essay." In the

Fawn McKay Brodie, age twenty, at the time of her graduation from the University of Chicago in August 1936. Courtesy Bruce and Janet Brodie.

process, she received excellent training in historical methodology. Such training would prove invaluable in her later historical research and writing activities. After less than a year at the university, Fawn completed her studies and was awarded her master's degree in English literature on 28 August 1936.[41]

Meanwhile, in the course of the year, Fawn had met and fallen in love with Bernard Brodie. Culminating a whirlwind courtship that lasted a mere six weeks, she married him on 28 August 1936, the very same day she received her master's. She had met Brodie while waiting on tables in the Hutchinson Commons, the University of Chicago cafeteria, a job she had taken to help pay school expenses. Because she was tall and could be seen easily, she was assigned to pour second cups of coffee. In this setting she and Bernard were introduced by a mutual friend. As Fawn recalled, "When I poured an extra cup for Bernard, he gave me two red carnations. He brought me flowers every day for the next six weeks, [until] we were married."[42]

Bernard Brodie came from a background radically different from Fawn's. He was born in Chicago on 20 May 1910 to Morris and Esther Block Brody, Jewish immigrants who had migrated from Latvia to the United States in the late nineteenth century. The Brody family settled in a predominantly Jewish section on Chicago's west side, where Bernard, the third of four sons, grew up. His father provided for the family as an itinerant peddler, selling produce and other commodities off of a horse-drawn wagon.[43]

Bernard's parents did not get along. The marriage itself, according to son Leonard, was one of convenience, arranged by family shortly after Esther's arrival in America. There was an age difference, Morris being some sixteen years older than Esther. But more serious were the Brodys' sharply differing values and attitudes. Morris was extremely bright; he enjoyed books and learning in general, and he passed these qualities on to Bernard. Bernard's mother by contrast, while a hardworking house-keeper, had minimal education and learning. She read very little and had difficulty writing. But apparently she encouraged her children to go to school and took pride in their educational achievements. When son Bernard graduated from the University of Chicago, she reportedly applauded his achievement as "the greatest thing in the world."[44]

Other differences involved Morris's and Esther's social interactions. Morris, who was very frugal, never attended a play or even a movie because he considered them extravagances. According to his son Leonard, he "had absolutely no friends [and] didn't associate with anybody." Esther, by contrast, was quite sociable. She had friends, liked to visit and to have people visit her. But if Esther offered her friends something to eat while entertaining them, her husband resented his wife's seeming extravagance. Thus their marriage did not survive, and by 1924 the two had separated. Esther was left to raise her four sons alone.[45]

Despite other irreconcilable differences, Morris and Esther Brody were in agreement on one subject. Both rejected all aspects of Jewish religious belief and practice. Morris was strongly antireligious, believing all religions to be based on fraud and designed to gouge money out of people. He was a decided atheist. Yet, on a social-cultural level, Morris and Esther maintained certain attributes of their Judaism. The Brodys, along with other recent Jewish immigrants residing in Chicago's distinctive Jewish section, retained certain customs and a sense of group awareness. They shopped in Jewish-run stores and even ate kosher meat, thus remaining at least culturally Jewish.[46]

Bernard, meanwhile, came of age, graduating from high school at fourteen and then leaving home to attend Crane Technical College. He was ambivalent about his Jewish heritage and "sought to disassociate himself from anyone, thing, [or] idea [that] might be considered Jewish, including his family." Such rejection was manifest in Bernard's identifying himself as "Brodie" rather than "Brody." In later years Bernard claimed that the change in spelling was due to an inadvertent error made when he first enrolled in college. Bernard's younger brother, however, asserted that the change was deliberate, an attempt to deny his Jewishness. Bernard's rejection of his family was also evident in his minimal contact with them after leaving home, even though he continued to live within an easy commuting distance for the next fifteen years. Bernard took time to visit his mother only once every six months and avoided all contact with his three brothers.[47]

Indeed, Brodie's alienation was not so much from things Jewish as it was from the members of his family, particularly his mother, with whom he had a difficult relationship. Even so, Bernard helped his family out financially throughout the Great Depression when he was employed as a meteorologist with the United States Weather Bureau, a position he secured after graduating from Crane Technical College.[48]

At the University of Chicago, Bernard pursed a bachelor's degree in philosophy. After completing that in 1932, he began graduate work at Chicago in international relations. In this setting, he met Fawn in the spring of 1936. Despite marked differences in their backgrounds, they were immediately attracted to each other. Fawn found Bernard appealing for a number of reasons. First, he was extremely intelligent, with an inquisitive mind and an insatiable thirst for knowledge. Then there was his personality. Bernard was dynamic and passionate. He was quick to show his feelings and emotions. Fawn's exposure to such behavior was a new, enormously exhilarating experience. Bernard, moreover, was charming. Despite a generally quiet, soft-spoken demeanor, he enjoyed interacting with others. Fawn particularly appreciated his eloquence, his mastery of the English language, both spoken and written, and his subtle, wry sense of humor. In addition to all these attributes, Bernard had a fondness for lyrical poety, good music, and beautiful flowers. He was quite a romantic, bringing Fawn flowers, reciting poetry to her, and taking her horseback riding in the park.[49]

In turn, Bernard was drawn to Fawn's striking presence and classic beauty. The fact that at five ten she was an inch taller than he did not bother him in the least. Bernard "saw a beautiful woman . . . and said, 'I want to get to know her.'" But beyond her physical attributes, and much more important, Bernard was drawn by her intellectual strength. She could talk his language.[50]

Disclosure of the whirlwind courtship and impending marriage caused consternation, bordering on hysteria, within the McKay family. Even though none of the McKays had yet met Bernard, the simple fact that he was Jewish generated strong opposition. Fawn's parents fasted and prayed that the objectionable marriage would not take place. Thomas E. McKay wrote his daughter a hostile anti-Semitic letter, which made Fawn extremely angry and only added to the growing alienation between father and daughter. Fawn's uncle David O. McKay also weighed in with strong objections; he even came to Chicago to personally counsel his niece against the marriage. But even David O. could not change Fawn's mind.[51]

Fawn's Mormon acquaintances in Chicago also sought to discourage the match. Shifting from religious to practical considertions, one friend warned Fawn about possible future consequences because of Bernard's speech impediment. While Bernard did not have any major difficulty in speaking, he did have a slight lisp. Fawn's well-meaning friend warned that Bernard's condition would be passed on to the couple's offspring.[52]

Finally, in a last-ditch effort, Thomas E. McKay dispatched his wife to Chicago, hoping she could stop the marriage and bring their daughter back to Utah. Thomas E. possibly felt that his wife, being closer to Fawn, would be more successful in talking their daughter out of the match, but the family's limited finances may have allowed only one parent to travel to Chicago.[53]

Also upset by Fawn's impending marriage was Dilworth Jensen, who had continued to believe that his relationship with Fawn was unchanged. This perception had been reenforced by the couple's almost daily exchange of letters for many months after Fawn's arrival in Chicago. Dilworth was shocked when, without warning, he received a brief letter from Fawn that simply announced that she was going to marry someone else. Extremely upset and hurt, Jensen attributed this sudden turn of events to what he saw as a flaw in Fawn's character: She was "a chameleon" who simply reflected her environment. When she lived in Utah, he claimed, she was attached to Mormonism, whereas after moving to Chicago, she lost her faith and adopted her new beau's beliefs, or rather lack thereof.[54]

Jensen's view of Fawn's disaffection from Mormonism was grossly oversimplified. The roots of her estrangement were complex, involving factors that had been at work long before her departure for Chicago, stretching all the way back to her childhood and later experiences at the University of Utah. She was also affected by a few experiences during her first year in Chicago, but none involved Bernard Brodie. The first resulted from a discussion that Fawn had with one of her roommates upon first arriving in Chicago. This roommate, not a Latter-day Saint, asked Fawn about the origins and development of the Mormon religion. After Fawn told her about Joseph Smith, the story of the "golden plates," and the Book of Mormon, the woman asked, "What happened to these golden plates?" When Fawn replied, "An angel came and took them back to heaven," the roommate rolled her eyes, and Fawn, suddenly realizing the preposterous nature of the story, experienced what she later described as a moment of truth.[55]

Fawn's second epiphany came as a result of her own investigation of American Indian origins. Up to this time, Fawn believed—in conformity with Latter-day Saint doctrine—that Native Americans were remnants of one of the tribes of Israel, a view asserted within the *Book of Mormon*. However, upon interacting for the first time with a significant number of American Indians, Fawn saw their clearly Oriental features. She came to the conclusion "that the whole *Book of Mormon* story was false," a conclusion that brought "great bitterness" over the deceit of her childhood.[56]

Thus, by the time of her wedding, Fawn was alienated from the Mormon Church. Nevertheless, out of consideration for the presence of her mother, she and Bernard decided to be married in the local Latter-day Saint meetinghouse near the University of Chicago. Fawn Brimhall was, in fact, the only one of the four parents attending the ceremony.

Wedding photograph of
Fawn and Bernard
Brodie taken in Chicago,
28 August 1936, the very
same day that Fawn
received an M.A. in
English literature from
the University of
Chicago. Courtesy Bruce
and Janet Brodie.

Although Bernard did not invite his father—with whom he had completely severed relations—he did invite his mother and three brothers.
The four refused to attend, however, offended as they were that Bernard
was marrying a "gentile woman," or *shiksa* in a church wedding.
According to his daughter, Pamela, Bernard's family interpreted the
marriage as a deliberate rejection not only of them but also of his Jewish
heritage.[57]

Fawn's marriage to Bernard and her own increasingly strong disaffection from Mormonism did not lead to immediate and complete disen-
gagement from the church. She actually took Bernard to at least one
Mormon service. But the sole message of the speaker at this meeting
was the necessity of using sales techniques to sell Mormonism to
potential converts. "Extremely embarrassed," Fawn never again went to
church.[58]

AN INITIAL WRITTEN CRITIQUE OF THE
MORMON CHURCH

Following Fawn's graduation and their marriage, the newlyweds remained in Chicago as Bernard completed his graduate work in international studies, which focused on naval strategy. Fawn sought employment to help with finances. Despite her advanced degree in English and her previous teaching experience, she was unable to secure a teaching position any-where in Chicago. The continuing grip of the Great Depression forced her to broaden her job search outside of academia, and she finally found employment selling hosiery at a Marshall Field department store. The salary was $16.50 a week. Even though she could earn a bonus if she sold more than her quota, she hated the work because she detested selling, and she continued to seek other employment.[59]

After nine miserable months as a salesperson, Fawn found more attrac-tive employment in the Harper Library at the University of Chicago. Her position, library assistant, was a modest one; she was a night clerk on the circulation desk. The pay was considerably more than she received at Marshall Field, one hundred dollars a month. She was much happier. "I was back in God's country," she said, "among my own people." Being on the night shift left her leisure time for reading. But the position had an even deeper effect, influencing as it did the nature and direction of her future research and writing. "Harper Library . . . changed the course of my life," she later noted. Here she renewed her interest in Mormon history, despite or, more probably, because of her disaffection from her heritage.[60]

Fawn's initial research into Mormon studies involved the Church Security Program, later known as the Church Welfare Program. This pro-gram, initiated in April 1936, was a Mormon response to the anticipated curtailment of federal relief efforts. It was touted by church leaders as a Mormon version of the Works Progress Administration, itself established by Franklin Roosevelt in 1935 under the direction of Harry Hopkins. In examining the Church Security Program, Fawn was encouraged by her uncle Dean H. Brimhall, a former administrative assistant within the WPA. Brimhall was critical of the church's new program, even though it admittedly aided many destitute Latter-day Saints. He felt that the Mormon Church had overstated its effectiveness in taking church members off government relief rolls. He found instead that the number of Mormons receiving public assistance remained high. According to Brimhall's own statistics, only six states placed a greater load on the federal Emergency Works Program than Utah.[61]

Brodie arrived at essentially the same conclusion as a result of her own research. In an April 1937 letter to Brimhall, she discussed her findings and disclosed her growing disillusionment with the Mormon Church. She agreed with her uncle that the church was deliberately creating the illusion that it had removed most or all of its members from public assistance rolls. But she went one step further, suggesting that the church, in collecting tithes and other donations used in its relief efforts, was actually making money on the whole business. If this was true, Fawn wrote, "I think it's too good to be kept hidden." She elaborated for him on her research and writing activities. "I have been working up this paper which I hope will be worthwhile to someone if it ever sees the light of publication," she wrote. But if it was to be published, she carefully noted, "I shall take the utmost pains to prevent anyone from home discovering who wrote it. I have too deep a regard for daddy and mother to let them know my present attitude toward the plan, and the Church as a whole since I am trying to make a minor move against it."[62]

Less than a year after Brodie told her uncle of her research, the essay was published, receiving national exposure under the title "Mormon Security" in the February 1938 issue of *The Nation* magazine. As her central argument, Brodie asserted that the Church Security Program fell far short of its advertised goal of keeping members off various New Deal relief programs. She maintained, instead, that the percentage of Utah workers on such programs was from 32 to 60 percent higher than in the nation as a whole. The church was actually benefiting materially from this program, largely through voluntary labor and donations from pious Mormons of the poorer classes, who already were heavily taxed. These contributions in turn had the pernicious effect of materially lowering the capacity of the average Latter-day Saint to save and invest independently, thus saving for periods of unemployment. To support her case, Brodie stated with more than a little irony, "The fact that in 1935 there were proportionally 25 percent more Mormons than Gentiles on relief in Salt Lake County is an indication of the serious depletion in personal resources resulting from the church's exactions from it members, for they cannot truthfully be said to be less thrifty or less industrious than are their Gentile neighbors." Brodie then warned that, because federal relief was being curtailed, Mormon leaders had good reason for worry about the effects of their policies on their followers. She gloomily concluded, "The Mormons have been preparing for the day of want. The day of want is upon them."[63]

Reaction to Brodie and her article from within the Mormon community is difficult to gauge, in that the fledgling author published the article under the pseudonym Martha Emery. She identified herself as "a daughter of the Mormon church"—an apparent allusion to her own ambivalent relationship with her parents as well as her childhood faith.[64]

Fawn Brodie, in fact, had already personally renewed her relationship with her folks when she traveled to Utah with her new husband in the summer of 1937. Back in Huntsville, Fawn's father, along with other family members, met Bernard for the first time. "My father was sort of reluctantly accepted into" the McKay family, son Bruce asserted years later. However, according to the recollections of other family members, Bernard's acceptance came more readily than Bruce acknowledged. Fawn's sister Barbara recalled that Bernard quickly won over the whole family. Younger sister Louise found him very bright, a bit intimidating, but with "a gentle heart." Members of the extended family also reacted favorably. Even Dilworth Jensen's immediate family, Flora's in-laws, were impressed, finding Bernard courteous, mild-mannered, and empathetic. All of this acceptance came despite the initial controversy generated by the marriage itself and despite strong anti-Semitic prejudices endemic to Huntsville.[65]

Also quick to accept Bernard were Fawn's favorite uncle and aunt, Dean and Lila Brimhall. Fawn's Aunt Lila, in fact, helped Fawn's new husband in a special way. After meeting Bernard, she took Fawn aside and told her, "You know, Bernard's speech impediment can be corrected by a speech therapist. He doesn't have to just live with it." Fawn subsequently talked Bernard into treatment, and his speech difficulty was completely corrected.[66]

Bernard's acceptance by Fawn's family undoubtedly was facilitated by firsthand observations of how well the young couple interacted. "Their relationship intellectually was absolutely superb," Flora said. Louise recalled the "great tenderness between them" and the great respect they had for each other. The family also noted an unassuming quality to their relationship. Bernard's pet name for Fawn was "Pert," which stood for "pretty." He tried to help Fawn deal with anxiety over her height by teasing her about it. "Fawn is so self-conscious about being tall," he explained, "that if I laugh at her enough maybe she'll quit worrying about it." But Fawn's concerns were not easily dispelled.[67]

From the first, however, there were difficulties in the Brodies' intimate relationship. Their "marriage . . . was not . . . easy," son Bruce recalled. "They were not affectionate with each other, at least not in public or even in front of their family." Fawn shared her private concerns with sister Flora, who like Fawn, was recently married. As Flora explained it, "Fawn never felt as though [her] sexual relationship [with Bernard] was good," though Fawn "tried desperately" to solve the problem. Her frigidity evidently frustrated Bernard, and Flora advised her younger sister: "I think you'll get along a lot better with Bernard if you'd let go." Perplexed, Fawn replied, "How can I let go?" Fawn's difficulties involving sexuality were undoubtedly rooted, at least in part, in her close relationship with her mother, who had her own sexual problems. Fawn's obsession with problems of sexuality not only affected her early relationship with Bernard but would apparently also influence her later biographical writing, where the sexuality of her subjects would emerge as a major theme.[68]

Fawn and Bernard's relationship was satisfying in virtually every other respect, however. Bernard, moreover, developed good relations with other members of Fawn's family and, indeed, found Huntsville much to his liking. Even so, his Jewish, big-city background made him a local curiosity. Upon his first visit to the town, he borrowed a horse and proceeded to explore the local community and surrounding countryside. As one old-time resident recalled, "The word went out" concerning Fawn's husband, and "he was the most observed rider in Huntsville that day."[69]

While in Huntsville on this visit, Fawn found time to drop in on Jarvis Thurston, her college friend. They discussed matters relative to the Utah cultural scene, a topic on which Thurston was well informed. (He was the literary reviewer for the *Ogden Standard-Examiner*, the region's major newspaper.) Like Brodie, Thurston had graduated from college with a degree in English literature. For the larger Utah literary community, the mid- to late 1930s was a time of intense creativity, an exciting time for aspiring writers. As Thurston noted, "Practically everybody . . . that I knew . . . intended to write a history of Mormonism, the history of Joseph Smith, or a novel based on it." Many such individuals were undoubtedly inspired by the success of fellow Utah native Bernard De Voto, who had written several essays on the Mormons, the earliest appearing in the *American Mercury* in 1926. De Voto, in fact, stood in the vanguard of an emerging group of Utah-born writers identified as "Mormondom's lost generation," even though De Voto himself was *not* a Latter-day Saint and indeed was less than flattering in his characterization of the Mormons and their culture.[70]

While Fawn indicated interest in Mormon history, she did not reveal to Thurston any intentions of writing in this field or pursuing a career as a biographer. Nor did she reveal to Thurston her soon-to-be published article in *The Nation* on the Church Security Program. Rather, their discussions focused on literature and writing outside of Mormon studies—specifically, James Joyce's recently published *Ulysses* and the works of William Faulkner and Sigmund Freud.[71] The latter's work and ideas would profoundly influence and affect Brodie's own research and writing.

The Brodies' 1937 visit to Utah was important in several respects. Besides visiting family and friends, many of whom she had not seen for two years, Fawn successfully dispelled the various fears, misconceptions, and prejudices concerning Bernard. In addition, the visit would be the last time that Fawn would see her parents and two younger sisters for another three years. Her immediate family was about to depart for Basel, Switzerland, where Thomas E. McKay had been appointed by the Mormon Church as presiding officer of the Swiss-Austrian mission. Thomas's call to serve as mission president, a paid position, apparently came through the efforts of his older brother, David O. McKay. At the time, Thomas was without income, having lost his long-held position on the Utah Public Utilities Commission in the spring of 1937.[72]

The departure of the McKay family for Europe also meant the family was leaving the Huntsville farm for good. While Fawn and her husband, along with other McKay family members, would return to Huntsville for occasional visits and reunions during the summers, never again would the family live in the community year round. The McKays' permanent departure ironically occurred just as the farm's heavy debt was substantially reduced. Mortgage relief came through a farm renegotiation program under the New Deal's Farm Credit Administration, an ironic twist, given Thomas E. McKay's partisan disdain for both Franklin Roosevelt and the New Deal. Though he remained a staunch conservative Republican, McKay found the aid offered by the FCA too attractive to pass up.[73]

In contrast to her father, Fawn moved politically in the opposite direction, becoming a liberal Democrat. One of the influences in her personal politics was her exposure to the strongly liberal environment of the University of Chicago and the pervasive dominance of the Democratic Party in Chicago. Also affecting Fawn's sympathies was the help provided her family though various New Deal programs. Then too her husband Bernard, and her uncle Dean R. Brimhall were both outspoken partisan Democrats. Brimhall, in fact, worked for several New Deal agencies throughout the 1930s, including the Civil Works Administration, the Federal Emergency Relief Administration, and the Works Progress Administration. Finally, the Democratic Party appealed to Fawn because it represented another means by which she could assert her growing independence not just from her father but also from the larger, extended McKay family, virtually all of whom were partisan Republicans.[74]

The departure for Europe of Thomas E. McKay, his wife, and daughters Barbara and Louise in August 1937 left Fawn McKay Brodie, just one month shy of her twenty-second birthday, with still more latitude to assert her growing independence from her family and from her culture. Fawn's quest for independence would be manifest in her continued research and writing on Mormon life and culture. Her efforts would focus on Mormonism's founder, Joseph Smith, a task that would absorb her energies over the next seven years and culminate in the controversial biography *No Man Knows My History: The Life of Joseph Smith*—a work that would profoundly alter the course of her own life while sending shock waves throughout the Latter-day Saint community.

THREE

"A Compelling Piece of Detective Work"

1938–1946

Fawn Brodie did not originally set out to investigate the life of Joseph Smith, the founder of Mormonism. Initially, she wanted only to satisfy herself as to how the *Book of Mormon* came to be written. Her curiosity was first piqued by a study of the anthropology of the American Indians that convinced her that—contrary to Smith's claim—they were of Mongoloid rather than Hebraic origin. But her search was also driven by her husband Bernard's many questions about her Mormon heritage, which he found both unique and fascinating. Soon realizing that there was no good biography of Joseph Smith to satisfy her curiosity, she decided to undertake the task herself. With "the whole problem of [Smith's] credibility . . . crying out for some explanation," Fawn Brodie began this "piece of detective work" that she found "absolutely compelling."[1]

A SOLITARY, SEMISECRET PROJECT

Few individuals were aware of Brodie's early efforts to research the origins and development of the *Book of Mormon*. It was a little-noticed enterprise started in 1938 and carried out whenever Brodie's schedule as a full-time librarian at the University of Chicago library and a part-time journalism teacher at nearby Crane Technical College permitted.[2]

In her research Brodie consulted various books and historical materials in the University of Chicago's Harper Library. "Every book I asked for was there," she remembered, including crucial books by Ethan Smith, Elias Boudinot, and others, all of whom believed that the American Indians descended from the Lost Tribes of Israel. Harper Library also housed a large collection of books on western New York history of the late eighteenth and early nineteenth centuries, enabling her to study the socioreligious environment from which Mormonism emerged.[3]

In June 1939, Fawn shared her initial findings with her uncle Dean R. Brimhall, noting that she "had the most fun with the *Book of Mormon* & was able to trace almost every idea in it right down to Ontario Co. New York 1827 [including] the lost tribe theory, the exterminated race theory, anti-Masonry, anti-Catholicism—the whole gamut of sectarian religious controversy." She then confessed to him her ambition to produce "a genuinely scholarly biography" on Joseph Smith. Anxious to tell someone besides Bernard what she was doing, she asked her uncle to look over some of her research on Smith, stating, "I think your own analysis is sane & judicious, perhaps because it conforms with my own." In fact, Brimhall, like Brodie, was no longer an active Latter-day Saint.[4]

In late 1939, when Fawn overcame her initial reluctance to share her work with her immediate family, she turned to her younger brother, Thomas. After returning from a Mormon mission to Germany, Thomas had enrolled as an undergraduate student at the University of Chicago for the 1939–40 academic year and was now living near his sister. Thomas was bright and inquisitive, and he immediately took an interest in what she was doing, actually examining many of the same materials on Joseph Smith and Mormon origins that Fawn was studying. This generated some intense discussions, with Fawn and Thomas sharply differing in their views. Thomas recalled, "I would look at it from the aspect of one who is thoroughly convinced that Joseph Smith was a prophet," whereas Fawn looked at the same information from the perspective of one thoroughly convinced that he was not.[5]

Fawn was particularly bothered by the discovery of Smith's "money-digging" activities, that is, the quest for hidden buried treasure. She told her brother that the Lord would never have permitted a prophet to engage in such activity. Yet Thomas insisted that Smith, as a very poor youth, engaged in money-digging to generate revenue for his impoverished family. Money-digging, Thomas added, was a respected profession at the time, and besides, at that period of his life, Smith had not yet proclaimed himself a prophet. Such arguments went nowhere, Thomas recalled: "Neither did [Fawn] change my mind nor did I change hers."[6]

More significant was the input Fawn received from Bernard, who acted as a sounding board for her ideas and evaluated her written drafts. She praised her husband as immensely helpful in judging her conclusions with a detachment that she herself lacked.[7]

The Brodies' main concern during this period was not Fawn's research but rather Bernard's academic work at the University of Chicago, where he was completing his doctorate in international relations. Bernard was naturally drawn to this field, given the momentous developments in Europe and Asia—specifically, the Spanish Civil War, Germany's rearmament and aggressive takeover of Austria and Czechoslovakia, and Japan's aggression into the heart of China.

The University of Chicago was a leader in the field of international relations, emphasizing an interdisciplinary approach that was novel for the time. The school set itself apart from most other universities, which continued to teach international politics from a static, organizational, strictly legalistic standpoint. At Chicago, the subject was taught in terms of *power*—who uses it, for what ends, in what political context, and against whom. Bernard was particularly influenced by two outstanding professors: Jacob Viner, a specialist in the politics of international relations and former advisor to Franklin D. Roosevelt, and Quincy Wright, a worldrenowned expert on the causes of war. As Wright's star student, Brodie was awarded the department's sole fellowship in 1939, which carried a stipend of $350 and enabled him to begin research for his doctoral dissertation. Focusing on the impact of naval technology on nineteenthcentury diplomacy, Bernard completed his doctorate in June of 1940.[8]

Meanwhile, Fawn viewed international relations from a particularly personal perspective because of her family's situation. Her parents and two younger sisters were living in Basel, Switzerland, while her father presided over the Swiss-Austrian mission. During the late 1930s, her father's responsibilities were expanded to include Mormon activities throughout Germany, causing Fawn particular concern. The Mormon Church in Germany had enjoyed relatively rapid growth, particularly during the years immediately following World War I. By 1930 Germany boasted some twelve thousand Mormons—a total larger than that found in any other nation outside the United States.[9]

Following the emergence of Adolf Hitler in 1933, the Mormon Church moved to accommodate itself to the new political order. Official Mormon policy, in the words of one writer, was to "get along" with the Hitler regime. German officials, in turn, allowed the Mormon Church to continue its varied activities, including missionary work, thus giving it a rather privileged position. By contrast, Nazi officials dissolved thirty-four other sects, including Jehovah's Witnesses, Anabaptists, Seventh-Day Adventists, and the Baha'i movement. Mormon accommodation came at a price. Like other functioning denominations in Nazi Germany, the Mormon Church remained ominously silent as the government perse-cuted Jews with greater and greater severity during the late 1930s.[10]

Fawn was particularly interested in the situation of German Jews. Her brother, Thomas, in fact, had been present as a Mormon missionary in Königsberg, East Prussia, during the events of *Kristallnacht,* or "the Night of Broken Glass," on 9–10 November 1938, which marked the beginning of the Holocaust. Mormon authorities, in both Germany and the United States, appeared insensitive to the plight of Jews. Fawn thought the church overly anxious to curry favor with Nazi officials, as evident in the actions of Alfred C. Rees, Mormon mission president for eastern Germany. Rees had written what Brodie considered a pro-Nazi essay, entitled "In the Land of the Mormons," which was published in the Nazi Party's official newspaper, the *Volkischer Beobachter.* In the essay, Rees described certain parallel features between Nazism and Mormonism that he felt should make the religion appealing to Germans. Further, Rees encouraged missionaries to write similar articles for other newspapers throughout Germany.[11]

Mormon actions within the United States also drew Brodie's ire. She criticized the editorial position of the *Deseret News,* the official Mormon Church newspaper in Salt Lake City. Brodie believed the *News* was falling over backwards in covering events in Germany to avoid offending Nazi officials because of a Mormon fear of complete banishment for its members. Upset at the *News* for failing to condemn Nazi persecution of Jews, she wrote her uncle, "I can just hear the good brethren . . . at home saying—'of course the persecution of the Jews is terrible but God moves in mysterious ways, his wonders to perform.'"[12]

Brodie also worried about her parents and sister Louise in Switzerland—Barbara had earlier returned to the United States to attend school—particularly as the international situation in Europe continued to deteriorate. Immediately after the start of World War II in September 1939, Thomas E. McKay assumed added responsibility, overseeing all Mormon activity in Germany. But in April 1940, with war spreading to western Europe, McKay, his wife, and their daughter were ordered to return to the United States after directing the evacuation all Mormon missionaries from Europe. After returning to Utah, McKay was given the title of acting president of the church's European mission. In that post he continued to oversee Mormon affairs in Europe as best he could, mainly through correspondence with local Mormon leaders.[13]

Thus Thomas E. McKay's role as a Mormon Church official continued to increase in importance during these difficult years. At the same time, his basic commitment to things Mormon remained strong and steadfast. This was not the case with his wife, Fawn Brimhall McKay. According to her daughter Fawn, she returned from Europe a thoroughgoing heretic. "Two years of playing hostess to itinerant apostles, plus some sophisticated literature and the overwhelmingly impressive spectacle of twenty centuries of European art," Fawn said of her mother, "really shocked her out of that provincialism in which twenty-five years in Huntsville had tried to enshroud her." Brodie noted that her mother's capacity for change "was always there . . . but I didn't think at her age there could come such delightful blossoming of courageous heresy." Brodie, of course, welcomed this development, proclaiming that she and her mother were now "closer in spirit than I had ever dreamed would be possible."[14]

THREE MOVES, MOTHERHOOD, AND ALFRED A. KNOPF

In the summer of 1940, shortly after Bernard completed his doctorate, the Brodies moved from Chicago to Princeton, New Jersey. It would be the first of three successive moves over the next three years, as Bernard experienced difficulty in securing an academic position, despite his outstanding record of scholarship at the University of Chicago and his excellent references. His lack of success was at least in part due to his

Thomas E. and Fawn
Brimhill McKay, the
author's parents, taken
in Salt Lake City in 1942.
By this time, Thomas E.
was a high-ranking
Mormon Church official,
while his wife remained
"a quiet heretic."
Courtesy Barbara McKay
Smith.

being Jewish at a time when many institutions still openly discriminated
against Jews.[15]

But that summer, Bernard secured a one-year research fellowship at
the Institute for Advanced Study at Princeton University, where he
continued research on the topics of war and strategy. The research was
timely, given the specter of full-scale warfare in Europe, including the fall
of France, the Battle of Britain, and the invasion of the Soviet Union.
Concurrently Brodie was caught up in the vigorous debate within the
United States between isolationists and interventionists. He himself
clearly favored American intervention, and he was active in the Committee to Defend America by Aiding the Allies. Meanwhile, thanks to a
Carnegie Corporation fellowship and promise of publication, he began
revisions on his doctoral dissertation on sea power.[16]

By September 1941 the Brodies had moved again, this time to Hanover, New Hampshire, where Bernard was hired by the political science department at Dartmouth College. The Brodies were ambivalent about their new surroundings. On the one hand, both Fawn and Bernard loved the New England countryside and the beauty of the changing seasons. But Bernard gradually became disenchanted with Dartmouth College, viewing it as an institution "for spoiled rich children . . . not smart enough to get into the better Ivy League schools." Dartmouth's faculty members were entirely oriented toward teaching—to the exclusion of research. This bothered Bernard, who loved research and never cared much for teaching. When he could find time, he continued the work of turning his doctoral dissertation into a book.[17]

In June of 1941 Princeton University Press brought out *Sea Power in the Machine Age*, Brodie's study of technological developments from the steam warship of Fulton's day to the modern dreadnought. The book was well received; reviewers praised it as an "excellent historical study," "clearly written," and "finely conceived." Particularly timely, *Sea Power in the Machine Age* assumed a special relevance following the Japanese attack on Pearl Harbor and America's entry into World War II on 7 December 1941. The U.S. Department of the Navy immediately purchased sixteen hundred copies of the book for its naval college, making it a best-seller by university press standards.[18]

Pleased by the book's success, Princeton University Press commissioned Bernard to write another. *A Layman's Guide to Naval Strategy*, published in September 1942, described the use and function of various tools of sea power, including battleships, aircraft, destroyers, and submarines, along with torpedoes and mines. *A Layman's Guide*, like Brodie's *Sea Power in the Machine Age*, was well received, garnering numerous favorable reviews. Better still, the *Guide* was adopted as a basic text by the Naval Reserve Officers Training Corps; the Department of the Navy ordered fifteen thousand copies in October 1942. Thus, Bernard Brodie, who had never served in the navy or even been aboard a naval vessel, came to be considered a leading expert on contemporary naval strategy.[19]

Meanwhile, Fawn, undoubtedly influenced both by her husband and the all-consuming environment of World War II, developed her own interest in strategy and warfare. During 1940 and 1941 she worked as a research assistant for the Committee for International Studies, collecting material for a small pamphlet, which was published under the title, *Our Far Eastern Record*. A short work of less than a hundred pages and containing a selection of official statements, treaty texts, and trade statistics, the book was designed as a reference aid. Despite its modest objectives, the pamphlet attracted the attention of the *Los Angeles Times*, which recommended it as "a veritable encyclopedia concerning foreign affairs," helpful in understanding "the hows and whys of our war with Japan."[20]

Fawn's interest in international affairs continued with her attendance at the International Peace Conference in Maine during the summer of 1942. Following that conference, she produced a second pamphlet, *Peace Aims and Postwar Planning: A Bibliography*. Published in July 1942, it listed pertinent pamphlets and articles that had appeared in the United States and England between 1939 and July 1942.[21]

By the summer of 1942 Fawn's primary concern was the expected birth of her first child. She and Bernard had been initially reluctant to have a child during the war but had changed their minds upon a visit to Utah during the summer of 1941. There Flora's happiness with her baby girl won Fawn and Bernard over to the prospects of parenthood, and a year later, on 9 November 1942, Fawn gave birth to their first child, a boy. The proud parents named him Richard McKay Brodie.[22]

In the meantime, Fawn's research on Joseph Smith had languished. The two pamphlets that had consumed her writing energies were not "in the least creative," Fawn admitted, but "more pertinent to 1942 than hunting up data on what happened in Nauvoo in 1842." Still, some months before the baby's birth, she had managed to draft a three hundred-page manuscript on Joseph Smith, characterizing it for Dean Brimhall as "very crude" and "far from finished." She described to him her findings on Smith's 1826 trial for "crystal-gazing," noting discovery of an old court record in which a witness had testified that Smith had laid a book upon a white cloth and "looking through [a] stone which was white and transparent, held the stone to the candle, turned his back to the book, and read." Brodie noted to her uncle that "the jump from this to translating the plates with a blanket stretched across the room is not a big one, I think." "Well, it's all very absorbing," she concluded, "and sometimes depressing. [Smith's] career continues to astonish me—as does the stubborn survival of the church." "The more I work with the man," she wrote her uncle, "the more of a challenge he becomes."[23]

Fawn Brodie with infant son Richard McKay, ca. 1943, taken at the time the author was working on *No Man Knows My History.* Courtesy Bruce and Janet Brodie.

The challenge did not daunt her. With her three hundred-page manuscript in hand, she pushed toward her ultimate goal of a complete biography. In early 1943, she approached Datus Smith, editor at Princeton University Press, undoubtedly encouraged by the publisher's success with Bernard's two books on naval sea power. Smith, however, after reading the manuscript, felt that, because of its controversial approach, it should be published by a nonacademic press. He also saw its potential for commercial success and encouraged Brodie to apply for an Alfred A. Knopf literary fellowship.[24]

Brodie followed Smith's advice. As part of her application, she submitted the first seven chapters, some forty-five thousand words covering the period from Joseph Smith's birth to 1831, when he was, in Brodie's words, "the leader of a fast-growing semi-communistic colony in Ohio." In her letter of application, she characterized Joseph Smith as "one of the most elusive and controversial figures" in American history. "I believe that the book will have a peculiar timeliness," she wrote,

not because [Smith's] life exactly parallels that of any modern
dictator, nor on the other hand, because persecution of the
Mormons is at all comparable to that of the Jews in this century, but
rather because the book is the story of a challenge to certain
enduring values which are a part of the American heritage. Both
the guilt and the honor lie at times with the Mormons, at times with
the "Gentiles," depending upon the issue at stake.[25]

The author asserted that she was not trying to "reinterpret" the
Mormon leader in light of the twentieth century but was endeavoring to
compose an accurate history on the basis of a myriad of scattered documents. Her ambition was "not to produce a fictionalized biography."
"Where so much controversy is rampant," she said "one needs documentation—not imaginary conversations." She then outlined her own unique
qualifications: "I believe that I am singularly well-equipped to do this study,
for I know the Mormon point of view intimately, having been reared in the
bosom of the church until I was twenty. Since then I have achieved an
attitude of complete objectivity toward Mormon dogma. . . . My point of
view has been shaped by the facts, not by any predilection for or prejudice
against the Mormons."[26]

In late May 1943, Fawn Brodie received the good news that her application was judged the best of the forty-four entries submitted. One of the
Knopf judges described Brodie's work as a "model of intellectual sobriety
and lucidity." The judge conceded that it was not "definitive," wryly
observing that "a definitive biography of [any] religious leader would
certainly be a contradiction of terms." He found the author's presentation "perspicuous, balanced, thought through, astringently sane," with
a narrative that moved with "unbroken smoothness." Overall, "Brodie's
portrait of Smith . . . [is] a very convincing one," he said, "for although
[Brodie is] aware of such special interpretations as those supplied by
psychoanalysis, economic determinism, religious bigotry, worship and
straight debunking, she steers a path that is not so much a mean between
these, as [something] simply better than any of them alone." In conclusion, he stated that the author's presentation "should satisfy the
scholar, impress the layman and absorb both." The fellowship carried a
stipend of twenty-five hundred dollars.[27]

Just prior to receiving this good news, the Brodies received some bad news: Dartmouth College had declined to renew Bernard's appointment for the 1942–43 academic year. The reasons for the school's negative decision were alluded to in a letter to Bernard written by college dean E. Gordon Bill: "There is a rather unanimous feeling in the Department of Political Science that you are too much of a specialist," the dean wrote, "and, in fact, too big a man in your field to fit into any future plans of the Department . . . as they are now being envisioned."[28] Bill's letter clearly suggested that departmental infighting and the petty jealousy of insecure academicians had doomed Brodie's career at Dartmouth.

In late 1942, Bernard Brodie decided to join the United States Navy, seeing it as the most appropriate place to contribute his skills in naval strategy. This meant yet another move for Bernard and Fawn—and now their infant son. The Brodies' move from Hanover to Washington, D.C., early in 1943 represented their third move in less than three years.

WARTIME WASHINGTON AND COMPLETING JOSEPH SMITH

The Brodies' move to wartime Washington, D.C., thrust them into an environment vastly different from placid, bucolic Hanover. Bernard's role as a newly commissioned lieutenant in the U.S. Navy, assigned to the Office of the Chief of Naval Operations, was a world apart from teaching government and politics to Dartmouth College freshmen. Because of his proven ability as a writer, Bernard was assigned to write "combat narratives"—short books describing various war campaigns, which were distributed as confidential documents to all fleet officers. He also served as chief ghostwriter for the chief of naval operations, Adm. Ernest J. King, and was assigned additional tasks in the Office of Naval Intelligence. He wrote propaganda tracts for broadcast to German U-boats in the attempt to get their crews to surrender.[29]

Meanwhile, even as she concentrated on Joseph Smith, Fawn worried about reaction within the Mormon community to the forthcoming biography. In writing her father and mother, she warned them that her work was likely to generate hostile criticism from Mormon Church authorities. "You will probably be criticized for having raised a wayward daughter," she told her parents, and then advised them, "When someone mentions [the biography], you'd better say, 'Well, I don't know what the girl is up to. It's all her own doing you know, and she's always been inclined to be a little headstrong,' or something like that." And she thanked her parents for teaching her "to revere the truth, which is the noblest ideal a parent can instill in his children."[30]

Fawn's worries were compounded by the elevation of her father within the Mormon Church hierarchy to the position of assistant to the Council of the Twelve. Some two years earlier, Thomas E. McKay, along with four other high Mormon officials, had been appointed to this newly created office. As a "general authority," McKay and the others were to assist the Council of the Twelve in its official duties. In apparent response to her father's appointment, Fawn confessed that winning the Knopf fellowship made her realize the responsibility of writing about Smith; "I am really a little scared," she wrote her parents, "and only hope I can do justice to the magnitude of the task."[31]

Extensive media publicity relative to Brodie's award was not long in coming. An official press release issued by Alfred A. Knopf and printed in newspapers throughout the country in late May quoted the author extensively. "Anyone who grows up with a Mormon background cannot escape [Joseph Smith]," Brodie was quoted as saying. "He is the first cause" for the existence of Mormonism as a religion. "I seem always to have known him, like Santa Claus and God," she said, yet confessed that she was troubled by his "baffling and elusive" character. "The more I read about him," she said in this press release, "the more I wanted to understand why the same man could have inspired such fanatical adoration in his followers and such venomous hatred in his opponents." She then concluded by critiquing those who had previously written on Smith:

> I found that Mormon historians had so deified their prophet that they had robbed him of the healthy, earthy qualities which endeared him to his people. The old anti-Mormon diatribes, on the other hand, gave Satan the whole credit for his success. Both biases blinded their authors to one of the most exciting and fabulous success stories in American history.[32]

Brodie was also featured in a special news story written by Peggy Preston for the *Washington Post*. Fawn modestly characterized her husband as the "real writer in the family," explaining that her own "book has yet to prove itself with the public." She then gave her reasons for focusing on Joseph Smith: "To most people, Mormonism means simply polygamy and Brigham Young," the biographer said, whereas "Joseph Smith and his influence [have] been largely overlooked." Besides the *Post*, Brodie was also featured in articles appearing in Utah newspapers, specifically the *Salt Lake Tribune* and the *Ogden Standard-Examiner*. The latter editorialized that the Ogden-born author's local friends were "eagerly anticipating her new volume."[33]

Brodie now pushed ahead with her writing. She had already completed the first seven chapters, taking her account of Joseph Smith to 1831, and had collected enough material to relate the Mormon leader's experiences in Ohio and Missouri up to 1839. There still remained research on the Nauvoo period, including Smith's introduction of polygamy and the critical events leading up to his assassination in June 1844. She characterized her book as still in a "very formative stage" in describing the immense amount of research left to do as well as "the sheer labor of writing and rewriting." She confessed that writing came "very hard and very slowly. I have to sweat over every line." The task was made even more challenging by her responsibilities as housewife and mother to her young son, Richard—or Dickie as he was called during his early years. All of this compelled her to organize her time carefully; from her daily routine she squeezed out four hours for the book and gave the rest of the time to her baby.[34]

Brodie's research took her to the Library of Congress, located close to her home in Washington, D. C. She also examined relevant materials in other libraries, thanks to money received from the Knopf fellowship. In doing such research she would leave her young son for short periods of time in the care of either close friends or family members. She traveled to the New York Public Library, where she found a significant amount of material on Mormon history. Particularly useful was a file of newspaper clippings on the Mormons and their activities in Missouri and Illinois. She visited the New York State Library in Albany, where she read the same newspapers Joseph Smith had read as a youth in Palmyra. Such publications contained articles on the Mound Builder Indians, along with the prevalent speculation on their descent from the Lost Tribes of Israel. Brodie also visited Kirtland, Ohio, where she examined documents on Joseph Smith's legal difficulties.[35]

More significantly, in the summer of 1943 Brodie visited Salt Lake City to do research and to consult with her family. She was particularly concerned about the sensitive position of her father as a high Mormon official. She told him that her biography would likely be an "embarrassment" to the church and that she did not intend to submit it for church censorship. She told her father she would publish it under a pseudonym to protect him—as she had her earlier *Nation* article—if he wished. To that offer Thomas McKay "said absolutely not," for which Fawn was always grateful.[36]

While in Salt Lake City, Fawn visited the Mormon Church Library-Archives, where she found access to research materials highly restricted. She gained access only by being "introduced about the place as Brother McKay's daughter," an artifice, she confessed, that made her feel "guilty as hell." Nevertheless, she pursued the research, being very discreet in not asking for anything remotely anti-Mormon and spending most of her time going through two early Mormon newspapers published in Nauvoo.[37]

Near the end of her visit, Fawn summoned enough courage to ask the assistant church historian, A. William Lund, for permission to see the 1832 diary of Joseph Smith, a rare, restricted manuscript. Lund, surprised by Brodie's awareness of this little-known document, referred Brodie to Apostle Joseph Fielding Smith, Mormon Church Historian, the only person who could grant access. In a tense, yet frank, meeting with Smith, Brodie told him that she "was trying to write scholarly and accurate history, to avoid sensationalizing and fictionalizing of any sort." In addition to the 1832 Smith diary, Brodie also asked about source materials dealing with polygamy in Nauvoo, which apparently also resided in the church archives. Apostle Smith, like Lund, was taken back by what he perceived as Brodie's audacity. "There are things in this library we don't let anyone see," he told her, then disclosed the existence of an 1831 revelation to Joseph Smith that sanctioned polygamy but that had never been printed lest it "be misinterpreted."[38]

Word of Brodie's frank discussion with Joseph Fielding Smith got back to her uncle David O. McKay, who angrily confronted his niece at her parents' home. In a painful, acrimonious encounter, David O. McKay forbade Brodie from doing further research in the Mormon Church Library-Archives, characterizing her presence as "an embarrassment" and stating that he would never "permit anyone to use the library who would distort the truth." But later that same day McKay changed his mind, sending his niece a formal note granting her permission to use the library.[39]

Brodie rejected her uncle's offer. To return to the church library would be impossible for her in light of their earlier confrontation, and she, in turn, wrote him a brief note expressing her desire to "spare him . . . further embarrassment." Never again would she ask to consult materials in the church library. She spent the remainder of her Utah visit doing research in the libraries of the University of Utah and the Utah State Historical Society.[40]

Leaving Salt Lake City, Brodie traveled to Independence, Missouri, where she spent ten days in the library of the Reorganized Church of Jesus Christ of Latter Day Saints. Her treatment by officials in charge there contrasted sharply with that of the Utah Mormon officials. At Independence, she was shown every courtesy. Particularly helpful was the former RLDS church historian S. A. Burgess, who, though semiretired, was still serving as a staff member. He opened the church library vault to her, bringing her "piles of material" without her having even asked for it. She was allowed to examine a good many original letters, the photostatic copy of the *Book of Mormon* manuscript, and various other manuscript and printed materials.[41]

While in Independence, Brodie also met several members of the so-called first family of the RLDS—direct descendants of Joseph Smith himself. These included the prophet's two grandsons, Frederick M. Smith, then president of the RLDS Church, and his younger brother, Israel Smith, a high-ranking RLDS official, who would eventually succeed his brother as president. Brodie's impressions of the Smiths were mixed. On the one hand, she came away convinced that the Utah church benefited enormously by not having the Joseph Smith heirs in their movement, noting, "They are interesting, intelligent people with a good deal of social presence, but they are such typical American bourgeois businessmen that the thought of a halo above any one of them is immediately incongruous. After conversing with Frederick and Israel, his brother, I felt that neither deifies his grandfather to nearly the extent that the average Utah Mormon does. They are inclined to be a little apologetic, and they are definitely on the defensive."[42]

In a later account, Brodie recalled Israel Smith in somewhat more positive terms: He was a thoughtful man and a scholar, she said, well acquainted with Ethan Smith's *View of the Hebrews*, which she believed to be an important source of the ideas in the *Book of Mormon*. But she argued with him over evidence of polygamy in the early days of the church, and Smith admitted quietly, "There were indeed strange things going on at Nauvoo."[43]

In general, Brodie's research trip to Utah and Missouri was profitable. Upon returning to Washington, the fledgling biographer felt that she had enough material to complete her account of Smith's Nauvoo years. But she conceded that a truly definitive study would have to await some future scholar granted unrestricted access to important manuscripts in the Mormon Church Library-Archives—specifically, the papers of key Mormon leaders, including Willard Richards, Wilford Woodruff, William Clayton, and especially Joseph Smith.[44]

As Brodie pushed ahead with her biography, she secured the services of Dale L. Morgan, whose role would prove absolutely crucial and with whom she would develop a lifelong association. Morgan was a contemporary of hers, born in 1914 and, like her, a graduate of the University of Utah. Despite his own deep fascination with Mormonism's past, Morgan, again like Brodie, was not a practicing Latter-day Saint. Although completely deaf, from the effects of meningitis suffered at the age of fourteen, by 1943, when Brodie met him, Morgan had already established himself as a respected scholar of Utah and western history. Working for the Utah Works Progress Administration on its historical records survey, he had risen to the position of supervisor of the Utah Writers Project in 1940. He also had numerous publications to his credit, including two major books, *Utah: A Guide to the State*, published in 1941, and *The Humboldt: Highroad of the West*, which appeared in 1943. Following the completion of his work on the Utah WPA survey and the outbreak of World War II, Morgan had moved to Washington, D.C., to assume a position with the Office of Price Administration.[45]

Almost from the moment of their first meeting in the summer of 1943, Brodie and Morgan became fast friends. Brodie characterized Morgan as a wonderful person, a sensitive writer, and a thorough scholar of Mormon history. She found Morgan's knowledge of that history "simply phenomenal." And despite his hearing impairment, she found him easy to communicate with. He verbalized fluently, albeit in a high, eerie monotone.[46]

His scholarly attributes—and the fact that he lived near the Brodies in Washington—enabled Morgan rapidly to assume the roles of mentor and critic. His "indefatigable scholarship in Mormon history" was a spur to Brodie's work.[47] He quickly demonstrated his skills in a thorough critique of Brodie's manuscript, which now consisted of ten chapters, taking the story of Joseph Smith and the Mormons up through 1832 and their expulsion from Jackson County, Missouri.

With alarming frankness, Morgan informed Brodie of the preliminary nature of her work. This draft, he said, was not yet, properly speaking, a "biography" of Smith but rather a "history" of the Mormon leader. He explained that she was "articulating the skeleton," that is, establishing a rationale by which to come "to grips with him as a human being." He found her manuscript oversimplified, "positive beyond what the facts will support when all the obscure lights and shadows of those facts are closely examined." Morgan went on:

> Your own point of view, as set forth in this manuscript, is much too hard and fast, to my way of thinking, it is too coldly logical in its conception of Joseph's mind and the developments of his character. Your view of him is all hard edges, without any of those blurrings which are more difficult to cope with but which constitutes a man in the round. I am particularly struck with the assumption your MS makes that Joseph was a self-conscious impostor.

Pursuing this point, Morgan told Brodie that what she had written was too much in the vein of an exposé. In conclusion, he recommended that the final manuscript "be so written that Mormon, anti-Mormon, and non-Mormon alike can go to the biography and read in it with agreement— disagreeing often in detail, perhaps, but observing that you have noted the points of disagreement and that while you set forth your point of view, you do not have Absolute Truth by the tail." He tempered his remarks by congratulating Brodie for what she had done thus far, predicting that her biography had the potential of being "a landmark in Mormon history."[48]

In general, Morgan was much more incisive and penetrating in his critique than the Knopf panel had been in awarding Brodie her fellowship. The difference was that Morgan knew Mormon history and the Knopf readers did not.

Responding to Morgan's suggestions, Brodie spent the next several months revising these first ten chapters. She also added chapters on Joseph Smith's experiences in Ohio: his difficulties in Missouri, culminating in his own imprisonment and the expulsion of his followers from that state; and his varied activities during the all-important Nauvoo period. In this work she had significant help from several other scholars, many of whom lived in Utah, and most of whom, unlike Brodie, were active, practicing Latter-day Saints. But, like Brodie, they were fascinated by certain disputable aspects of Mormonism's past and willing to examine them in a critical, dispassionate light.

One such scholar was Vesta Crawford, a Utah-based poet and writer whose own research focused on Emma Smith, the first wife of the Mormon prophet, research she shared with Brodie. Crawford, like Brodie, was interested in Joseph Smith's practice of plural marriage, but unlike Brodie, she remained close to the Mormon Church, becoming editorial secretary and later associate editor of the *Relief Society Magazine,* an official Mormon publication.[49]

Also helping Brodie was Utah writer and photojournalist Claire Noall. Like Crawford, Noall was interested in the practice of Mormon polygamy in Nauvoo, an interest that stemmed from her ongoing research on her grandfather, Willard Richards, a onetime confidant of Joseph Smith's and one of the first Latter-day Saints to embrace polygamy. Noall's research ultimately culminated in a fictionalized biography of Richards, *Intimate Disciple.* Like Crawford, Noall shared her research with Brodie.[50]

Brodie and Noall developed a close friendship and had frank discussions concerning the operation and morality of Mormon polygamy in Joseph Smith's time. "The more I work with the polygamy material," Brodie told Noall on one occasion, "the more baffled I become." With Noall she speculated on Joseph Smith's motives for entering and endorsing polygamy. She believed that he came to view monogamy as an intolerably circumscribed way of life. As church leader he was also in a position to "define the nature of sin." Thus it was "ridiculously easy" for him "to transform relative promiscuity into a religious duty." As Brodie wrote Noall,

> I think polygamy was disguised whoredom. But the disguise was so good that it metamorphosed the system into something quite different. After all the difference between fornication and sacred matrimony is merely a few mumblings from any mangy justice of the peace. The word is the thing, after all. Most of the polygamous women were very certain that it was a commandment of God. Read the revelation again, and see how shockingly specific it is. "Unless a man enters this covenant he shall be damned, etc."

Brodie also speculated that the secrecy of polygamy lent an attractiveness to the practice, noting that "there was more trading around among married couples in those days. . . . Women as well as men have an impulse to variety, and when that impulse is loosed under the guise of a profound religious duty, there is no telling where it will lead."[51]

While acknowledging polygamy's mutual attraction for men and women, Brodie expressed to Noall her moral outrage at Joseph Smith for taking as plural wives women married to other men. According to Brodie, four out of five of Joseph's wives were already married to other men when they married Smith. "What about these poor husbands?" Brodie moralized. "Some of them left the Church; some of them took several more wives; none of them could have been very happy about the arrangement, either for time or eternity."[52]

A third Utah writer who aided Brodie was Juanita Brooks, a teacher and administrator at Dixie College in St. George. Like Noall and Crawford, Brooks was interested in certain controversial aspects of early church history, in particular the Mountain Meadows massacre. This was an 1857 incident in the "Utah war," when tensions between the Mormons and non-Mormons were at their peak. It involved the murder of the Fancher party—a group of non-Mormon immigrants passing through southern Utah, nearly one hundred individuals in all, including women and children. The massacre was actually carried out by a group of Indians, but they were aided and abetted in the act by local Mormons, who later attempted to cover up their involvement. Despite the controversial nature of her research, Brooks remained an active, practicing Latter-day Saint, though she admired Brodie's courage in tackling Joseph Smith and offered to share any useful information she found in her own research. Eventually, Brooks obtained and passed on to Brodie an auto-biography of one of Smith's wives, Mary Elizabeth Rollins Lightner.[53]

A fourth Utah-based scholar, the one who provided Brodie with the greatest amount of help, was M. Wilford Poulson, professor of psychology at Brigham Young University. Like Dale Morgan, whom he knew well, Poulson was very interested in early Mormon church history, and he was an avid collector of old Mormon books and diaries. According to at least one writer, Poulson was a disaffected Mormon. Quite possibly, Brodie's initial contact with him came through her uncle Dean Brimhall, a fellow psychologist who had at one time taught with Poulson at BYU.[54]

Wilford Poulson not only provided Brodie with information on the plural wives of Joseph Smith, he significantly influenced her views of some crucial aspects of Joseph Smith's career. Through Poulson, Brodie became aware of certain parallels between Joseph Smith and the schis-matic Mormon leader James J. Strang. Poulson had deciphered the coded portions of Strang's diary, which revealed Strang to be intensely ambitious but frustrated—until he deliberately faked prophecies in order to gain the trappings of authority, the wealth from tithes, the adulation of the flock, and the choice of pretty girls for plural wives. According to the noted Mormon writer, Samuel W. Taylor, Brodie took Poulson's findings relative to Strang and imputed like attitudes to Joseph Smith. She also took from Poulson the belief that Joseph Smith wrote the *Book of Mormon* to make money. In turn, Poulson agreed with Brodie that Thomas Dick's *The Philosophy of a Future State* "was extremely important in fixing the source of many of [Joseph Smith's] metaphysical conceptions."[55]

Wilford Poulson exerted influence in another significant way: He assumed the role of literary critic, reading though and critiquing the final draft of *No Man Knows My History*. His critique was much more severe than Dale Morgan's. He actually gave Brodie a preview of the kind of criticism her work would encounter from within the Mormon establish-ment. "Frankly," he said, "I had hoped your presentation would be more worthy of being characterized as DEFINITIVE. I had hoped [that] you would bring to bear the appropriate canons of historical criticism upon your sources." Then he got to the nub: "I believe the future truly great biography of the Prophet Joseph Smith will not ungenerously trim him down to the proportions of a liar, an impostor, an adulterer, and anything else mostly bad," he admitted to Brodie. Still, he praised Fawn for her effort, asserting that many good things would result from her book—perceptively predicting that it would stimulate wide and careful reading, pro and con, into sources dealing with the early history of the church. This, in turn, he said, would result in "a really objective and truly critical work in this field."[56]

All of the help from Wilford Poulson, Juanita Brooks, Claire Noall, and Vesta Crawford notwithstanding, Brodie relied most heavily on Dale Morgan, drawing on his expertise as she continued work on the manuscript. She lamented to Morgan in a November 1943 letter that the book was already getting much too long. She chastised herself: "[I] simply must stop trying to write the history of the church, and start writing a biography," she told Morgan. And then she admitted, "Perhaps I am dodging the man because I am still not quite certain what I want to do with him."[57]

Brodie encountered other problems as she moved ahead during the winter of 1943–44 and into spring. She was becoming tired of basic research. She told Morgan that she was getting to the point where the thought of hunting down stray pieces of information now appalled rather than excited her. By mid-December of 1944, she had finished writing the chapters dealing with the Missouri period and was well into writing up Joseph Smith's Nauvoo activities. But she was having difficulty in finding the right way to introduce polygamy.[58]

Moreover, Fawn was, of course, forced to balance time devoted to the biography with time demanded by her role as wife and mother, looking after the needs of her husband and her very active toddler. "The boy is getting to be more demanding of my attention all the time," she told Morgan. "Dickie is pulling at my arm," she wrote him. "He demands to be fed. My life is one series of interruptions. If I could get three consecutive hours of uninterrupted work, I could do wonders—maybe even finish the book." But she confessed ambivalence; her year-old son was such fun to play with that she generally succumbed to his begging—and as a consequence her writing suffered.[59]

Fawn was also affected by her growing alienation from the Mormon Church. She maintained a lively interest in individuals and incidents

involving the church, clearly evident in her response to news of the
November 1943 excommunication of Richard Lyman, a high Mormon
official who was a member of the church's Council of the Twelve. Lyman
was excommunicated for an extramarital affair—or as it was termed
"unchastity." He rationalized his relationship by characterizing it as a
plural marriage. "Too bad [Lyman] didn't live in the days of Brigham
Young," Brodie observed, "when the 'celestial law' [of polygamy] . . . was
a surer way to glory than the 'Christian law'" of monogamy.[60]

Brodie's alienation was also reflected in her response in late March
1944 to the apparent involvement of Mormon Church officials in the
arrest and prosecution of Mormon fundamentalists in Salt Lake City
earlier that month. These Mormon fundamentalists, a dissident Mormon
faction, had become a major embarrassment to the main body of Latter-
day Saints because of their forthright advocacy of plural marriage—once
a major pillar of the Mormon faith but now vigorously rejected. Brodie
saw J. Reuben Clark, member of the church's elite First Presidency, as
"largely responsible" for the arrests of the dissidents. The incident, she
speculated, resulted from Clark's "pathological obsession on the subject
of chastity." "The whole prosecution may have been originally motivated
by frustrations in [Clark's] own sex life," she added, an observation that
clearly reflected Brodie's fascination with Mormon things sexual, be they
historical or contemporary.[61]

Fawn Brodie's own church activity as a practicing Latter-day Saint had
long since ended, even though she was still officially listed as a member
of the Mormon Church. Her membership records continued to follow
her: first from Chicago to Princeton, New Jersey; then to Hanover, New
Hampshire; and then on to Washington, D.C. "The Church is always
catching up with me," she lamented, and she described to Morgan how
Edgar A. Brossard, a Mormon official in Washington, had recently contacted her, inviting her to attend services at the local Mormon ward. She
speculated that her own fiercely devout father, with "just a shade of malice
in his heart," had set Brossard after her. Brodie was deeply bothered by this
persistent "personal problem," as she termed it. She told Morgan how
she had handled an earlier situation involving two Mormon missionaries,
who had confronted her in Hanover. "I retaliated by giving them a typewritten list of all the extracts from Joseph [Smith's] history where he
admits drinking wine," she told Morgan, "challenging them to show the

list to their superior, the local mission president." Triumphantly, she reported that she never again heard from the missionaries in question.[62]

Fawn meanwhile moved ahead with the manuscript. In early April of 1944, she wrote Morgan, announcing that she was in a celebratory mood because she had essentially completed her manuscript—as she put it, "I finally succeeded in putting five bullets in the prophet." In other words, she had written on Joseph Smith up though his murder by an armed mob in Carthage, Illinois, in June 1844.[63]

But Brodie's euphoric mood was short-lived as she encountered new problems in the process of revision. In confronting her early chapters on Mormon origins, she confessed to Morgan, "I am quietly tearing my hair over the Book of Mormon again. Those chapters are the ones I have worked over the most and are still the least satisfactory." Difficulties in revision continued: "I am too prone to cling to what I have written before, even though it doesn't satisfy me." She then lamented that what she had rewritten did not satisfy her either.[64]

Brodie was further distracted in late May upon receiving news that her father had suffered a heart attack and was bedridden. She was extremely anxious about his condition, sensing a relationship between it and her own writing and research. She was haunted by the thought that her father might die shortly after her book came out; "the consequences for my own peace of mind [in that case] would be simply unbearable," she admitted to Morgan. She then shared with him the complex, ambivalent aspects of her relationship with her father: "If I didn't have such an affection for my father, who is the soul of kindness, perhaps I wouldn't be so troubled. . . . This whole business complicates an already melancholy personal problem. Sometimes I wish to God I'd never started the book."[65]

Fawn's father did not die. In fact, he recovered to the point that he was soon able to resume his church duties as an assistant to the Council of the Twelve. And his daughter continued with her revisions. In early June she indicated her great interest in finding definitive evidence that Joseph Smith had fathered children through one or more of his polygamous wives. Frustrated, she lamented that it piqued her to think that the Reorganized Church might be right in its assertion that the only children fathered by Smith were those through Emma Hale—proof, according to the Reorganized Church, of its long-standing claim that Mormonism's founder never practiced polygamy.[66]

By mid-July Brodie had completely revised the first fourteen chapters and had pretty well completed revision on another thirteen; all together, these twenty-seven chapters constituted the bulk of her biography. But the chapters on Joseph's wives and on Mormon metaphysics still required extensive work. She noted her ability to handle "the political narrative much better than the theological matter, most of which bores me."[67]

At this point, Fawn felt she had made sufficient progress to leave the manuscript long enough to accompany Bernard and twenty-month-old Dickie to New England for a two-week vacation. But in preparing for the break, she experienced new anxieties, worries about possible personal mishap and what it would mean for the completion of the biography. "I've got such a vested interest in the damned [manuscript]," she told Dale Morgan, "that I simply couldn't bear not to see it published in case we all got smashed up by a truck or something. So this letter, however absurd it may seem to you, is something in the nature of a 'what to do if I die' letter." She gave Morgan explicit instructions relative to the manuscript, her notes, and other materials.[68]

These concerns, however, proved unfounded. Safely home two weeks later, she wrote Morgan of visiting old friends in Hanover and of hiking over the hills that she and Bernard had enjoyed while living there. "Unfortunately my weariness with the book was not dissipated by the vacation," she lamented.[69]

In late August 1944, Brodie completed her revisions and sent the manuscript on to Morgan for evaluation and comment. Morgan quickly responded, finding it "thoroughly engrossing" and "downright fascinating." He characterized the research as "wide and deep without being ostentatious; the prose . . . admirably muscular," and the text full of stimulating ideas with a rapidly moving storyline. Most important, Morgan felt that Brodie now had a true biography rather than a mere history of Smith's life. She was clearly the master of her material, writing with insight and understanding and exhibiting "practical shrewdness and deftness," particularly in those chapters dealing with Smith's life through the Missouri period.[70]

Morgan, however, still had several concerns. He saw serious defects in Brodie's handling of the Nauvoo period, telling the author that more

work was required to make it credible, feeling that she was not in command of her material as she had been in earlier chapters. He was also
critical of what he termed her "bold judgments on the basis of assump-
tions." He warned her that if such generalizations were carried into the
final manuscript, they would expose her to strong attack from those
Mormons already negative toward the book and looking for ways to
discredit it. Finally, he urged Brodie to add a chapter focusing on Smith's
character. The manuscript belied a certain tentativeness toward the
Mormon leader. Morgan felt Brodie had not adequately explained the
extraordinary magnetism that Smith had for his followers. She should
provide readers a much-needed analysis of the Mormon leader in all his
complexity, particularly within the context of the final events of his life,
Morgan said.[71]

Brodie responded positively to Morgan's varied suggestions, but the task
of incorporating them into her final draft was interrupted by a two-week
visit from her mother and father in early September. Fawn was relieved by
her father's improved condition, but her difficult relationship with him
continued. The two disagreed on virtually everything—a situation complicated by Thomas McKay's avoidance of all topics of debate and controversy.
Thus, there could be no talk of her forthcoming biography. "We [both]
simply act as if it did not exist," she told Morgan. Though her mother,
fortunately, expressed her enthusiasm for the work, the whole experience
made Fawn painfully aware of the "unpleasantness" likely to occur when
the book finally appeared. She feared she would never be able to enjoy the
fruits of her labor because she would know the pain it had caused her
father. "I suspect some Freudian [psychologist] would explain my whole
five-year toil [relative to the book] on the basis of an unconscious desire to
wound him," she wrote Morgan. "God knows the compulsion I have been
laboring under has been emotional rather than intellectual, but it certainly
doesn't have its roots in that kind of complex."[72]

Causing Brodie additional anxiety was the sudden appearance in late
1944 of two books: *Joseph Smith: The Prophet*, by Preston Nibley, and *Joseph,
the Prophet, as He Lives in the Hearts of His People*, by Daryl Chase. Both were
published by the Deseret News Press, a publishing house owned and
operated by the Mormon Church. These two books thus enjoyed semi-
official church approval. Brodie conceded that both "really beat me to

the draw." She believed, with some justification, that high Mormon Church officials had actively promoted both books in order to lessen the impact of her own forthcoming work.[73]

Brodie meanwhile finished her own revisions, sending the completed manuscript on to Knopf in October 1944. Knopf moved Brodie's work through the final phases of editing in response to the suggestions made by Dale Morgan and by two other reviewers—namely, Wilson Follett, an in-house editor at Knopf, and Milo M. Quaife, an outside reader who was curator of manuscripts at the Detroit Public Library. Follett praised Brodie's manuscript as thoroughly viable and alive, predicting that it would be viewed as the final authority on Joseph Smith "by everyone except those speaking for the official point of view by the Mormon hierarchy."[74]

Milo M. Quaife was likewise impressed with the work, characterizing it as "excellent . . . scholarly [with] an easy, pleasant narrative style." While calling it "[as] laudably free from bias . . . as [is] reasonably possible to achieve," he, like Follett, predicted that it would by criticized by the Mormon Church, but he cautioned that "this possibility should not deter any publisher from bringing it out."[75]

Brodie's manuscript received final in-house editorial clearance in January 1945.

Meanwhile, the author focused on other important concerns. She was pregnant once more, but in early January of 1945 complications developed and she was hospitalized. Two weeks later, Fawn suffered a miscarriage. The whole experience was a "bad dream," she said. "I had all the pain and misery of childbirth without anything to show for it." In addition to the trauma of the miscarriage, she received the shocking news that her cousin McKeen Eccles Brimhall, only son of Dean and Lila Brimhall, had been killed in combat in France. McKeen was her favorite cousin, "practically like a brother," and Fawn found it difficult to get the tragedy out of her mind. The young lieutenant left behind a wife and two-year-old daughter, and Brodie's sense of deep personal loss prompted her to dedicate the forthcoming biography to his memory.[76]

Meanwhile, Brodie stumbled onto an unexpected surprise. While working at the Library of Congress on some final details, she came across a photograph of Oliver Buell, the son of Prescindia Huntingon Buell, one of Joseph Smith's plural wives. Examining this photograph closely,

Fawn Brodie at age thirty, in late 1945, at the time of the publication of *No Man Knows My History,* Brodie's controversial biography of Mormon Church founder Joseph Smith. Courtesy Bruce and Janet Brodie.

Brodie was convinced that Buell was the son of the Mormon leader, so similar was he in appearance to Smith. With a bit a wry humor, she told Morgan, "if Oliver Buell isn't a Smith then I'm no Brimhall." She ultimately included the photograph of Buell in the biography alongside a photograph of Emma and Joseph Smith's four sons.[77]

In late March, Brodie received the copyedited manuscript back from Knopf with instructions to correct the occasional errors and omissions. She then had to wait several months for the final galleys, which arrived in early August 1945. She was pleased with the type-setting and with the fact that Knopf had elected to include twenty-six of the twenty-seven pictures that she had submitted as illustrations. These she placed in spots most appropriate to heighten the effect of the narrative. The only thing left was actual publication, scheduled for 22 November 1945.[78]

NEW HAVEN AND INITIAL REACTION TO THE BIOGRAPHY

Bernard Brodie's situation changed as World War II entered its final stages in 1945. The D day invasion of France the previous June, followed by the collapse of Nazi Germany in May 1945 and the American advance in the Pacific, meant a gradual winding down of the war effort. This, in turn, affected Brodie's status as a naval intelligence officer, making his services less essential. In March 1945, he was offered, and accepted, a position in the Institute of International Studies at Yale University, and the Brodies moved from Washington, D.C., to New Haven, Connecticut, in July 1945. Bernard's new appointment commenced on 1 August 1945.[79]

Within a week, on 7 August, the Brodies, along with other Americans, were startled by news out of Hiroshima. The dropping of the atomic bomb, followed three days later by the explosion of a second nuclear bomb over Nagasaki, abruptly ended World War II. Upon reading the first newspaper accounts of these momentous developments, Bernard expressed doubt to Fawn concerning his role and relevance: "Everything I have written is obsolete," he told her. In truth, he was being overly pessimistic. Adjusting his thinking to the new realities of the atomic age, he would soon emerge as a leader in the field of nuclear strategic deterrence. In the words of one writer, Brodie was "first—both in time and in distinction—among America's nuclear strategists." But now, in the fall of 1945, Brodie—along with his colleagues at the Yale Institute of International Studies—set about the task of developing new strategic theory for the atom bomb.[80]

Brodie articulated his concepts in *The Absolute Weapon: Atomic Power and World Order*, published in early 1946. He concluded there that the A-bomb, because of its great destructive power, had changed not only the magnitude of war's destructiveness but indeed the very nature of war itself. According to Brodie, the deterrence of war was the only rational military policy in the nuclear age. Bernard Brodie was thus among the first to come to grips with the fact of everyday living with the bomb.[81]

Fawn Brodie, meanwhile, encountered greater difficulty in adjusting to the sudden changes in her own life. The move to New Haven and the completion of *No Man Knows My History* left her both "deflated and a little bit lost," causing her to ask rhetorically of Dale Morgan, "What, in God's name is there in New Haven for *me*?" She was clearly in a quandary. Bernard suggested that she enroll in a Ph.D. program in American history at Yale. But that possibility "rather appalled" her. She also considered being simply a housewife and mother, but quickly admitted, "I'm not a domestic person in any sense except that of training."[82] In effect, she was confronting the new postwar reality—pressure on all married women to conform to the ideal and to remain at home full-time.

Fawn had other concerns. Because of an acute housing shortage that affected New Haven, as it did almost all other communities across the United States immediately following World War II, the Brodies were compelled to live in a tiny duplex within a government housing project, where, according to Fawn, "the houses [were] about as utilitarian and uninspired as any you will find anywhere." In just a few weeks, however, she was much more upbeat in describing her situation to Morgan. Her New Haven residence, she told him, was "high on a hill overlooking one of Connecticut's lovely green valleys." She had a most impressive view. She had also found a fine nursery school for three-year-old Dickie, who was now off her hands from 9 A.M. to twelve noon each day. She was getting "as much satisfaction out of redecorating a room as from turning out a reasonably well-written paragraph." "All my resentment against New Haven has vanished," she concluded, "and life here promises to be very pleasant indeed."[83]

But a month later, Fawn was again ambivalent. She lamented her situation to Morgan. It was gender that limited her options, she said. "I envy you males the continuity in your work. The mere necessity of making a living enforces some kind of continuity in the first place." With most women, by contrast, the only factor working toward such continuity was childbearing. She found "that once you have raised a child to the ripe age of three and sent him off to nursery school there isn't anything else to turn [to] except to having another—which is of course satisfying enough in itself, but only for another three or four years. Then where are you?" "As you can see," she confessed, "I'm still floundering. . . . I need another labor of love like the one I just finished." A part of Brodie's melancholy was the realization that she had reached a milestone on 15 September, her thirtieth birthday, which she characterized as "a dreadful day for a woman!"[84]

Despite such complaints, Fawn had pretty well decided to pursue research and writing for a second book-length biography. Even while she was awaiting the publication of *No Man Knows My History*, Brodie had spoken of such plans to Morgan. "I know . . . that eventually I shall have to sink my teeth into something else," she had said, and she had had hopes of discovering what it was "pretty soon." "It can't be another Mormon book," she had insisted, "that I am sure about."[85]

She was now seriously considering a dual biography of two nineteenth-century newspapermen, the James Gorden Bennetts—father and son. The book would be "a history of the New York *Herald*," she said. But she quickly abandoned the idea upon discovering a new book in print on the topic. She then looked at Margret Fuller, a nineteenth-century transcendentalist and author, but quickly discarded her upon discovering that the subject "had been more than adequately taken care of" by other writers. Next, at Morgan's suggestion, she looked at Horace Greeley, nineteenth-century editor of the *New York Tribune* and one-time presidential candidate. That idea too was soon aborted: The newspaperman simply did not excite her enough. "Heaven knows who will after Joseph [Smith]," Brodie remarked.[86]

Brodie's anxious search continued into late 1945. In December 1945, she confessed to Morgan that the only people who really interested her were characters like Aaron Burr and *Chicago Tribune* owner-publisher "Bertie" McCormick—both of whom she also considered, albeit briefly. She then revealed, with deep insight, a primary motive behind her compulsion to craft biography, particularly on controversial subjects. She put it in the form of two profound questions: "Why is it, I wonder, that I prefer someone I can tear into? Is it because until I was twenty I was such a supremely good and obedient child that I am still trying to make up for lost time?"[87]

Thus Brodie continued her relentless search for a new biographical subject. By January 1946, she was giving serious consideration to Mary Todd Lincoln, carefully weighing the pros and cons. Going through the Lincoln material would be a monumental job, she told Morgan, "but not an unfeasible one for me, with the Yale library close at hand." In certain respects, she noted, it would be like writing a biography of Emma Smith, the wife of Joseph Smith, in that "telling the wife's story without having the husband dominate the book would be difficult technically." Brodie found Mary Todd "an extremely interesting character in her own right," but she had abandoned her by March 1946, turning once more to Horace Greeley.[88]

Brodie knew herself well enough to pinpoint the source of her difficulty in finding a subject for a second biography. The problem stemmed at least in part from her first biography, which she labeled a "'labor of love'—or 'hate' or what you will—at least a labor all bound up with my emotions." Then too there was the intense work involved in writing a book. It was hard to assess just how much the writing took out of her—and her family—"in terms of energy, time, and youth." "I don't write easily," she confessed, while also pointing to the difficulty of research. Such difficulties were compounded by her never-ending responsibilities as wife and mother. "Children are a twenty-four hour job," she said, "an easy and wondrously satisfying job . . . but a job, nevertheless, which involves constant interruptions all day long and meticulous planning for every hour of 'escape.' All this means that I've got to be thoroughly satisfied that a new subject is worth my tackling." She was, moreover, "callous enough to want to write a book that will sell reasonably well [which] means picking a subject in whom there is rather wide interest already."[89]

Meanwhile, *No Man Knows My History* was itself attracting widespread interest. Even before publication, Brodie's book had generated anger from leaders of the Reorganized Church of Jesus Christ of Latter Day Saints. RLDS officials actually tried to stop publication upon receiving and reading an advance copy of the galleys. They were upset over Brodie's presentation of irrefutable evidence of Joseph Smith's involvement in polygamy, which went against the official RLDS position that Mormonism's founder had never practiced nor sanctioned plural marriage. Israel Smith strongly denounced the biography for alleging "that there were bastard children born to Joseph" and for presenting Emma Smith, Joseph's first wife, in an allegedly distorted light. Worse still, RLDS officials even spoke of suing both the author and the publisher on behalf of his descendants for defamation of Joseph Smith's character.

This alarmed Alfred A. Knopf, the publisher, which immediately contacted Brodie, asking her if there was anything in the book that the Reorganized Church could bring suit over. Brodie sought to reassure

Knopf that this controversy was little more than pure face-saving on the part of the Reorganized Church. But RLDS officials appeared ready to press ahead. Israel Smith wrote Knopf in October 1945, suggesting legal action under what he termed a "libel of the dead suit." He charged that Brodie's book was full of error that would greatly damage not only the Latter Day Saint organization but also the family and descendants of Joseph Smith. The Mormon founder had been "the most lied-about man in American history," he said, and launched an attack on the author: "Mrs. Brodie, it is claimed, is a renegade Mormon, born into a Mormon family, an apostate from the Utah Church. If so, we are reminded of the old saying, which now appears to be truer than ever: 'It is an evil bird that fouls its own nest.' "[91]

Brodie initially reacted to Smith's comment with humor: "The old boy is pretty mad," she told Dale Morgan. "If it is true, as Israel says, that Joseph Smith is the most 'lied-about man in American history,' one reason is certainly that the Reorganites have been so indefatigable in supporting this reputation." But Brodie was stung by the attack, and angry: "Those old hypocrites know perfectly well they haven't any evidence worth a damn. It was, in fact, a glimpse of their opportunism and hypocrisy that gives me further insight into the original Smith. It seems to be a universal human trait to do selective thinking and to ignore troublesome data when it interferes with one's prejudices—but the Reorganites have developed that trait to absolutely astonishing proportions."[92]

Although the Reorganized Church did not press ahead with threatened legal action, spokesmen were quick to attack the biography. Again, Israel Smith took the lead, using the pages of the *Saints' Herald*, official publication for the Reorganized Church, on two different occasions. In one essay, entitled "Apostates and Joseph Smith," he engaged in a play on words: "[The book] purports to be history," he wrote, "although the title is *No Man Knows My History*. Being a woman—not a man—we suppose [the author] is at least an exception: she knows her history." But this was not the case, Smith quickly added, denouncing Brodie's volume as "another vicious assault on the church, its founder, and the Restoration . . . by a renegade Mormon." In a second article, entitled "The Brodie 'Atrocity,'" Smith asserted that the author had been entirely controlled by her animosity toward the church and its founder in producing "a very unworthy book."[93]

As for Brodie, she expected the quick reaction to the biography from within the Reorganized Church to be replicated by spokesmen from within the much larger Utah-based Church of Jesus Christ of Latter-day Saints. Her uncle, David O. McKay, had been given a copy of the galleys of the book prior to publication. "The fat is in the fire out in Zion," Brodie said upon hearing that. Her humor aside, she had deep anxieties over the situation, anxieties that apparently affected her subconscious. She related a dream wherein she was giving a speech before a group in Salt Lake City, when she suddenly realized the presence of the Council of the Twelve, whose members got up one by one and denounced her. Within this same dream, two of the twelve—John S. Widtsoe and Joseph Fielding Smith—informed Brodie that her "father was dying of a heart attack, and I, wretch that I was, was responsible for it."[94]

In reality, the Utah Mormon Church did not respond immediately to the biography, even in the wake of actual publication. *No Man Knows My History* "met a thunderous silence in Utah," Brodie said wryly. But there was response from within Brodie's own family. Reaction was mixed. Fawn's mother and three sisters were enthusiastic and supportive, describing the book as "wonderful." Fawn's father and brother were both ambivalent. The elder McKay was in a particularly awkward situation because of his high Mormon Church position. He had supported his daughter's right to write the book and do the research, but he did not endorse the book's content or its interpretations. He refused to discuss the book with his daughter or even acknowledge its existence. Years later, Brodie disclosed deep-seated feelings of frustration, hurt, and anger: "My father never did read the Joseph Smith biography. . . . I always felt . . . that his not reading it was an act of real hostility . . . and his refusal to discuss it hurt me more, I think, than an angry argument about the contents would have done. At any rate, we both found it impossible to communicate on the subject, as on most others." Fawn's brother was also ambivalent. The younger McKay, like his father, was a devout, practicing Latter-day Saint; but unlike his father, he was willing to discuss and debate with his sister the contents of *No Man Knows My History*. In such discussions, he defended Fawn's right to publish the book, but did *not* defend the book or its interpretations.[95]

Outside the immediate family, reaction was also mixed. Fawn's favorite uncle, Dean Brimhall, was extremely enthusiastic. His niece "had a hero

in her book and that hero was TRUTH," Brimhall said, noting that she
had raised the family to new levels of achievement. A second uncle, Joel
Ricks, professor of history at Utah State University and husband of Fawn's
aunt Katherine McKay, also reacted positively. It was a fine scholarly
effort, he said, even though it did not alter his Mormon beliefs.[96]

A third uncle, Julian Cummings, also a devout Mormon and husband
of Fay Brimhall, twin sister of Fawn's mother, was extremely negative. In
a sharply worded letter, he accused his niece of "laboring under a false
premise" and arriving at false conclusions. He called on Fawn to repent
immediately her "sins," warning her that failure to do so would result in
dire consequences after her death. He predicted that Brodie "would have
no place to hide [her] sins" in the hereafter, adding, "Your shame will be
so mortifying that it will place you in an environment of darkness where
you will see no one else and 'think' that no one else sees you. There you
will wander until you become so tired with your condition and so
weakened that a feeling of repentance will begin to manifest itself." Fawn
did not respond directly to Cummings, but in quoting Cummings's letter
to Dale Morgan she commented, "Let this be a lesson to you, Dale. But
don't heed the warning too seriously. I want a little company out there
in the outer fringe of darkness!"[97]

Also denouncing Brodie's biography was her father's cousin Ernest
McKay. He used a more public forum. A capable public speaker, he made
himself available to speak on the book at various Mormon wards in the
Ogden-Huntsville area. According to one observer, McKay knew how to
choose those parts of the biography he wanted to tear to pieces, convincing his audience that Brodie "was a very naughty girl." His attack
included, on at least one occasion, a vicious anti-Semitic slur: He referred
to Fawn as "Mrs. Jew"—a clear allusion to what McKay mistakenly perceived as Bernard's influence on her interpretation of Joseph Smith. Also
reacting in a nasty fashion was Fawn's physician-uncle, Joseph Morrell of
Ogden, husband of Fawn's aunt Jeanette McKay. Morrell was so upset
that he warned Fawn through a mutual acquaintance that "she had better
stay the hell out of Utah from now on." Fawn's response was a simple "I
shall of course go back [to Utah]."[98]

Outside the Brodie family, reactions to *No Man Knows My History* were
as varied as within. One historian, Herbert O. Brayer, writing in the
Mississippi Valley Historical Review, predicted that Brodie's book would

"probably be one of the most highly praised, as well as highly condemned, historical works of 1945." Praise was forthcoming from many reviewers in the eastern press. Orville Prescott of the *New York Times* characterized the work as "one of the best of all Mormon books, scholarly, comprehensive and judicious." *Newsweek* described Brodie's book as "a definitive biography in the finest sense of the word," while *Time* magazine praised the author for her "skill and scholarship and admirable detachment."[99]

Likewise, *No Man Knows My History* was favorably reviewed in various midwestern newspapers, particularly in Ohio and Illinois, states where Joseph Smith and the Mormons had been influential during the 1830s and 1840s. Elsewhere, reviews were less positive, particularly in professional historical journals. Ralph H. Gabriel through the pages of the *American Historical Review* characterized Brodie's work as "fresh, well organized and well written" but found fault in the book's failure to carefully consider the various factors affecting the growth of Mormonism, dubbing the treatment "a surface portrait of the prophet." James Burnett, in *New York History*, credited Brodie with bringing both new detachment and new material to bear in creating "a scholarly and readable biography" but felt that the author was less sure when moving beyond Mormon history proper, betraying limited understanding of various socioreligious developments within the larger society in which Mormonism developed.[100]

These various mixed reviews frustrated Brodie. "Why [should I] bother trying to make my [next] book good history," she asked Dale Morgan, "[when] historians are bound to find errors, and the public won't give a hang for it. Is it all worth the effort anyhow?" She was especially upset by the review written by noted Utah-born novelist Vardis Fisher in the *New York Times Book Review*. He praised Brodie as "zealous and industrious and about as impartial as any biographer can be," but he criticized her for quoting "copiously . . . from books by embittered apostates" and accused her of stating "as indisputable facts what can only be regarded as conjectures supported by doubtful evidence."[101]

Fisher's remarks distressed Brodie. "I spent a bad day reflecting on the futility of writing books at all, and particularly of spending seven years at it," she complained to Dale Morgan. In writing her parents, she questioned the thoroughness of Fisher's evaluation, asserting that "he was completely blind to my scholarship" and alleging that he hadn't even bothered "to look at the footnotes."[102]

Also rendering a mixed review was Bernard De Voto, writing for the *New York Herald-Tribune.* He had some good things to say, calling Brodie's work "the best book about the Mormons so far published," putting it "in a class by itself." But he also found deficiencies. He noted gaps in Brodie's knowledge of the America of the 1830s and alleged that the author had credited Joseph Smith with innovations and inventions that, in fact, were not his. He criticized the author for her failure to explore adequately Joseph Smith's basic drive or motives. A religious skeptic himself, De Voto agreed with Brodie's basic assertion that Smith's ideas were not divinely inspired but found that the author had not provided a satisfactory alternative explanation. He dismissed as inadequate her view that Smith was an artist whose "prose fiction" provided for "the natural expression of his fantasies and religious perceptions." A more plausible explanation, according to De Voto, was his own long-held view that Smith was paranoid.[103]

Brodie took De Voto's mixed review much better than Vardis Fisher's, finding the former's comments "on the whole . . . extremely satisfying" and actually more positive than she had expected. She wrote Dale Morgan of her reactions:

> De Voto is quite right in saying that my accounting for "the basic drive" in Smith's early years is weak. I was never wholly satisfied with it, . . . I remain absolutely convinced that the Book of Mormon was conscious deception. And where can you point to the first vision or revelation of Joseph Smith which you can honestly identify as "Hallucination." At what point, in other words did he become so intoxicated that he honestly believed he was communing with God? I don't think anyone can answer that.

She had rejected De Voto's thesis of paranoia after reading several textbooks and several hundred case studies on the subject early in her research, yet she was not completely satisfied with her own, "at least not with the presentation of it," admitting to Morgan, "The more I think about it the more the old bafflement seizes me." In the end, she agreed with De Voto that a psychological analysis of Joseph Smith was essential and conceded that she herself "hadn't gone far enough in this direction."[104]

Dale Morgan himself was asked to review Brodie's book for the *Saturday Review of Literature*, despite his central role in the biography's production. Inexplicably, he accepted. Not surprisingly, Morgan characterized his good friend's work as "the finest job of scholarship yet done in Mormon history, . . . a work distinguished in the range and originality of its research, the informed and searching objectivity of its viewpoint, the richness and suppleness of its prose, and its narrative power." He praised Brodie for "having faced up to the hard fact that Joseph Smith must have been initially a conscious fraud and imposter"—the central thesis of her work—while at the same time remaining essentially sympathetic toward her subject. He did offer some criticism, specifically that the author's overall judgment concerning Joseph Smith's life might be "subject to both a kinder and a far more . . . objective reinterpretation," but he proclaimed the work "definitive" or "at the very least . . . the book that had to be written before a finally authoritative biography could be written." The book was, in sum, Morgan wrote, "a benchmark and a corrective in Mormon scholarship."[105]

MORMON DENUNCIATION AND EXCOMMUNICATION

Latter-day Saint spokesmen, official and otherwise, were extremely slow to comment publicly on *No Man Knows My History*. Various Mormon publications, most prominently the *Deseret News*, the Salt Lake City-based daily newspaper owned and operated by the Mormon Church, declined to review, or even to acknowledge the book's existence for months after its release. In the meantime, Brodie's biography was being noted and/or reviewed in dozens of newspapers and periodicals across the United States. Both author and book received further notice during Fawn's trip to New York City in January 1946, an event arranged by Alfred Knopf. Brodie's itinerary included newspaper and radio interviews. In these interviews, Brodie discussed frankly her personal feelings. She knew she had "burned [her] bridges" within the Mormon community, she confessed, by characterizing Joseph Smith as a man whose life was an "outrageous melodrama," and she wryly conceded that her biography had not been "widely heralded in certain Mormon centers."[106]

By this time, spokesmen from within the Mormon Church were beginning to respond. The biography could no longer be ignored. In addition to extensive media publicity, the book was enjoying brisk sales. It had exhausted its first printing by early January 1946, and a second just two months later. Total sales reached over 7,700—far exceeding the expectations of both author and publisher. Widespread interest in Brodie's book was clearly evident in Utah, the heart of Mormon country, despite deliberate church silence. In Salt Lake City, in Ogden, and in other outlying communities, demand for the book was high. Even in Provo, home of Brigham Young University, the local bookstore sold out its supply in two days, and the university library had an endless waiting list for its three copies.[107]

Mormon spokesmen finally opened their attack. It was indirect at first. Leading the way was J. Reuben Clark, counselor in the church's First Presidency. Without mentioning Brodie or her book by name, he addressed a December 1945 gathering at Brigham Young University: "He wounds, maims, and cripples a soul who raises doubts about or destroys faith in the ultimate truths. God will hold such a one strictly accountable, and who can measure the depths to which one shall fall who shatters in another the opportunity for celestial glory."[108]

Two months later, in February 1946, Fawn's uncle, David O. McKay, also spoke obliquely on the subject. In the course of an address at BYU, he told a story that clearly alluded to his niece. It was the story of Dandy, a well-bred colt with a "good disposition, clean well-rounded eyes, . . . well proportioned, and all in all, a choice equine possession." But Dandy resented restraint. "He was ill-contented when tied and would nibble at the tie-rope until he was free." One day Dandy broke out of his pasture and got into a neighbor's sack of grain that had been poisoned as bait for rodents. Within a few minutes, Dandy was in spasmodic pain, and shortly thereafter he died. McKay concluded his story: "My heart aches this morning because one who was pretty close to me failed—violated conventions in childhood—later broke through the fence of consideration and decency—found the poison grain of unbelief, and now languishes in spiritual apathy and decay."[109]

Fawn's only response to her uncle's public denunciation was one of mild curiosity: What could McKay have been referring to when he said that she "violated conventions in childhood," she wondered. Within

David O. McKay, Fawn Brodie's uncle, who served as Mormon Church president from 1951 until his death in 1970. Extremely angry with his niece over publication of *No Man Knows My History*, he reportedly played a key role in her excommunication from the church in May 1946. Reprinted by permission, Utah State Historical Society, all rights reserved.

family and community she had always been considered a model child; she had never engaged in even a healthy amount of mischief.[110]

David O. McKay's pronouncement opened the way to more direct denunciations. John A. Widtsoe, a member of the Council of the Twelve attacked *No Man Knows My History* through the pages of *The Improvement Era*, the church's official periodical. There Widtsoe assailed Brodie's "purported history of Joseph Smith" for its attempt to portray the Mormon leader as a deceiver. While conceding that the author had labored to give the book a scholarly color by use of numerous footnotes, Widtsoe claimed that some of these were from doubtful sources. Everything in the book had already been presented by other anti-Mormon writers, he said. The book presented "only a preconceived estimate of [Smith's] mind, and . . . [did] not analyze [his] works." Brodie's biography was "of no interest to Latter-day Saints who have correct knowledge of the history of Joseph Smith."[111]

Other Mormon leaders responded to *No Man Knows My History* during the church's April 1946 semiannual General Conference. The responses, though less direct—not one mentioning the author or her book—were no less strong. Mormon Church President George Albert Smith asserted, "Many have belittled Joseph Smith, but those who have will be forgotten in the remains of Mother Earth and the odor of their infamy will ever be with them." A second Mormon leader, Apostle Albert E. Bowen, "made a stirring defense of the Prophet Joseph Smith," defending his mission and accomplishments while denouncing "the poisonous slander of those who would make him out an imposter". They may have gone unnamed, but Fawn Brodie and her book cast a long shadow over this gathering. The conference "didn't exactly neglect me," Brodie observed.[112]

In May 1946, Mormon Church spokesmen stepped up their attacks against the author and her book. The "Church News" section of the *Deseret News* presented an "Appraisal of the So-Called Brodie Book," a lengthy critique that assailed *No Man Knows My History* as wholly atheistic, allowing no place in human experience for the transcendental. This review conceded that it was easy to grant the author "the merit of a fine literary style . . . which makes the book altogether enticing reading," but it was the style of the novelist and not the historian. It concluded that "little more can be said for the book than that it is a composite of all anti-Mormon books that have gone before, pieced into a pattern conformable to the author's own particular rationale and bedded in some very bad psychology." This critique apparently mirrored the official position of the Mormon Church, for it was soon reprinted as a pamphlet and circulated as a missionary tract.[113]

Soon thereafter came a second Mormon pamphlet, *No Ma'am, That's Not History*, written by Hugh Nibley, an articulate young BYU professor. Produced under the apparent direction, or at least with the encouragement, of Mormon Church leaders, it was subtitled *A Brief Review of Mrs. Brodie's Reluctant Vindication of a Prophet She Seeks to Expose*. Nibley's pamphlet assailed *No Man Knows My History* on several fronts. He attacked the book for its use of historical parallels—that is, Brodie's assertion that Joseph Smith drew heavily from the social and cultural environment in which Mormonism developed—and for its theory that all of Smith's thoughts and actions were the result of slow and gradual evolution. But Nibley, unlike other church spokesmen, conceded that the book was not animated by violent hatred, that it stood in contrast to polemical anti-Mormon biographies of earlier times that had painted Mormonism's founder in total depravity. Brodie's Joseph Smith, if a "complete impostor," at least *"meant well."* *No, Ma'am, That's Not History* was destined to become the most famous of all Mormon Church–sanctioned publications refuting Brodie's biography. It sold briskly, thanks to its clever, readable style and to strong advertising.[114]

In response to the sudden appearance of two pamphlets, Brodie remarked that Mormon authorities had "really let go both barrels." She found "Appraisal of the So-Called Brodie Book" a well-written, clever piece of Mormon propaganda, but she had nothing but contempt for Nibley's *No, Ma'am, That's Not History*, dismissing it as "a flippant and shallow piece."[115]

At the same time, Brodie was writing an essay for *American Mercury*. Highly critical of the Mormon Church, the article, "Polygamy Shocks the Mormons," focused on the arrest, conviction, and imprisonment of fifteen fundamentalist (or polygamous) Mormons by Utah law enforcement officers some two years earlier, in June 1944. This action, aided and abetted by Utah Mormon authorities, represented, according to Brodie, a strange reversal of Mormondom's earlier vigorous defense of polygamy and defiance of the United States government. How was it, Brodie asked, that the overwhelming majority of Mormons could "so soon forget the savage persecution of their fathers and grandfathers," while condemning the very practice that had been "a fundamental tenet of [their] theology"? She answered her own question in clearly psychological terms, attributing Mormonism's current antipolygamist position to "a legacy of unconscious shame." She noted that by the 1890s, when the Mormons moved to abandon polygamy, they longed for respectability. "Mormon historians are now not only anxious to forget the past, but actively suppress the activities of would-be researchers in Mormon archives," Brodie said, in clear allusion to her own experiences. Forgotten in the current campaign to suppress fundamentalist practices, Brodie added, is "the magnificent immoderation with which Joseph Smith embraced polygamy." The fundamentalists were now an embarrassment to the church, "for by practicing and advocating polygamy [they] not only revive the general sense of shame and guilt which has been so successfully buried beneath a complexity of rationalizations and dimming memories, but also they cast a blight on the holy image of Joseph Smith," an image carefully crafted by Mormon spokesmen.[116]

The appearance of the *American Mercury* article coincided with the decision by Mormon Church officials to excommunicate Fawn Brodie. Although Brodie had long before ceased all involvement with the church, she was still officially listed on the membership rolls of the New England Mission, headquartered in Cambridge, Massachusetts. The formal process of excommunication began on 25 May 1946, when two Mormon missionaries arrived at the Brodie home in New Haven with a summons for Fawn to appear before a Church Mission court in Cambridge. The proceedings were scheduled for 1 June 1946.

In the summons, signed by Mission President William H. Reeder, Brodie was charged with apostasy: "In a book recently published by you, you assert matters as truths which deny the divine origin of the Book of Mormon, the restoration of the Priesthood and of Christ's Church through the instrumentality of the Prophet Joseph Smith, contrary to the beliefs, doctrines, and teachings of the Church."[117]

Now in the late stages of another pregnancy, Fawn Brodie chose not to appear at the proceedings, which would have required a long trip from New Haven to Boston less than two weeks before the anticipated birthdate. The tribunal opened in her absence. It was directed by Reeder and included nine other individuals, most of whom were young male missionaries. The proceedings were brief, concluding in "a matter of minutes." President Reeder, after considering the evidence, declared that Fawn McKay Brodie, through her book, was guilty of teaching false doctrine, specifically of denying the divine nature of Mormonism and the prophetic calling of Joseph Smith. It was thus his judgment that she be excommunicated from the church. All present concurred, and Brodie was declared excommunicated. Shortly thereafter Reeder drafted a letter to the excommunicant, officially notifying her of the action.[118]

Mormon officials themselves made public Fawn Brodie's excommunication. It went out on the AP newswire and was written up by newspapers throughout the United States. Locally, the *Salt Lake Tribune*, 16 June 1946, buried a short news article on page 8B. The *Deseret News* did not accord Brodie even that much recognition, merely listing the church's official actions in its weekly account of those "Excommunicated from the Church" in its Saturday section, "Church News." According to Brodie's mother, the excommunication was announced over local radio in the Salt Lake City area.[119]

The summons had caught Fawn Brodie "completely off guard," and the excommunication "upset [her] a good deal more than [she] would care to have the [Mormon] authorities know," Brodie told Dale Morgan. The action could not really have been a complete surprise, however. Brodie had been informed by her mother, immediately following the publication of her book in late 1945, of the possibility of such drastic action. David O. McKay had reportedly initiated a resolution before the Council of the Twelve suggesting that local Mormon authorities in New England institute a court to consider her excommunication. But McKay's resolution had been voted down on the basis that such action would make a martyr of Brodie.[120]

McKay's precise role in his niece's ultimate excommunication is difficult to determine, because meetings of the Mormon Church's ruling elite, the Council of the Twelve, are kept strictly confidential. But Fawn suspected his leadership in the affair: "I suppose I shall never know exactly what brought the action about," she said, "but if my uncle did push the thing through, such an action wouldn't surprise me." McKay, according to Brodie, would have felt the necessity of disassociating himself from her "in the most dramatic fashion possible," believing that he would be condemned if she were treated leniently. And his anger at her, personally, would have moved him to take drastic action against her.[121]

For Fawn, excommunication brought emotional vulnerability. She admitted to family and friends that the action "symbolized so dramatically the fact that my bridges really are irrevocably burned. Home will never be the same again," she said. She sought out her uncle, Dean Brimhall, reportedly in tears. Members of Brodie's immediate family discounted the report of her emotional response, recalling her as less conflicted by the excommunication. Whatever her emotional state, Brodie was clearly sensitive to her parents' situation. She sought to reassure both her mother and father that the excommunication itself meant nothing "except insofar as it may make you unhappy." "It's really a very little thing," she told them, "and perhaps the logical outcome of the evolutionary process in my own thinking and acting." She was, in fact, quite satisfied to be considered "a rebel" by church authorities. To be taken this seriously, she added, "might almost be considered a compliment."[122]

Fawn Brodie sought to put the whole affair quickly behind her, focusing her attention on other matters. By June 1946, the Brodies had been in New Haven for almost a year and were beginning to put down roots. In early 1946, they had purchased a two-acre plot of land in Bethany, a small community just north of New Haven, and had made plans for a custom-built home. They engaged an architect, who drew up plans for a modern house, featuring an enormous living room with forty feet of windows, a large fireplace, and an adjacent study. In March 1946 they started clearing their land in preparation for construction. Fawn threw herself into the task. Despite the fact that she was in late pregnancy and was tending a three-and-a-half-year-old, she spent every leisure hour on the lot, chopping, cutting, and burning the brush and other unwanted foliage. This task she did not mind in the least. The whole "house business," as she called it, was "a pleasant madness."[123]

But construction plans were brought to a halt by the scarcity of building supplies and materials as an aftermath of World War II—and by Bernard's appointment to teach at the National War College, newly created for high-ranking army and navy officers and State Department officials. The new responsibilities would require Bernard's presence in Washington from September to December, allowing him to return to New Haven only on weekends.[124]

Fawn's most immediate concern was the expected birth of a second child in early June 1946. On the one hand, she was experiencing that "placid feeling of contentment that comes in the later months of pregnancy," but she was also haunted by the 1945 trauma of her miscarriage. She was increasingly anxious toward the end of this pregnancy. On the scheduled due date of 9 June she climbed a hill behind the Brodies' home "in an effort to encourage the process of nature." As it happened, the birth of a healthy eight-pound boy, whom the Brodies named Bruce Robertson, occurred on 11 June after a four-hour labor. "He came in such a God-awful hurry that I didn't get any medication until practically too late," Fawn noted. "As a result I had a taste of honest-to-goodness labor pains such as I hope never to experience again." "The whole delivery convinced me more than ever that the female procreative apparatus is one of God's most inefficient creations," she added.[125]

Following the birth of her second child, Fawn's plans for a second biography grew even more indefinite. If she got "broody," given to the feeling "that nothing is more important than having a very little baby around again, . . . why God knows if I will ever finish another book," she wrote Dale Morgan. She also faced the very real problem of finding an appropriate topic. By this time, she had abandoned Horace Greeley once more. Coming to terms with her Mormon heritage may have been the major factor in her inability to settle on a proper subject for a new book. With abrupt frankness, Dale Morgan told her, "I have an idea that you haven't come full circle yet in liberating yourself from [Mormonism]."

> I don't think you fully recognize the extent to which your book was written out of an emotional compulsion, and the extent to which that compulsion persists. You are looking for something that will occupy and satisfy your emotions as Mormonism has done, and it is hardly likely that you will find such a topic or subject. Because writing Joseph [Smith's] biography was your act of liberation and of exorcism. You might write on Mormonism again with the same pleasure and intensity—but this violates your idea of your growth as an artist, to be so limited in your subject matter; you want to find something that will let you develop in new dimensions your mind.[126]

Brodie was quick in responding to Morgan: "When you start psychologizing about me, you do it with more sagacity [than] you perhaps realize." She admitted that "I never could have spent the time and energy on the book that I did without a pretty powerful emotional compulsion." Then she added, with probing insight of her own, "The book served for me what an autobiographical novel usually does for the young novelist. . . . [T]here was a compulsion to self-expression . . . as well as a compulsion to liberate myself wholly from Mormonism, and perhaps also certain family relationships." Without doubt, the publication of *No Man Knows My History* had purged some of those compulsions, though. Brodie conceded that "emotional disturbance" may still be "coloring [her] attitudes."[127]

By mid-1946, then, Fawn Brodie was secure in her roles as wife and mother of two small children. But she was still seeking fulfillment as a writer. Over the next thirteen years her efforts at research and writing while carrying on those demanding roles at home would receive their most severe test.

FOUR

"An Enormously Fulfilling Role"

1946–1959

From 1946 to 1959, Fawn Brodie channeled her major literary energies into a second biography, one completely outside of Mormon studies. Published in 1959, it dealt with Thaddeus Stevens, congressional leader of Radical Reconstruction and acknowledged father of the Fourteenth Amendment. In her recollections, Brodie called *Thaddeus Stevens: Scourge of the South* "a total about face in terms of intention" from her biography of Joseph Smith. The more she studied Stevens, the more she felt he had been unjustly vilified. This stood in stark contrast to her reactions in researching Joseph Smith, whom she saw as undeserving of the high opinion of his followers.[1]

Brodie brought some preconceived notions of Stevens and his times to her work. "Like other Mormon kids I had been taught [in school] that Reconstruction was a brutal period of revenge on the South and that Stevens was a vindictive, evil old man," she said. She now engaged herself in rebuilding a reputation. "It was good to be doing a positive thing rather than the destructive thing," she said, "because I had always felt guilty about the destructive nature of the Joseph Smith book."[2]

Other factors drew Brodie to Thaddeus Stevens. The most important was the issue of race. For Brodie, Stevens was "the greatest champion of black people" during the Civil War and Reconstruction era—with the obvious exception of Abraham Lincoln.[3] Her interest in Stevens, vis-à-vis African Americans, mirrored the contemporary struggle over rights for blacks, evident in Harry S. Truman's executive order desegregating the American armed forces; various landmark Supreme Court decisions, including *Brown v. Board of Education*; and in the growing civil rights movement led by such activists as Martin Luther King, Jr., Whitney Young, and Thurgood Marshall.

Brodie was also sensitive to the problem of the status of blacks within the Mormon Church, where they were denied full fellowship in the priesthood, which was open to males of all other racial groups. In her Joseph Smith biography, Brodie had speculated on the historical origins of this practice, which she characterized as "the ugliest thesis in existing Mormon theology." Her long-standing concern over Mormon discrimination against blacks now drew her to Thaddeus Stevens.[4]

Stevens fit well as a subject of research for Brodie because of growing interest in the field of psychohistory and psychobiography. The larger fields of psychology and psychoanalysis were very much in vogue during the late 1940s and 1950s. Appropriate for such analysis was the effect of deformity—a club foot—on Thaddeus Steven's life. What would this "physical crippling" do to a man's psyche? Brodie asked herself. In preparing her biography she researched the clinical literature and ultimately saw her finished work as "an important piece of psychohistory."[5]

Brodie's decision was prompted by one other important consideration—the limitations imposed by home and family. Necessary source materials on Stevens were contained in the Yale University Library, which meant that her research could be conducted close to home. Indeed, before settling on Stevens, she had given serious thought to doing Eleanor Roosevelt but had discarded the idea because the necessary materials were not readily available. She was "too confined," she said, to research Roosevelt's life.[6]

A NEW HAVEN HOUSEWIFE

Fawn Brodie's lament at being "too confined," and thus limited in choice of a biographical subject, may seem the bitter statement of a dissatisfied woman thrust into the role of housewife and mother. The immediate post–World War II period emphasized the ideal of feminine domesticity, valuing above all else for a woman the "traditional" role as wife and mother. This was a jarring readjustment for those women who, during the war years, had been employed outside the home while their husbands were far away on the battlefields of Europe or in the Pacific theater. While relieved at the safe return of loved ones at war's end, these same women now lost a certain independence and at the same time were forced to readjust to the presence of spouses deeply affected by the trauma of their wartime experiences.[7]

Such did not apply to Fawn Brodie. Although her husband had served in the navy during the war years, he was never sent abroad. Despite short periods of absence, he remained at home with his family. Thus for Fawn, her responsibilities—those typical of wife and mother—had continued, even as she completed *No Man Knows My History*. For her, the postwar period was a time of continuity rather than change. She extolled the virtues of motherhood as "enormously fulfilling" and "wonderfully rewarding." Such domestic duties, she repeatedly affirmed, had unquestioned priority over writing and research—but still allowed for the latter. Brodie recalled years later that she had enjoyed "the perfect life," in that she was able to write at home while raising her children, not having to abandon them to nursery schools or baby-sitters.[8]

Family and children were without doubt, Brodie's first priority. "Children are more rewarding than books," she once said, adding, "once a book is finished it is the deadest thing in the world." The birth of her second child, Bruce, only confirmed her feelings in regard to motherhood: "My newest child is lying on his stomach on the table in front of me," she wrote Dale Morgan. "He laughs back at me every time I talk to him, and I am absolutely gratified. . . . He makes me want six children."[9]

But Fawn also betrayed some ambivalence over this role of wife and mother. She felt women were at a great disadvantage: "No one expects creative work from them, as they do from men, and it's taken for granted universally that home, husband and children should have first precedence on a woman's time and interest." As a housewife, she said, she was lucky to find three or four hours in a day for "some kind of intellectual activity." That kind of activity, she concluded, "must always take the last ounces of your energy rather than the first." She clearly saw the basic irony of life: "I believe that a woman who can do everything—husband, home, children, and art—is probably the luckiest person alive. For sheer richness of experience no one does any better. But the penalty is likely to be stomach ulcers or gray hairs at thirty-five."[10]

Brodie's situation was complicated by continuing difficulty in finding a satisfactory biographical topic. Her ultimate choice of Thaddeus Stevens did not come easily—nor quickly. Ever since completing her work on Joseph Smith, she had entertained the possibility of researching at least six other subjects, but none of them held her interest for long. In early September 1946 she seriously considered a dual biography on Margaret and Katherine Fox, two principals in the nineteenth-century spiritualist movement. The Fox sisters, like Joseph Smith, had lived and worked in western New York. While their lives and activities lacked the drama of Smith's, Brodie felt that their spiritualism had much wider repercussions. As with Smith, there was "a mixture of fraud, trickery, and falsehood with what seems to have been a very real sincerity and conviction." Brodie's interest in spiritualism and the Fox sisters, however, was short-lived. She abandoned the topic, having become "utterly fed up with all the hocus pocus. It was bad enough reading about a million seances, most of them alike, without having to write about them too."[11]

Brodie's search for a suitable topic then languished, preempted by family concerns. Her two young sons, infant Bruce and Dick, just barely four, demanded almost constant attention. She did not seem to mind. Describing Bruce at six months, she noted that he "is now mobile and squirms around on his stomach in a comical fashion. He continues to delight me and leaves me precious little leisure." Fawn found her motherly role much more appealing than book writing, which she characterized "the hardest of all possible ways to get an income." Although anxious to supplement the family's income, she rejected employment outside the home, turning down the offer of a steady job as a research assistant with the Yale University Institute of International Studies because it would mean turning her sons over to baby-sitters. "If my boys turn out badly," she told Dale Morgan, "I want it to be because of my incompetence and not that of a series of maids."[12]

There were other concerns. The Brodies were still anxious to begin construction of their new house in Bethany, plans that had been scuttled by the postwar scarcity of building materials. Thus they remained in the New Haven government housing project, where they had been living since August 1946. Then, in January 1947 they received the alarming

news that the project was about to be liquidated by the federal government. Thus they had to either buy the tiny duplex in which they were
living or face eviction pending its sale to someone else. In describing her
family's situation, Brodie told Dale Morgan, "We're so crowded now that
I can't bear to think of buying anything that doesn't have more elbow
room, but I shouldn't like the particular kind of elbow room provided
by an eviction into the street either." In the end, the Brodies were able to
avoid eviction, and to remain in their duplex, thanks to timely federal
legislation retaining government control.[13]

Also keeping Fawn from research and writing was the time she spent
on the Bethany property, clearing the land of brush and undergrowth in
anticipation of construction. It was work she liked. "I feel more like
clearing brush in Bethany than wearing my eyes out [doing historical
research]," she wrote Morgan. She viewed Bethany in idyllic terms; it was
the only place she had ever spent time, since Huntsville, where she felt
"completely at peace with the world." Later that spring, she and Bernard
planted two gardens on their Bethany property, one containing vegetables and the other flowers. Although gardening was time-consuming,
she found it both rewarding and satisfying. For Bernard, gardening provided an effective counterweight to the atom bomb—the grim focus of
his research and writing activities at Yale.[14]

Early in 1947, though, Fawn was compelled to return to historical
research. There were charges of sloppy research in the Joseph Smith
biography. In discussing Smith's youthful role as a "money-digger"—prior
to his founding the Mormon Church—Brodie had asserted that in 1826
he had been arrested, tried, and found guilty of disturbing the peace,
citing as documentation the text of the court record published in the
Scaff-Herzog Encyclopedia of Religious Knowledge. Mormon scholar Francis
Kirkham characterized the document a forgery in *The Improvement Era,* an
official Mormon Church periodical. Brodie now felt compelled to check
the authenticity of the court record in question.[15]

In March 1947, leaving her two young sons in the care of her younger
sister Louise, Fawn set out for upstate New York—specifically Chenango
County, the site of Joseph Smith's alleged trial—in search of the lost court
record. Traveling by automobile, she ran into a blizzard while crossing
the Alleghenies. In making her way slowly over the icy mountain roads,
she wondered "forlornly why I had ever set out on this seemingly foolish

quest." Upon reaching Norwich, the seat of Chenango County, Brodie learned much to her dismay, that the court record in question had been lost years earlier in a fire that destroyed the original courthouse. Out of desperation she expanded her search to the Norwich library, where the librarian directed her to a previously undiscovered account of Joseph Smith's 1826 trial. Much to Brodie's relief, the so-called Purple account— it had been written by a local physician, W. D. Purple—affirmed her original contention in *No Man Knows My History* that Joseph Smith had been brought to trial for "disorderly conduct" as a money-digger in 1826. She sent a copy of the Purple account to Francis Kirkham, who not only acknowledged it but included it, with commentary, in his own work on Joseph Smith, *A New Witness for Christ in America*.[16]

Brodie did other research and writing during the early part of 1947— specifically, an essay on the Mormons for the *New York Times* on the occasion of the centennial of Brigham Young's 1847 arrival in the Great Salt Lake Valley. She agreed to do this against her better judgment, and after completing the essay, she was less than satisfied. It was published in the *New York Times* in July 1947 under the title "'This Is the Place'—And It Became Utah." It began with a generally conventional historical overview of the Mormon Church in its first hundred years, focusing on the changes that had occurred as it slowly and imperceptibly receded from its position of complete domination over the political, economic, and moral aspects of Mormon life."[17]

In the last part of the essay, however, Brodie became more contentious, asserting that a combination of idealism and solidarity in the Mormon heritage was responsible for some "strange contradictions." Among the most evident was its emphasis on obedience to church authority, while at the same time promoting the individual ideal of human perfectibility through knowledge. "The church organization is strictly authoritarian and the leaders, tenaciously aware of their traditions and of their power, exhort their people first of all to be obedient," Brodie said. "But if obedience to ecclesiastical authority is the primary law of the church, a belief in human perfectibility is its loftiest theological ideal." "There results," she concluded, "an increasing conflict between uncompromising fundamentalism and the eager striving for perfection which is the basis of Mormon educational philosophy. For the very education of which Mormonism is so proud breeds skepticism and often outright rejection of Mormon doctrine."[18]

The author was clearly alluding to the origins and evolution of her own alienation from Mormonism. While the essay was a succinct reflection of her feelings as a skeptical observer of Mormonism, past and present, Brodie was unhappy with what she had written, or at least with the essay as published. "I was extremely annoyed to find that [the *Times*] had cut it almost beyond recognition with consequent distortions that I shall hate to have blamed on me," she lamented to Dale Morgan. "They took a good deal of the meat out of it and invariably left in what was just plain obvious. It was never really good in the first place, but it was a hell of a lot better in the original."[19]

Brodie's unhappiness with her *New York Times* essay was undoubtedly a manifestation of frustrations over her continuing uncertainty concerning the direction of her scholarly and literary pursuits. She questioned whether she should be writing at all, even while she continued her quest for a suitable topic for a second book-length biography. In March 1947 she announced to Dale Morgan her intention to do a biography on Andrew Johnson, Abraham Lincoln's hapless successor in the White House and staunch opponent of Radical Reconstruction. "I don't know why I should choose so difficult a man . . . but I have, and God willing, I may finish it ten years hence," she told Morgan. She found the period of Johnson's life fascinating. She believed the subject would be of contemporary interest in that the problems of race and sectional conflict were still current.[20]

Brodie's interest in Johnson and his times continued strong over the next six months. In August 1947 she again wrote Morgan, telling him of her fascination with the "Radical Republican revolution, which so fantastically misfired." She was intrigued "that the figures of Johnson and Thaddeus Stevens have never been adequately described, either in terms of what they were or what they symbolized." Still, she was all but immobilized by ambivalence, and she temporarily shelved all thoughts of historical research after reviewing "the facts" of her own life. Instead, she intended to take another fling at fiction, "an old ambition," she said. She felt it would be less arduous in terms of preparation and "a lot more fun" than historical research. And fiction might prove a better fit with her domestic situation. "You cannot imagine how much it takes out of you in terms of nervous energy," she wrote Morgan, "to have three people utterly dependent on you. I think I am a bad administrator—as my mother was—and am quite unable to shift portions of the burden."[21]

Fiction proved a passing fancy. In early 1948 Brodie gave that up and returned to Radical Republicans and Reconstruction. And by May she had shifted her focus from Andrew Johnson to Thaddeus Stevens, jutifying her choice of the Radical Republican leader by labeling him one of the most significant figures in American legislative history. The revolutionary character of his work, Fawn felt, had been completely obscured by the flood of histories written from the defensive southern position and by the fact that the revolution that was Reconstruction had failed. She characterized Stevens as a true revolutionary, "further to the left than any significant figure in American political history." His "idealism, tenacity, and enormous drive," along with his "mercilessness and ruthlessness," were qualities evident in outstanding leaders of both the French and Russian revolutions.[22]

Despite her newfound enthusiasm, Brodie expressed continued anxiety. There was the daunting nature of the research, not to mention the writing. Nevertheless, she began to devote "every spare minute" to gathering material and compiling research notes. There were, undeniably, feelings of guilt. It was hard to keep from chastising the boys when they bothered her, especially since she knew they could not understand "what unceasing interruptions can do to a train of thought." Bruce, an active toddler, hated to see his mother sit down at the typewriter. Whenever she sent him away, he would say, "Mommie, bad boy!" Fawn found that the only time she could "get any real research done is when he is asleep." "I am not by nature a patient person," she wrote Morgan, "but believe me, I am learning pateince. The boys really know how to discipline me in that respect."[23]

By April 1948, much of Fawn's attention was also directed toward the building of the Bethany house. Once started, construction moved along with astonishing speed, but it required much of Fawn's time and energy over the next six months. She wrote Dale Morgan that she had been "living in a madhouse of activity for so long now, I am close to getting accustomed to it." Her daily schedule involved eating a hasty breakfast, "and then out to Bethany, where we alternately gloat and work and return for an equally hasty lunch." In the afternoon there was a round

of errands for various items needed, concluding with another visit to
Bethany in the evening.[24]

The Brodies moved into their new residence on 30 August, but much
remained to be done—specifically, painting the interior, which the
Brodies chose to do themselves, and making the drapes. "I have been
painting by day and sewing . . . by night," Fawn noted, while "neglecting
everything else." All of this "naturally, plays hell with my research, and
has deteriorated my cooking to a disgraceful point."[25]

BUCOLIC BETHANY

Settling into their dream home, Fawn and Bernard knew that all the time
and effort had been more than worth it. "We are really enjoying our
house tremendously," Fawn wrote Morgan. "Bernard's chrysanthemums
are beginning to bloom in all their gorgeous profusion of color, and it is
wonderful to be able to enjoy them all the time." The best thing about
the new home, according to Fawn, was the picturesque view provided by
the six big living-room windows.[26]

The house was so striking that it attracted national media attention
through *Your House and Home*, being featured in that publication's
inaugural 1950 issue. The Brodie's so-called Hilltop House was praised
for its tasteful planning and careful attention to detail. The huge windows
in the living-room/dining-room area afforded a "glorious view" of nearby
Gaylord Mountain and gave the entire first floor a monumental cheer-
fulness. The intimate comfort of a tasefully planned, modern interior
complemented the fresh outdoor atmosphere. Also on the first floor was
given over to four bedrooms and two larger-than-usual bathrooms.
Another outstanding feature was the home's radiant heating system,
specially designed to ward off the effects of harsh New England winters.
Radiant heat extended throughout the whole house, utilizing a maze of
prefabricated panels of half-inch copper tubes built in the ceiling on both
floors. This feature was carried even into the quarters of Dash, the
Brodies' English setter.[27]

In their new spacious home, the Brodies hosted dinner parties for
friends, both personal and professional, and entertained house guests.
Their very first overnight visitor was M. Wilford Poulsen, the BYU

professor who had provided Brodie significant help and encouragement while she was working on *No Man Knows My History*. Fawn's parents arrived for Thanksgiving in late November 1948, and no one was as excited over the house as was Fawn Brimhall, who joyed in seeing her daughter have the kind of house she herself had always wanted but was denied by circumstances surrounding the joint family ownership of the old McKay house in Huntsville.[28]

Fawn understandably had difficulty returning to Thaddeus Stevens once she was settled in the new house. She told Claire Noall she had not "touched the typewriter for weeks," except for an occasional letter to family or friends. The new house was proving to be a deterrent to writing. The living room was so beautiful she wanted nothing more than to sit and look out its windows. Watching the birds at the feeding station was "infinitely" more attractive then researching Reconstruction history.[29]

The research, in any event, was presenting problems. Although she had already spent two years gaining knowledge of the Civil War and Reconstruction periods, she still felt inadequate to write about them. Documentation of Thaddeus Stevens's life was hard to come by. No one had collected his speeches, which meant that Brodie had to go through the *Congressional Globe*. Making matters worse, given Brodie's bent in biography, was the fact that Stevens rarely referred to himself in his public pronouncements; it meant she would have to analyze his character by circuitous means. Still another obstacle involved deciphering the documents in Stevens's handwriting, a script Brodie found "practically illegible."[30]

All this caused Brodie to doubt the viability of what she was doing. "I have no faith that a life of Stevens will begin to have the market [that *No Man Knows My History* had]," she told Dale Morgan. Why should she spend her leisure on an enterprise of questionable monetary compensation? Well aware that successful sales were driven by controversy, she acknowledged, "There was plenty of controversy in Stevens' life, but little drama." She had been "utterly spoiled," she admitted, by the drama and controversy she had found in researching Joseph Smith's life.[31]

All in all, Brodie was struggling through a period of inertia. She saw such inertia as the curse of gender. "If one wanted to discover the laws of inertia the best place to go for data [is] the female mind," she wrote Morgan. "So many fathers pass their genius on to their daughters, but as a general rule the talents lie dormant and are passed on to flower in the sons." A woman's failure to live up to her intellectual potential, Brodie felt, was reinforced by "the extraordinary satisfaction a women gets from taking care of small children. It makes ambition seem ridiculous, and shows up fame for the hollow thing it is." The paradox, she continued, "is that children grow up, and then a woman's life is unutterably barren, and it is generally too late to fill it up with anything."[32]

Such views clearly conformed with Fawn's long-standing belief that her role as a wife and mother took priority over research and writing. Not surprisingly, therefore, Fawn was pregnant once more, anticipating the birth of a third child in the fall of 1949. However, in early June, well into her pregnancy, Fawn received the alarming news that her father had suffered another heart attack. The initial prognosis was uncertain. Against the advice of her doctor, she traveled to Salt Lake City to be with her stricken parent, who, shortly after her arrival, made a remarkable recovery. But the trip took its toll on Fawn. She was bedridden in Utah with a threatened miscarriage. Initially, she appeared to recover, but when her condition worsened, she was hospitalized. She not only lost her baby but very nearly died.[33]

The entire experience proved traumatic. Upon leaving the hospital, Fawn experienced severe depression, largely attributable to a second miscarriage in five years. The depression took the form of "pessimism & bitterness." "If all the venom that accumulated in my soul could have been harnessed in some kind of explosive [the whole] state [of Utah] would simply have been blown to nothing," she told Dale Morgan. At the root of this anger was the behavior of certain members of the extended McKay family who indicated that the loss of her child and near-fatal illness were "just punishment" for her "sins." This was "the worst thing" that had ever happened to her, she said, but she found one "positive good emerging from the whole wretched experience": It had brought a "complete erasing of the feelings of guilt" she had had since the Joseph Smith biography had come out.[34]

Rather than returning to Bethany after her recovery, Fawn traveled to California for a period of rest and recuperation. She spent five weeks that summer in a cabin on Huntington Beach, just south of Los Angeles. Keeping her company were her two sons and two of her sisters, plus their children. This change of scenery helped Fawn to complete recovery, both physical and emotional. "Being around a flock of children and my two cheerful and plucky sisters worked a miracle in erasing my despair," she claimed.[35]

Despite the recent trauma, Fawn's desire for more children was stronger than ever. She was willing to go through anything to have another baby, she said. "This is priority number one, and everything else is going to be sacrificed to it." Research on Thaddeus Stevens now seemed "remote & tedious & unimportant." "I haven't even thought about Thaddeus Stevens for six months," she said in September 1949, "and doubt if I'll get back to that study for another year."[36]

Just two months later, however, Brodie found herself under pressure from her publisher. She received a blunt letter from Alfred Knopf, asking about progress on the biography. Knopf's sudden inquiry was prompted by information that Ralph Korngold, a popular biographer of minor renown, was working on Thaddeus Stevens, having signed a contract with Little, Brown of Boston. Knopf asked Brodie a series of short, to-the-point questions: "What do you think about this? How far along are you? Would you like me to tell my friend, the President of Little Brown, something about your plans? Please let me know."[37]

Brodie promptly replied to Knopf, giving him a frank assessment of her situation. She told him of her shattering illness and her slow recovery. She informed him of her lack of progress, noting that she did not expect to finish the biography for at least another two to three years. She had barely begun the writing, she said, and needed to do more research. She asserted that Ralph Korngold's volume would not be formidable competition; he was more a journalist than a biographer, she said, and his treatment of Thaddeus Stevens would not preempt the field.[38]

Knopf responded in his usual curt manner. Hers was "not good news," he wrote, but he expressed sympathy for her situation. He also indicated his intention to write Little, Brown to inform them of the delay in her work.[39]

Brodie's brief exchange with Knopf did prod her to take up research again late in 1949. It proceeded, however, at "a leisurely pace," and she lamented to Dale Morgan, "I peck away at research on Stevens, but without any real conviction that the book will be finished before I am forty." Further discouraging Brodie was news that still another person— George Fort Milton, who like Ralph Korngold was a semipopular writer—

was doing a Thaddeus Stevens biography. As with Korngold, Brodie dismissed both the author and his work. In *The Age of Hate*, Milton had characterized Thaddeus Stevens as "an evil and vindictive old man." If Milton now did no more than build on that thesis, there would still be plenty of room for another book.[40]

Meantime Brodie sought to channel the knowledge and information gained from her research into an article-length essay on military rule in the South following the Civil War. She described the work as "a straight historical piece with contemporary overtones." In early 1950, she submitted this essay, entitled "Denazification, Our First Experiment," to *Reporter* magazine, a small but highly regarded journal of opinion on contemporary affairs. When the essay was rejected, the disappointed author despaired of her ability to "combine research and child-rearing," deciding that perhaps she should "chuck the former for another five years or so."[41]

Such disappointment was more than offset by the good news that Fawn was once again pregnant. Despite her previous problems in carrying a baby to term, she was optimistic. She selected a gynecologist who was fully aware of her previous difficulties and in whom she had complete confidence. The next several months were nevertheless difficult. Her activities were greatly restricted, and she was "practically jailed to the house." The loneliness and isolation were difficult to bear. Her medication made her so lethargic she found it virtually impossible to do anything more than the essential tasks of motherhood and housework. The bulk of her time was spent resting or sleeping. "I am absolutely good for nothing except as an incubator," she said, "and I'm not sure how good I am at that."[42]

Despite this, she remained in reasonable good spirits, getting along far better than during any of her previous pregnancies. For this she was most grateful, although the nine-month wait seemed more "like nine years." To make time pass more quickly, she took up knitting, an activity she had previously scorned as "the nadir of female degradation." Now she found "it wondrously relaxing and satisfying."[43]

On 9 October 1950, Fawn gave birth to a daughter. "She came late, but precipitously," the mother reported. The "breakneck ride to the hospital" made it "all very exciting." Much to Fawn's relief, the birth was without complication, with "just enough of the famous 'Read' method of natural childbirth to miss the worst of the pain and yet be fully awake for the last push." "It was a great thrill to hear the first cry, and see her completely in the raw in the first minute of birth, something that had not happened to me before. . . . It was just as if I had had three stiff cocktails. I never felt happier in my life." The infant was named Pamela Beatrice.[44]

A RETURN TO WASHINGTON, D. C.

At the time their third child was born, Fawn and Bernard were preparing to move back to Washington, D. C. Bernard had just accepted a position as consultant with the Air Targets Divison of the U.S. Air Force. In accepting this position—thus moving his family from their much-loved, recently completed Bethany home—Bernard was motivated by several factors. First, the position involved research for the air force in nuclear strategy, a "subject . . . dear to Bernard's heart." As direct advisor to the air force's chief of staff, Gen. Hoyt Vandenberg, he would be at the center of national strategic planning. He had achieved recognition as the leading civilian military thinker of the day.[45]

The position appealed to Bernard for a second reason: He was tiring of Yale; he found his colleagues at the Institute of International Studies stagnant in their thinking, still focusing on the ramifications of the atom bomb. Brodie had moved beyond such fundamental issues to more complex, practical questions of military strategy, including possible deployment of nuclear weapons in warfare, a particularly timely topic with the outbreak of the Korean War in June 1950. And there was also a very practical appeal to the new position; The air force was offering him twice his Yale salary—this when the Brodies faced increased expenses, including the need to replace the family's twelve-year-old automobile.[46]

Despite the advantages, the move to Washington was wrenching, particularly for Fawn. The Brodies had lived in the New Haven–Bethany area for over five years. Their two youngest children, Bruce and Pamela, had been born there, and the oldest, Dick, now eight, had attended his first three years of public school there. The years in New Haven–Bethany were important in the family history and were full of significant memories. For Fawn, the selling of the Bethany home was "heart-breaking." "For two blessed years I cherished the illusion that I could take root somewhere and live with a sense of permanence," she lamented to Dale Morgan. "I never really believed we were building this house for our children—only for us—but even that illusion is shattered. Now I know we will hop around every few years or so.[47]

Bernard, sensitive to such feelings and seeking to ease the family's difficult adjustment, commissioned a contractor to build a new home in a wooded area just south of Alexandria, Virginia. Known as Hollen Hills, it was a modern housing development close to historic Mount Vernon, George Washington's plantation home. Because of the outbreak of the Korean War, construction went more slowly than expected, and the Brodies were forced to live temporarily in a small furnished apartment in southwest Washington when they first arrived. In this less-than-ideal situation, Fawn fought homesickness for New England.[48]

In spite of her discontent, Fawn was grateful for the opportunity to see and once more interact on a personal level with Dale Morgan, who was still living in Washington, D. C., and still doing research on Mormon history. Besides exchanging historical information, the two discussed contemporary developments within the Mormon Church, most significantly a major change in church leadership. In April 1951, with the sudden death of George Albert Smith, who had served just six years as Mormon president, David O. McKay was elevated to the top office of the church. In discussing the development with Morgan, Fawn admitted ambivalence over her uncle's ascendancy. She had "maliciously hoped," she said, that this highest of positions "would always be denied him."[49]

In addition to being close again to Dale Morgan, Brodie found another benefit to living in Washington. She now had convenient access to the Library of Congress, which contained materials essential to her Thaddeus Stevens research. When Brodie could arrange for sitters to look after her children, she spent time in the library going through relevant newspapers and manuscripts.

On 1 May 1951, after three months in their cramped, temporary quarters, the Brodies moved into their newly built Hollen Hills home near Alexandria. Located in a nice wooded area, the new residence was described by an admiring Dale Morgan as "[as] beautiful [a] place [as] anyone might want to own." Fawn and Bernard, however, were much less enthusiastic. They were, in fact, actually quite dissatisfied with a number of its features. It lacked any scenic view and the living space covered two levels, creating a problem for a family with two very young children. Less than two months after moving into the house, Fawn and Bernard were formulating plans for a new, one-level home. Attempting to replicate their Bethany house, they drew in a large living room and chose a site on a nearby hill. These new house-building plans distracted Fawn once more from her research and writing.[50]

There were other distractions. In June 1951, after less than a year on the job, Bernard Brodie resigned his position as civilian consultant with the Air Targets Division of the U.S. Air Force. He found his concepts of nuclear strategic bombing in opposition to those of important high-ranking air force officials, particularly Gen. Curtis LeMay, head of the Strategic Air Command. While Brodie advocated precision bombing of selected military targets, LeMay favored blanket bombing of both civilian and military targets. Unfortunately for Brodie, LeMay's views were in ascendency in the climate of the Korean War and the intensified cold war.[51]

Bernard next accepted an offer from the RAND Corporation, a pioneering think tank based in Santa Monica, California, to serve as a full-time staff member. Established by the air force, RAND initially had focused on engineering studies and low-level operations research analysis. With its recruitment of Brodie, it made long-range strategic planning an important part of its research program, and Brodie was soon joined by other outstanding strategic thinkers, including Herman Kahn, Albert Wohlstetter, William W. Kaufmann, and Thomas Schelling. Later, other notables joined RAND—Henry Kissinger, the future secretary of state, and Charles Hitch, a future deputy secretary of defense and later University of California president.[52]

Although the move to RAND provided Bernard a more congenial work environment, it made the Brodie family situation more difficult, particularly for Fawn. Bernard was required to divide his time between RAND's Washington, D.C., office and corporate headquarters in Santa Monica. This meant frequent, extended trips to California that took him away from home for days, sometimes weeks on end. Fawn was compelled to assume additional responsibilities in looking after the family. She disliked this situation: "I hate these two-week stretches [of separation]," she wrote Bernard once. "They seem four times as long as a single week."[53]

Bernard, sensitive to his wife's discontent, tried to remedy the situation. During the two months of July and August 1951, when he was required to be at the Santa Monica headquarters, he took the entire family west with him, giving them an extended vacation. The Brodies spent the time in a beautiful house right on the water at Malibu Beach, for which they paid a "perfectly bankrupting rental" fee. But it was more than worth it, allowing the family to be together and enjoy the California beach, while escaping the "hellish summer" heat of Washington. The Brodies were joined by Fawn's older sister, Flora, and her three children and a niece, which made for pleasant days on the beach and relaxing evenings. Even Bernard, despite limits on his own leisure time, enjoyed himself, telling a close friend, "I feel like a real patriarch when I sit down to dinner each evening, what with two women and seven kids, but it's a nice feeling." For Fawn, the carefree environment of Malibu Beach meant minimal concern for Thaddeus Stevens.[54]

However, Thaddeus Stevens *was* of concern to Fawn's editor and publisher, Alfred A. Knopf. Knopf had written a cryptic letter to Fawn in early June 1951, apparently his first communication in some two years. "Have you any news for me? It is a long time since I have heard anything from you," the publisher wrote. Fawn quickly answered in a longer but equally blunt letter. "If I had had any good news for you, I should have written long ago." As it was, Brodie noted "all my good news has been personal." With disarming frankness, she told Knopf: "I have a new baby daughter who with her two brothers is filling up not only my days but also all of my needs. I find them infinitely more rewarding than writing books." Thaddeus Stevens, she said had "been reduced to about fifth place among [her] interests."[55]

But Fawn was also careful to inform Knopf that Stevens had not been entirely neglected. She had completed research in the materials at the Library of Congress, she said, though the manuscript remained to be written. She had no idea how long it would take, she told her publisher, but she had good intentions of "beginning serious writing" by fall. "Please be patient with me," she pleaded. Knopf responded with another short note, congratulating Fawn on her new baby and acknowledging her busy schedule, but concluding, "I do hope the book will make some progress."[56]

CALIFORNIA AND PACIFIC PALISADES

Brodie's work on Thaddeus Stevens was further interrupted by yet another family move. In February 1952, because of Bernard's work with RAND in Santa Monica, the Brodies relocated to nearby Pacific Palisades. Bernard had begun planning the move in June 1951 after a visit to the community. He was impressed with the spectacular views of the sea and the mountains from bluffs two hundred to three hundred feet above the Pacific Ocean. Equally enticing were the bright sun, the cool air, lovely flowers, and the striking examples of modern architecture in the homes already built there.[57]

Fawn initially opposed the move. "I am putting up stiff resistance for many reasons," she told Morgan, "not the least of which is that I know that I should vegetate completely." Such fears stemmed, in part, from her long-held perception of California as a vestige of the "fleshpots of Egypt"—her own oft-used phrase. But late in 1951 Fawn changed her mind, having been won over, like Bernard, by the picturesque and pleasant location of Pacific Palisades. More important, Fawn was ready for any move that would allow her to resume what she considered a normal family life after a year of Bernard's frequent prolonged absences. Still haunted by memories of the wrenching move from their Bethany home just a year earlier, however, she extracted from Bernard a promise that he would never sell whatever home they built in Pacific Palisades.[58]

Following the Brodies' move west early in 1952, Fawn adjusted quickly and enthusiastically to life in California. After just one month she confessed to being "a hopeless convert to the West all over again," enjoying as she was, "more genuine wonderful sunshine, with all of the clear blue marvelous western air that accompanies it, in my four weeks here than in the last four years in the East." The winter rainfall had made the nearby hills lush with vegetation. "The June grass all over the foothills must be the thing God had in mind when he decided to invent greenness," Fawn noted, "and the Pacific is actually as blue as all the pictures make it out to be."[59]

The Brodies had chosen as a site for their new house a lot high on a hill overlooking the Pacific Ocean. It "is so wonderful that I cannot conceive of ever living anywhere else, and already [I] am making plans . . .

to see my daughter married in the house," she wrote back to Dale Morgan, "and to see my grandchildren, one of them at any rate, inherit it." Both she and Bernard were as "hopelessly lost" in house-building plans now as they had been in Bethany five years earlier. While awaiting actual construction, the Brodies were living in a little cottage some three miles from the home site. Despite rather cramped quarters, Fawn coped much better than she had in similar conditions in Washington the previous year.[60]

Construction of their home started in the spring of 1952. Fawn and Bernard were caught up in the entire process, and it occupied their energies over the next several months. Bernard exhibited the same passionate interest in every detail he had with the construction of their Bethany residence, and Fawn spent several hours at the construction site each day, planting shrubs and other foliage as ground cover to prevent the severe erosion caused by winter rains that was a recurring problem in the hills and bluffs of Pacific Palisades.[61]

By fall, construction was complete and the Brodies moved in. The house contained two thousand feet of living space, all on one level, with a large combination living room-dining room, reminiscent of the Bethany home. The most striking feature of the house was its extensive window space—again reminiscent of the earlier residence. From its windows one could see a wild mountainous area to the north and east, and the whole of Santa Monica bay and a portion of the vast Los Angeles skyline to the south and east. The 270-degree panoramic view offered an astonishing contrast in moods: a vast ocean, a crescent of city lights at night, and a rugged mountain range—the latter reminiscent of the mountains encircling Huntsville.[62]

Meanwhile, Fawn's writing further languished as the new home consumed her time and energy. Although she still had ambitions to work on Thaddeus Stevens, she found her days filled with one long series of interruptions. The little time she found to write, she devoted not to Stevens, but to the Mormons. She had been approached by the editor of *Frontier*, a recently established western periodical, to do an article on the influence of Mormonisn on American writing. Again against her better judgment and despite a previous vow never to touch Mormonism again, she consented. "It might be fun to write about 'The Impact of the World on the Mormon writer,'" she wrote her uncle Dean Brimhall, "because obviously

there is no such thing as the impact of Mormonism on the writing world."
The subject actually seemed an easy one, since "everything would come
out of my own head, and I wouldn't have to check sources and footnotes."[63]

Brodie's essay appeared in the December 1952 issue of *Frontier* under
the title "New Writers and Mormonism." It discussed the phenomenon
of the Mormon writer by focusing on novelists Vardis Fisher, Virginia
Sorenson, Maurine Whipple, and Ardyth Kennelly and on several non-
fiction authors, including her good friend Dale Morgan and Juanita
Brooks, author of the recently completed, controversial *Mountain
Meadows Massacre*. Fawn also dealt with two prominent non-Mormon
writers who had grown up in Utah—namely Bernard De Voto and
Wallace Stegner. All these writers had been raised either in the Mormon
Church or alongside it and had found Mormonism so fascinating or
provocative that they could not "resist the urge to reckon with it in print."
More important, these writers stood "outside of the Church altogether,
in spirit if not in fact." But they stood in sharp contrast to the classic anti-
Mormon writers of the nineteenth and early twentieth century who
"counted Mormonism a dragon to be slain." Later writers had "the
ambition to be serious novelists and historians, striving earnestly, if not
always successfully, for impartiality."[64]

These writers, Brodie noted, "however determined to be detached,
urbane and if possible philosophic about the society which irrevocably
shaped their childhood, still find themselves torn between filial loyalties
and a fierce hunger for independence." Clearly she was alluding to her
own situation, to the irresistible attraction of her family and her heritage,
and to the urge to break free from its narrow, confining aspects. She noted
the uneasy relationship of the new writers with the Mormon Church, which
was not officially nor publicly proud of the best Mormon novelists—and
was even more suspicious of its young historians, viewing them, with some
validity, as a potential threat. Mormon officials, instead of blasting such
writers out of the church, as they would have done for the same literature
a half century earlier, were content to issue negative book reviews through
official church publications. "The old terror of persecution has vanished,
with the result that within the Church there is in general far greater
tolerance of the dissenting voice and the genuinely creative spirit." This
tolerance, Brodie suggested, was due to Mormonism's relatively secure
position in mid-twentieth century, in contrast to the situation in the

nineteenth century when the church was under siege from within and without. The present-day Mormon Church Brodie said, was readily seen to be "well entrenched, powerful, and marvelously cohesive."[65]

The appearance of this essay represented Brodie's first publication in some five years. After such a long drought, she expressed pleasure at seeing her name again in print. Her pleasure was short-lived, however, when the precocious Dick asked his mother, "Can't you ever write about anything but the Mormons?" Initially taken aback, Fawn could only concede that the boy's reproof was all too justified.[66]

BACK TO THADDEUS STEVENS

Although shaken by her ten-year-old's bluntness, Brodie actually was refocused already on Thaddeus Stevens. By June 1953, she had finished writing four chapters. Four months later, she informed Alfred Knopf that she had finished her research and had written two more chapters, bringing the total number of text pages completed to one hundred and fifty. She assured Knopf that despite all the interruptions she was working fairly steadily, with the certain conviction that she would finish the book." "Stevens has gotten hold of me and is not likely to let go," she told her publisher. But she could not say precisely when the manuscript would be completed. Knopf replied quickly to Brodie's letter; he found the news encouraging, he said.[67]

Throughout the rest of 1953 and into 1954, Brodie continued to push ahead. "I am still hammering away at Thaddeus Stevens," she wrote Dean Brimhall in February 1954, adding, "Nobody who has not tried to write history can possibly realize how much time is consumed with the mere matter of organizing material." She was now so immersed in Thaddeus Stevens literature that she was doing absolutely no other reading, except for newspapers and current newsmagazines. While such discipline was good for book writing, she said, it was "bad for the soul." By the fall of 1954, she had completed nine chapters, and she sent them to Knopf for evaluation. Knopf in turn sent them out to several outside historians for assessment.[68]

In November 1954, Brodie received bad news from Knopf. The historians Knopf had consulted gave her manuscript "the kiss of death," as she put it. The major problem was concern over the seemingly limited appeal of the topic itself—the life and times of Thaddeus Stevens, which presented the publisher a clear sales problem. Brodie ruminated over the book's seemingly limited marketing potential: "The Democrats won't buy it because it is about a Republican; the Republicans won't buy it because it is about a Radical; the Southerners won't buy it because I am more inclined to defend him than to make him out the monster history has pronounced him to be. The Northerners won't buy it cause they don't really give a damn about Negro rights; and the Negroes won't buy it because they don't buy books, anyway."[69]

Knopf, however, had not completely given up; he advised Brodie to rewrite the whole thing in order to make it marketable, a prospect the author found extremely unappealing. She could not resist commenting sarcastically to Dale Morgan—with the contemporary American fascination with Joseph McCarthy in mind—"If I really wanted to make money I would title [the book] 'Thaddeus Stevens and the Rape of the South' and make him out to be a prototype of Joe McCarthy. This could be done. But not by me, I am afraid." She still thought that Thaddeus Stevens, as a subject, was just as good as Joseph Smith. But she lamented, "I often have grave doubts if I am the person to write the biography. If I were really smart, I'd give up writing and have a couple more children. They are in every way so much more rewarding than writing."[70]

Old conflicts surfaced. In weighing her responsibilities, she berated herself for not devoting her complete energies to the children that she already had, but then her children had now grown to the point of being sufficiently independent that they did not demand her time, even though they were so much fun, she said, that they robbed her of any compulsion to engage in the "really hard work" of writing.[71]

Despite her ambivalences and the negative reactions to her early chapters, Brodie continued with her biography during the rest of 1954 and into 1955. "I am beginning to think [it] will be a lifetime project," she told her uncle Deam Brimhall. "It is turning out to be an extraordinarily difficult book to write. . . . Defending a radical in this day and age is something that requires guile as well as passion." She was, after all, made constantly aware of the conservative, sometimes reactionary, political climate of the 1950s—specifically, the deep suspicion of all forms of liberalism and the anti-Communist hysteria of McCarthyism. When political commentators likened Joseph McCarthy to Thaddeus Stevens, Brodie was appalled. "I don't know that I can ever rescue him from such an association," she told her uncle. "But I shall keep on trying, even though historians are certain to hurl brickbats in my direction." These challenges only invigorated her work.[72]

Brodie's presentation of Thaddeus Stevens as an enlightened reformer clearly reflected her own liberal Democratic orientation. Such bias was evident in all her reactions to contemporary political developments. She was greatly disappointed in the outcome of the presidential campaign of 1952, sharing as she did the views of her husband, who had had a great deal of firsthand experience with the military mind and was particularly suspicious of the leadership qualities of World War II hero Dwight D. Eisenhower. Fawn lamented the defeat of Democratic candidate Adlai E. Stevenson; his loss, she said, "demonstrated that Americans have no faith in the articulate man."[73]

Fawn was further appalled by Eisenhower's appointment of Mormon Church Apostle Ezra Taft Benson to serve in his cabinet as the secretary of agriculture. Brodie's disdain for Benson intensified as the apostle-turned-agriculture secretary became increasingly outspoken in his conservative views. Fawn and Bernard both got a good chuckle out of a speech Benson gave in 1955 wherein he blamed the fall of Rome on "creeping socialism." Her strongly partisan views complemented those of Bernard, who expressed his own harsh criticism of Eisenhower and his advisors, particularly his pugnacious secretary of state, John Foster Dulles, whom Bernard privately characterized as "a boob and a national disaster."[74]

Fawn Brodie's liberal Democratic views were evident in the tone and tenor of her approach to Thaddeus Stevens. Her presentation of Stevens as a enlightened liberal reformer set her work apart from Richard Current's biography of the Radical Republican leader that had been published in 1942. Brodie recognized Current to be an able and disciplined historian and acknowledged that his *Old Thad Stevens, A Story of Ambition* was written "with . . . restraint and scholarship." But she took issue with Current's interpretation as being too negative, noting that whatever he could find in Stevens's life that was "tricky, unscrupulous, and demagogic [was] meticulously assembled and copiously documented."[75] Current's work obviously opened the way for a more sympathetic treatment of the Radical Republican leader.

But, alas, Ralph Korngold's long-awaited biography, *Thaddeus Stevens: A Being Darkly Wise and Rudely Great*, which came out in 1955 as Brodie labored over her manuscript, was a very favorable biography, appearing to preempt her efforts. Brodie conceded that "Korngold's admiration for Thaddeus Stevens permeates every chapter and his occasional derogatory criticisms are offered with apology and regret." This disappointment was immediately followed by even worse news. Alfred Knopf informed Brodie of his decision not to publish her biography. The official reason for rejection was that the work would not sell, but underlying this practical consideration was a related ideological concern. Knopf was apparently uncomfortable with Brodie's interpretation of Stevens as a reformer within a liberal political tradition; in her view, Knopf was reluctant to handle anything on the Radical tradition in America.[76]

Knopf's rejection only brought to the surface again Brodie's ambivalence toward the entire project. "At the moment," she told Dale Morgan, "I am saying 'To hell with writing' and just enjoying our garden & the children." Despite such rhetoric, however, Brodie was not quite ready to give up. "There must be publishers who are not afraid to be as far 'left' as Arthur Schlesinger Jr. and [Bernard] De Voto whose opinions on American history I respect profoundly, and who have, in fact, greatly influenced my [own] thinking." So saying, she submitted her manuscript to Princeton University Press, a decision influenced by Bernard, who approached his editor there, Herbert S. Bailey, on his wife's behalf. Bernard knew Bailey well, both professionally and personally; his first two books, *Sea Power in the Machine Age* and *A Layman's Guide to Naval Strategy*, had been published by Princeton University Press in the early 1940s. Bailey found the manuscript "exciting" and passed "it on to a historian or two," raising both anxiety and hope in the author." "God knows what their verdict will be," she wrote Dale Morgan.[77]

PSYCHOANALYSIS AND PREOCCUPATION WITH FAMILY

By the time Brodie submitted her manuscript to Princeton, she had become acutely interested in the field of psychology and psychoanalysis—

an interest that would profoundly influence the focus of the Stevens biography. Her interest in psychology had predated Thaddeus Stevens, of course; it first became evident while she was working on *No Man Knows My History* and came across Bernard De Voto's theory that Joseph Smith was a "paranoid personality"—though she ultimately rejected that theory. Her interest in psychoanalysis deepened with her move to California and apparently came through Bernard's work at RAND, where he used psychological methodology in developing theories involving nuclear defense strategy. In the course of his work, Bernard became acquainted with a number of psychoanalysts in the Los Angeles area, whom he in turn introduced to Fawn.[78]

Initially, Fawn's reactions to contact with these professionals was mixed. She was "amused at how much their work has become a religion to them," she wrote Dean Brimhall. Still, she couldn't help finding much of their theory impressive. Among the psychoanalyst friends on whom Brodie relied for help in evaluating the character and behavior of Thaddeus Stevens were some who had acquired national and even international renown, including Nathan Leites, Milton Wexler, Hanna Fenichel, and especially Ralph R. Greenson. It was with Greenson that Fawn, as well as Bernard, developed a particularly close professional and personal relationship. Fawn turned to Greenson for insight on Stevens as she rewrote her manuscript. Although he did not take on the role of mentor, as had Dale Morgan, Fawn greatly respected his judgment.[79]

Greenson's interaction with Fawn Brodie came at a time when psychoanalysis was very much in vogue, with treatment sought not just by individuals in genuine mental or emotional crisis but also by those who felt this therapy was useful in handling life's ordinary demands. Fawn and Bernard Brodie themselves chose to go into therapy, since psychoanalysis was particularly popular with RAND people and RAND's health insurance paid most of the costs of anaylsis for employees and their spouses. Greenson referred Fawn to another Los Angeles psychiatrist, Dr. Lewis Fielding, who was as prominent as himself, for help with what she presented as her two major problems: chronic mild depression and continuing difficulties with sexuality, a condition that had plagued her throughout her marriage and even prior. Bernard sought help for his chronic insomnia, which was adversely affecting his work with RAND. In the end, analysis brought some success for Fawn, who at least found ways to deal with both her depression and her sexual problems. Bernard, however, was not successful in alleviating his insomnia.[80]

Fawn and Bernard Brodie also interacted socially with Greenson and others within the Los Angeles psychiatric community. They became noted for their magnificent dinner parties—small, intimate gatherings limited to eight to twelve people and focusing on stimulating conversations covering topics from politics to the arts. A carefully prepared meal, sometimes featuring exotic dishes cooked by Fawn herself, was served, and the usual guests were the Greensons, who throughout the 1950s remained among the Brodies' closest friends. Others invited on a rotating basis were individuals from the local psychiatric community and friends and associates of Bernard's at RAND. Among the most prominent of these were Edward Teller, father of the hydrogen bomb, and Henry A. Kissinger, the future national security advisor and secretary of state.[81]

Interacting with their circle of friends proved much less challenging to the Brodies than dealing with Fawn's aging parents, who were both suffering from various afflictions. Initially, Fawn was grateful for the opportunity to visit with her mother and father on a more regular basis after moving to California. In early 1953 Thomas E. and Fawn McKay visited the Brodies in Pacific Palisades. During this visit, Fawn drove her father over to the construction site of the new Mormon temple in Los Angeles.[82]

In July of that same year, the Brodies traveled to Utah to attend a family reunion on the occasion of Flora's fortieth birthday. With all of the children and grandchildren of Thomas E. and Fawn McKay gathered together, a group photograph was taken in front of the old McKay home in Huntsville. Several months later, the photograph was published in the Mormon Church magazine, *The Improvement Era*, to illustrate an article featuring Thomas McKay and his work as a Church General Authority. It seemed both amusing and ironic to Fawn that church officials allowed the picture of an excommunicated Mormon to appear in the *Improvement Era*.[83]

In April 1955 Thomas and Fawn McKay traveled once more to California. And once more, Fawn took them to the site of the Los Angeles temple, by then further along in construction. After a tour of the partially completed structure, Fawn reported to Dale Morgan "that nothing could be more appropriate to Los Angeles than this building and all that it

Three generations of the Thomas McKay family at a McKay family reunion in Huntsville, Utah, in July 1953. This is the only known image of all five members of Fawn and Bernard Brodie's family in a single group photo. Fawn and Bernard Brodie are standing on the extreme left of the back row; next to Bernard is Fawn's older sister, Flora, and next to her is Fawn's brother, Thomas. Fawn's younger sister Barbara is in the back row, third from the right, holding the child, and her youngest sister, Louise, is in the middle of the back row, fifth from the right. The Brodies' oldest son, Richard, is to the left and slightly behind his grandmother, Fawn Brimhall McKay. Daughter Pamela is held by her grandfather, and son Bruce is third from the left in the front row. Courtesy Flora McKay Crawford.

stands for. . . . As a pretentious monument to the most outlandish nonsense it is head and shoulders above any Hollywood set or local shrine."[84]

By this time, Thomas McKay's health was in decline. In fragile shape since his near-fatal heart attack in 1949, he had been diagnosed in early 1954 with an inoperable cancer on his neck. But he responded to X-ray treatment, and the cancer went into remission. There were other problems, however. The seventy-eight-year-old was almost blind and so physically weak that he could not walk about for more than a few minutes at a time. Yet according to Fawn, he remained as alert as ever and continued to enjoy extensive travel with his wife, who willingly drove the two of them on extended vacations throughout various parts of the West. Included were trips to Arizona and California in the winter, Yellowstone and Jackson Hole in the summer. All the while Fawn Brimhall appeared "busy and happy," but Fawn Brodie worried about her mother's state of mind should her father precede her in death.[85]

Ironically, it was Fawn's mother who presented her daughter and other family members with the most immediate problem. In July 1956, Fawn McKay attempted suicide by slashing her forearm with a piece of broken glass. Responding to this crisis, Fawn flew to Salt Lake to consult with her sisters and brother—and the doctors treating her mother. Efforts to help her mother were complicated by two major problems. First, Brodie found it impossible to communicate with her mother's psychiatrist, Dr. Louis Moench. The second problem was Fawn's father. Fawn already had a strained relationship with him, but during this crisis the two became further estranged as Fawn grew increasingly frustrated trying to get her father to accept care for himself from a visiting nurse or other home-care person, thus relieving Fawn's mother of such overwhelming responsibility.[86]

Though conditions were not totally satisfactory to Fawn's way of thinking, her mother appeared to recover. But just one month later, Fawn Brimhall attempted suicide a second time, this time cutting herself with a Catholic crucifix. Fawn returned to Salt Lake City once more to consult with family members. And again, as after her mother's first suicide attempt, she met the same two problems—her mother's psychiatrist, Dr. Louis Moench, specifically, his techniques, and her father's behavior. Fawn and other family members quickly dealt with the first problem, dismissing Dr. Moench, whom they considered completely incompetent because of his use of shock therapy and his failure to advise follow-up treatment. By contrast, the new psychiatrist enlisted by the family, a Dr. Anderson, appeared more willing to prescribe follow-up treatment. The family had Thomas McKay temporarily hospitalized, and the prognosis for Fawn's mother appeared to improve.[87]

In the fall of 1956 Fawn returned to Salt Lake, this time to evaluate her mother's situation. Fawn was now convinced that her father was primarily responsible for her mother's condition because of all his demands on her. "My disillusionment with my Father," she told her uncle Dean Brimhall, "reached the lowest possible point . . . absolute bottom." "Maybe in years to come," she continued,

> I can be more forgiving, but he makes any kind of detachment so
> difficult because of continuing pretentions to purity and saintliness.
> And of course I started out as a child thinking he was next to God
> in gallantry and goodness. Then, too, there is the factor that I have
> hurt him, and having hurt him I must believe the worst about him
> lest I suffer too much from guilt myself.[88]

But Fawn had some positive feelings for her father, recalling an incident in which he had defended her while the two were shopping together in Salt Lake City during her 1956 visit. Fawn had taken him to ZCMI, a Mormon Church–owned department store in the center of the city. During the course of a conversation between her father and the salesclerk, who knew Thomas McKay well, Fawn was introduced as "my daughter from California." The clerk, apparently unaware of who Fawn was, asked brusquely, "Are you the worst daughter or the best daughter?" Before a startled and mortified Fawn could respond, her father drew himself up and promptly replied, "I have four daughters and they're all wonderful." In recalling her father's behavior on that occasion, Fawn admitted, "I cherish this memory and will cherish it till I die."[89]

But Fawn's overall relationship with her father remained ambivalent. "A daughter's relationship with her father is unquestionably the most important single factor in determining the course of her life," Fawn once stated, but quickly added, "Of course, the relationship with both parents is equally significant."[90]

Her father's behavior aside, Fawn's most immediate concern was in finding treatment for her mother's psychological problems. Drawing on her own knowledge of psychoanalysis, she detected several complex, interrelated causes. The most evident involved the unbearable pressures imposed on Fawn McKay in caring for her blind, enfeebled husband. A second related factor, she knew, was that "every suicide contains a murder." Her mother's suicide attempts, Fawn speculated, were triggered by a secret desire to have her husband dead. The only way that she could live with this forbidden wish "was to punish herself through slavish and genuinely masochistic nursing devotion." Finding that scenario intolerable, Fawn Brimhall chose suicide as the only way way out.[91]

Fawn suggested a third, even deeper-seated cause, one rooted in her mother's youth—a traumatic childhood experience that involved her mother's shock at seeing a younger sister, who had been left in her care, killed in an accident. This tragedy, Fawn theorized, may have caused her mother to take on a terrifying burden of guilt that was reactivated, Fawn further speculated, by the recent deaths of three cows on the family farm in Huntsville for which Fawn Brimhall had been held responsible. In general, Fawn felt her mother "had a fairly ample reservoir of hatred and guilt," which, being systematically repressed, had ultimately turned inward.[92]

A fourth, more direct explanation for Fawn McKay's psychological problems was simply that she suffered from bouts of acute depression. In looking to suicide as a way out, she reflected the behavior of her father, George H. Brimhall, whose cancer and physical agony had led to his own suicide twenty-five years before. Fawn McKay's depression had been exacerbated in earlier years by the difficulties of living in the old McKay family home in Huntsville under less-than-idyllic conditions. Two other factors, Fawn figured, could have contributed to Fawn Brimhall McKay's acute depression: the sudden departure of her three youngest children, Louise, Thomas B., and Barbara, all of whom had left home and married within a nine-month period in 1942–43, and the care of her own aged widowed mother, Flora Brimhall, who was suffering from Alzheimer's disease.[93]

Whatever the causes, Fawn Brimhall McKay's condition improved following the change in doctors. She went through clinical treatment based on shock therapy. Initially, daughter Fawn reacted negatively to the prescription of such treatment, but she changed her mind upon observing her mother's much-improved condition. "Had I not seen the extraordinary dramatic results with my own eyes," Brodie said, "I would [still] be extremely suspicious of it." Following completion of shock therapy, Fawn and her siblings looked for the most appropriate long-range therapy to ensure their mother's continued recovery. Fawn was advised by her Los Angeles psychiatrist friends that the best recipe for a depressed individual was hard, even dirty, work that involved a serious task and occupied all of one's time and energy. For Fawn McKay, her children thought, the best solution was to buy or build a house in Huntsville, fulfilling "a consistently frustrated, life-long dream" of hers. Fawn and other family members sold a portion of the family's Huntsville farm land to secure the necessary funds for the project.[94]

Even before this project was actually begun, Fawn McKay's condition appeared to improve. She was back to normal, it seemed to Fawn, which didn't "mean she is happy, but at least she bitches a little more than she used to, which is certainly what she needs to do most." In May 1957, during a visit to Utah, Fawn could only marvel at her mother's recovery. She "was very much in control of everything, and quite her old self," Fawn noted. But she was still frustrated that her mother was "back in the old groove" of having to look after her husband. Fawn could readily see her father's increasingly feeble condition and her mother's dogged determination not to be responsible in any way for his death.[95]

Despite all of Fawn McKay's efforts, her husband weakened to the point of requiring hospitalization in September 1957. He continued to hang on for several months longer. Then, on 15 January 1958, Thomas E. McKay died of what his obituary described as a heart ailment. He was eighty-two. His death and funeral received extensive coverage in the Utah press; the *Salt Lake Tribune* and *Deseret News* carried tributes from various church and public officials, including Utah governor George Dewey Clyde. The funeral was held in Assembly Hall on Temple Square in Salt Lake City, with J. Reuben Clark, Jr., of the church's First Presidency presiding and eulogies given by a number of high-ranking Mormon Church leaders. Following the service, the funeral entourage traveled north to Huntsville, passing the old McKay family home and the Huntsville Ward meetinghouse, en route to the town cemetery, where another short service was conducted before burial.[96]

Thomas E. McKay's funeral evoked a variety of emotions and memories for Fawn, both good and bad. "I found the whole experience most exhausting," she told Dean Brimhall, "but in some ways most memorable and even 'healing.'" The funeral was appropriate for her father as one who had "lived by ritual all his life"; his daughter found the services "not only bearable but somehow fitting and proper."[97]

Even while giving all the attention to her parents, Fawn still considered the welfare of her own immediate family of primary importance. Her three children were "lively, happy kids who give their parents an untold amount of obvious and secret delight," she wrote Morgan. She was a doting mother who wished only that she "had two or three more [children]."[98]

There was much in the children in which to take pride, particularly in the oldest, who was bright and talented. An outstanding student, Dick pulled a straight A average all through his elementary, junior high, and high school years. He was, moreover, an accomplished violinist. In junior high, he served as concertmaster in the school orchestra and played center on the football team. He was also an adventurous boy, somewhat of a free spirit. During the summer of 1958, when he was fifteen, he and three friends traveled through Baja California, hiking and camping on their own. The following summer, he and a friend hitchhiked across the United States, clearly inspired by the adventures of contemporary beat writer Jack Kerouac as articulated in *On the Road.* In viewing her oldest son's activities, Fawn worried as any parent would. "Dick is absolutely without fear and yearns for great adventures," she noted as the boy set out on the cross-country hitchhiking venture. "There isn't much I can do except to say 'Yes' and cross my fingers."[99]

The future seemed bright for Richard Brodie as he graduated from high school in 1959 and prepared to enter college. It appeared he would excel in whatever field of enterprise he chose to pursue. He was blessed with an impressive physical appearance, clearly inherited from the McKay side of the family. Standing 6 feet 2 $1/2$ inches by age seventeen, he was big and rugged-looking, with an outgoing personality to match. While Fawn found Dick's adolescent high spirits "sometimes difficult to cope with," she considered him "far more exciting than troublesome."[100]

The Brodies' second son, Bruce, differed from Dick both in physical appearance and personality. While even taller than his brother, Bruce was much leaner. He was also more reserved in behavior and general demeanor. And he possessed different talents. As a young child, he became interested in drawing and painting. Encouraged by his abilities, his parents financed art lessons, and Fawn proudly displayed his work throughout the house, describing it as "very gay and imaginative." But Bruce, who suffered from dyslexia, had more difficulty academically than his older brother. He was motivated and hardworking, but he struggled to achieve good grades. Concerned about his difficulties, Fawn consulted her older sister, Flora, herself a teacher, seeking her counsel in finding ways to make schoolwork easier for Bruce.[101]

Meanwhile, the Brodies' youngest child, Pamela, was a typical preteen, at nine years of age, with pretensions of being older. This was evident in such behavior as dressing up in her mother's clothes and getting into her lipstick and other cosmetics. Because of her interest in dance and ballet, she was dubbed "Bernard's ballerina" by at least one family member, and her father pampered Pam in much the same way that Fawn fussed over Dick. Every Sunday Bernard took Pam and Bruce ice skating at a local rink or horseback riding into the Santa Monica Mountains, just to the east of Pacific Palisades.[102]

Spending time on a regular basis with his children was important for Bernard, not only as a devoted parent but also as a diversion from his work at RAND. Although the work was stimulating and fulfilling, it was intense, high-pressure, and always grim, focused as it was on questions of strategic deterrence of thermonuclear warfare and mass destruction.

Another important pastime for Bernard was gardening. He was "a mad gardener, . . . terribly intent on having beautiful surroundings." He carefully maintained gardens containing all types of flowers around the Brodies' home; specific varieties were planted to bloom at different times of the year. Another leisure activity for Bernard was classical music. He was not much of a concertgoer but enjoyed listening to his music at home, thanks to his state-of-the-art high-fidelity stereo system, which he built himself and continually upgraded in response to technological improvements. Over time, he also amassed an impressive collection of classical recordings.[103]

Through such varied interests and activities, Bernard found it much easier to relax than Fawn did. Although she occasionally accompanied Bernard and the children on their horseback rides, she lacked their enthusiasm for it. She spent time in the garden with Bernard, working just as hard, and sometimes even harder—particularly in the strenuous tasks of weeding, pruning, and basic maintenance, tasks Bernard was unable to perform because of chronic back problems. And she did most of the work involved with construction of a concrete retaining wall around the Brodie home. But Fawn considered such yardwork a necessary task, whereas Bernard saw gardening as a pleasurable diversion.[104]

Fawn did, however, enjoy the walks that she and Bernard took on a regular basis along a trail just above their home that led into the wilderness of the Santa Monica Mountains. She also enjoyed contemporary politics and current events. On a daily basis, she read the *Los Angeles Times*, and on a weekly basis, both *Time* and *Newsweek* as well as other lesser-known publications.[105] Her lively interest in contemporary events was the natural product of her father's involvement in politics and was reenforced by Bernard's strong interest and his work at RAND.

Fawn's opinions on various contemporary issues invariably reflected her liberal Democratic bias—including her support of Tennessee senator Estes Kefauver, a major contender for the Democratic presidential nomination in 1956. But in general she admitted to great ambivalence concerning American presidents, past and present. Except for Lincoln and Jefferson, she said, "I don't think we have ever had [a president] who had a great and profound gift with language combined with [the] subtle faculty for reaching out and 'touching' the people." Such ambivalence reflected her skepticism towards male authority figures in general, yet she longed for heroes, political and otherwise, men she could look up to.[106]

Fawn was *not* ambivalent about remaining busy. "I like working hard," she stated on more than one occasion. "In this respect," she added, "I'm like my parents. . . . I think it's part of the Mormon heritage."[107] Thus when not doing housework or devoting time to her children, Fawn always sought some productive activity. The most satisfying of these activities remained research and writing.

FINISHING THADDEUS STEVENS

Despite numerous delays, Fawn pushed ahead with Thaddeus Stevens. In 1956, while doing research at the Gettysburg (Pa.) College library, she came across what she characterized as "sensational material" about Stevens's early years. There was evidence that Stevens had possibly killed "a colored girl who was pregnant with his child." Although Stevens was never brought to trial, neither was he actually cleared of the charge. Brodie agonized over the validity of the charge, ruminating that this issue made her problem as a biographer "pretty complicated." She wrestled with how to treat the episode. To gain further insight, she read Freud and his followers on the problem of guilt. At one point, she wrote up the episode as though Stevens had murdered the woman in question and shared her conclusions with Bernard. When he was not convinced by the evidence and her arguments, Fawn reexamined the case and came to the same conclusion Bernard had. In this and other ways, Bernard's editing

Fawn Brodie in 1955, sitting on the patio of the Brodies' Pacific Palisades home at the time she was working on her second biography, *Thaddeus Stevens: Scourge of the South*. Reprinted by permission, Utah State Historical Society, all rights reserved.

proved crucial to Fawn's work. He continued to be chief critic and editor, exercising the same role he had played some ten years earlier with *No Man Knows My History.* "Bernard is my severest critic," Fawn confessed, and she was extremely grateful for his careful evaluations and his "stimulation and support."[108]

As Fawn moved toward completion of the manuscript—a long, arduous process requiring at least five complete drafts—there remained the problem of publication. For some two years, from early 1955 until 1957, it appeared that Princeton University Press would publish Brodie's work, for Fawn had formed a close working relationship with Herbert S. Bailey, editor of the press, as she readied her manuscript. Late in 1957 she sent Princeton the final draft. The press sent it out for review and then, for reasons that were never made clear, decided not to publish the work. Instead, Bailey encouraged Brodie to submit the biography to a commercial publisher, New York–based W. W. Norton.[109]

Brodie followed Bailey's advice. After spending the early summer months of 1958 cutting and revising what she had written, she submitted her manuscript to Norton. By this time, she was less than optimistic, relaying her frustrations and anxieties to Dean Brimhall. She confessed that "it is not easy for me to face up to the possibility of failure with this book." But late in 1958, Norton informed her of their decision to publish the manuscript. And they moved quickly. In February 1959 Brodie received the final galley proofs to examine and correct. It was an enormous relief for Brodie, for the work had been "a real millstone." Still, there was inevitably "a deep sense of loss" once the biography was finished, for in the course of her research she had become very fond of her subject.[110]

In September 1959 came actual publication of her *Thaddeus Stevens: Scourge of the South.* It brought one more disappointment: The book enjoyed limited commercial success, selling a mere fifteen hundred copies in the first seven months after publication and shortly thereafter going out of print. The author had not really expected it to sell well, but she had hoped for better than that.[111]

Offsetting commercial failure was the almost universal praise *Thaddeus Stevens* drew in reviews in various newspapers and professional journals. Patrick Riddleberger, writing for the *Washington Post,* called the biography a "sensitive study," "exceptional," and "filled with insight." Richard Hooker, in the pages of the *Springfield (Mass.) Republican,* went further, praising

Brodie for "what must be saluted not merely as one of our better American biographies, but as one of the few best." In the *Baltimore Sun,* David S. Sparks characterized Brodie's portrait of Stevens as "filled with compassion and understanding." It was "great history as well as great biography," he said, and his personal nomination for a Pulitzer Prize.[112]

The biography also earned the praise of important American historians of the Civil War and Reconstruction. David Donald, writing in the *New York Herald Tribune,* praised Brodie for going beyond the earlier biographies of Richard Current and Ralph Korngold in probing the reasons behind Stevens's behavior. He called her psychoanalysis of Stevens "a tour de force." C. Vann Woodward, another eminent historian, writing for the *New York Times,* praised Brodie for her "balanced account." The biography, he said, was "a siginficant and readable contribution to the understanding of Stevens and Reconstruction.[113]

In a personal letter written to Brodie, Allan Nevins, considered at the time the dean of American historians, complimented the author on her excellent work. "You give us our most convincing portrait of a repellant leader," he told her. Brodie found Nevins's letter particularly gratifying, more than compensating her for all the times she had "felt bitterly that the rewards for writing this book simply weren't worth all of the toil."[114]

Brodie was also pleasantly surprised by the favorable reviews that appeared in the southern press. These reviews, while certainly not favorable toward Stevens the man, had good things to say about Brodie's treatment of him. The *Nashville (Tenn.) Banner* praised her research and called her book "very well-written, readable and important." The *Louisville Courier-Journal* proclaimed Brodie's study "objective and judicious," avoiding "emotional retreat or surrender."[115]

Outside the South, from the district Stevens had represented in the U.S. Congress, the *Lancaster (Pa.) News* lauded Brodie's biography, characterizing it "as among the finest of the publishing season." It also noted the timeliness of the subject matter, stating that "the lively ghost of Thaddeus Stevens . . . limps into the center of the [contemporary] strife" over civil rights and segregation then being debated in Congress. Stevens, the review concluded, "is just about as controversial a figure today as he was in the late 1860s."[116]

Praise also came from two unexpected quarters. The first was none other than historian Richard N. Current, whose earlier protrait of Stevens

Brodie had critiqued. Writing in the *American Historical Review*, Current credited Brodie for making "a real contribution" in examining Stevens's private life and personality relative to his public and political career. Current even conceded that he had "possibly overemphasized considerations of personal ambition and partisan politics" in his own earlier study, though he registered a complaint that Brodie had perhaps paid too little attention to such issues.[117]

And totally unexpected was the praise that came from Salt Lake City. Not surprisingly, the Mormon church-owned *Deseret News* ignored both the author and her new book, but the book review editor of the independent *Salt Lake Tribune*, Ernest L. Linford, praised Brodie for her wonderfully sharp insight into the character of Thaddeus Stevens. Like other reviewers, he alluded to the volume's timeliness and recommended it to readers who wanted to gain greater understanding of the origins of contemporary racial problems. Linford echoed the *Baltimore Sun* in recommending the book for a Pulitzer Prize.[118]

For Fawn Brodie, all such reviews were particularly gratifying, given the work, energy, and time expended on the biography over the previous thirteen years. But *Thaddeus Stevens*, with all of its disappointments and difficulties, made her reluctant to undertake yet another biography. The precise direction of her future work was uncertain in late 1959, a situation hauntingly reminiscent of where she had found herself following publication of *No Man Knows My History*. Once more, Fawn toyed with writing fiction. "Fiction is so tempting, and it looks so easy. No weary hours in the library, no stacks of notes to be taken and sorted, and filed," she told Dean Brimhall in January 1960. But she conceded that fiction "takes a very special kind of talent, and I am not at all sure that I could do it if I tried. The fact is, I have tried, but have never been content with the results."[119]

Fawn's major concern in late 1959 and early 1960 was not her future writing plans; rather, her time and energy were focused on preparing the family to live in Paris for a year. Bernard Brodie had been awarded a Carnegie Corporation Reflective Year Fellowship, to commence in July 1960. Under the terms of this fellowship, he was to live abroad while engaged in what was termed "reflective scholarship." The award was meant to free him from the pressures of research and writing at RAND. Joining him in Paris would be Fawn and their two younger children,

Bruce and Pamela. Dick would attend the University of Grenoble, south of Paris. To help cover the costs, Bernard signed a contract with Dell, a paperback publisher, to produce a history of the impact of science on military technology. The book was intended for the college market, specifically for courses in military science and related disciplines. Although Bernard assumed primary responsibility for the authorship of this volume, clearly within his own area of expertise, he enlisted Fawn's help in doing the research. In the end, Fawn would do most of the actual writing as well.[120]

Thus Fawn Brodie's plans for her own future research and writing were both uncertain and deferred as 1959 drew to a close. She and her family looked forward to the 1960s with a combination of optimism and uncertainty.

FIVE

"A Fun Book to Write"

1960–1967

For most of the 1960s Fawn Brodie focused on Sir Richard Francis Burton, a multifaceted and eccentric nineteenth-century Englishman. Burton, a noted explorer, traveled throughout Africa, the Middle East, and to North and South America; he was best known, perhaps, for his attempts to discover the headwaters of the Nile. He once disguised himself as a devout Muslim and penetrated the forbidden holy cities of the Sind, El Medina, and Mecca, daring feats that, if discovered, would have resulted in his immediate execution. He was also an accomplished scholar, conversant in some forty tongues and dialects. He was the author of forty-three books, all focusing on his varied and far-reaching travels; and he was a translator of Arab erotica. Particularly noteworthy in this regard was his unexpurgated version of *Arabian Nights.*

Brodie's initial exposure to Burton arose out of Alfred Knopf's decision to publish a new edition of Burton's 1862 travel account, *The City of the Saints and Across the Rocky Mountains to California.* Knopf asked Brodie to edit and write a new introduction for this volume—a work relating Burton's experiences in visiting Salt Lake City and the Mormon-dominated Great Basin. Finding herself doing twice as much research as necessary for the introduction, she realized very quickly that she "was lost" to the man. She described Burton as "fascinating beyond belief" and her biography of him, *The Devil Drives: The Life of Sir Richard Burton,* "a fun book to write and research."[1]

While the editing of *The City of the Saints* served as the initial impetus, Brodie was drawn to Burton for a number of reasons. She was intrigued by the range of his interests; they made the drama of his life "fabulously exciting." Brodie also identified with several aspects of his personality. Among these was his interest in religious customs and rituals, even though he "scoffed at all forms of religious superstition—whether the fetishism of the Fan cannibals or the death ceremonies of his own Church of England."[2]

Brodie also identified with Burton's compulsive nature, which she picked up on immediately and chose to emphasize in the title of the biography: "The Devil Drives." This she took from a statement made by Burton as he reflected on his willingness to risk his life to penetrate the jungles of central Africa: "I ask myself 'Why?' and the only echo is 'damned fool! . . . the Devil drives.'" Brodie identified with this driven, compulsive personality, specifically, with Burton's "demon, the source of his restlessness." She knew that demon, attributing it to "some kind of mad, inner compulsion which has to do with God knows what." Describing herself as a "compulsive woman racing around frantically," she asked, "Why do I do it? Because I'm unhappy when I'm not doing it."[3]

Then, too, Brodie found Burton relevant to her own life and times in an even larger sense. Burton symbolized the restlessness and rebellion that Brodie found evident in the organized protests, assassinations, riots, and social upheavals of the 1960s. The state of California, especially up in Berkeley, where all three Brodie children would attend school that decade, clearly epitomized the unrest of this period. The Brodie kids gave their mother firsthand accounts of the various waves of student protest, beginning with the free speech movement of 1964 and culminating in the 1969 "People's Park protest." Fawn personally witnessed aspects of the restless rebellion in her oldest son during his four-year sojourn at Berkeley—and after.

Another factor that made Burton appealing was his fascination with all things sexual. With unabashed admiration, Brodie characterized Burton as "a great sexologist." He wrote with courage and exactness about sexual customs in the various countries he visited; as Brodie noted, Burton "sampled everything in the sexual market."[4] She was also intrigued with his androgyny, his combination of masculine and feminine traits. The author detected certain homosexual tendencies in Burton, evident in his fascination with the male brothels in Karachi, India, and in his close relationship with John Speke, onetime friend turned bitter rival.

Also drawing Brodie to the flamboyant Englishman was his complex relationship with his wife, Isabel Arundell. The marriage seemed an improbable match. Burton, an avowed agnostic, was attracted to Isabel, a devout Catholic. Though deeply in love with Burton, Isabel was repelled by certain aspects of his character, specifically, his robust interest in sex. In reading through her husband's forty-year collection of diaries and journals after he had died, Isabel was so appalled by their explicit contents that she ordered them burned, thus destroying what Brodie characterized as one of the greatest anthropological collections in history. In their place, Isabel wrote an idealized account of Burton's life, designed for public consumption, making her late husband out to be "pure, innocent, guileless," scrubbing his image so thoroughly clean that it became unrecognizable.[5] In confronting this sanitized portrait, Brodie was undoubtedly reminded of the equally implausible image of Joseph Smith presented by Mormon officials.

Fawn also saw in the Burtons' marital relationship a reflection of certain aspects of her own marriage to Bernard. Like Richard and Isabel Burton, Bernard and Fawn Brodie were both intelligent, strong-willed individuals, each pursuing separate interests, literary and otherwise. On the positive side, the Brodies, like the Burtons, were fiercely devoted and mutually supportive of each other's creative activities. But the Brodies, like the Burtons, experienced difficulties in relating intimately to each other. Isabel was apparently frigid. Fawn had known such feelings before undergoing psychoanalysis in the 1950s. Though she had overcome her sexual inhibitions, Fawn remained more reserved and less affectionate than Bernard. Still, her own sexual liberation prompted her lively interest in the "great sexologist" and translated into a fascination with and admiration for the man. Fawn was, in fact, "passionately in love" with Richard Burton according to her son Bruce.[6]

A YEAR IN PARIS

In early 1960, however, Fawn Brodie's strong feelings for Richard Burton were yet to emerge. She had other, more immediate preoccupations—

specifically, preparations for the family's departure for Paris in fulfillment of Bernard's fellowship. Bernard eagerly looked forward to the year away from RAND, where he had become increasingly dissatisfied. The experience in Paris, he hoped, would regenerate his spirits and enable him to return to California with renewed enthusiasm. The Brodie children had varied feelings about living abroad. Seventeen-year old Dick was the most enthusiastic of the lot, being a seasoned traveler and quintessential seeker of adventure. Fourteen-year old Bruce and nine-year-old Pam were more ambivalent. This new adventure in a different environment might offer some excitement, but they were worried about leaving their schoolmates, friends, and familiar surroundings. Even Fawn expressed anxiety about having to learn and communicate in a new language.[7]

Besides preparing for the trip, Fawn completed research for *From Crossbow to H-Bomb*, the Brodies' treatise on weapons and military technology. Fawn had assumed primary responsibility for the manuscript, even though Bernard had been the one to sign the book contract with Dell publishers. All of this work, plus plans for the trip, served to clutter her mind with a thousand and one details. But work on the volume brought unexpected benefits, invigorating her with a scholarly enthusiasm that had waned following completion of *Thaddeus Stevens*. She found the research for *From Crossbow to H-Bomb* "quite exciting," providing a crash course in European history. This, in turn, whetted her appetite for Europe.[8]

On 30 June 1960, the Brodies departed California, traveling by auto across the United States. There were stops at Fruita, in southern Utah, to visit with Dean Brimhall, and then in Salt Lake City to visit with Fawn's sisters. In Utah, Fawn also spent time with her mother, who was still coping with bouts of depression exacerbated by the death of her husband two years before. Fawn worried about her mother's condition, concerns heightened by the realization that she would be far from her for a whole year.[9]

In late July—following a nostalgic visit to their old home in Bethany, Connecticut—the Brodies arrived in New York, where they boarded the *Rotterdam* for the seven-day crossing of the Atlantic. Once in Paris, the family secured a pleasant, sunny apartment on Boulevard Victor, a major thoroughfare. Dick had little trouble adjusting. He learned French quickly and fluently during his short stay in Paris before moving on to Grenoble and the university in November. In Paris, Bruce and Pamela enrolled at nearby schools, which took special account of their language deficiencies. Both adjusted well. The Brodie children, in fact, learned French more quickly and more easily than either of their parents.[10]

Fawn had particular difficulty in adjusting to the city and the language, having to remain by herself in the apartment, where she was responsible for maintaining the household and preparing the meals. She also spent significant periods of time working alone on *From Crossbow to H-Bomb*. Although Bernard was nominal co-author, he was away most of the time at his office in another part of Paris, engaged in study and in meetings with various government officials, diplomats, and academicians. Fawn's confined, circumscribed situation caused her to complain to Dean Brimhall: "I rather regret having committed myself to working on this weapons book . . . it means that until February I shall have no leisure, and I doubt if I shall learn much French."[11]

Such cares were abruptly pushed into the background by the shocking news from Utah of yet another suicide attempt by Fawn's mother. This time Fawn McKay set herself on fire while in Huntsville, having gone to the mountain community to put the finishing touches on a small house she had built for herself with the help of her children, the project recommended as therapy by doctors and designed to realize her long-cherished but unfulfilled dream of having her own home. It was not enough, and she once again chose to try to end her life. She was discovered in extreme pain by next-door neighbor and distant relative, Gunn McKay. McKay took her to the local hospital, where she lingered for several days in critical condition. On 6 October 1960 she died. She was seventy-one years old.[12]

The funeral was held in the old Huntsville Mormon meetinghouse, and Fawn Brimhall McKay was buried in the Huntsville cemetery, next to her husband. The local newspapers discreetly avoided mention of the precise circumstances of her death.[13]

Fawn Brodie's efforts to deal with her mother's death were compounded by her inability to return to Utah. "I wish I were not so far away," she wrote Dean Brimhall. She knew there was little point in flying home. "The children need me here—and I need them," she told her uncle. "Why did she?" Fawn asked. "Her life really wasn't so bad. Why couldn't she have settled into [the role of] being a successful grandmother? And above all why did she punish us all so much by punishing herself in such a horrible fashion?"[14]

Fawn was newly mindful of the close relationship she had had with her mother, and she poured out her feelings to her uncle. "She gave me that special encouragement and affection all my life which goes far in explaining what kind of a person I am." "I think I understand some of her terrible inner conflicts." she continued, "because I have had the same kind. Two and a half years with a gifted psychoanalyst in California taught me a great deal about us both. The terrible pity is that there was no outlet for her guilt and fury, and she turned it all in upon herself."[15]

A month later, in early November, Fawn wrote more of her reflections to her uncle. Her feelings about her mother's death changed every day, she told him, and she still found it difficult to face. She was attempting to gain a clinical perspective on her mother's illness in order to reach "some kind of detachment." Getting to the essence of her own analysis, Fawn theorized:

> I still feel that much of her suffering was unnecessary, and that she could have had some pleasant years at the end, but she was caught in a Victorian society and trapped in the patriarchal traditions of the Mormon Church. . . . The worst thing, I think, was that there were so few to whom she could speak honestly, and so she turned her hatreds and furies inward, and this proved in the end to be a corrupting thing.[16]

With the coming of the new year, Fawn was finding her mother's death "easier to bear . . . than in the beginning." She took some solace in her environment, describing her experiences to Brimhall in buoyant, upbeat terms, ironically in the very same letters in which she spoke of her anguish over her mother's death. "We are beginning to enjoy Paris, despite the continuing rains," she wrote. One could not help but find the city beguiling, she continued. Shopping was fun, and museums and churches wonderful. "It is impossible not [to] be continuously delighted by the French food, which is remarkable as much for its cheapness as for its superb quality. We eat out a great deal, and I find this a very special luxury." Fawn found the French people friendly, honest and helpful, and she was captivated by their uninhibited manners.[17]

The family had taken a ski vacation in the French Alps over the Christmas break, spending several days in a tiny village halfway up the mountain on the southern side of Lake Geneva. The village was so much like Huntsville that Fawn felt as if she were back in Utah. The sojourn in such a setting helped the healing process. As did the passage of time. Winter yielded to spring, and Fawn was struck with the realization that "when one is happy, time flies and when one is wretched it drags." The Brodies' year abroad, unbelievably, was almost over. The Algerian crisis that spring brought unrest to the city streets, and Dick barely avoided being caught up in a violent student demonstration down in Grenoble. But it all took on aspects of comic opera to Bernard, and Fawn felt that the family was "in far greater danger from Paris traffic than from any bombs."[18]

The Brodies' one-year sojourn in France concluded in July 1961. For Fawn, it had been an extremely fulfilling experience. Despite initial difficulties learning the language, she was utterly charmed by both the country and its people. In describing her overall impressions, she told Dean Brimhall: "I came away with an immense respect for the French way of life, with a love for their landscape, their magnificent churches and castles, the beauty of their language, and not least the lavish care they take with the art of eating well and making love." She had also found satisfaction in completing *From Crossbow to H-Bomb*. Her marriage, she noted, had survived the collaborative effort, despite advanced warnings that this was "an excellent way to precipitate a divorce."[19]

A RETURN TO CALIFORNIA AND TO MORMON HISTORY

The Brodies returned to the United States after some additional travel in Italy, Germany, Holland, Belgium, and England. They drove back across the country, taking time for a necessary stop in Utah to see Fawn's family, a visit Fawn faced with "a certain dread." Visiting Utah was for her a little like being "stretched out on a rack." There were all the old conflicts, never completely resolved, "of wanting to flee as well as wanting to stay forever."[20]

The Brodies finally arrived home in Pacific Palisades in August 1961. Despite the familiar surroundings, Fawn experienced initial dissatisfaction at being back in California. She was surprised at such feelings, having expected to be delighted with home and garden. Instead, she found herself thinking nostalgically of Paris and "the wonderful medieval things . . . left behind." She was appalled by the commercial materialism of America, which was particularly pronounced in the Los Angeles basin, a region growing rapidly.[21]

Such feelings gradually abated as Fawn and her family settled into familiar routine. But the year in France had undeniably caused subtle changes in Fawn, her husband, and her children. Bernard returned to his duties at RAND a thoroughgoing Francophile. Such sentiments added a new dimension to ongoing difficulties with various RAND colleagues, a significant number of whom were strong Anglophiles who looked upon the flamboyant, independent Charles de Gaulle with suspicion and disdain for having pulled France out of NATO, seeming to abandon the United States and other cold war allies. Bernard, by contrast, admired France for asserting itself as an independent third force between the United States and the Soviet Union, and this pro-French position accentuated his loner status at RAND.[22]

Bernard was also disappointed at not having been asked to join the New Frontier defense analysts in Washington following John F. Kennedy's 1960 election. His expectations had been raised as the new secretary of defense, Robert S. McNamara, recruited a number of Brodie's colleagues at RAND. Brodie himself seemed destined for appointment, given his well-known Democratic leanings—and the fact that John F. Kennedy himself had personally expressed his favorable reaction to Bernard's recently published *Strategy in the Missile Age.*[23]

But Brodie's views on tactical nuclear warfare were at variance with those of important officials in the Kennedy administration. His reputation as a loner—not a team player—also worked against his appointment. He was, according to at least two close RAND associates, outspoken and unwilling to "adapt his views to . . . conventional wisdom." Brodie himself blamed his longtime nemesis at RAND, Albert Wohlstetter. Wohlstetter had been able to "gather round himself a veritable court" of individuals at RAND, including Alain Enthoven, Henry Rowen, William Kaufmann, and Daniel Ellsberg—individuals who, according to Brodie, were "not quite of the first rank intellectually, but nevertheless very able." Yet Wohlstetter had an inside track that enabled him to get his people appointed. "All of the so-called 'whiz kids' around McNamara were either members of [Wohlstatter's] original RAND following . . . or people who were intellectually beholden to them," Brodie claimed, whereas he himself, not being one of Wolhstetter's favored persons, was passed over.[24]

Bernard made the best of his situation. He even rejected the offer of a one-year visiting professorship at Yale, turning it down out of consideration for his family, none of whom wanted to leave California again. The two younger children, Bruce and Pam, returned to school in Pacific Palisades, and Dick moved on to Berkeley, where he enrolled at the University of California in the fall of 1961.[25]

Fawn, meanwhile, settled in to resume her role as full-time housewife and mother, which was unexpectedly interrupted when she was drawn back into the field of Mormon history. Harvard's Howard Mumford Jones asked her to edit a nineteenth-century travel account focusing on the Latter-day Saints in Utah—Frederick Hawkins Piercy's *Route from Liverpool to Great Salt Lake Valley*, originally published in 1855 and scheduled to be reissued as part of the John Harvard Library Series. Fawn was initially ambivalent about accepting the assignment and finally took it mainly to pay for new living-room drapes. "And I really have nothing else at the moment to do," she wrote Dale Morgan, "except the routine housework."[26]

Just as she started her editing assignment, Brodie received the request from Alfred Knopf to edit Burton's *The City of the Saints and Across the Rocky Mountains to California*, also a nineteenth-century travel account. Burton stood in sharp contrast to Frederick Piercy, who was, for Brodie "a dull fellow."[27]

The work on these two books immediately engaged her. "I am thoroughly enjoying being back in the field [of Mormon history] after such a long absence," Brodie wrote Dale Morgan. She did not limit her scholarly activities to Mormon history, though. Drawing on knowledge gained from *Thaddeus Stevens*, she wrote a provocative essay, "Who Won the Civil War Anyway?" that was featured in the book review section of the Sunday *New York Times* in August 1962. It was essentially a critique of so-called revisionist scholarship she saw dominating current writing of Civil War history. The "vindication" of the Southern viewpoint put forth by the revisionists, Brodie asserted, distorted and misrepresented the past. In its "glorification of the Southern hero"; in its benign view of

Southern slavery, minimalizing the institution's horrors and immorality; in its misrepresentation of Northern abolitionists as "villains"; and finally in its distortion of Abraham Lincoln, this new history presented a skewed version of this period. She viewed this whole phenomenon in ironic terms. "By some quixotic reversal," she stated, "the Lost Cause seems no longer lost."[28]

Brodie's essay provoked varied responses from writers interested in the Civil War. A portion of these were published in a subsequent issue of the book review section of the Sunday *Times*. Thus Fawn Brodie found herself, once more, at the center of historical controversy, reminiscent of the firestorm generated over *No Man Knows My History* seventeen years earlier. She clearly relished the attention. But she was simultaneously preoccupied with pressing concerns closer to home. In November 1961 extensive forest fires in the nearby Santa Monica Mountains threatened Pacific Palisades. Residents of the area were told to prepare for possible evacuation. The Brodies experienced two and a half days of intense anxiety as the fire swept down a nearby canyon, coming within three-quarters of a mile of their home before the winds died and the blaze could be contained.[29]

"The sight of billowing clouds of smoke and flame so close, and the knowledge that a rise in the wind could start the same kind of holocaust that swept the other areas made my own anxiety difficult to control," Fawn wrote her uncle in admitting that the fire had triggered unpleasant memories. She knew she had inherited her mother's "life-long fire anxiety." She was always struggling to keep it under control while at the same time seeking to understand its causes. She could only paraphrase Freud: "There is, I know, something of a wish with every anxiety." She was drawn to reflect on her mother's death. "I can't help feeling that mother wanted to set fire to things all her life, without knowing it," Fawn said, "and in the end chose to take vengeance on herself rather than on whatever it was she hated."[30]

Fawn, meanwhile, moved ahead with the editing of the two Mormon travel accounts. She finished *From Liverpool to the Great Salt Lake Valley* in February 1962. She had spent a lot of time on it, but was disappointed with the result. Still, she was glad to be rid of it. In contrast, she was completely absorbed with Richard Burton's *City of the Saints*. The research was "absolutely fascinating," and the writing of it was actually enjoyable in that Burton was a fabulous person, and his story captivating. She finished that work in June 1962.[31]

BEGINNING THE BURTON BIOGRAPHY

Upon completing *City of the Saints*, Brodie had all but made up her mind to do a book-length biography of Richard F. Burton, and she shared her plans with Alfred Knopf, who responded enthusiastically. But W. W. Norton was also pursuing Brodie now, hoping to sign her to another book contract. With characteristic bravado, Knopf took a swipe at his rival, the publishers of Brodie's *Thaddeus Stevens*. "I am vain enough to think that we are much better publishers for you than Norton will ever be," he said, asserting that the latter's editorial standards in the field of history and biography did not begin to approach Knopf's.[32]

Brodie, however, rejected Knopf and elected to go with Norton. She was candid with Knopf in explaining her decision. While satisfied with Knopf's handling of her Joseph Smith biography, she praised Norton for the quality of her *Thaddeus Stevens*, noting that George Brockway, her editor at Norton, had been extremely kind and easy to work with. Besides, Norton offered her a generous advance. More to the point, Brodie told Knopf that she very much regretted his lack of faith in her Thaddeus Stevens manuscript eight years before.[33]

Initially, Brodie expected Richard Burton to be a much easier subject than either Joseph Smith or Thaddeus Stevens. He was, in many ways, "as colorful and baffling" as Joseph Smith and at the same time "less melancholy and tragic" than Thaddeus Stevens. As she got into actual research, however, she found him more complex than she had anticipated.[34]

By the spring of 1963, Brodie was well into gathering materials. She acquired an almost complete collection of Richard Burton's writings, more than a hundred volumes, an acquisition that made research and writing easier. Then in midsummer, she received the alarming news of publication of a book-length biography of Richard Burton by Byron Farwell, an American author of minor renown who had written several books on the Victorian era, including a biography of the British explorer Henry M. Stanley. This unwelcome news came from none other than Alfred Knopf and revived bitter memories of the author's experience some ten years earlier, when Knopf had rejected Thaddeus Stevens after publication of Ralph Korngold's, biography of the man. Brodie, however, put on her best face, telling Knopf frankly that she could not "help but hope, selfishly" that Farwell's *Burton* was an inferior biography. "Still," she added, "Burton is worth more than one good treatment, and even a first-rate biography need not wholly swallow up the market." With ill-disguised condescension, Knopf replied, "I hope, for your sake, that the new Burton biography is an inferior one, because as a publisher, I would have grave doubts of the [market's ability] to absorb two."[35]

Despite Knopf's gloomy assessment, Brodie was fully committed to her own book-length biography. Burton "is a wonderfully fascinating and exasperating man," she wrote Dale Morgan, "and his wife is almost as interesting a person in her own right, and even more exasperating. It was an extraordinary marriage," she confided "This book will be the closest thing I'll ever come to writing a novel."[36]

In October 1963, Brodie traveled abroad to examine Burton materials contained in various museums and libraries in England. Although she limited her research time in London to just two weeks, she accomplished a great deal. At the British Museum she found some useful material—in particular, a few pages of Burton's original diary, written during his trip to Utah. Brodie found his "handwriting . . . almost indecipherable," a discovery that made her "glad that there is so little manuscript material to see." Yet she was also glad that at least some materials had escaped destruction by Burton's wife following his death. Besides the British Museum, Brodie visited the Royal Anthropological Institute in London, which had all of the printed volumes from Richard Burton's own private library. And she visited the library of Trinity College, Cambridge, where she found a crucial, previously undiscovered letter written by Burton to one of his best friends, containing the quotation—"the devil drives"—that she would use as the title for her biography.[37]

While in London, Fawn also examined Burton material belonging to a private collector, Quentin Keynes, a noted filmmaker. Coming from patrician British stock, Keynes was a direct descendant of Charles Darwin and a nephew of the famous British economist, John Maynard Keynes. Brodie gleaned useful information from Keynes's collection of books, pamphlets, and manuscripts. The filmmaker also provided a previously unknown, extremely striking 1854 photograph of the British explorer.[38]

In addition to research, Fawn found time for sightseeing and for travel with Bernard, who was already in Europe on RAND business. The Brodies visited Cairo, Luxor, Athens, and Istanbul; these sites particularly intrigued Fawn because of their connection with her Burton research. She found Egypt rewarding beyond all expectations. She was awed by the pyramids and by the great temples at Karnak and Luxor. Continuing on to Greece, the Brodies visited Athens and Delphi. At Delphi, the site of the great temple of Zeus, Fawn was strangely reminded of her childhood home in Huntsville, finding the mountains there so much like the Wasatch range that she was overcome by feelings of intense familiarity. She described the scene to Dean Brimhall: "Imagine yourself on the rocky and partly wooded slope of Ogden Canyon just before it opens out into Huntsville—eliminate the lake—add fragments of an old temple, amphitheater and stadium progressively spaced up the mountain, and you have Delphi." By contrast, Fawn found Istanbul far less compelling than any of the cities of Greece or Egypt.[39]

By February 1964, Brodie had begun writing the biography. The task was as exhausting as writing had always been for her. After a day of writing, she said, "I'm not much good for anything else." But it was also "rewarding in a very subtle fashion." In March she informed her editor, George P. Brockway, that she had "75 pages in fairly decent shape." The research itself was essentially complete, although she continued to pursue leads on certain documents she felt crucial to her story. In particular, she spent a significant amount of time in an unsuccessful effort to locate a lost manuscript, Burton's account of the Karachi male brothels, a study that his superiors had condemned and that had ruined his army career. Brodie even enlisted the help of Mian Muhammad Sadullah, official keeper of the records for the government of Pakistan, but to no avail.[40]

Engaged as she was with her work, Fawn was also involved with home and family. All three Brodie children were busy with their varied activities. Completing his undergraduate studies at Berkeley, with a major in English, Dick graduated in 1964, but he remained undecided about a profession. Fawn voiced some concern as he weighed various options. At first, he considered joining the army but quickly dismissed that option, much to Fawn's relief, given escalating American involvement in Southeast Asia. He then looked into graduate school, finally deciding to attend UCLA, which brought him back to the Los Angeles area. Bruce, meanwhile, graduated from high school the same year his brother finished college and, like Dick before him, enrolled at the University of California. In the fall of 1964, as Bruce went off to Berkeley, Pamela, fourteen, began her freshman year of high school.[41]

Bernard, meanwhile, was active with his own research and writing. He continued to be outspoken and blunt regarding American foreign policy, and his views reflected the deep division of opinion among RAND people. An article he published in the May 1963 issue of *Reporter* magazine, "What Price Conventional Capabilities in Europe?" further isolated him from various RAND colleagues. According to one observer, Bernard "occasionally displayed a savage temper and a bristling ego, especially if he thought others were robbing his ideas."[42]

Bernard was also plagued by back problems resulting from deteriorated disks, which had affected him for a number of years. As the condition became increasingly debilitating, he sought relief through a surgical procedure performed in November 1963. The surgery eased the pain somewhat, but he would have the problem for the remainder of his life.[43]

AN ENVIRONMENTAL CRUSADE, GEORGE ROMNEY, AND MORMONISM'S BAN ON BLACK PRIESTHOOD

As Bernard recovered from his surgery, Fawn involved herself in an environmental controversy that distracted her from Richard Burton—a crusade to save the nearby Santa Monica Mountains from real estate development. The Santa Monica Mountain region consisted of sixteen thousand acres of unspoiled greenery teeming with deer, foxes, raccoons, and rattlesnakes. Cutting across the Los Angeles basin, the mountains rose in some places to two thousand feet.[44]

Fawn had become alarmed as developers moved into the area near her Pacific Palisades home. With their big Caterpillars, they began destroying the mountain to the east of the house. Green ridges were stripped of natural vegetation and the mountain "skinned . . . gouged and flattened." The natural contours were "terraced into tiny rice-paddy platforms." Irate, Fawn dubbed the developers "the Mountain Mafia." The only way to save the Santa Monica Mountains, she concluded, was to make the entire region a state park.[45]

Fawn joined Friends of the Santa Monica Mountains State Park, a local citizens lobbying group. A broad-based coalition, "Friends" was led by Donald Douglas, Jr., president of Douglas Aircraft. The group cut across party lines and included such diverse individuals as the liberal Democratic mayor of Beverly Hills, Leonard Horwin, and the prominent Republican conservative businessman, Henry Salvatori. Also allied with "Friends" were movie star Burt Lancaster, the Sierra Club, the League of Women Voters, and various civic groups. Their goal was to have sixteen thousand acres set aside as a regional park.[46]

Through the summer and fall of 1964, Brodie involved herself in the crusade. She took the lead in gathering signatures on petitions, organizing meetings—frequently held at her home—and attending meetings with Los Angeles public officials. On one occasion, she and her neighbors confronted the land developers directly. When one of the developers' spokesmen listed all the advantages that their plans would bring to the area, including tennis courts, swimming pools, and parks, Fawn allegedly snapped her head to one side and said, "Oh, you are a living deceit, sir. I write you down for a scoundrel." And that was the end of the meeting.[47]

Brodie also confronted the local political establishment, including Los Angeles mayor Sam Yorty. She called her meeting with the mayor "an illuminating and dismaying experience." "Why these people have to be pushed, wheedled, cajoled, and educated into the idea of a park," she lamented, "I do not know. Everyone in City Hall seems to think the mountains should be destroyed to take care of the population explosion."[48]

As time went on, Fawn found herself more and more embroiled in the fight to save the mountains. Their fate was eventually tied to a $150 million bond measure, which appeared on the California ballot in the November 1964 election, asking voter approval to appropriate that amount for the purchase of park land. Even after the proposition passed, Brodie stayed involved. "I am still in this frustrating crusade to save the Santa Monica Mts from the bulldozers," she told Dale Morgan in a 1964 Christmas note. "If we lose," she said, "I shall be tempted to write a small very angry book—*How to Lose a Mountain*."[49]

The outcome of the crusade remained in doubt into 1965, largely because of the ambivalent position of three leading Democratic politicians: Los Angeles mayor Sam Yorty, California assembly speaker Jesse Unruh, and California governor Edmund G. (Pat) Brown, none of whom were willing to support a state park. Frustrated, Fawn wrote an article entitled "Parks and Politics in Los Angeles," which was published in *Reporter* magazine. In the article, Brodie lamented that the fate of the Santa Monica Mountains had become a political football and expressed alarm that political infighting could result in loss of the park altogether. The article caught the attention of politicians and bureaucrats in the state capital, and lively exchanges, both public and private, followed. Brodie sent copies of her *Reporter* article to California state legislators and to other politicians and park people. Her efforts had impact. Ultimately, the State Parks Commission threw out their original staff report, which had minimized the need for such a reserve, and released a new report in April 1965 that called for a two thousand-acre state park. This relatively modest proposal—considerably less than the sixteen thousand acres originally envisioned—seemed "hardly worth all the fight" to Brodie. But she supported it, viewing it as a beginning. Her optimism was eventually rewarded. A portion of the Santa Monica Mountains was first set aside in the creation of the Will Rogers State Park, and, in 1978, a 153,500-acre national recreational area was established there.[50]

Concurrent with the crusade to save the Santa Monica Mountains, Fawn involved herself in another controversial issue, one that also had political overtones. This was the Mormon policy of excluding black males from ordination to the priesthood. Long bothered by the Mormon-black issue, Brodie was among the first to address its questionable origins in *No Man Knows My History.*[51] She also alluded to it, indirectly, in *Thaddeus Stevens: Scourge of the South.*

Until the early 1960s, interest in the issue had largely been limited to the Mormon Community. This all changed, however, with George Romney's emergence as a national political figure. Romney, a Mormon businessman, had first gained attention as president of American Motors in the late 1950s. By promoting efficiency in production and clever marketing, Romney had pulled American Motors back from the brink of bankruptcy and turned it into a flourishing enterprise. In 1962 he entered the political arena as a Republican, declaring his candidacy for the governorship of Michigan. Immediate attention focused on Romney's Mormon background and, in turn, on the church's controversial position regarding blacks, a relevant issue in Michigan, given its large black population.[52]

All this prompted Fawn's renewed interest in the issue. She was now frequently running into people who asked her about the attitude of the Mormon Church toward African Americans. Brodie knew that Romney had been out to Salt Lake City to consult with Mormon Church leaders about the matter of black priesthood, and she commented on his dilemma: "It is hard for me to believe that it won't cost him the election. But I should be most surprised to see any relaxation on the part of the church leaders."[53]

But Brodie had misjudged Romney's political prospects, for in the fall 1962 election, Michigan voters elected the Mormon Republican over the favored incumbent Democratic governor. Almost immediately, Romney was touted as a possible presidential candidate by political pundits. All this caused Brodie to speculate, overly optimistically, as it turned out, about the possible lifting of the Mormon ban on black priesthood. When the national press carried rumors that the leadership of the Mormon Church was seriously considering abandonment of its historic policy of discrimination against blacks, Brodie commented to Dale Morgan, "It will be fascinating to see what form the policy change takes—revelation, manifesto, or some kind of weasel-worded advice to the elders." Then, with ironic family pride, she speculated, "It would really not surprise me to see my uncle [David O. McKay] issuing the first revelation since B.[righam] Young. He has the conviction and necessary self-assurance; moreover he is a dedicated Republican, and I think would even conquer his anti-Negro feeling to make Romney president. Moreover, I'm sure he would love to have a revelation. And this is an issue truly worthy of it."[54]

Brodie's optimism was premature. But her lively interest in the race issue continued. In February 1964 she announced her intention to write a piece on the Mormon-black issue if Romney was placed on the 1964 Republican ticket as a vice-presidential candidate. When this did not happen, Brodie abandoned her earlier optimism, asserting that "there isn't much likelihood of real change in the [Mormon Church's] attitude toward Negroes." Not only had political pressure from outside the ranks eased off, but Brodie knew who was likely to succeed David O. McKay as church leader—the hard-line, orthodox Joseph Fielding Smith.[55]

COMPLETING RICHARD BURTON

Brodie's major literary efforts from mid-1965 to early 1967 focused on completing her work on Richard Burton. In May 1965 she traveled to England once more to examine some recently discovered Burton manuscripts, materials that had escaped Isabel Burton's fires. Fawn characterized these materials "as good stuff—and revealing though not sensational." After completing her research, she and Bernard spent time vacationing in Europe.[56]

Following her return to California, Fawn settled into the serious work of completing the manuscript, hoping to be finished by Christmas 1965. But the writing took longer than expected, and she failed to meet her self-imposed deadline. The task actually took her well into 1966. "A book is really a pile of trouble," she complained to Dean Brimhall in April 1966, "as I realized all over again." She found the final draft "a great nuisance"; everything required a lot of checking. "Always it takes much longer than you plan for," she said.[57]

Throughout the entire process, Fawn received significant help from Bernard, on whose editorial skills she had long depended. He acted as a sounding board, or, as she put it, he at least "tolerated endless 'Burton talk' with good humor." He also gave "the manuscript his characteristic thorough and perceptive scrutiny and criticism." Also of help once more were Fawn's acquaintances in the Los Angeles psychoanalytic community—in particular, Ralph Greenson, Nathan Leites, Lewis J. Fielding, and Maimon Leavitt, all of whom helped Fawn in clinically defining some of the complexities of Richard Burton's personality.[58]

Inspired by the psychoanalysts, Brodie utilized the innovative, but controversial, process of free association in examining Burton's personality. She conceded that no historian can put a subject "on the couch," so to speak. "When a person is dead, we must make do with what we have," she said, and "free association was one technique she used. As Brodie explained,

> When Burton wrote about his mother, in his short autobiography, if you look at the paragraphs in which he mentions his mother and note what he said before and afterward, you will find he talks immediately about cheating, decapitation, mutilations, smashing—all the

stories and metaphors are violent, negative, and hostile. After he began to write about his mother he was reminded of a mother who killed her children and was guillotined. He saw this woman executed. The immediate association to her from his own mother is very interesting.

The careful analysis of such free associations, Brodie felt, provided essential insights into both Burton's feelings about his mother and underlying motives for his later actions. It was part of the psychoanalytic approach. It was like listening with a third ear. "It is treacherous," she conceded, "but I think [it is] important technique."[59]

In June 1966, Brodie sent her completed manuscript off to Norton. Her editor, George Brockway, gave it strong initial praise: "It lives up to my every expectation. You've done yourself proud." But Brockway also suggested significant revisions. His major suggestion was for one or two additional chapters or subchapters. He cited the need to summarize in a systematic manner the analytical conclusions scattered throughout the book. Brockway felt that Burton was an enormously difficult person to grasp and that most readers would welcome a little more explicit characterization.[60]

Brockway suggested other changes. He felt that Brodie made excessive use of quotations, noting that she often quoted writers with no greater claim to authority than herself. Foremost among these was Alan Moorehead, a contemporary popular author, whose books on Africa and the Nile River were current best-sellers. Brockway, with a touch of ribald humor, then went on to comment on how Brodie frequently misspelled Moorehead's name as "Morehead." "What would Freud have said about that paraprax?" he asked her.[61]

Brockway also felt that Brodie was excessive in her use of quotes from Burton's wife, Isabel. Such quotes illuminated her character but added nothing about Burton that could not be as well conveyed without the direct quote. This tendency indicated a more fundamental problem, said Brockway: "Isabel seems always on the point of taking over the book; so it would be a good tactic to eliminate unnecessary quotes from her passim." Brockway conceded that these revisions would mean a lot of work for Brodie, but to make his suggestions palatable, he noted that "the book is so very good, it deserves to have every chance to reach the widest possible public."[62]

Brodie reacted to Brockway's critique with relief and delight. In general, she accepted his suggestions but resisted his specific recommendation for two new chapters. She agreed that more summing up was essential but countered that such summation could be incorporated into existing chapters. As to her misspellings of Moorehead: "I have always envied him his talent and his success. Now I have disconcerting evidence that I have felt all along he has 'more head' as well."[63]

Brodie completed the necessary revisions in a month, and in August the manuscript was sent on to London for conversion to British spellings for an English edition of the biography, to be issued concurrently with Norton's American edition by the British publisher, Eyre and Spottiswoode. Thus Brodie was confronted with the task of reviewing the copy-edited manuscript not only for Brockway but also for John Bright-Holmes, editor of the English edition.[64]

Brodie reacted negatively to the whole process, complaining to Brockway about "the incredible copy reading" called for by the British editor. She was also upset by what she considered excessive editorial changes made by Bright-Holmes. Further aggravating the procedure, the British editor took three and a half months to complete the editorial process, which threatened to push back the projected date of publication. But when she received the final galleys in December 1966, Brodie was extremely pleased. "In some ways I think it is [my] best book yet," she told Dale Morgan, "though it didn't come out of my gut the way Joseph Smith and Thaddeus Stevens did."[65]

Actual publication of *The Devil Drives: A Life of Sir Richard Burton* came in May 1967. It had taken longer than Brodie's original expectations, but not as long as she had feared. More than compensating for the delay was good news that the biography had been chosen as a featured selection by the Literary Guild Book Club, guaranteeing the sale of at least ten thousand copies and earning the author significant royalties. "I am terribly pleased and astonished," Brodie told George Brockway. *The Devil Drives* was also chosen by the History Book Club as its featured selection. Their review, an essay commissioned for its "Editors' Choice" column and written by noted historian Louis B. Wright, praised *The Devil Drives* as "beautifully written, with understanding, candor, and good taste."[66]

The Devil Drives gained additional attention through book reviews published in newspapers and magazines throughout the United States and in the United Kingdom. The reviews were generally positive. The *New York Times* reviewer praised Brodie for capturing "the strange contradictions" of the man and for not trying "to smooth things out" with oversimplifications. The *New York Times Book Review* promoted *The Devil Drives* in its "New and Recommended" column as an "Excellent biography of a bizarre man who had a bizarre wife—and life." Josh Greenfeld, writing in the *Washington Post*, characterized Brodie's biography as an "eminently readable, accurate, and fully annotated biography," and literary critic Orville Prescott, writing in the *Saturday Review*, credited Brodie for her diligent research, deftness in keeping her narrative "moving briskly, and unshockable when confronted by material that can still raise eyebrows even in our outspoken age."[67]

Also heartening to Brodie was the praise given *The Devil Drives* in various publications in Utah. Ernest Linford, reviewer for the *Salt Lake Tribune* and Brodie's longtime friend, called her biography a most readable book, adding to "Brodie's stature as a leading American biographer." An anonymous reviewer writing in the *Utah Alumnus*, a publication of the University of Utah Alumni Association, called the biography "a formidable achievement, a work of demanding and thorough scholarship, carefully done" and written in "a style suitable to her subject."[68]

Abroad, the London *Observer* praised the book as scholarly and well-written, providing the reader with "a marvelously vivid surface narrative." "Not the least of this fine book," the reviewer continued, "is the discreet yet illuminating use which Mrs. Brodie makes of depth-psychology." But it was on this precise point that a number of other reviewers criticized both author and book. *Newsweek* writer Paul D. Zimmerman accused the author of "too often" wrestling Richard Burton "onto the analyst's couch for some instant Freudian forays into his psyche." Close to home, the *Los Angeles Times* called Brodie's efforts to analyze Burton a failure. "The spirit that drove this eminent Victorian eludes us still," the reviewer wrote.[69]

In general, Fawn Brodie could take pride in the overall response to *The Devil Drives*. A British reviewer, Gordon Waterfield, writing in the scholarly *Geographical Journal* went so far as to proclaim *The Devil Drives* "the best biography so far written" on Richard Burton, superior to any of the dozen full-length biographies published earlier on the eccentric Englishman.[70]

A RECOGNIZED BIOGRAPHER AND HISTORIAN

With the publication of *The Devil Drives*, Fawn Brodie achieved status as a prominent biographer, acknowledged not just in the United States but also abroad. But Brodie had, in fact, already acquired significant recognition as a biographer and historian on the basis of her earlier writings. Some four years before, in 1963, she received her first international exposure with the publication of an English edition of *No Man Knows My History*, brought out by Eyre and Spottiswoode as part of their Frontier Library series—a collection of well-known, previously published books focusing on the American frontier experience. *No Man Knows My History* thus joined such distinguished nonfiction works as Francis Parkman's *The Discovery of the Great West*, George R. Stewart's *Ordeal By Hunger*, Alvin M. Josephy's *The Patriot Chiefs*, and Walter Van Tilburg Clark's fiction classic, *The Ox-Bow Incident*.[71]

Recognition had also come with the 1965 publication of a paperback edition of Brodie's second biography, *Thaddeus Stevens: Scourge of the South*. This work, originally issued in 1959, had gone out of print because of limited commercial appeal. In now bringing out a paperback edition, Norton was acting at the suggestion of none other than Richard N. Current, who urged republication, indicating his willingness to use the biography in the history courses he taught. Current, moreover, wrote a blurb for the cover of the paperback edition, praising the author for writing "more imaginatively" and "more resourcefully . . . than any other Stevens biographer." Brodie's biography "must be taken into account by all serious students of the Civil War and Reconstruction," Current said. His effusive endorsement validated Brodie's status as a recognized biographer and historian.[72]

Further affirming Brodie's status were several articles written and published from 1959 to 1965. "A Lincoln Who Never Was," published in the *Reporter* in 1959, appeared concurrently with her Thaddeus Stevens biography. Three years later her noteworthy "Who Won the Civil War Anyway?" appeared in the *New York Times Book Review*. Also in 1962, Brodie's essay "Lincoln and Thaddeus Stevens" was included in *Lincoln: A Contemporary Portrait*, a volume edited by two distinguished popular writers, Allan Nevins and Irving Stone. Three years later, Brodie penned "Who Defends the Abolitionist?" at the request of the eminent Civil War historian, Martin Duberman, for inclusion in an anthology entitled *The Antislavery Vanguard: New Essays on the Abolitionists.* Essentially the same essay was published under the title "Abolitionists and Historians" in the scholarly journal *Dissent* that same year, giving Brodie further exposure. And concurrently, utilizing her skills in psychobiography, Brodie produced "Thaddeus Stevens, the Tyrant Father," an essay essentially drawn from her biography and published in an anthology, *Psychological Studies of Famous Americans: The Civil War Era.*[73]

In September 1967, Brodie received recognition—from a surprising source—when the Utah State Historical Society made her a fellow, that organization's most prestigious honor. This special recognition, given annually to a prominent individual, was awarded Brodie on the basis of her scholarly contributions in both the national and international realms. Everett L. Cooley, director of the historical society, asserted that the controversial Utah-born author was long overdue in receiving recognition. Brodie described the award as both "astonishing" and "gratifying" and indicated her intention to travel to Utah to receive her award in person, asking—and receiving—permission to give a brief acceptance speech at the society's annual banquet at the University of Utah.[74]

Brodie's return to the University of Utah was of special significance, for it was there some thirty years earlier that she had begun her quest for independence from things Mormon, or the "quiet kind of moving out," as she had termed it. She found the entire occasion deeply moving. In a two-and-one-half-minute acceptance speech, she discussed frankly her feelings as a dissenter from Mormonism. "I never return to Utah without being forcibly reminded of the overwhelming significance of the past," she said. She quoted the noted British philosopher Bertrand Russell: "The past is an awful God, though it gives life almost the whole of its haunting beauty . . . [including] . . . the weight of tradition, the great eternal process of youth and age and death. . . . Here the past is everywhere with us." Then Brodie quoted William Faulkner: "The Past is not dead; it is not even past." Employing clear personal allusions, Brodie elaborated:

> Certainly it is true that the way a person brought up in . . . [Utah] chooses to reckon with the past—either to wrestle with it, to abominate it, to submit to it, or to adore it and try to convert others to its overwhelming significance—has major consequences for his

life. It determines the quality of his intellectual life; it very largely determines the nature of his friends; and has important consequences whether for good or ill upon his peace of mind.

Brodie praised the Utah State Historical Society for making its resources and documents available to all, opening its doors to everyone, including the devout proselytizer, the detached scholar—or the scholar trying his best to be detached—the crackpot, and even the paranoid. In conclusion, Brodie thanked the society for her award, noting that it paid tribute to the right to dissent from the past.[75]

While Brodie took pride in her numerous accomplishments, she was already looking toward a fourth book-length biography. Immediately after completing Richard Burton, she spent six months researching the life of Eleanor Roosevelt. She thought a biography of the former first lady particularly timely, given her death four years earlier. Her fascination with Roosevelt was of long standing, going back to the mid-1940s when she had toyed with the idea of a Roosevelt biography after completing No Man Knows My History. But as she had before, Brodie abandoned Eleanor Roosevelt, this time because she was informed by George Brockway in October 1966 that Joseph Lash was already at work on what would ultimately become his best-selling two-volume study. Brockway advised her not to undertake the work because Lash was Roosevelt's very good friend and "had a much better opportunity to meet and know many of her friends and members of her family." Lash's was, moreover, a quasi-official biography in that the Roosevelt family was supporting his efforts.[76]

Brodie then seriously considered a biography of Brigham Young, Joseph Smith's successor as Mormon leader and important western colonizer. Ever since completing Joseph Smith, Brodie had been periodically haunted by the desire to do Young. She had been encouraged by many people and more than one publisher but was initially reluctant to proceed because another writer, Madeline McQuown, also a very close friend of Dale Morgan, had been working on Brigham Young for a number of years. However, as years went by and no McQuown publication appeared, Brodie became curious. She asked Morgan for a progress report on McQuown's work. "I have considered many possibilities other than Brigham Young, since finishing the Burton biography," she told Morgan, "but keep returning to him."[77]

Morgan had discouraging news: McQuown had been working determinedly on her Brigham Young manuscript for two years. It was substantially complete and so massive that it might end up a two-volume work. And she had approached Alfred A. Knopf as a possible publisher. On the basis of this information, Brodie abandoned her plans for Young.[78]

In the meantime, Fawn's attention was drawn to the burgeoning field of Mormon studies. In late 1967, Wesley P. Walters sent her a copy of his recently published and extremely provocative essay, "New Light on Mormon Origins from the Palmyra (N.Y.) Revival," which vindicated much of Brodie's own earlier research on Joseph Smith. She also received a copy of F. L. Stewart's recently published *Exploding the Myth about Joseph Smith the Prophet*, which took Brodie and her scholarship to task. Stewart had done a lot of digging in original documents, Brodie noted, and appeared to have read every source quoted in *No Man Knows My History*— except those on polygamy, which she had "religiously avoided." Stewart had found "some real errors and plenty of things she chose to call errors," Brodie conceded.[79]

Brodie also found her work under attack from Leonard J. Arrington, a leading exponent of the so-called new Mormon history by virtue of his highly regarded *Great Basin Kingdom: Economic History of the Latter-day Saints*. In an essay, "Scholarly Studies of Mormonism in the Twentieth Century," published in *Dialogue: A Journal of Mormon Thought*, Arrington was critical of *No Man Knows My History*. Brodie declined a formal reply to Arrington's critique, dismissing the Mormon author with the curt observation that he was of the school that was "so emotionally committed to the church that the truth will always elude [them]." In contrast, Brodie was extremely impressed with Klaus Hansen, who had sent her a copy of his recently published *Quest for Empire*. She described Hansen's study as "full of fascinating things I had never suspected" and expressed pleasure at seeing the younger generation of Mormon historians doing "serious and exemplary work."[80]

Brodie's own long-range plans remained uncertain. She was "torn between the desire to do more work in the Mormon field, and the burning necessity to stop the skyrocketing of Ronald Reagan." The 1966 election of Reagan as governor of California over incumbent Pat Brown was a profound shock to Fawn Brodie and other liberal Democrats in the state. She—and most political pundits—had dismissed the former movie actor and television host as a political lightweight, lacking the experience and stature necessary to be governor. But Reagan's election represented the culmination of a strong conservative trend in the Golden State. In 1964, despite the overwhelming defeat of the ultraconservative Republican, Barry Goldwater, for president, California voters had elected two conservative Republicans to high offices—namely, George Murphy, a former actor and song-and-dance man, to the U.S. Senate and Max Rafferty to the position of state superintendent of public education.[81]

During the 1966 campaign, Brodie lamented that with "Rafferty heading our education system, Murphy in the Senate and Reagan threatening to oust Brown, California should hide her head in the sand for shame," adding, "It's a wonder how much punishment our system of government can take without serious damage, though, and I suppose we could survive even four years with Reagan in office. But I hate to think of it."[82]

Brodie's dismay only increased following Reagan's election, as he pushed his conservative agenda upon taking office in January 1967. Particularly upsetting were his proposed cuts in the California state college and university budget by 10 percent, accompanied by a request for a two hundred to four hundred dollar increase in fees, proposals that represented a shrewd attempt to capitalize on the conservative backlash against student unrest at Berkeley and on other California college campuses. For Brodie, Reagan's proposed cuts in higher education had strong personal implications since all three of her children had attended, or were planning to attend, the University of California. And Bernard had just joined the political science department at UCLA. She viewed Reagan's attacks on the schools on an even more ominous level: "It marks him as a true 'anti-intellectual' and an individual to be greatly feared," she wrote Dean Brimhall.[83]

Brodie went public with her disdain for Reagan in a highly critical essay, "Ronald Reagan Plays Surgeon," published in the April 1967 *Reporter*. His proposed cuts, she said, posed a direct threat to California's tuition-free system of higher education—a system that was a model not only for the rest of the nation but a fundamental factor in California's industrial growth. She saw this budget slashing as reflective of Reagan's anger over student unrest at Berkeley. It was an appeal, she said, "to a deep-seated anti-intellectual tradition in America, which included hostility to universities, and fear of being manipulated by the expert." Reagan's methods reflected the meat-ax approach of an old-time butcher-surgeon. The governor was cutting up the body politic of California with all the zeal of the doctor who had cut off both Reagan's legs in the movie *Kings Row*, and in the process, he was subjecting vital programs to near-fatal amputations.[84]

A year after the publication of her 1967 *Reporter* essay, Brodie publicly attacked Reagan once more, this time assailing the California governor for cuts in the state's mental health program. For Brodie, the issue of mental health, like education, had direct relevance from both a personal and professional perspective. In "Inside Our Mental Hospitals: How Did We Get Here Anyway?" published in the *Los Angeles Times West Magazine* in February 1968, Brodie reiterated that "cutting" was a real necessity for Reagan. The governor was "a frighteningly destructive man," she wrote. "The bland, toothy smile, and the good-guy manner is a great coverup and fools almost everyone." She was deeply alarmed that by now Reagan was already a national political figure with presidential aspirations. The prospect that Reagan might one day occupy the White House appalled her, and she felt a particular urgency to expose his alleged flaws and misdeeds to the largest possible audience. She considered doing a book-length study of Ronald Reagan but eventually abandoned the idea, and the *Los Angeles Times* article was her last printed attack on the California governor.[85]

A UCLA LECTURER

By this time, Fawn Brodie was busy as a part-time lecturer in history at the University of California, Los Angeles, having been appointed at the beginning of the fall 1967 quarter. The appointment came in the wake of a significant expansion of the school's history department. In a department that already consisted of some fifty-five faculty members, Brodie was one of five new individuals added in 1967.[86] She entered at the rank of lecturer rather than at the traditional entry-level rank of instructor or assistant professor because she did not possess a doctoral degree in history. In fact, she had not earned any degree in history. Both her bachelor's and her master's were in English.

Despite her unconventional academic background, Brodie was eminently well qualified. She had initially been recommended to the department by Isser Woloch, a history professor familiar with and impressed by her writings. Also enthusiastic was Peter Loewenberg, another UCLA history professor. Loewenberg was an expert in modern European history and a trained psychoanalyst who knew Brodie through their mutual involvement in the Los Angeles Interdisciplinary Psychoanalytic Study Group. It also helped that Brodie's expertise was in the fields of psychohistory and psychobiography, areas of growing interest during the late 1960s.[87]

Despite all her attributes, there were also concerns. Brodie was a woman joining a department that was overwhelmingly male—there were only two other women on the UCLA history faculty in the fall of 1967. More than that, she was a middle-aged woman, of fifty-two years, and also a novice to the academic scene; certain faculty considered her an amateur biographer, a mere housewife and mother who dabbled in history.[88] Such reservations, however, were not of sufficient weight to block her appointment to the department in 1967—though they would be used against her when she sought promotion to full professor years later.

The new appointee concentrated on class preparation for teaching undergraduate upper-division American history courses along with specialized graduate seminars in American political biography and psychobiography. Brodie's first course, taught during the fall 1967 quarter, was an upper-level class in United States history, focusing on Jeffersonian America, the period from 1800 to 1830. A large lecture class, it contained some two hundred students. Her lecture style was conversational and matter-of-fact, her subject matter meticulously prepared and carefully presented. She wrote out each and every lecture, evidence of an overriding need to be carefully prepared but also of a deep-seated fear of public speaking—surprising, given her extensive forensic experience.[89]

She was much more at ease before small groups—a situation she took advantage of in her graduate-level courses, beginning with a seminar on American political biography taught in the winter 1968 quarter, where she found the intimate setting of ten to twenty students much more to her liking. She was also more at ease with the subject matter—biographical treatment of American political figures.[90]

In addition to adjusting to the new regimen of teaching, Fawn faced significant changes on the family scene. Bernard was busy with his own writing and research, having published *Escalation and the Nuclear Option* in 1966. The controversial study called for deployment in Europe of tactical nuclear weapons, with the threat of using them, if need be. In arguing this position, Brodie took issue with strategists promoting the deployment of large conventional forces, which he thought a waste of hundreds of billions of dollars. He discounted the threat of war posed by nuclear deployment, arguing that the very existence of such weapons— and the adoption of an unequivocal polity to use them—were prime guarantees of preventing war in the first place. This thesis opposed the conventional-war position of the then secretary of defense, Robert S. McNamara, and the stance of many of Brodie's RAND colleagues.[91]

Brodie also found himself at odds with certain RAND associates on another relevant issue—American involvement in the Vietnam War. By the late 1960s Brodie had discarded his earlier position of support for American intervention in Southeast Asia—in particular, the bombing of North Vietnam, which he had previously endorsed "as both warranted and effective." His new antiwar position came in response to two developments. First, he was influenced by Konrad Kellen, a RAND colleague, neighbor, and close friend. Kellen, an expert on Vietnam and Southeast Asia, expressed early opposition to the war, first debating Brodie and then converting him. Bernard was influenced as well by the situation faced by his two sons, Dick and Bruce, who were in their early to mid-twenties and eligible for the draft. All this occurred as Lyndon Johnson, at the urging of Robert McNamara and other military strategists, drastically escalated America's military commitment to over 500,000 American troops by 1968.[92]

In the fall of 1966, at the same time Bernard was changing his views about Vietnam, he left RAND to accept a teaching position in the political science department at the University of California, Los Angeles. His departure was not completely unexpected. At RAND he found himself out of step with more and more of his associates on policy matters and increasingly at odds with certain key individuals. In particular, there was his acrimonious relationship with Joe Goldson, chairman of RAND's social science division and Brodie's immediate supervisor. Small in stature, Goldson was vain and "extremely insecure intellectually," according to a former RAND associate, and Brodie had nothing but contempt for him.

Brodie's departure from RAND became inevitable. In fact, he had been offered a position at Harvard the previous year but had turned it down out of consideration for Fawn and the children, who were reluctant to leave California. The offer of the position at UCLA, then, proved the perfect answer to his situation.[93]

The Brodies' three children also went through significant changes in the mid-1960s. Dick, after a year of living with Fawn and Bernard in Pacific Palisades, left for Europe in the fall of 1965. There he enrolled in graduate studies at the Sorbonne. In the fall of 1966, he moved on to Holland, finding temporary employment in Amsterdam. A year later, he was in Sweden, where he taught at the University of Stockholm, while pursuing graduate studies in English. Fawn had some anxiety about her eldest son, confiding to Dale Morgan that Dick was "a wanderer and a romantic, with so much talent going to waste." Bernard put it more bluntly. Dick, he said, remained "committed to be uncommitted."[94]

Bruce, meanwhile, continued his undergraduate studies at the University of California, Berkeley. By the fall of 1967, as he entered his senior year, he expressed an interest in medicine, but some C grades in biochemistry "shot his grade average out of the medical school market." Meanwhile, seventeen-year-old Pam completed high school in the spring of 1968 and moved to UC Berkeley the next fall. She expressed interest in a career in acting, which both Fawn and Bernard viewed with some ambivalence. Pam had "so much grace and talent," Fawn told Dale Morgan, that her parents were "not actively discouraging her [from a career in theater], though we look . . . askance at the profession."[95]

• • •

The decade of the 1960s had been one of profound change for Fawn Brodie. By the late 1960s she had achieved status as a widely recognized biographer and historian, thanks to the widespread recognition accorded *The Devil Drives: A Life of Sir Richard Burton, Thaddeus Stevens: Scourge of the South,* and *No Man Knows My History.* She "was absolutely thrilled" with her 1967 appointment to teach at UCLA, viewing it as acceptance of her status as a professional historian.[96] She had moved beyond being a mere part-time biographer limited to writing when family and household duties permitted. Now she could look to the future with confidence as she pursued both her teaching and research.

SIX

"An Elaborate Psychological Exploration"

1967–1974

Thomas Jefferson: An Intimate History is undoubtedly Fawn Brodie's best-known biography. Certainly it was her most popular, appearing on the *New York Times* best-seller list for thirteen weeks. Going through five printings during the first year of publication in 1974, it ultimately sold a total of 80,000 copies in hardback. Issued as a Bantam paperback a year later, the book sold 270,000 additional copies from 1975 to 1979 and netted its author some $350,000 in royalties.[1] More important, *Thomas Jefferson* affirmed Brodie's status as a preeminent American biographer.

The book's great success was ironic, given the author's own frank characterization of it as a "limited study." Brodie did not attempt to present Jefferson's entire life; such a task was made hopeless, she said, by the multifaceted nature of the man and his activities. Instead, Brodie presented a portrait of "the private man." Hers was "an elaborate psychological exploration of Jefferson, looking into his feelings, sexuality, [and] capacity for love and hate." Despite its limited scope, Brodie considered *Thomas Jefferson* her "most rewarding" book. Its popularity and monetary rewards exceeded her wildest fantasies—and it provided the great satisfaction of dealing with a timely topic.[2]

Brodie was drawn to Thomas Jefferson in preparing materials for the class in American political biography that she taught at UCLA. In turn, the work complemented her role in the classroom: As she explored new areas for the biography, Brodie communicated to her students the enthusiasm and excitement of producing a book. They had the benefit of observing, firsthand, various techniques of research. And the author had the benefit of receiving feedback from these students as well as from her colleagues.[3]

Also stimulating Brodie's interest in Jefferson was the bicentennial of the American Revolution, the celebration of which brought renewed attention to the author of the Declaration of Independence. And Jefferson's status as a slaveholder intrigued Brodie, who approached the issue as a problem: Why did this man who wrote the Declaration of Independence go to his death without freeing his slaves? she asked herself. The answer, she believed, was rooted in his personal life—specifically, his twenty-eight year liaison with Sally Hemings, one of his slaves but also the half-sister of his deceased wife, Martha Wayles Skelton. Jefferson could never publicly acknowledge this relationship—which produced seven children—because he was trapped in what Brodie labeled "a complex of taboos."[4]

Jefferson was also trapped by a fundamental dilemma: If he freed his slaves in conformity with his self-proclaimed ideals of liberty and equality, they would have been banished from the state as freedmen in accordance with Virginia law. Thus, the only way Jefferson could maintain his relationship with Sally Hemings was to keep her enslaved. This made the larger issue of slavery too complex to deal with. And so Jefferson drifted along apathetically through the remainder of his life, leaving it to later generations of Americans to contend with the slavery issue.[5]

Brodie's focus on the Jefferson-Hemings liaison was especially timely, given the state of American society during the late 1960s and early 1970s, when race, sex, and gender were issues of prime concern. The problem of race turned to violence in the late 1960s, with urban race riots sweeping the United States—beginning with the Watts riot in Los Angeles in 1965 and culminating in the widespread destruction that followed Martin Luther King Jr.'s 1968 assassination. Gender issues also commanded major attention, with unequal treatment of women being the focus of an emerging feminist movement sparked by activists Betty Friedan, Gloria Steinem, Helen Gurley Brown, and others.[6]

Brodie's examination of Jefferson's personal life had contemporary relevance during this period when many Americans were cynical about their elected leaders, particularly their presidents. Fueling such cynicism were Lyndon Johnson's troubles in Vietnam followed by Richard Nixon's problems over Watergate. Then there were the revelations concerning past presidential behavior, including the extramarital affairs of Franklin D. Roosevelt and John F. Kennedy. Brodie's treatment of Jefferson's carefully concealed intimate relations with women other than his wife seemed both timely and titillating, and it all went toward the making of a best-selling book.

On a personal level, Fawn found Jefferson's intimate relations with women other than his wife painfully relevant in light of the behavior of her own husband. Bernard was drawn to other women, projecting the same charm that had so captivated Fawn years earlier. Such flirtatious behavior was usually limited and vicarious, but he became deeply involved with one particular woman, which led to an extramarital affair during the late 1960s. Upon discovering her husband's infidelity, Fawn was so mortified she considered divorce, according to one close friend. But in weighing her husband's indiscretion against the overwhelmingly positive aspects of their relationship, Fawn concluded that their marriage of some thirty years was worth preserving.[7]

Brodie found Jefferson relevant for other personal reasons. His home at Monticello reminded her of that "wonderful, old white house with pillars" in Huntsville, Utah. And she found important resemblances between Thomas Jefferson and her own father. Like Jefferson, Thomas McKay exhibited deep affection for his offspring—and equally strong expectations. "My father would say to his children, perhaps not in so many words, 'I will not love you if you do not do such and such.' That is how Jefferson dictated his daughter's affection," Brodie said. Both men "insisted on orderliness. Both stressed self-control. Both admired 'adoring, deferential daughters.' Both were chronically in debt." And finally, like Jefferson, "My father was a gentle, courtly man, but a benign despot in his own family," Brodie recalled.[8]

A CONTINUING INTEREST IN MORMON STUDIES

Despite all the varied factors that were drawing her to Thomas Jefferson, Brodie continued to focus much of her attention on Mormon studies.

In early 1968, she reconsidered her plans for a biography of Brigham Young. She was skeptical about Madeline McQuown's long-heralded biography, despite reports of its imminent publication. At her behest, George Brockway, Brodie's editor at Norton, approached Alfred Knopf in an attempt to verify Dale Morgan's report that McQuown had signed a contract there. When Brockway reported that no communications had yet transpired between McQuown and Knopf, Brodie approached Morgan once again concerning McQuown's plans. She told Morgan that Brockway was still trying to persuade her to do Brigham Young and indicated her desire to proceed if McQuown's biography was to be delayed another two years. Brodie was also encouraged by friends and professional acquaintances in Utah. Morgan urged Brodie not to proceed; McQuown's book was soon to be published, he said. In fact, however, McQuown had done very little and her biography was never completed. Still, the persistent rumors circulated by McQuown and Morgan had their desired effect, and Brodie abandoned her plans for Brigham Young.[9]

Brodie, nevertheless, maintained a lively interest in other Mormon issues, particularly the issue of black-Mormon priesthood, which had drawn national attention again because of a statement by Stuart Udall, then secretary of the interior under Lyndon Johnson. Udall, a nominal Mormon, publicly spoke out against Mormonism's racial policy, expressing his views in an essay published in *Dialogue: A Journal of Mormon Thought* in 1967. He asserted that the offensive Mormon policy was merely a social and institutional practice, with no real sanction in essential Mormon thought. Udall sought Brodie's personal reaction to what he had written. At the same time he thanked her for helping to liberate him from Mormon dogma through *No Man Knows My History* years earlier.[10]

Concurrently, Brodie was caught up in controversy relative to the historicity of the "Book of Abraham"—a collection of Mormon scriptural writings providing justification for denial of the priesthood to blacks. This work, according to Mormon belief, was translated from a set of Egyptian papyri acquired by the church in the 1830s. Brodie had been originally interested in the "Book of Abraham" years earlier, in researching the black-Mormon priesthood problem for *No Man Knows My History*. Her renewed interest resulted from rediscovery in late 1967 of the long-lost Joseph Smith Egyptian papyri in the Metropolitan Museum of Art in New York City. Following their rediscovery, the papyri were turned over to the

Mormon Church. This alarmed Brodie, particularly when the Metropolitan Museum declined to release copies of the original papyri to the general public. She reacted angrily to this development, believing that the Metropolitan Museum had been intimidated by the Mormon Church into covering up or suppressing the papyri. As she told Dale Morgan,

> Has the Church become so powerful [that] it can intimidate the Metropolitan Museum? If so, we have come to a pretty pass and must do something about it. I have fired off a letter [to the museum] myself asking for a photocopy of the negatives [of the papyri] they kept, and pointed out in the letter the names of great scholars of Egyptian art who have not in the past hesitated to comment on the unscholarly character of the Book of Abraham.[11]

Brodie also told Morgan that if the museum failed to respond, she would contact Wallace Turner, a hard-hitting investigative reporter for the *New York Times* who was noted for his highly critical book-length study of the contemporary Latter-day Saint movement, *The Mormon Establishment.* Brodie planned to have Turner look into the matter, hoping that he would expose what she characterized as "ridiculous censorship & cowardice."[12]

Brodie's fears of a Mormon Church–sanctioned cover-up were overstated. Mormon officials actually appeared anxious to resolve the issue of the Egyptian papyri and their precise meaning. They enlisted Hugh Nibley, professor of languages at Brigham Young University, to translate them, and the results were published in *Brigham Young University Studies.* Brodie was less than impressed with Nibley's analysis, dismissing it as "damned irrelevant." All Nibley had to say, she concluded, was "Look at this fascinating piece of research I have done supporting Joseph Smith." Nibley had dodged the whole issue. Through clever, diversionary tactics, he had managed to "worm out of the problem" of dealing with the precise relationship between the Egyptian papyri and the "Book of Abraham." In critiquing his work, Brodie alluded to the more direct conclusions arrived at by virtually all Egyptologists, who asserted that the recently rediscovered papyri did not even remotely resemble the contents of the "Book of Abraham" as transcribed by Joseph Smith. The former, the scholars asserted, were actually funeral scrolls from a work known as the *Egyptian Book of the Dead.*[13]

Brodie's interest in the Egyptian papyri had the effect of plunging her into the larger controversy over the status of blacks within the Mormon Church. Debate over this issue increased during the late 1960s and early 1970s, not just among concerned Latter-day Saints, but among non-Mormons within the larger American society as well. Activists from within and outside the Latter-day Saint community exerted pressure on the Mormon Church to lift its ban on black priesthood. Various colleges and universities throughout the United States, including Stanford and San Jose State University, canceled athletic competition with Mormon Church–sponsored Brigham Young University in protest over this policy. Such agitation reflected a fundamental shift in the American civil rights movement, whereby activists moved beyond criticism of civil acts of discrimination and began to attack its alleged roots—specifically, fundamental racist concepts and doctrines.[14]

Clearly fitting in this category was the Mormon practice of denying priesthood to African Americans. Fawn Brodie confronted this issue directly in a public address entitled "Can We Manipulate the Past?" given in October 1970 to a standing-room-only crowd of over five hundred in the Hotel Utah's Lafayette Ballroom in Salt Lake City. Brodie's appearance was sponsored by several local civic groups, including the Salt Lake branch of the American Association of University Women, the Utah State Historical Society, the University of Utah Division of Continuing Education, and the Center for Studies of the American West. Brodie approached her task with some anxiety, confessing to her good friend, Everett Cooley, then director of special collections at the University of Utah, that making speeches in Utah was difficult because there were "too many ghosts." Initially she worried that it might be the wrong speech at the wrong time in the wrong place. But after completing the written text she felt it would be a useful statement, and after delivering it, she concluded it had been the right thing to do.[15]

In her speech, Brodie accused the Mormon Church of manipulating its own past over a period of many decades to justify its policy of denying male African Americans the priesthood. She called the policy, "Jim Crowism in the Mormon Church." She asserted that Joseph Smith's approach to questions involving race was not static but evolutionary. Granted, Smith affirmed Mormon anti-abolitionist sentiments and provided scriptural precedent for the ban on black priesthood in the

1830s, but his views had gone through an astonishing change by the mid-1840s. For instance, she said, during his 1844 campaign for the U.S. presidency, he "took a very strong abolitionist stand, calling for an end to slavery by 1850." In every respect except intermarriage, Smith had favored total equality for black Americans, a stand Brodie labeled "dangerously revolutionary, and far more radical" than the position Abraham Lincoln took on these same issues.[16]

But this enlightened Mormon position, Brodie asserted, was forgotten following Smith's death, and the "Book of Abraham" was ever since used as a justification for the denial of priesthood to blacks. This was "a repudiation of the best, the most forward-looking, the most compassionate, in Joseph Smith," she said. It was also "manipulation [or] at least a misreading of the Mormon past for the purpose of social control."[17]

Brodie noted the mounting pressure on the Mormon Church to repudiate its restrictive practice. The issue had forced the Mormon Church into an agonizing dilemma, she pointed out. On the one hand, truly devout Mormons found it impossible to accept the findings of Egyptologists, whose translations of the newly discovered papyri from which the "Book of Abraham" was derived totally differed from the earlier interpretations of Joseph Smith. But giving blacks the priesthood without a new revelation or new manifesto would mean "implicit repudiation of countless quiet decisions made by Mormon leaders in the past." For the Mormon Church to continue denying black men the priesthood on the basis of the "Book of Abraham" was "to an increasing number of Latter-day Saints . . . unjust and alien to the ideals of the Declaration of Independence." "The past should not control the decisions we make today, especially if they are decisions reinforcing injustice," Brodie concluded.[18]

Brodie's speech was, on the whole, favorably received, and Brodie herself characterized the audience as "most sympathetic." Because of this enthusiastic response, the entire text of her address was reprinted as a pamphlet by the University of Utah Press, and a run of some thirty-five hundred copies was distributed under the title *Can We Manipulate the Past?* Thus Brodie added her voice to the widening chorus of critics assailing the Mormon Church on the black priesthood issue.[19]

Reaction to Brodie's speech from within the official church was noticeably muted. Not surprisingly, the *Deseret News* did not mention Brodie or her presentation, despite the fact that she had spoken in the Mormon Church–owned Hotel Utah, which was located across the street from historic Temple Square and adjacent to the church's world headquarters. This position of absolute silence stood in sharp contrast to the church's robust reaction, albeit belated, to the publication of her Joseph Smith biography almost twenty-five years earlier.[20]

Fawn Brodie, in fact, revised and updated *No Man Knows My History* in 1970, adding a supplementary chapter to the main body and making what she characterized as "numerous changes in the text." Actually, such changes were minimal, with the pagination remaining the same as in the original 1945 edition. But the author found it "a real effort to get back into the old morass" of Mormon history. Her twenty-five page supplement analyzed new information discovered since the first edition had appeared. In it, she backed away somewhat from her original contention that Joseph Smith was a conscious impostor. She noted, instead, that Smith's situation relative to various prophetic claims was "a very special, complicated story" rooted in a complex, interrelated "identity problem."[21]

Despite such modifications, Brodie stood steadfastly by her original thesis, asserting that Joseph Smith had emerged as a religious leader through an "evolutionary process." Also remaining intact was her basic contention that the *Book of Mormon* was the product of Smith's imagination, that the book was of an "unmistakable fraudulent nature." Although her biography had been in print for some twenty-five years, Brodie felt it still did a better job than any other in dealing with its subject, though she confessed that "she was never satisfied that she had solved the mystery of Joseph Smith." She was frankly astonished that "a better biography" had not been produced over the years.[22]

CONTEMPORARY POLITICS AND JESSE UNRUH

Besides her continuing interest in the Mormons, past and present, Brodie was equally, if not more, fascinated by the contemporary political scene. She found compelling the trends of the late 1960s and early 1970s, which brought a whirlwind of change. Her earlier writings on Gov. Ronald Reagan were clear evidence of this. During the early phases of the 1968 presidential campaign, Brodie faced the "happy" dilemma of having to choose between Eugene McCarthy and Robert Kennedy in the California primary.[23]

On the Republican side, Brodie viewed with more than passing interest the rise and fall of Michigan's Mormon governor, George Romney, as a major presidential contender—and then the emergence of Richard Nixon as the Republican front-runner, despite the former vice-president's ignominious defeat for the California governorship just six years earlier. Brodie received a firsthand evaluation of Nixon's leadership potential from none other than Henry Kissinger at a dinner party she and Bernard hosted in late 1967 or early 1968. Kissinger at the time was acting as a foreign policy advisor to New York governor Nelson Rockefeller, another Republican presidential hopeful and major rival to Richard Nixon. When asked what kind of a president he thought Nixon would make, Kissinger reportedly replied, "Well, he will be a strong president, but he will choose weak advisors," an ironic prediction, given Nixon's subsequent selection of Kissinger to serve as national security advisor and later as secretary of state.[24]

Brodie's fascination with contemporary politics was also evident in a 1968 article she wrote on a powerful California politician, Jesse Unruh, speaker of the California Assembly. Entitled "Big Daddy vs. Mr. Clean" and published in the *New York Times* in April 1968, Brodie's essay presented Unruh, a liberal Democrat, in an extremely positive light—at variance with the speaker's longtime image as a fat, cigar-smoking party boss, brainy, dedicated, but tactically ruthless, whose abiding ambition was to replace incumbent governor Pat Brown. Brodie's discussion focused on Unruh's current, more positive image: a "slimmed-down, tough-muscled and tough-minded champion of higher education, mental health programs and parks, battler of the anti-intellectual, budget-chopping Ronald Reagan." Brodie took special note of Unruh's rural roots and values—clearly similar to those of the essayist herself—which had helped shape him as a liberal Democrat.[25]

Brodie also discussed Unruh's contemporary political activities, presenting the California speaker as a party unifier who had become a militant partisan for liberal causes. She praised his decision to back the 1968 candidacy of Sen. Robert F. Kennedy for the Democratic presidential nomination and predicted a bright political future for Unruh as either a vice-presidential running mate on a Kennedy ticket or contender for California governor in 1970. The article drew praise from Unruh, who tried, unsuccessfully, to commission Brodie to write a book-length campaign biography.[26]

BEGINNING THOMAS JEFFERSON

By May 1968, Brodie was focusing her major literary energies on Thomas Jefferson. Stimulating her interest was Winthrop D. Jordan's recently published, widely heralded *White over Black: American Attitudes toward the Negro 1550–1812.* Particularly intriguing was Jordan's extensive discussion of Thomas Jefferson's complex and often ambiguous posturing on the issues of slavery and race—specifically, Jordan's tentative speculations of a possible sexual relationship between Jefferson and his mulatto slave, Sally Hemings.[27] Brodie felt that Jordan had not gone far enough in pursuing the nature of the relationship. In beginning to examine this piece of Jefferson's life, she found herself caught up in the much larger story of America's third president.

Brodie's attention was also caught by a controversial article entitled "Thomas Jefferson and Sally Hemings," which had been written by Pearl N. Graham and published some eight years earlier in the *Journal of Negro History.* Intrigued by Graham's arguments, Brodie quickly established contact with the author, attempting to get at the sources of her information. Through Graham's contacts, Brodie was able to communicate with some of the individuals who claimed to be descendants of Sally Hemings.[28]

Further facilitating Brodie's research was the ready accessibility of primary sources on Thomas Jefferson in the Los Angeles area. Many of his original papers had been microfilmed and deposited at the Huntington Library in nearby San Marino. Other extensive writings were available in edited collections at UCLA and other nearby libraries.[29]

Between classes and during summer, Brodie did further research outside the L.A. area, traveling to archives in Washington, D.C., and at the University of Virginia, Charlottesville. She first visited Charlottesville in March 1969, where she had the opportunity to interact with members of the so-called Jefferson establishment, including Dumas Malone and James A. Bear. Initially, Brodie's relationship with these individuals was cordial, especially her relationship with Malone, at the time the foremost living Jefferson scholar.[30]

Brodie was unable to meet personally with another renowned Jefferson scholar at Charlottesville, Merrill D. Peterson, who was on leave. But Peterson responded by letter to Brodie's written inquiries, expressing mixed feelings about the subject that was becoming a major focus of her research—Jefferson's alleged interracial affair with Sally Hemings. Peterson told Brodie that, frankly, this subject did not interest him.[31]

More helpful was James Bear, head of the Thomas Jefferson Memorial Foundation, who provided information on the alleged descendants of Jefferson and Hemings. In evaluating Bear's information, Brodie admitted, "At this point I simply cannot sort out fact from family folklore in this material and I am not at all sure that I ever will be able to." To others, Brodie was less equivocal in criticizing the work of traditional Jefferson biographers, including Malone and Peterson. She was intrigued at the degree to which such scholars tried to cover up anything controversial in Jefferson's life—specifically, "fathering a family by his favorite slave"— in order to "keep their hero shining."[32]

Nevertheless, Brodie's cordial relationship with the Jefferson community at Charlottesville continued, and the University of Virginia invited her to present a lecture in conjunction with that institution's sesquicentennial celebration in the fall of 1969. Brodie's lecture, "The Political Hero in America—His Fate and His Future," focused on what she characterized as five threats faced by American political heroes. The first was the danger of assassination, which seemed particularly ominous during the turbulent 1960s. A second was what Brodie described as a "general disenchantment" with all political leadership evident in the aftermath of the Johnson administration and during the early Nixon years. The third was the "widespread distortion and denigration of the true magnitude of the hero to fit contemporary fashions." A fourth, she stated, was the biographer or historian who felt compelled "to tell everything" in pursuit of truth. This so-called threat, Brodie noted, worried her "very little" but concerned certain other historians. The final danger she stated in the form of a question: "Can our political heroes survive the impact of new clinical techniques that explore the hitherto hidden mysteries of the inner man?" Brodie quickly answered her own question. "No man," she said, "is a hero to his psychoanalyst."[33]

Then, getting to the heart of her research, Brodie asserted that an intimate knowledge of Freudian concepts would help solve "the major mystery in Jefferson's life"—what she termed "the great Jefferson taboo." This she also put in the form of a question: "Did Jefferson, who all his life indicated that he was in favor of the separation of the races and who wrote specifically against miscegenation, did he after the death of his wife have a family by a slave woman? If so, what does this do to the heroic image?" Brodie felt her efforts to probe the inner man were particularly timely in that "Jefferson is the most presently relevant of all our heroes, for his ambivalences are our ambivalences."[34]

The Jefferson scholars were there in force on that occasion of course, and Brodie felt as if she were in the lion's den. "But everyone was gracious," she acknowledged, "even Dumas Malone, who hates what I am researching."[35]

By that fall of 1969, Brodie had made sufficient progress to approach W. W. Norton with a proposal for a Jefferson biography. She submitted to George Brockway a tentative draft of the first three chapters, written earlier and given at a UCLA seminar. The theme of her proposed volume was Jefferson's inner life. To her mind, the relationship between his inner life and his political life presented "fascinating opportunities for speculation." Her study would be limited, she admitted. She did not intend to "do the whole life" as she had with Joseph Smith, Thaddeus Stevens, and Richard Burton. Merrill Peterson and Dumas Malone were both writing the political story in such detail as to make additional work in this area superfluous. But, Brodie concluded, "I think there is great potential in the material I have already uncovered for a truly original and provocative book, one that will sell well, and one that will be enthusiastically received by everyone save the most protective of the Jefferson scholars."[36]

George Brockway wasted little time in responding. He read Brodie's draft "with great admiration and great excitement"; he felt that the author had "something important here—and saleable as well. We certainly want the honor of publishing it." He immediately offered Brodie a contract calling for an advance of fifteen thousand dollars. This she promptly accepted, telling Brockway she hoped to have a completed manuscript by January 1972.[37]

To meet this goal, Brodie requested and received a leave from her teaching responsibilities for the 1970–71 academic year. The leave, combined with a light teaching load during the spring 1970 quarter, would allow her to concentrate for the better part of two years on research and writing. Though she enjoyed teaching and the contact with her students, the Jefferson material was so fascinating that she was eager to get the text written. She hoped to finish quickly but confessed to finding Jefferson "so magical I may end up taking 5 years or so." The process itself she found "extraordinarily challenging."[38]

Among the noteworthy challenges was the extreme hostility she faced from one of Jefferson's white descendants, Harold Coolidge. Coolidge was angry over the author's interest in Jefferson's alleged black progeny, and he rejected Brodie's request to use a quotation from the letters of his ancestor, Ellen Coolidge, replying, "I am distressed that the subject which seems to interest you most relates to the controversial matter of Mr. Jefferson's children and I can assure you categorically that this is not a subject which I wish to have raised."[39]

Predictably, Brodie found the pace of research slower than anticipated, and in January 1971 she informed George Brockway, "I do not want this book to be a mere gossip piece, but a serious study." She found the quality of the writing and research done by other Jefferson scholars "so distinguished that it sets very special standards." She wanted to hold to those standards. "I do not want to sacrifice quality for haste, she told Brockway, adding that she hoped to complete a first draft by October 1971.[40]

Also slowing progress was time taken to prepare short papers based on her research and published or presented at gatherings of historians. These allowed her to test her ideas, which invariably generated sharp debates. Among the most significant was a paper delivered at the Organization of American Historians meeting in New Orleans in April 1971. Entitled "Thomas Jefferson and Miscegenation," it contained the major arguments that would eventually appear in the biography. Brodie asserted that Jefferson, widowed at thirty-nine, took as a mistress his slave Sally Hemings, the quadroon half-sister of his late wife. To support her claim, Brodie presented a variety of circumstantial and other evidence. Jefferson, she began, was at Monticello nine months before the births of each of Sally Hemings's children, as recorded in his own "Farm Book." Second, the two men whom Jefferson most revered, George Wyth, his law teacher whom he called his second father, and John Wayles, his father-in-law, had both fathered children by black slave mistresses on their respective plantations, thereby setting precedents for the young Jefferson. Third, Brodie had found two accounts written by early-nineteenth-century Richmond newspaper editor James T. Callender that testified to a Jefferson-Hemings liaison. Fourth, Brodie presented what she termed hard evidence that Jefferson had treated Sally Hemings with special consideration, providing her with material comforts and giving preferential treatment to her immediate family. And finally, Brodie offered psychological evidence, which she admitted was highly controversial in nature: She noted Jefferson's frequent use of the word "Mulatto" in a daily journal he kept during his sojourn in Europe and immediately after he had begun his relationship with Hemings; and she pointed to his description of himself as "an animal of warm climate, a mere Oran-ootan." "Oran-ootan," Brodie explained to her audience, was a term applied to those men who preferred black women over those of their "own species."[41]

Brodie's New Orleans presentation sparked intense controversy. Merrill Peterson, in his role as a commentator, blasted the speech. By contrast, Winthrop Jordan, the other commentator, liked the presentation and found the documentation impressive. The audience, according to Brodie herself, was "deeply divided." All of this caused her to confess to George Brockway that her forthcoming biography would be "very controversial."[42]

A RICHARD BURTON SCREENPLAY

In addition to working on Thomas Jefferson, Brodie found herself involved, once more, with Richard Burton—through a movie script based on *The Devil Drives*. The actual writing of the script was initially commissioned to a young Englishman and professional screenwriter, John Hopkins, in May 1968. At first Brodie was impressed with Hopkins, but his completed script proved to be a "bitter disappointment." It was "a typical Hollywood phantasmagoria of sex and violence which can only end up being dull as well as prurient." Brodie herself had emphasized Burton's sexual behavior and preferences in her biography, but she felt Hopkins's screen play exceeded the boundaries of good taste. The script featured scenes of Burton reveling in homosexual brothels; one such scene was actually intended as the opening for the movie. Brodie labeled Hopkins's treatment a "terrible waste of the [larger] man," and she finally intervened, informing producers that without significant changes any movie based on the existing script would be a disaster. She gave them some forty pages of criticism and called for a rewrite. The script, she said, had been "badly bungled." Hopkins was asked to rewrite.[43]

Less than a year later, Brodie's frustration over the movie script was offset by an unexpected windfall. She received twenty thousand dollars from moviemakers Eddie Lewis and John Frankenheimer for the film rights to *The Devil Drives.* Now there was speculation concerning casting for the projected movie. Seriously considered for the title role was Sean Connery, then noted for his movie portrayals of James Bond. Connery was apparently a great Burton fan and keenly interested in the role. There was also talk of having none other than British actor Richard Burton portray his namesake. Brodie sent Burton a copy of *The Devil Drives* in a not-too-subtle effort to interest him in the project.[44]

However, there remained the problem of a satisfactory script, let alone ultimate production. Another year passed without a screenplay. In the summer of 1971 Brodie herself took over the task of rewriting the Hopkins screenplay. Although this meant valuable time away from Jefferson, she found herself enthusiastically caught up in the project. She told George Brockway that "it was great fun, and I felt an enormous sense of liberation at not having to fool around with footnotes. Anyway, this screenplay is now being used to try and get some financing. If it doesn't work, we will simply have to wait till the contract expires, and I'll look around for a new producer-director."[45]

Despite Brodie's efforts, the movie project languished. In a January 1972 letter to George Brockway, she described plans for the Franken-heimer-Lewis production as "bogged down in God knows what kind of difficulty, mostly financial." To make matters worse, Columbia Pictures severed relations with both Frankenheimer and Lewis, apparently because the studio had been disappointed in Frankenheimer's recent films.[46]

Then came the news that the British Broadcasting Company was planning a six-part television series, *The Sources of the Nile.* The series, to be narrated by British actor Richard Burton, would come to the United

States after an initial airing in Great Britain. Brodie was at first optimistic that the series would have the salutary effect of stimulating interest in the entire life of the adventurer, Richard Burton, and she hoped that Christopher Ralling, the British producer of *Sources of the Nile* might be interested in a movie project. Attempting to promote this possibility, she urged George Brockway to approach Ralling through Norton representatives in London. But nothing came of this effort, and production of a Richard Burton movie was once more frustrated.[47]

All of her time and energy notwithstanding, Brodie was never able to generate a Richard Burton movie. Having long since signed away her movie rights, she could only stand by as a helpless observer as these rights were passed from studio to studio and producer to producer.[48]

TEACHING AND TENURE AT UCLA

Taking even more time away from Thomas Jefferson were Fawn's teaching and professional responsibilities at UCLA. She had joined the history department in the fall of 1967 as a part-time lecturer. She was ambivalent about her position from the beginning, and after completing her first quarter at UCLA, she was not sure if she wanted to continue. It had been a difficult quarter, and she had doubts about her ability to research, write, and teach all at the same time.[49]

Brodie's dilemma was further complicated in early 1968 when her department chairman asked her to teach full time commencing with the fall 1968 quarter. "I cannot do serious research . . . and teach full time," she lamented to Dale Morgan. "I have no energy for that kind of double regimen—and there aren't enough hours in the week." Nevertheless, Brodie accepted the full-time appointment, partly because she found the prospect of a steady income too tempting to pass up.[50]

Brodie's ambivalence continued. Late in 1968, after completing her first quarter of full-time teaching, she reassessed her position. It was not only difficult to find time to write, but "the simple joys of being a housewife [turned] into onerous chores at the end of a hard day." Although she found her contact with students energizing and her colleagues stimulating, she all but decided to ease out of teaching gracefully.[51]

It was a decision Brodie could not bring herself to carry out. A major inducement to continue teaching was the added income. Even though the Brodies never had cause to worry about money, Fawn was by nature a worrier—especially over money matters, a carryover from her formative years, when her family had struggled through hard times. Other factors made teaching attractive. She liked an audience. She was exhilarated by performing before any group, and lecturing college students filled a strong need. She was also, quite simply, "terribly fond of young people." She took an interest in her students' personal lives, inquiring about their varied activities both within and outside of academia. This—and the opportunity to guide students in their research and writing—appealed to her nurturing tendencies. Despite her own highly opinionated and controversial writings, Fawn was extremely gentle in advising students in historical research. She allowed them great latitude in developing their own ideas and encouraged them to follow their intuition and only then consult with her in evaluating the results.[52]

Still, despite the fulfillment it brought, Fawn found teaching taxing and exhausting. Much of this resulted from her basic nervousness. No matter how many classes she taught or how well she prepared, she never got over a certain amount of stage fright in standing before a group of students. On days she had a seminar to teach, she would get her hair done beforehand, just for added confidence. A former graduate student who considered Brodie a "fantastic teacher" noticed that her hands would always shake. But few others were aware of the nervousness, and Brodie impressed all her students as a "very, very powerful" lecturer; her every presentation was a "major performance," it seemed, and always extremely well prepared.[53]

Weighing the pros and cons, Brodie decided that she could not give up the immense satisfaction she received from teaching, nor was she in a position to give up the institutional support for her research and writing. In the spring of 1971, she asked for promotion in rank from senior lecturer to full professor. She felt she was entitled to this promotion by virtue of her extensive scholarship plus four years of teaching experience. In that time she had developed and taught six different courses in American history, three graduate and three undergraduate. Her publications included three major biographies, two edited book-length works, and numerous articles in both scholarly and popular publications. This record equaled, and in many cases exceeded, that of the vast majority of her history department colleagues.[54]

Initially it appeared that Brodie would have little difficulty in securing promotion. She was "doing a splendid job," according to her immediate supervisor, Eugen Weber, chair of the history department. Letters solicited from Brodie's students were "highly laudatory." Echoing such views were student evaluations independently administered in Brodie's courses. Students in her Civil War and Reconstruction course described her as an enthusiastic lecturer who had a sense of humor and a great command of her material. Students in her American Political Biography course found her interesting and stimulating. However, there were admittedly some students who found her highly opinionated and her classes lacking in open discussion.[55]

Brodie encountered unexpected opposition to promotion from a number of her colleagues. Such opposition focused not on teaching but on other issues. First, there was lingering concern about her nontraditional academic background and training, including the lack of any degree in history. Second, certain department traditionalists discounted Brodie on the grounds that she was a biographer and not a scholar of conventional history; viewing biography as a less-than-legitimate field, they dismissed her as a mere popularizer of history. These same traditionalists were especially doubtful of the scholarly validity of psychobiographical analysis. Certain European specialists found Brodie's work too narrowly limited to the field of American history—ironic as that was, given that her most recent biography was *The Devil Drives*. Finally, opposition was based simply on the fact that she was a woman seeking advancement within an overwhelmingly male-dominated department.[56]

Despite all such opposition, Brodie's promotion petition received initial approval from a UCLA history department ad hoc committee in the spring of 1971; a substantial majority voted in her favor. Brodie's promotion, however, was not yet secure; it required approval by two committees at the next level—specifically, the ad hoc social science division promotion committee and the campus budget committee. At this level, in July 1971, Brodie's opponents prevailed, blocking promotion. Opposition was spearheaded by certain of Brodie's own history department colleagues who were not reconciled to the initial approval granted at the departmental level. The leader of this opposition was Robert Wohl, newly installed as chairman of the history department. As Brodie herself recalled, Wohl justified his action in a vague statement criticizing Brodie's scholarship as limited to personal biography. Without doubt, Wohl was also biased against Brodie because of her avowed liberal views, the department chair being "inclined against liberals," according to at least one fellow faculty member.[57]

Brodie's situation was made worse by her own lack of confidence in the leadership of Wohl. She expressed "moral outrage" at what she saw as a systematic purging of junior faculty hired during the late 1960s and early 1970s but denied tenure and thus terminated. This purge was justified by the chair with the rationale that many of these junior faculty had been hired with undue haste and were not up to the standard deemed worthy of permanent tenured faculty. Although Brodie had been hired during the same period as the junior faculty members now under siege, she was not in danger of being terminated since her position as senior lecturer included a grant of tenure. But Wohl and his allies were determined to deny Brodie promotion to full professor, which implicitly placed her in the same category as the endangered junior faculty.[58]

Brodie reacted to this treatment with a combination of outrage and indignation. The whole affair was "a grave departure from university standards of fairness and equity," she said. Bernard himself was furious at what he perceived as a humiliation of his wife. He talked of confronting those responsible, and he threatened physical violence. "Whom do I confront and hit?" he thundered to several of his close friends in the political science department. The confrontation was a real possibility, given that Bernard's office in the political science department was located in the very same building as the history department.[59]

But cooler heads prevailed. Fawn sought and received support from various allies within the history department, including Profs. John Galbraith, Stanley Wolpert, and Theodore Saloutos. Particularly helpful was Brodie's close friend and colleague, Peter Loewenberg, who, like Brodie, had focused much of his research and writing in the field of psychohistory. More significantly, Brodie gained the support of Chancellor Charles E. Young, the highest administrator on the UCLA campus. She wrote Young a letter in July 1971, protesting what she characterized as her "unjust and prejudiced" treatment and pointing specifically to

Bernard Brodie, ca. 1974, after leaving RAND to join the political science faculty at the University of California, Los Angeles. Courtesy Bruce and Janet Brodie.

Robert Wohl as leader of the action against her. Two months later, Brodie asked for, and was granted, a personal interview with Chancellor Young. Convincing Young of the merits of her case, she gained his support, and in December 1971, the chancellor approved Brodie's promotion to full professor, step I, at an annual nine-month salary of $17,500.[60]

FAMILY AND FRIENDS IN TRANSITION

Meanwhile, important changes were taking place within Fawn Brodie's immediate family. Her oldest son, Dick, focused on graduate studies in English at the University of Stockholm during the period 1968–70. But in mid-1970, for reasons not completely clear, he withdrew from the graduate program and returned to the United States. He lived briefly in Los Angeles, where he had hopes of starting a rock and gem business, but that September, he moved to Salt Lake City, where he had been accepted into the graduate program in English at the University of Utah. At the same time, he considered newspaper journalism and looked at possible career opportunities with the city's largest daily, the *Salt Lake Tribune*. However, by December 1970, he was back in southern California, his mind made up. Music was the field he wanted to pursue, he told his parents; it was a field he'd had an interest in since childhood.[61]

Not surprisingly, Fawn was deeply concerned over Dick's continuing indecision. Worse still, Fawn had difficulty communicating with her son. "I find that everything I say to [Dick] is the wrong thing, and I wish I could discipline myself to say nothing at all," she confessed to Dean Brimhall. "Part of the problem is that I have always known what I wanted for myself . . . and I am impatient with young people who cannot seem to find a direction in their life."[62]

By contrast, her younger son, Bruce, had a clear sense of direction. Immediately after receiving his bachelor's degree from the University of California, Berkeley, in June 1968, he joined Volunteers in Service to America. VISTA, a federal agency established by Pres. Lyndon Johnson as the domestic equivalent of the Peace Corps, provided assistance to Americans living in depressed areas of the United States. Volunteering for a one-year term of service, Bruce was sent to an Appalachian region in West Virginia, where he worked in a local mental health clinic treating alcoholics. With characteristic humor, Fawn described her son's work as "sobering," both for him and for his clients. It is "a totally new world for him," Fawn told Dean Brimhall, "a little bit like being a missionary, except, thank God, he isn't preaching Mormonism."[63]

As Bruce was completing his year of VISTA service in the spring of 1969, he received word of acceptance into graduate school at the University of Chicago, along with news of a fellowship awarded by the psychology department. Fawn was particularly pleased that Bruce had been accepted at Chicago, the institution at which she and Bernard had completed their own graduate studies thirty years earlier. But Bruce's schooling, scheduled to begin in the fall of 1969, was threatened by the draft. Not yet formally enrolled in graduate school, he was classified 1-A, thus subject to immediate induction into the armed forces. This was particularly alarming given continuing American involvement in Vietnam, despite newly elected Pres. Richard Nixon's announced intentions to reduce American military involvement there. This was of no immediate help to Bruce Brodie, who, in May 1969, at the very moment of Richard Nixon's promise to "Vietnamize" the war, was called in by his local draft board.[64]

With the help of family and friends—including a lawyer the Brodies hired to advise their son—Bruce pursued various options for staying out of the military. Initially, he sought an occupational deferment on the basis that his University of Chicago fellowship was being paid for by the U.S. Public Health Service. The fellowship, Bruce reasoned, should entitle him to the same selective service classification accorded U.S. Public Health Service employees, who were exempted as health-care workers. But the Los Angeles draft board denied Bruce such status, classifying him a mere graduate student, subject to immediate induction. The young man then asked to be classified as a conscientious objector, but this request too was denied, for reasons not clear.[65]

Bruce then sought reclassification on the basis of his health—specifically, his hay fever and other allergies. In August 1969 he won a temporary reprieve from the draft by changing his legal residence from Los Angeles to Salt Lake City, which delayed imminent induction for two to six weeks and allowed him time to secure the necessary documentation of his health problems. With Bruce now in Utah, Fawn confessed her sense of moral outrage concerning her son's precarious situation. "I have hated the war for a long time," she wrote Dean Brimhall, "but it never seemed as vile as recently, when the personal threat was so close and so overwhelming." Meanwhile, in Salt Lake City, where doctors looked with greater favor on requests for deferments on the basis of allergies, Bruce was able to secure letters from two different doctors that recommended his classification as 1-Y, a status he ultimately achieved and thus avoided the draft, much to this parents' relief.[66]

Thus Bruce commenced his graduate studies in psychology free of the threat of induction. Meanwhile, he became engaged to Janet Ferrell, a fellow student at the University of California, Berkeley. Janet, whose mother was a native of England and whose father was a Berkeley professor of agricultural economics, had graduated from the university with a bachelor's degree in history. Like Bruce, she had been accepted into graduate school at the University of Chicago, where she planned to pursue a doctorate in history. The young couple was married in August 1970 in a garden ceremony at sundown at the Brodies' Pacific Palisades home. The marriage was performed by a Lutheran minister, in accordance with Janet's wish. Fawn described the occasion as one of the greatest days of her life. Calling it "a very special marriage," she told Dean Brimhall, "I could wish for nothing more than the same kind of blessedness for Dick and Pam."[67]

Meanwhile, the Brodies' youngest child, Pam, also pursued her undergraduate studies at the University of California, Berkeley, receiving a bachelor's degree in anthropology in 1971. During her years at Berkeley, she dated a fellow student, Jonathan Kuntz; in May 1970, some months prior to her brother's wedding, she announced her intentions to marry. In contrast to her feelings about Bruce and Janet's situation, Fawn had reservations about this relationship. Pam had just turned nineteen, and her mother was concerned that she was too young to marry. In addition, Fawn and Bernard were ambivalent about Pam's fiancé. Although Jonathan Kuntz, like Bernard, came from a Jewish background and was well educated, having earned a bachelor's degree in theater arts from UC Berkeley, the Brodies, particularly Bernard, had difficulty accepting him. In Bernard's case, the long-standing bond between father and daughter created a natural barrier to any potential son-in-law, but Bernard found Kuntz less than acceptable for other reasons. Kuntz was short and slight of build, not the all-

American type that Bernard envisioned for his daughter. In addition, Bernard found fault with Kuntz's choice of a career in moviemaking; it was at variance with Bernard's ideal of scholarship within academia. He also had problems with Kuntz's religious beliefs as an orthodox Jew, having long since abandoned his own beliefs. Thus Fawn and Bernard did what they could to discourage the pending marriage, but without much hope.[68]

In the midst of all the wedding talk, Fawn and Bernard Brodie observed a matrimonial milestone of their own—their thirty-fifth wedding anniversary. They celebrated the date in August 1971 with a lawn party, hosting their immediate family and a few close friends. "Except for the fact that we have 3 young adults in the family, plus a new daughter-in-law," Fawn noted, "I feel thirty [years old], and so does Bernard. We are both keeping fitter than before."[69]

Then, in July 1972, at the bride's home in Pacific Palisades, in rites performed by a Reform Jewish rabbi in accordance with the wishes of the groom, Pamela Brodie and Jonathan Kuntz were married.[70]

In addition to the changing situation of Fawn's immediate family, there were changes affecting others close to her. In December 1970 Fawn had received news that Dale Morgan had been diagnosed with terminal cancer. Over the course of some twenty-five years Morgan had played mentor to Fawn, particularly during the 1940s while she worked on *No Man Knows My History*. Since that time, the two had maintained a close friendship that was perpetuated through frequent correspondence and periodic personal contact. Fawn's reaction to Morgan's illness was one of both denial and anger. "I simply refuse to face the fact that your life is in danger," she told him. "You are a great fighter, and have so much to live for," she encouraged, "and I know that [your] indomitable will, will be working in your favor now." She continued:

> Meanwhile I shall pray for you, with every confidence that my prayers, under the circumstances, will be heeded with even more respect than those of the brethren in Salt Lake City. This is a time when, damn it all, a seeker after truth should have a little miracle. Nobody knows your great worth as a scholar and writer better than I do. And nobody knows how much, over the years, I have valued your friendship.[71]

Dale L. Morgan, ca. 1950s, Fawn's good friend and mentor who not only provided significant help on *No Man Knows My History* but who remained close to the author from 1943 until his untimely death in 1971 at age 56. Reprinted by permission, Utah State Historical Society, all rights reserved.

But all of Brodie's determined optimism could not stay the course of the disease. Dale Morgan died on 30 March 1971. He was fifty-six years old.

As if Dale Morgan's death were not enough, Fawn was concurrently forced to cope with the declining health of Dean Brimhall. Brodie had confided her innermost thoughts and feelings to her favorite uncle through a forty-year correspondence, and their closeness was reinforced during Fawn's frequent visits to Utah. When, in February 1971, she had first received word from his doctors that her uncle was suffering from emphysema brought on by his heavy smoking, her reaction was denial, just as it had been upon receiving news of Morgan's illness. "I cannot think of you as ill and unable to roam the mesas and climb in and out of your canyons," she wrote Brimhall. With an air of confidence, she reassured him that she knew several people who suffered from emphysema and had lived with it for years and years.[72]

Fawn now began to work in earnest with her uncle on a major study of the distinctive Indian pictographs in southeastern Utah's scenic canyonlands region, a work based on Brimhall's discovery of extensive archaeological remains and a task that had occupied his major energies for some two decades. To facilitate the publication of what was envisioned as a book-length study, Brodie approached Alfred A. Knopf on her uncle's behalf.[73]

The work was never completed. Brimhall's health continued to worsen over the following year. In April 1972, he was hospitalized for what was diagnosed as pneumonia and malnutrition, and one month later, on 14 May 1972, Dean Brimhall died. Fawn accepted her uncle's death more easily than she had Dale Morgan's a year earlier. After all, her uncle had suffered through a protracted illness—and at eighty-five, he had lived a long, productive life.[74]

COMPLETING THE JEFFERSON BIOGRAPHY

Through all of this, Brodie pushed ahead with Thomas Jefferson. Her return to full-time teaching in the fall of 1971 at the end of her sabbatical meant less time for research and writing. In addition, her promotion to full professor required more departmental committee work, which she detested. Despite such distractions, however, Brodie had the biography three-fourths finished by January 1972. The completion of the work now depended on tying up some loose ends in research. Accordingly, the author traveled east in April to examine a Thomas Jefferson account book at the New York Public Library, filled other holes through that spring, and gave the summer of 1972 to revising and editing. But there were still at least four chapters to be written.[75]

To expedite this process, Fawn applied for, and received, another leave from UCLA for the fall 1972 quarter. She hoped to have a complete first draft by the end of 1972, but loose ends in research and an inordinately slow typist prevented her from meeting this deadline. In mid-December she sent Brockway twenty-five chapters of the projected thirty-two-chapter manuscript, seeking his impressions of what she had completed thus far.[76]

In late December, Brockway responded favorably. Brodie's manuscript was "successful in presenting the man and his times," he said. His only complaint was that the author "had underplayed the Maria Cosway story a little too much." Brockway considered Thomas Jefferson's romantic involvement with Cosway, a married woman, analogous to the Lucy Mercer story involving Franklin D. Roosevelt. "Both stories were more or less widely known," Brockway said, and both had "a taint of sensationalism about them." He wanted "a more complete retelling of the Maria Cosway story." Otherwise, he was satisfied, characterizing Brodie's work "a delight."[77]

Despite Brockway's favorable report, Brodie continued to worry about gaps in her research. She sought information on certain alleged African American descendants of Thomas Jefferson through his purported relationship with Sally Hemings. In this search, she called upon her son Bruce and daughter-in-law Janet, then living in Chicago, to visit the nearby communities of Watseka, Illinois, and Chillicothe, Ohio, where such information reportedly was located.[78]

Brodie now planned to complete the writing of her manuscript by early 1973, though she met constant frustrations in her task. With the end of her one-quarter leave and the resumption of her academic responsibilities at UCLA, there were classes to teach and always the hated committee work. In the final honing of the manuscript she enlisted the editorial services of husband Bernard, who offered numerous suggestions. She also gave copies to several of her psychoanalyst friends and incorporated their suggestions in her revisions. And she sought input from the eminent psychobiographer, Erik Erikson, himself preparing a short volume on Thomas Jefferson.[79]

In early March 1973, Brodie mailed Brockway her complete Jefferson manuscript, some 674 pages long, with 140 more pages of notes. All of this, she told Brockway with wry humor, "goes to show that one can't encompass Jefferson in an afternoon." Brockway responded quickly and enthusiastically, praising Brodie's work as "absolutely brilliant." His own editorial suggestions were slight, focusing mainly on a dozen instances where the author had written unclear sentences and perhaps two dozen instances where he suggested deletions of repetitious passages. Brockway also asked Brodie to remove her psychological analyses of persons other than Jefferson, finding such material superfluous.[80]

After Brockway had finished his reading, he sent Brodie's manuscript on to Thelma Sargent, an in-house copy editor. Sargent was much more critical, finding a lot to question. In one instance, she discovered four or five discrepancies between the way the Madison Hemings story appeared in the main text and in the appendix. Sargent outlined her concerns in an April 1973 in-house memo to Brockway. Worried about the manuscript, she told Brockway that Brodie needed "to do a thorough checking job on names, dates, places, and quotations—the who-what-wheres-whens her argument depends on—before typesetting." Sargent queried numerous discrepancies but was not confident of having caught them all. Sargent noted two other major concerns. The first involved Brodie's case for an affair between Jefferson and Maria Cosway, which Sargent felt did not stand up on the basis of the evidence present. "Doesn't [Brodie] know about making the theory fit the facts instead of trying to explain the facts to fit the theory?" Sargent asked rhetorically. "It's pretty fascinating, like working out a detective story, but she doesn't play fair."[81]

The second specific problem involved Brodie's failure to discuss the Lewis and Clark expedition. According to Sargent, this event "must have meant more to Jefferson than a change of secretaries. He had a strong interest in natural history, and in mountains, rivers and Indians. But there's not a word about it. Instead, we get that same tiresome old duel between Hamilton and Burr that has nothing to do with [Jefferson] at all."[82]

After Sargent finished, Brockway returned the copyedited manuscript to the author. It is not clear if he disclosed to Brodie the copy editor's more probing comments. Brockway called Sargent's efforts "a careful, not to say finicky job," adding, "What you do with the various queries I of course leave to you." Brodie responded, praising the copy editor's skills in uncovering her "fatal weaknesses" at arithmetic and catching other errors that would have been most embarrassing. Though Brodie carefully considered the copy editor's suggestions and made some deletions, she declined to delete the various passages that Sargent characterized as "dubious psychologizing."[83]

Even as the copyediting went on, Brodie was jolted by news that Norman S. Fiering, editor of the *William and Mary Quarterly*, was considering publication of "The Jefferson Scandals," an essay written by the late distinguished Jefferson scholar Douglass Adair, which argued directly against Brodie's assertion that Jefferson had fathered Sally Hemings's children. Adair argued instead that Jefferson's nephews, Peter and Samuel Carr, were the responsible parties. In sending a copy of the Adair essay to George Brockway, Fiering offered Brodie an opportunity to comment on the article, noting that it would be useful to him if she found Adair in error on any fact.[84]

Brodie responded to Fiering through Brockway, curtly dismissing the Adair piece. She noted that an earlier article she had written for *American Heritage*, "The Great Jefferson Taboo," underscored the errors in Adair's arguments and concluded, "If the *American Heritage* article isn't sufficient answer to Adair, then the whole of my book ought to be. But you can be sure that historians will be pointing to the Adair article as the answer to Mrs. Brodie, for all time."[85]

There was a sense of déjà vu in the mounting controversy over Brodie's forthcoming work. "I have seen this before with devout Mormon reactions to my life of Joseph Smith," Brodie wrote Brockway, "And here [with Jefferson] we have a deity as important to many Americans as Joseph Smith is to many Mormons." Then revealing the range of her inner feelings, she declared, "I am prepared for incomprehension as well as controversy. I am prepared for distortion, and am prepared for indignation. But I still think the time is ripe for what I have written, and that in general the response will be favorable, and good. It may even be overwhelmingly enthusiastic."[86]

Brodie did what she could to ensure an enthusiastic response to her book insofar as potential reviewers were concerned, confiding in Brockway, "The three reviewers I most dread are Dumas Malone, Merrill Peterson, and Julian Boyd," all distinguished members of the Jefferson establishment. On the other hand, she felt that

> Denis Brogan, J. H. Plumb, and Max Beloff in England would review it favorably. Among the historians here [in America], I think Winthrop Jordan and Eric McKitrick would be fair and favorable. My hunch is that the best reviews would come from literary critics like Lionel Trilling, Justin Kaplan, and Leon Edel. Robert Coles . . . should do a favorable and sensitive review . . . [and] if Erik Erikson would review it—that of course would be my good fortune.[87]

Brockway immediately sent a memo to the publicity department at W. W. Norton discussing potential reviews of Brodie's book for various newspapers, magazines, and other publications. He characterized her study as "one of the most important" on Norton's fall list but also "most controversial" because it "proved that Jefferson had a mistress in France and that he also had several children by a slave." He warned that there was a big Jefferson industry in this country, with many people anxious to avoid "the besmirching," as he termed it, of Jefferson's name. Brockway continued,

> It is very important, if at all possible, to see that the following be waived off as reviewers: Dumas Malone, Merrill Peterson, and Julian Boyd. On the other hand, it is conceivable that among Englishmen Denis Brogan, J. H. Plumb, and Max Beloff would be likely to approach it with an open mind, and among prominent American historians Winthrop Jordan and Eric McKitrick. The best reviewers might well come from among literary critics like Lionel Trilling, Justin Kaplan, and Leon Edel. Also Robert Coles, since there's quite a bit of psychiatry in the story.[88]

Meanwhile, through the summer and fall of 1973, Brodie confronted the tedious task of preparing her manuscript for publication. She received the page proofs to check in June, and in August came instructions to prepare the index. Suddenly Brodie found herself under added pressure to complete these two tasks even more quickly than first designated, for the biography was chosen as a main selection by the Book-of-the-Month Club; bound books were now needed by mid-September.[89]

After rushing through the page proofs and completing the index, Brodie received the disappointing news that her book would not appear as a Book-of-the Month Club selection until April 1974. Dismayed that her biography would not be available for the Christmas market, she tried to have it moved forward by the BOMC. But she found the club locked into its publication schedule by long-standing commitments to Gore Vidal's *Burr* and to a newly published biography on Benjamin Franklin. Anxious to avoid issuing three books dealing with the same period of American history in successive months, BOMC pushed Brodie's biography to the later spring date, on the basis that it was the last of the books to have been designated as a BOMC selection. As if this were not enough, Brodie received additional bad news that as a result of BOMC's delay, W. W. Norton had decided to postpone its own printing of Thomas Jefferson until January 1974.[90]

Brodie expressed deep disappointment over Norton's decision. She asked if Brockway could not "run off a couple of thousand copies and store them in a closet somewhere, meanwhile distributing some to various scholars asking for their opinions?" The author also argued that this would solve her Christmas gift problem, for she had previously planned to give copies of her book to members of her family and close friends. This would, moreover, provide time to secure blurbs for the dust jacket from early reviews for advertising. But it was not to be: In mid-November Brockway informed Brodie that the books would not be ready until late January.[91]

As it turned out, this last-minute delay was actually in the best interests of both author and publisher. Gilbert Highet of BOMC, assigned to write a piece for the club's newsletter, found time to pick up some typos and misquotations in rereading the page proofs and forwarded to Norton a four-page, single-spaced typewritten list containing the errors. These in turn were sent on to Brodie for her consideration and correction in early December. When Brodie promptly returned the corrections, Brockway assured her that all was in order and that the presses would soon roll.[92]

A POPULAR BUT CONTROVERSIAL BIOGRAPHY

Finally, in February 1974, *Thomas Jefferson: An Intimate History* appeared in bookstores. It was made available to members of the Book-of-the-Month Club in April as its main spring selection. From the onset, Brodie's biography enjoyed great commercial success. In early April the author received the good news that the book's first printing of 20,000 was oversubscribed; the book was well into a second printing, with a third ordered. By July sales of the biography had reached 56,000 and one month later had climbed to over 64,600. Beginning in late spring 1974, *Thomas Jefferson* was on the *New York Times* best-seller list for thirteen weeks. Within the first year of publication, the book made for its author some $200,000. Such overwhelming commercial success exceeded Brodie's wildest fantasies.[93]

Part of the book's success was due to Norton's promotional efforts. In late April the publisher sent Brodie on a publicity trip to New York City and Washington, D.C., where she was interviewed by both the print and

Fawn Brodie in 1974, age fifty-nine, at the time of publication of her fourth biography, *Thomas Jefferson: An Intimate Portrait*. Reprinted by permission, Utah State Historical Society, all rights reserved.

the electronic media. Feature articles appeared in the *Washington Post* and the *New York Post*. In New York City Brodie received national exposure through an interview on NBC's *Today* show. In Washington, Brodie's biography quickly became a topic of comment in elite social-literary circles. It was the focus on conversation at a birthday dinner party given for Ethel Kennedy, the widow of Robert F. Kennedy. And a number of prominent Washingtonians, including David Brinkley and Art Buchwald, were all reportedly deeply engrossed in the biography.[94]

Along with popularity came controversy, most evident in the book reviews. The *New York Times* gave the book two reviews, both in early April 1974 shortly after the book's publication. The first, by noted literary critic Alfred Kazin, was generally favorable, characterizing the biography as "fascinating and responsible . . . except for a few rhetorical exclamations over what Jefferson-on-the-couch really meant to say here and there in the letters." Less positive was in-house *Times* reviewer, Christopher Lehmann-Haupt, who described Brodie's line of reasoning as hard to follow, accusing her of groping for "extremely subtle evidence." He dismissed Brodie's biography as "speculations about Jefferson's private life." At the same time, however, the *New York Times Book Review* staff made Brodie's biography an "Editor's Choice," calling it "a fascinating, and generally convincing, speculative study focusing on Jefferson's inner life, especially his tragic irresolution about slavery." This latter endorsement doubtless helped propel the book onto the *New York Times* best-seller list.[95]

Meanwhile, the noted novelist Larry McMurtry, reviewing Brodie's biography for the *Washington Post*, praised the author for the combination of boldness and tact with which she addressed the central issue of Jefferson's relationship with Sally Hemings. By contrast, distinguished Cornell University historian Michael Kammen, also reviewing this work for the *Washington Post*, lambasted Brodie as little more than "a historical gossip incapable of distinguishing between cause and effect." Also extremely harsh was noted author and syndicated columnist Garry Wills who, in the *New York Review of Books*, assailed Brodie's scholarship. He noted that the author had "managed to write a long and complex study of Jefferson without displaying any acquaintance with eighteenth-century plantation conditions, political thought, literary conventions, or scientific categories—all of which concerned Jefferson." Wills also criticized Brodie for consistently finding double meanings in colonial language and basing her arguments on the present usage of key words.[96]

By contrast, other noted writers praised the biography. Ray Allen Billington, at that time considered the dean of western American historians, found Brodie's biography "thoroughly fascinating, opening vistas into Jefferson's life and thought that were fresh and exciting." Page Smith, himself a Bancroft Prize–winning biographer of John Adams, lauded Brodie for "an extraordinary human drama told with great insight, compassion and literary skill." Justin Kaplan, the noted biographer of Mark Twain, praised Brodie for giving Thomas Jefferson a "human and recognizable dimension" through her "finely-shaded portrait." And Brodie's good friend, Wallace Stegner, a Pulitzer Prize–winning novelist and biographer, praised Brodie's *Thomas Jefferson* as "meticulous history . . . carefully researched, discriminating, and intuitive . . . [and] a powerful and touching portrait." Stegner went on to characterize Brodie's biography as a serious contender for the 1974 Pulitzer Prize in biography, a remarkable statement given that his own recently published biography of Utah-born Bernard De Voto was itself being touted as a Pulitzer Prize contender.[97]

Historians were more mixed in their reactions in reviewing the book in various professional journals. Lois W. Banner, in the *American Historical Review*, conceded Brodie's book to be "a tour de force in the imaginative reconstruction of the historical past," but Banner was critical of the "unrelenting rigor of Brodie's psychologizing" and her "questionable speculations." According to Paul F. Boller, writing in the *Southwest Review*, "Brodie undoubtedly overpsychologizes and occasionally she reads too much between lines and forgets that sometimes, with people, there is less (rather than more) there than meets the eye." But he also credited Brodie with "loosening up" our thinking about the third president by breathing "life and spirit" into a man who had heretofore appeared "cold, aloof, elusive, and impenetrable." Writing in the *William and Mary Quarterly*, Winthrop Jordan, whose own work on early American slavery and Thomas Jefferson, *White over Black*, had so influenced Brodie, was surprisingly negative, accusing the author of bad psychology and noting that on the question of Jefferson's relationship with Sally Hemings, the centerpiece of Brodie's work, he remained "persuaded that it does not much matter."[98]

T. Harry Williams, himself a distinguished biographer, dismissed Brodie's book as "not biography as the art is understood by its better practitioners." Psychological tools, Williams observed, "can be useful to writers of biography and should be employed by those who cherish the art. They must, however, be used with some restraint and recognition of their limitations." Brodie, he concluded, had misused them, and in so doing, "badly set back the calling of psychobiography." Similarly, Bruce Mazlish, like Brodie a recognized psychobiographer, dubbed the book "a disappointment," one that came off as "flat and one-dimensional."[99]

Reactions to Brodie's biography by the three most prominent historians in the Jefferson establishment—namely, Dumas Malone, Merrill Peterson, and Julian Boyd—were predictably negative. Although none formally reviewed the book, each reacted through other venues. Malone, after telling a newspaper interviewer that as a rule he did not discuss "other people's books on Thomas Jefferson," nevertheless described Brodie as a "determined woman [who] runs far beyond the evidence and carries psychological speculation to the point of absurdity. The resulting mish-mash of fact and fiction, surmise and conjecture" he continued, was not history as he understood the term. He also dismissed Brodie's biography as "dirty graffiti" on the monument of Thomas Jefferson. In a similar vein, Merrill Peterson observed that "Brodie has her obsessive theory and she sends it tracking though the evidence, like a hound in pursuit of game . . . [but] in the end nothing is cornered and we are as remote from the truth as when we began." Julian Boyd claimed that "among the whole chorus of adulatory critics of Mrs. Brodie's book not a single Jefferson scholar is to be found."[100]

Despite such intense controversy, or more probably because of it, *Thomas Jefferson: An Intimate History* continued to sell well, going through eight printings by November 1974. A total of eighty thousand books were in print within the first year of publication.[101]

Meanwhile, looking to further capitalize on the success of *Thomas Jefferson*, Brodie pursued the possibility of a movie or television series based on the book. She had actually begun contacting various individuals in the Los Angeles film community in July 1973, some six months before publication. She continued to pursue possible production of a movie or television series into 1974. It seemed a particularly timely project, given the approaching bicentennial. In February, through an agent, she sought to get NBC involved in financing a television series. She also hoped to get British Broadcasting Corporation people involved in the production, feeling that they would do a more faithful and skillful representation of Jefferson's life than American producers. The BBC, she noted, had "a feeling for history and tremendously talented actors." In pursuit of this goal, she traveled to London in April, where she personally met with a group of actors and directors. Director Richard Marquand expressed keen interest in the project. Concurrently, Lamont Johnson, Hollywood filmmaker, neighbor, and good friend of Brodie's, indicated his willingness to work with the BBC group—or independently, depending on financing.[102]

Financing was, in fact, the critical issue. Brodie applied for a grant from the National Endowment for the Humanities in April 1974. In her application, she noted that "the extraordinary drama in Jefferson's life, particularly as developed in my new biography, would make possible a dramatic and faithful portrayal of the man's life which would command a wide audience, not only in the bicentennial year, but for many years to come." Money was no small matter, since the estimated cost to produce each episode ranged from $200,000 to $300,000, placing the entire enterprise in the million-dollar range.[103]

Despite such high production costs, NBC committed itself to a projected Jefferson television miniseries based on Brodie's biography. The network's involvement remained strong throughout 1974 and into 1975. They hoped to have production completed by 1976 in time for the bicentennial. Lamont Johnson, as designated producer, traveled to Virginia, to Monticello, to look into the use of Jefferson's home as a location for filming. But officials in charge at Monticello blocked all access upon learning that Brodie's biography was to be the basis for the screenplay. As a result, the entire production was hopelessly delayed, mired in controversy. When NBC withdrew all support, the project simply died.[104]

Disappointed though she was by the failure of the idea for a television series, Brodie found personal matters of much greater concern. Bernard, who had undergone back surgery in 1963 to relieve chronic back pain, was again suffering. In early March, a neurological surgeon with the University of California Los Angeles Medical Center suggested that Bernard's condition was the early stages of Lou Gehrig's disease. The

Brodies sought other opinions. After further evaluation, two other doctors ruled out Lou Gehrig's disease, much to the couple's relief. Following treatment, Bernard's condition improved to the point that more surgery appeared unnecessary.[105]

But such relief was only temporary and Bernard's back problems continued to grow worse with the deterioration of his disks and the involvement of arthritic nodes on his spine. Ultimately, he was compelled to undergo a second major operation in the fall of 1974. The surgery appeared to go well. But this operation, like the first, brought only temporary relief; it was, in fact, less successful. Bernard continued to teach his classes on the UCLA campus, though he walked bent over in order to alleviate the back pain. At home, he carried on his research and writing in the one-thousand-square-foot study the Brodies had built in 1970 on a small bluff on their Pacific Palisades property, just above the main house. The funds for its construction had come from sale of the film rights to *The Devil Drives*.[106]

In his study, Bernard had completed his last book-length work, *War and Politics*, published in 1973. Reflecting Bernard's continuing interest in American foreign policy, the book was clearly influenced by American failure in the Vietnam War. The author took note of the failure of the United States to deal effectively with the relationship between strategy and politics in the last four wars in which the country had been engaged. Brodie maintained that a military force should always be subservient to a nation's political goals and purposes, a dictum the United States had not followed in prosecuting its wars in the twentieth century, particularly the Vietnam War.[107]

Unfortunately, *War and Politics*, which Bernard regarded as his most important work, was not initially well received, although in time it did gain the recognition it deserved. The book's early failure was due, at least in part, to the fact that neither Bernard nor his ideas were attracting the attention of important foreign policy experts. Contributing to Bernard's diminished visibility since the forties and the fifties was his physical condition, as well as the "writer's block" he had suffered during the 1960s. Removed from the public spotlight, he had lost the prominence he had once enjoyed in the field of American foreign policy.[108]

All of this occurred at the very time that Fawn was becoming increasingly prominent in her own field. Even though Fawn and Bernard excelled in vastly different arenas and were strongly supportive of each other's efforts, there was, nevertheless, an element of rivalry in their relationship. Bernard even exhibited a little jealousy when Fawn's *Thomas Jefferson* made the Book-of-the-Month Club, though he quickly admitted that Fawn had "hit the jackpot" when the biography made it onto the *New York Times* best-seller list. Mostly, Bernard Brodie's jealousy was directed at his wife's feelings for Thomas Jefferson. "God, I'm glad that man is out of the house," he reportedly said upon completion of the biography.[109]

Fawn's deep affection for—even infatuation with—Jefferson had only grown during the course of her research and writing. She found, by her own report, that in her nighttime dreams, she and Jefferson became "man and wife." She related to her subject on even a deeper level: "If I had been [born] a man," she told her son Bruce, "I would have been a man like [Jefferson]."[110]

Hence her mixed feelings upon completing *Thomas Jefferson: An Intimate History.* On the one hand she felt a strong sense of accomplishment: She now had published four major biographies and was recognized as a biographer of national renown. But at the same time, she asked, "Where does one go [after Thomas Jefferson] but down?"[111] In fact, this question would turn out to be prophetic in an ominous way as Fawn Brodie turned her research and writing energies to a fifth and final book—a biography of Richard M. Nixon.

SEVEN

"The Hardest Book"

1974–1981

In a 1978 television documentary focusing on her life and work, Fawn Brodie characterized her current work-in-progress, a biography on Richard M. Nixon, as "the hardest book I'll ever try to write."[1] It was a poignantly accurate prediction: The biography was completed under extremely difficult circumstances, and the author did not live to see it in print. *Richard Nixon: The Shaping of His Character* was published in September 1981, eight months after Brodie's death.

Brodie's interest in Nixon—as with the subjects of her four previous biographies—was rooted in a complex set of factors. Like most Americans during the early 1970s, she viewed the besieged president with morbid fascination as he found himself increasingly ensnarled in Watergate. In her classes at UCLA, she and her students attempted to explain Nixon's behavior to each other. "The students were so keyed up, and I was so keyed up . . . ," Fawn recalled. "How could a Quaker boy have ordered all those bombs dropped on Asia? How could the man who had promised to bring truth to government enter into a situation of telling so many lies?" The questions "multiplied like ripples in a stream." And the seeds for a biography were planted.[2]

As early as October 1972 Brodie expressed both frustration and indignation at the failure of the media to grasp the full magnitude of the Watergate scandal—the efforts of *Washington Post* reporters Bob Woodward and Carl Bernstein notwithstanding. Frustration turned to exasperation in the wake of Nixon's 1972 landslide reelection victory over George McGovern. In November 1973, as the crisis over Watergate deepened, Brodie expressed her feelings in print when her essay, "President Nixon's Distortion of History," was published in the *Los Angeles Times*.[3]

At the same time, Brodie was absorbed by the drama of Watergate as it played out on television, first in the Senate hearings during the spring and summer of 1973 and then in the 1974 House Judiciary Committee hearings—the latter culminating in Nixon's resignation from office in August 1974. All this compelled her to do the book. Fawn was so goal-oriented, recalled daughter Pamela, that after spending a year watching Watergate on television there was nothing for her to do but produce something concrete from it.[4]

Brodie was drawn to Nixon by certain aspects of his personality and behavior. He represented a classic case study of lying versus truth telling—a major theme in all of Brodie's biographies. Particularly fascinating was his seemingly "overwhelming tendency to falsehood." Brodie found Nixon a unique case—a "plain damn liar," standing apart from others who engaged in falsehood, those she categorized as "ignoramuses, self-deluded individuals, or charlatans."[5]

Nixon's sexuality was also of interest to Brodie. She alleged that he had homosexual tendencies, calling this his fatal flaw and a key to his destructive behavior. Nixon's homosexuality, Brodie claimed, was evident in his extremely close relationship with Bebe Rebozo, a Miami business-man of Cuban descent—though because of a lack of definitive evidence, she had to mute her suspicions concerning the nature of the relationship in the final published biography.

Nixon was, without doubt, a fit subject for Brodie's well-honed skills in psychoanalytic methodology. Her psychobiographical approach had evolved, both in intensity and sophistication, through her previous biographies—moving from limited use in the first edition of *No Man Knows My History* to a highly theoretical, almost clinical approach to *Thomas Jefferson: An Intimate History*. Turning now to Nixon, she examined the pathology of his childhood and youth, focusing on what she considered his dysfunctional family, especially his angry and volatile father, whose behavior, Brodie said, warped the young boy's character and led to the development of childhood patterns of deception that carried over into adulthood.[7]

Brodie thoroughly despised Nixon. To her, he was an aberration in the American democratic process; he had tarnished both the American presidency and the Constitution. A repellent fascination developed as she researched his life and work. It was like "examining a rattlesnake," she said.[8]

There were personal factors involved in her abhorrence of this individual. Attempts to draft her son Bruce in 1969 at the height of the Vietnam conflict had occurred during Nixon's presidency—after Nixon had won the 1968 election on his promise to end the war. Yet well into his first term, Nixon kept the nation actively engaged not only in Vietnam but expanded the war into neighboring Cambodia and Laos, clearly symptomatic of deceptive behavior. There was another personal aspect driving Brodie's vendetta. This involved the Watergate break in itself. Nixon operatives had looted the office of Los Angeles psychiatrist Dr. Lewis Fielding, seeking information to discredit Daniel Ellsberg in response to the latter's leaking of the Pentagon Papers. Ellsberg was a close friend and former RAND associate of Bernard Brodie, and Dr. Fielding was Fawn Brodie's longtime personal therapist. Brodie considered Nixon the perpetrator of an assault on her privacy.[9]

Then there was Brodie's personal identification with the man. She detected striking parallels between her own early life and that of the former president—high irony, given her disdain for Nixon. "I am reliving my own life," Brodie said at one point, noting Nixon had been born in a small Quaker town in California in 1913 and she in a small Mormon town in Utah in 1915. Both were debaters in college; both went east to school; he to Duke and she to Chicago. In both cases, the experience "changed our lives—mine for the better—I never went home again." By contrast, Nixon returned home to Whittier, "which he hated, to the practice of law—which he did badly—and corruptly." He "looked to politics for his liberation—the train back east—he lied and defamed to win his liberation." By contrast, Brodie indicated that she won her liberation by marrying Bernard, from whom she learned integrity.[10]

Finally, Brodie was attracted to Nixon by a number of parallels that she detected between the ex-president and Joseph Smith. Both men, she asserted, engaged in numerous lies while purporting to tell the truth. Nixon, like Smith, presented himself as something more than what he was. Nixon denied any wrongdoing relative to Watergate, just as Joseph

Smith denied he had practiced polygamy. Nixon tried to destroy John
Dean, who exposed him, just as the Mormon leader sought to destroy
William Law, who exposed Smith as a polygamist. Nixon promised to
bring truth to government but continued to prevaricate, while Smith,
purportedly in quest of religious truth, lied to cover his actions. Further,
Nixon was an impostor like Joseph Smith, though not the "charming
impostor" the Mormon leader was. And finally, the two men continued
to enjoy the support of their followers, despite the exposure of their
numerous lies and deceptive behavior. Brodie was perplexed by the
intense affection shown Nixon by people who supported him throughout his career, even after Watergate. Similarly, Joseph Smith's integrity
and credibility had been questioned for over a century as a parade of
critics and skeptics exposed his weaknesses. Still, devout rank-and-file
Latter-day Saints retained their affection for Mormonism's founder, and
the church continued to grow, becoming a major American denomination that numbered some 4.5 million members worldwide by the time of
Brodie's death.[11]

IN QUEST OF A NEW TOPIC

Despite all the compelling factors drawing Brodie to Richard Nixon, the
author initially considered other possibilities and focused on other pro-
jects. During a visit to Salt Lake City in late April and early May 1974,
Brodie was urged, once more, by Utah friends and acquaintances to do
a biography of Brigham Young. A definitive life of the Mormon leader
was long overdue. Stanley P. Hirshson's 1969 publication, *The Lion of the
Lord*, had proved shallow and superficial, and Madeline McQuown's long-
expected biography was still not forthcoming.

Everett Cooley, curator of special collections at the University of Utah,
urged Brodie to do Brigham Young, as did Utah writer-scholar Helen Z.
Papanikolas. Cooley described the situation at the Mormon Church
Library-Archives as the ideal climate for doing Mormon research; it was
now under the direction of a new church historian, the professionally
trained academician Leonard J. Arrington, and a policy of remarkably
open access to primary documents and other materials prevailed during
the early 1970s. An added inducement came from prominent Salt Lake

jeweler and philanthropist Obert C. Tanner, who offered Brodie several thousand dollars to undertake the project.[12]

Following her return to California, Brodie consulted with her good friend and colleague, Norris Hundley, a prominent western historian and longtime editor of the *Pacific Historical Review*. After careful consideration, Brodie decided against Brigham Young. She noted that a similar work on Young would mean "a return to old ground . . . and this I am reluctant to do." Nor did she care to "live with [Brigham Young] for five years."[13]

Brodie then gave brief consideration to a biography on a prominent woman. In this, she was encouraged by some of her female students at UCLA. But she was ambivalent, given what she perceived as the limited choices of women as viable subjects. She dismissed all of the wives of American presidents as an "unimpressive, dreary group," with the obvious exceptions of Lady Bird Johnson and Eleanor Roosevelt, the latter of whom Brodie had seriously and briefly considered doing years earlier. Brodie did not consider the American suffragists "terribly exciting" either. She simply could not find a female subject she was willing "to spend five years with."[14]

Meanwhile, Brodie continued to focus on varied matters related to her most recent biography. In May 1974, she negotiated, successfully, with Bantam Press for publication of a paperback edition of *Thomas Jefferson: An Intimate History*. Its total sales far exceeded the earlier hardback edition, going through numerous printings. She was less successful in promoting either a movie or television production based on the biography, though she sold the production rights for several thousand dollars, a windfall that enabled the Brodies to remodel their Pacific Palisades home.[15]

The biography itself continued to attract attention. The author was featured at a National Town Meeting in the Kennedy Center for the Performing Arts in Washington, D.C., where she appeared with noted fellow writer-historian Garry Wills in August 1975. Wills had published an extremely harsh review of Brodie's *Thomas Jefferson* in the *New York Review of Books*. The National Town Meeting was organized to bring the two together to discuss "Jefferson Revisited: How Relevant?" Bernard tried to dissuade Fawn from appearing, feeling that any confrontation with Wills would be "degrading," but she believed that her appearance would afford her the opportunity to answer Wills's earlier attack. She was also urged on by George Brockway, who had motives of his own. The confrontation should stimulate sales of Brodie's biography. Brockway promised to make sufficient copies available in local Washington, D.C., bookstores "for those who want to find out what the shouting is all about."[16]

The 27 August "town meeting" was well attended, with an audience of eight hundred gathering in the Eisenhower Theater of the Kennedy Center to witness the Brodie-Wills confrontation. It was also broadcast live to a national audience over National Public Radio. The discussion focused on the central dilemma: "How could the man who wrote 'all men are created equal' have been a slaveholder?" The predictable antagonism between Brodie and Wills colored the entire proceeding. Brodie could hardly contain her outrage at Wills's remark that Jefferson treated Sally Hemings "as he would a healthy prostitute." She denounced this "denigration of Jefferson." Wills countered, attacking both Brodie and her book: "I'm afraid that Professor Brodie, despite her estimable qualities," Wills said, "is the worst thing to happen to Jefferson since James Callender"—the latter the pamphleteer who first alleged a Jefferson-Hemings liaison in 1802.[17]

Following this "scrappy debate," Brodie characterized Wills as a "very opinionated young man," who "simply doesn't know the Jefferson literature." Wills was not even a historian, she added, but "a classics scholar turned free-lancer. He writes about a great many things and he does not do his homework."[18]

Six months later, Brodie appeared in a second public forum, this one decidedly nonconfrontational. Before the American Bar Foundation's annual meeting of the fellows in Philadelphia in February 1976, Brodie spoke on "Thomas Jefferson the Lawyer." She took particular pride in this presentation, given both the place and time—the cradle of American Independence during the bicentennial.[19]

Brodie also pursued further research on Thomas Jefferson, focusing now on his alleged black descendants. She eventually found what she characterized as "exciting new data about the heirs of Eston and Madison Hemings," supposed black offspring of Jefferson. She claimed to have unearthed a direct family link to Charles G. Dawes, vice-president under Calvin Coolidge, and she wrote an essay incorporating her new data, including four never-before-published photographs of four Jefferson grandchildren. The results were published in the October 1976 issue of *American Heritage* under the title, "Thomas Jefferson's Unknown Grand-children: A Study in Historical Silences." Following publication, Brodie gave serious thought to a book-length study on this same topic, and she continued to collect material on Jefferson's varied descendants. But she abandoned the idea after George Brockway reacted lukewarmly to the proposal.[20]

CONFRONTING RICHARD NIXON

By this time Brodie was directing her major attention to Richard Nixon. As early as April 1974, barely two months following publication of *Thomas Jefferson*, she indicated interest in the besieged president. This early research was prompted by an invitation to speak to the Friends of the University of Utah Libraries in Salt Lake City the following October.[21]

Brodie's presentation, "A Judgment on Nixon: The Historical Hazard," was given to a standing-room-only crowd in the fine arts auditorium at the University of Utah. Revealing her own fascination for the recently resigned president, Brodie warned her audience that a judgment of Nixon presented many hazards to historians. "Will Nixon be rated as the worst of our presidents, or the most paranoid?" she asked rhetorically. "Or will he emerge as a genuinely tragic man who went from poverty to the Oval office to a national nightmare?" Brodie admitted that these were difficult-to-answer questions. She noted that while the ex-president was a very private man, his feelings showed through in his public statements. For example, Nixon warned in his first book, *Six Crises*, that "the informer destroys himself," but Brodie predicted that Nixon would go down "as one of the great informers of all time."

Nixon was notorious for his slips of the tongue, Brodie continued. These slips happened because he was always so tense, and they provided clues as to what was troubling him. Historians "will have to learn to read some of Mr. Nixon's statements backwards," she stated, "such as his remark in his resignation speech that, 'I leave with no bitterness.'" Alluding to what she perceived as Nixon's paranoia, Brodie continued that the recently resigned president was fearful that "history will hang and blacken him for generations."[22]

Despite her fascination, Brodie was initially ambivalent about doing a major work on Nixon. In August 1974 she issued a disclaimer to George Brockway about a book-length biography, stating her intention to write a short essay on Nixon as part of a larger work on the "political hero" in America. Other individuals to be included were Robert E. Lee, Abraham Lincoln, and Thomas Jefferson. She was granted a sabbatical from UCLA to work on such a volume during the 1974–75 academic year. For this volume, Brodie drew inspiration from earlier studies written on political heroes by Dixon Wecter and Sidney Hook.[23]

But by October 1974 Brodie had changed her mind and was toying with the idea of a book-length biography of Nixon alone. "I find myself unable to do research about anyone else," she told George Brockway. She then outlined her basic thesis: She intended to focus on Nixon's youth and early years as a lawyer; she would deal with his "sainted" mother and "punishing" father, both of whom she saw "responsible for his predilection for lying."[24]

Brodie encountered a mixed response—and not just from Brockway. Bernard was strongly opposed. Doing Richard Nixon, he said, was a work utterly unworthy of Fawn's time, talents, and energy. Brockway himself was less than enthusiastic. The editor understood Brodie's obsession with Nixon and agreed that there was a pathology crying out for analysis. From a hard-boiled business perspective, however, he wondered if there would be a market for such a work. Given the recent success of *Thomas Jefferson*, he conceded "that any big book on any big subject by Fawn Brodie is going to get taken seriously" and further conceded that a biography of Nixon would probably be better received than a collection of studies of heroes and antiheroes, as originally proposed by Brodie. If she decided to do Nixon, he advised, the book "should be a big one," one that by the end the reader could say, "Well, I don't have to read about that son-of-a-bitch ever again." She had to decide, he said, if she could "stand living with Nixon" for the five or six years it would take to complete such a book.[25]

Despite all the potential pitfalls, Brodie pushed ahead. In November, she informed Brockway of her intention to use her sabbatical during the winter of 1975 to do "some research in the Whittier area on Nixon's childhood." There, in the Whittier College library, she discovered a marvelous archive on Nixon's prepolitical activities. Just months later, Brodie started interviewing various individuals who knew and had interacted with Nixon during his formative years and throughout his political career. She started with one of Nixon's aunts and Jack Anderson, a syndicated columnist. Interviews were terribly time-consuming when compared with library or archival research, Brodie decided, but they were also "great fun."[26]

As her interviews expanded to take her all over the country—Richard Nixon "quite literally, carried me off and changed the course of my life," the author said—Brodie decided to resign from her position at UCLA, effective the end of the 1976–77 academic year. In the meantime, she began the task of reviewing some four hundred oral interviews previously conducted by other scholars and available in the oral history collection at nearby California State University, Fullerton. She herself would interview one hundred and fifty individuals during the period from 1975 to 1980. Among the most noteworthy of these were onetime counsel John Dean; former California governor Pat Brown; onetime California lieutenant governor and former cabinet member Robert Finch; former U.S. congressman Jerry Voorhis, whom Nixon defeated in his first political contest in 1946; and Nixon's first girlfriend, Ola Welch Jobe.[27]

Through oral interviews Brodie sought psychiatric insight into what she perceived as the pathology of Richard Nixon's character, particularly his sexuality. She interviewed Dr. Joelyn West, head of the UCLA Neuropsychiatric Institute, attempting to probe rumors of alleged Nixon's homosexuality. West told Brodie that Nixon never "performed an overt homosexual act, save maybe once or twice in adolescence." As for Nixon and Bebe Rebozo, West saw no evidence of a homosexual relationship, characterizing their interactions as platonic and symbiotic. Rebozo was simply a good friend with whom Nixon felt comfortable, and the relationship provided the president a needed escape from the stress of office, West said. Rebozo, in turn, found fulfillment in keeping company with this powerful man of affairs.[28]

Brodie, however, remained unconvinced and continued to probe the issue of Nixon's alleged homosexual behavior with a second therapist, Dr. Arnold Hutschnecker, a psychoanalytic internist with special expertise in psychosomatic illness. In the 1950s Hutschnecker had actually treated then-Vice-President Nixon for stress. Brodie interviewed Hutschnecker on two different occasions—first in November 1976 and a year later in October 1977. Brodie questioned Hutschnecker about the impact of

Nixon's troubled relationship with his father. She also asked Hutschnecker point-blank about gossip surrounding the Nixon-Rebozo liaison. The therapist, Brodie reported, said, quite simply, "I cannot help you on that"—but , she hastened to note, he did not deny it.[29]

In a second interview with Hutschnecker, Brodie again questioned him on Nixon's homosexuality. Hutschnecker expressed skepticism about this line of questioning. Such inquiries, he said, were fraught with hazards; he warned "against pat formulae," noting that solid evidence was essential for any assertions made concerning sexuality. But he conceded that Nixon's paranoia could be rooted in "latent as well as overt homosexual problems." Although Brodie repeatedly questioned the therapist about Nixon's relationship with Rebozo, Hutschnecker would say nothing, only that he would advise her to rely on direct quotes, if she did pursue the topic further, allowing the reader to make up his or her own mind.[30]

Brodie actually attempted to set up a interview with the ex-president himself. Initially she tried to utilize Hutschnecker as in intermediary. Failing this, she wrote Nixon directly in January 1978, describing her work on what she hoped would be "a compassionate and accurate study, if not of your whole life, at least of your early years." She made a simple appeal: She was having difficulties, she said, in resolving numerous contradictions about his early years. "Could you find time to give me an hour, just to resolve some of the major problems?" she asked. Nixon made no response to the letter.[31]

Brodie was similarly unsuccessful in interviewing Henry Kissinger, even though both she and her husband knew the former national security advisor and secretary of state on a first-name basis. In a February 1978 letter to Kissinger, she posed a number of penetrating questions she wished to pursue in a possible interview. Kissinger refused the invitation, putting Brodie off with a short, curt reply, noting that the present spate of revelations about Nixon reinforced his own "aversion to discussing things like this." He "would be delighted to see" both Fawn and Bernard again, he said, "but let's find something else to talk about."[32]

Despite her failure to gain interviews with either Kissinger or the former president, Brodie received encouragement from other prominent individuals with whom she corresponded on a first-name basis: journalists James Reston, Jim Bishop, and Bob Woodward; fellow writers

Wallace Stegner and Irving Wallace; and onetime director of the CIA, Stansfield Turner. Writing James Reston in June 1977, Brodie confessed that there were times when she felt oppressed by the Richard Nixon project "and wish to God I'd never started it," noting that she had never felt that way with Thomas Jefferson.[33]

Such doubts notwithstanding, Brodie pushed ahead and by August 1977 was into the actual writing. It was then that she advised Brockway, "The book is likely to be a big one, as you once recommended. You may remember telling [me] that if I must do this book let it be so big and so conclusive that anyone reading it will never have to read about the son-of-a-bitch again. That's presently my ambition."[34]

Two months later, in October, she submitted a draft of the first ten chapters to Brockway. In describing the basic structure of her work, Brodie indicated that it was not "a conventional birth to death biography" but a work of biographical analysis that did "a lot of bouncing back and forth from childhood to the presidency." The emphasis would be on connections and interrelationships. She indicated her intention "to get at the genesis of his lying, his manipulation," and his "deep, dark rage." She claimed to have unearthed information "that illuminated the beginning of . . . his trickery," along with "evidence that throws light on his uncertainty about his masculinity." As to what she hoped to do in subsequent chapters,

> I hope to explore the major paradoxes of his life as they continue from his childhood through the presidency and into the exile years. Among other things I hope to explain is how it happened that a good Quaker boy ended up decorating the Oval Office with 307 battle flags, proclaimed "Amnesty, Never!" [for Vietnam War draft resisters], and ordered more bombs dropped than any man in history.[35]

Brockway was extremely impressed with what Brodie submitted. Her manuscript was "marvelous. It's full of fascinating stuff of a sort I never dreamt existed." He found it "full of fascinating people," slyly adding that "snakes are fascinating, too." He offered the author a contract calling for an impressive seventy-five thousand dollar advance. Brodie's ability to command such an advance undoubtedly resulted from the commercial

success of *Thomas Jefferson.* But the author had also entered into negotiations with Asbel Green at Alfred A. Knopf, who offered her a sixty thousand
dollar advance. Brodie shrewdly played Knopf off against Norton, probably
never intending to go with Knopf and signing with Norton in November
of 1977.[36]

In addition to the research and writing she was doing during this
period, Brodie also addressed several professional audiences, testing her
preliminary findings. In October 1977 she delivered "Nixon, the Child
in the Man" to the San Francisco Psychoanalytic Institute. Later that
month, she gave this same address at the Western History Association
annual meeting in Portland, Oregon, in response to an invitation by that
organization's president, W. Turrentine Jackson. Her less-than-flattering
presentation of Nixon, focusing on the ex-president's childhood traumas,
was provocative, and it generated challenges from certain politically
conservative members of the WHA.[37]

FAMILY CONCERNS AND BERNARD'S CANCER

Notwithstanding the time and energy spent on Richard Nixon, Brodie
was also involved with her family and related activities. In March 1974,
she and Bernard spend ten days in Israel. Bernard had been invited to
participate in the opening of the Leonard Davis Institute of International
Relations at the University of Jerusalem. During the visit, the Brodies
managed to see a great deal of the country and interact with its people.
The effects of the Yom Kippur War were evident everywhere, but both
Fawn and Bernard were impressed with the resilience of the young
Israelis and with their determination to make necessary changes in
political outlook and institutions. The couple traveled abroad again the
following year, this time to Greece, where Fawn developed a particular
fondness for the people, "the best hosts in Europe." Greece itself she
found romantic and fun.[38]

As Fawn approached her sixtieth birthday, in September 1975, she and
Bernard observed a major milestone with the birth of their first grand-
child, Jedediah, born to Bruce and Janet on 22 July 1975. A second
milestone came one year later with Fawn and Bernard's fortieth wedding
anniversary. The Brodies celebrated at their Pacific Palisades home,

inviting forty of their closest friends and family, including Fawn's three sisters and her brother.[39]

It was a time for reflection concerning a marriage that had survived numerous difficulties. The Brodies shared with guests recollections of family opposition, on both sides, to the improbable match of Fawn, the onetime Mormon from rural Utah, and Bernard, the son of Chicago Jewish immigrants. Fawn remembered enduring more abuse from certain members of the extended McKay family for marrying a Jew than for writing *No Man Knows My History*. She recalled that immediately following their marriage some of her good Mormon relatives told Fawn's mother, who had opposed the match, not to worry—that the marriage was doomed to inevitable failure and that Fawn would ultimately find "a good Mormon boy."[40]

But the match had survived. It was "not an easy marriage": the couple frequently aired their disagreements openly in front of family and friends. Bernard could be crotchety and irritable; he would sometimes complain in front of their guests about the food Fawn served at dinner parties the couple hosted. And he flirted with other women, which was a continuing source of tension and of earlier marital difficulties. But such problems were minor given the overall strength of their marriage—a mutually supportive relationship that had not only endured but appeared to grow stronger with the passage of time. Theirs was an intense relationship, characterized by strong bonds and extremely rewarding to both partners.[41]

The strength of their devotion was evident in Fawn's reaction to news that came in November 1977 that Bernard had cancer. This was a particularly bitter turn of events. Bernard, like Fawn, had just retired from UCLA the previous June, and, like Fawn, he had planned to focus his creative energies on research and writing. He was interested in Carl von Clausewitz, the German military strategist who had been a major focus in his recently published *War and Politics*, and he planned to edit a number of von Clausewitz's writings. He was also urged by the University of Indiana Press to revise and update *From Crossbow to H-Bomb*, the short history of weapons and tactics of warfare that he and Fawn had jointly written in Paris some fifteen years earlier. Beyond that, he had intended to enjoy time riding "Freckles," a Tennessee walker he had recently purchased, on the trails through the nearby Santa Monica Mountains, in an area just above the Brodies' Pacific Palisades home.[42]

Fawn reacted with frantic anxiety upon first hearing the diagnosis of malignancy in Bernard's sinus and lymph glands. Unable to think of anything other then her husband's condition, she stopped all work on Richard Nixon. She informed George Brockway of the situation and promised to try to get back to Nixon after the first of the year. "That son of a bitch can wait," she told her editor.[43]

Initially, Bernard responded well to chemotherapy treatment. His condition was so improved by early December that Fawn optimistically predicted a great Christmas for the Brodie family. By early January 1978, he was almost back to normal though there was some huskiness in his voice and he experienced exhaustion from chemotherapy.[44]

This improvement in Bernard's condition enabled Fawn to return to Richard Nixon in April 1978. By this time, she was examining Nixon's role relative to the Alger Hiss case, noting that Allen Weinstein's recently published *Perjury: The Hiss-Chambers Case*, which she characterized as a marvelous piece of detective work, greatly simplified her own work. Even though Weinstein's work vindicated Nixon in the Hiss affair, Brodie's disdain for the ex-president remained undiminished, and she had to question her own efforts: "Does a scoundrel deserve all this effort?" she asked. "I wonder." Bernard's improvement also prompted plans for a visit to Japan in June; both Brodies had been invited to lecture at Japan's National Defense Academy. Fawn looked forward to the trip, intending to make it a vacation even though it meant having to prepare and deliver twelve lectures.[45]

In the end, the Brodies were forced to cancel their Japanese journey. Bernard's lymphoma returned, despite six months of chemotherapy and one month of radiation treatments. To make matters worse, the lymphoma was causing other physical problems and Bernard became bedridden. "I am playing nurse," Fawn told Brockway, "resenting it—but not too badly, I think." She continued to push ahead with her writing but temporarily stopped all interviewing. With no little irony, Fawn found "working with Nixon . . . very therapeutic" in helping her to cope. But she was "terribly tired" of both Bernard's illness and the depression that beset her because of the situation.[46] Undoubtedly aggravating her depression were vivid reminders of her mother's similar situation years earlier in looking after her own sick husband.

Fawn continued to express optimism, even when Bernard's condition worsened to the point of requiring hospitalization in late July 1978. It was merely "a bad time," she said, partly because of ineptness in his initial diagnosis. In early August he was given radiation treatments on his spine where the original cancerous lesion was belatedly located, lending hope for remission. He recovered the use of his left leg and was able to walk with a cane and some help.[47]

Improvements were short-lived, however, and Bernard's condition deteriorated. By late August there was no real hope for remission, let alone recovery. By late October, he was paralyzed from the waist down and was experiencing weakness in his arms and hands. He tried his best to hide his discomfort and despair from Fawn and other family members, but it was difficult for him. He hated the idea of dying and could not even talk about it until the final week of his life—by which time he was so crippled and weak that he actually welcomed the thought of escape. His only consolation seemed to come from directing the planting of daffodil bulbs and lilies in his beloved garden—and from listening to music, in particular, to Richard Strauss's "Death and Transfiguration," which he played over and over again. He refused to eat or to take medication, though at the end he begged for chemotherapy in the forlorn hope for recovery.[48]

Fawn had difficulty in coping during the final days. "We both felt terribly cheated . . . there were times of black despair," she confided to friends.[49] On 24 November 1978, one day after Thanksgiving, Bernard Brodie died. He was sixty-eight years old.

The loss deeply affected Fawn. She entered into a depression from which she would never really emerge. "I am in a quandary," she confessed to her older sister, Flora. "I don't have Bernard to help me." There was also a lot of anger involved in her sense of helplessness. How could "someone as wonderful . . . productive, kind, and good [as Bernard] . . . die," she wondered, while "a son of a bitch like Richard Nixon [is] still . . . alive." She found the loss insupportable. "I didn't know how much I depended on him," she admitted to fellow historian Jan Shipps. "Ours was a very special marriage, with sharing on every level." In comparing the loss of Bernard with that of her parents years earlier, she found Bernard's death infinitely more difficult to accept. "Every now and then I dream most vividly that Bernard is back walking with me, or eating in a Paris restaurant, or driving somewhere," Fawn told good friends. "Such dreams shake me, upon waking. But I would rather have them than not."[50]

To George Brockway, on whom she became increasingly dependent for moral support, Fawn mused that although she had mourned Bernard's death in advance, it was no real preparation for his loss. "The loneliness . . . is as evil as I feared it would be," she said, and she then foresaw its impact on her work: "I will never write as well without him, or with as much zest." The sense of loss brought with it a distaste for the whole Nixon project. "I find it very difficult to get back to work in Nixon," she confessed, "whose life at the moment seems like a total obscenity." But she promised Brockway that she would resume work on the biography. She felt bound by her commitment to Norton—and by Bernard's insistence that she complete it.[51]

There were other worries involving immediate family during this extremely difficult time. In 1977 daughter Pam separated from, and ultimately divorced, Jonathan Kuntz. The couple had faced difficulty from the very beginning of their relationship, including initial opposition from Fawn and Bernard. Kuntz proved so domineering that Fawn actually rejoiced when Pam decided to leave him. Undue complications were avoided in the final divorce settlement because the couple had no children. The twenty-six-year-old divorcée returned to Pacific Palisades, moving into her father's oversized study next to the Brodie home and turning it into an apartment. Fawn enjoyed having her daughter close by, finding her "good company." Returning to school, Pam entered an environmental studies program at UCLA, and after completing her studies in 1979, found employment with the Sierra Club, working in Los Angeles while continuing to live in Pacific Palisades.[52]

The situation of Fawn's oldest son, Richard, by this time in his midthirties, was more complicated. Still looking into various career options, Dick announced his intention to return to college in March 1977. He enrolled at UCLA, majoring in art history. But within a year, he turned his creative energies to painting, returning to an avocation in which he had shown talent during the late 1960s. Fawn supported and encouraged her son, taking motherly pride in his artwork.[53]

Dick's relationship with his father, however, was much more difficult, involving conflict stemming from Dick's continued difficulty in finding a profession Bernard deemed worthy of his abilities. There were bitter confrontations between the two, mostly verbal, even shouting on occasion. Fawn was upset by the tension caused by the father-son conflict and was relieved by the reconciliation evident between the two at the time of Bernard's death.[54]

Meanwhile, the Brodies' younger son, Bruce, secured employment in Boston as a clinical psychologist following completion of his doctorate at the University of Chicago. At the same time, his wife, Janet, completed a doctorate in history from that same institution, writing a dissertation on the history of birth control in America. Bruce and Janet seemed content living in Massachusetts, despite the distance from both of their families on the West Coast. When they began talking of buying a home in Weston, a suburb of Boston, Fawn had mixed feelings, having hoped that Bruce and Janet would soon settle in California. Perhaps, she lamented, she should have known "they would eventually lose their hearts to New England as we once did."[55]

POLITICS, THE MORMONS, AND THOMAS JEFFERSON

Fawn had concerns outside the family through the late seventies, some of them political. As a Democrat, she applauded the 1976 election of Jimmy Carter over incumbent Gerald R. Ford for the presidency. And she viewed with personal satisfaction the decision of the newly elected president and wife, Rosalynn, to send their eight-year-old daughter, Amy, to the Thaddeus Stevens Elementary School, an integrated public school in the heart of Washington, D.C. This prompted Brodie to write a short article entitled "The Hero of Amy's School" in which she stated that Stevens, "the club-footed old 'Father of Reconstruction'" for whom the school was named, would have gained a "certain sardonic satisfaction . . . to see the enrollment there of Amy Carter, daughter of a Georgia planter and the President of the United States." Brodie's piece was initially published in the *Los Angeles Times* in late 1976 and reprinted in at least two other periodicals. She sent the essay and a copy of *Thaddeus Stevens: Scourge of the South* to Amy, a gesture that earned the author a personal thank-you letter from Amy's mother, the new first lady.[56]

Brodie, however, garnered less favorable reaction—and from a wider public—to a second article with political overtones. Entitled "Hidden Presidents" and appearing in *Harper's* in April 1977, the essay evaluated the memoirs of certain past presidents, from Thomas Jefferson through Richard Nixon, looking for what the author characterized as involuntary truths—examples of the use of nuance, omission, and self-concealment in efforts to reconstitute a damaged reputation.[57]

The essay generated a minor firestorm in suggesting that Lyndon Johnson's writings as vice-president betrayed an "unconscious death wish" directed toward then-president John Kennedy. Influential Democrats associated with both former presidents—namely, the assassinated president's mother, Rose Kennedy; his widow, Jacqueline Kennedy; and the advisor to both presidents, Kenneth P. O'Donnell—were all upset. Finding fault with Brodie's assertion, O'Donnell stated that Kennedy and Johnson "were friends politically and socially." In response, Brodie discounted the outcries as evidence of the resistance to the fundamental idea that "hatred and love can be felt simultaneously between political opponents." She also asserted that what the article was speaking to was ambivalence, not hatred.[58]

Brodie manifested her own particular ambivalence in a different venue—the Utah Mormon environment. Brodie returned to her native state on a regular basis, at least once a year, to visit family and friends and to address various professional and academic groups—the latter with increasing frequency during the 1970s. In June 1978, Fawn was in Salt Lake City at the invitation of the University of Utah to accept honorary membership in Phi Beta Kappa. As luck would have it, she was in Utah at the very moment the Mormon Church announced the revelation mandating an end to its long-standing ban on ordained black males to the priesthood. As a longtime critic of the practice, Brodie was ecstatic at the news: "It was a great day to be [in Salt Lake]," she said.[59]

Later that same year, she was in Utah again, this time at the invitation of the Friends of the Weber County Library Association. This was Brodie's first opportunity to speak in Ogden since moving away in the 1930s, and she accepted the invitation with great pleasure. "I spent many hours in the Ogden Public library when I was going to Weber High School and Weber College and I have very happy memories of the place, and friends I made while studying there," she recalled.[60]

Union Station in downtown Ogden, where Brodie delivered the speech, also evoked vivid memories. She found it extraordinary to be back in the recently refurbished depot "so familiar to me when . . . I was saying goodbye" before going off to Chicago in 1935. In the speech itself, "Richard Nixon: The Child in the Man," delivered to an audience of nearly nine hundred, Brodie put aside all pleasantries and expressed her disdain for the former president. She characterized him as an individual who "went up the walls of life with his claws—lying, manipulating and benefitting by the misfortunes of others to become the most damaging President the country has ever had."[61]

The 1978 visit to Ogden's historic Union Station was not the first, nor the last, opportunity for Brodie to reflect nostalgically on her youth. Some three years earlier, in November 1975, she had been interviewed by Shirley Stephenson of the Fullerton State University Oral History Center, an institution whose interest in Brodie was prompted by the author's extensive use of its large Richard Nixon oral interview collection. In a thorough, wide-ranging interview, a portion of which was subsequently published in *Dialogue: A Journal of Mormon Thought*, Brodie provided significant information on her personal and professional activities, past and present. She also provided illuminating insights into her research methodology, philosophy of history, and motives behind the writing of each of her four published biographies.[62]

A year and a half later, Brodie allowed herself to be interviewed once more, this time by Judy Hallet, a reporter for Salt Lake City television station, KUTV. The March 1977 interview, while not as extensive as that conducted by Fullerton State University, received greater exposure. It was broadcast as a segment on *Extra*, KUTV's newsmagazine show on 8 March 1978, reaching a large audience of television viewers throughout the Mormon-dominated Great Basin. With her audience clearly in mind, Brodie discussed in some detail her Mormon background, including the reaction of her family to the publication of *No Man Knows My History* some thirty years earlier. Particularly illuminating were the author's frank insights concerning her father's difficult position relative to the biography, a topic she had never discussed publicly.[63]

On a third occasion, Brodie chose to reminisce, in some detail, about her youth and family to yet another Utah audience. In March 1979 she spoke to the annual convention of the Utah Library Association meeting in Salt Lake City, discussing what she described as "the libraries of my life." Brodie confessed that libraries taught her about deceit, treachery, and illicit love, which she knew nothing about in her very sheltered life growing up in Huntsville. She also described how various libraries had provided invaluable information for the books she wrote. With her Utah audience clearly in mind, she focused most of her speech on her controversial *No Man Knows My History*, describing how information from various libraries had aided her in the process of research and writing. Describing the reactions to McKay family members to her work, Brodie frankly recalled her 1943 visit to the Mormon Church archives, including her acrimonious encounter with uncle David O. McKay.[64]

The latter incident was immediately picked up by the *Salt Lake Tribune*, which quoted Brodie as saying, "This caused a [McKay] family fight." Dismayed, Brodie fired off a letter to the newspaper's editor. The phrase, "a family fight," she said, was "an invention of the *Tribune* reporter." Even so, she privately blamed herself for the unwanted publicity. It was a "mistake [to speak] autobiographically," she realized belatedly, instead of discussing her research on Nixon, and she vowed never to talk about herself in public again.[65] The incident illustrated the paradox of a woman who was reluctant to disclose details of her own personal life yet as a biographer was more than willing to expose the most intimate side of her subjects.

This resolve not to speak of personal matters publicly did not prevent Brodie from speaking out on various controversial issues involving Mormonism. She took an active interest in the status of Mormon women—an increasingly provocative topic by the late 1970s. In reviewing Marilyn Warenski's study, *Patriarchs and Politics: The Plight of the Mormon Woman*, for the *Los Angeles Times* in November 1978, Brodie denounced the "obstructionist techniques" used by Latter-day Saint officials to block ratification of the Equal Rights Amendment. She found it ironic that the current Mormon president, Spencer W. Kimball, permitted black males through revelation to hold the Mormon priesthood while prohibiting similar offices to women.[66]

Brodie's interest in the status of Mormon women was further piqued by the church's treatment of dissident Sonia Johnson for her outspoken support of the Equal Rights Amendment. A measure calling for legal equality of the sexes, the ERA had enjoyed initial broad support from both Democrats and Republicans. It was overwhelmingly approved by both houses of Congress in 1917 and promptly moved on to the states for ratification. But by the late 1970s, it had run into stiff opposition, primarily from conservative Christians, including Latter-day Saints, who saw in its vague wording an implicit threat to the traditional family. Finding Johnson's outspoken, aggressive pro-ERA stance offensive, Mormon officials excommunicated her, a drastic action that received as much media attention, if not more than, Brodie's own celebrated excommunication some thirty years earlier. When the two women actually met shortly after Johnson's excommunication, Brodie reportedly remarked, "I think you [have] usurped my place as the leading female Judas Iscariot [within Mormondom]."[67]

Besides her interest in these Mormon issues, Brodie remained actively interested in Thomas Jefferson. She continued to pursue the idea of a play, movie, or television production based on her biography, and in February 1977, she approached Jane Fonda, whom she had met previously, with a proposal. Brodie envisioned the actress's father, Henry Fonda, playing Thomas Jefferson, with Jane herself taking on the multiple roles of all of the major women in Jefferson's life—his mother, his wife, Maria Cosway, and Sally Hemings, and his daughters Martha and Polly. Brodie suggested that Jane could also perhaps play the role of Abigail Adams. The frame of the storyline would be Jefferson as an old man remembering—with the women appearing and disappearing. The emphasis would be on the heart of Jefferson rather than on his intellect. "Only an actress of your talent and versatility could play so many roles," Brodie told Fonda. But Fonda did not share Brodie's vision or her enthusiasm, and she politely responded that because of her busy schedule she could not "even consider undertaking what would be a major commitment." The actress also saw the problems inherent in herself playing mother, wife, and mistress to her father as Thomas Jefferson.[68]

The idea of a Thomas Jefferson production, however, was revisited some two years later—this time *not* at the instigation of Fawn Brodie, although she found herself involved. The 1979 proposal promoted by Warner Brothers envisioned a four-part television miniseries for CBS, based not on Brodie's *Thomas Jefferson* but on black writer Barbara Chase-Riboud's recently published novel, *Sally Hemings*. Although *Sally Hemings* was a work of fiction, Chase-Riboud confessed to being inspired and influenced by Brodie's earlier *Thomas Jefferson.*[69]

Brodie herself was approached by CBS to serve as a consultant. She had decidedly mixed feelings. On the positive side, she saw her direct involvement as providing an opportunity to ensure accuracy in the overall production. There was, moreover, the potential of vast new sales for her *Thomas Jefferson* as a result of such a television series. But she worried about her role and rights as a historical advisor. She was anxious that the production be "done with delicacy, restraint, and good taste, understated rather than overstated. The story in its essence is dramatic enough without spelling it all out in Jefferson's bed." She was particularly concerned about the novel from which the screenplay would be drawn. She found Chase-Riboud's Sally Hemings too sophisticated and too talented, given the female slave's actual background. Privately, Brodie expected little of the project, but after weighing the pros and cons, she signed a contract with Warner Brothers agreeing to act as a story and historical consultant. In return, Brodie received an immediate payment of eleven thousand dollars with provisions for an additional thirty thousand to fifty thousand dollars upon commencement of actual production.[70]

In the end, the Warner Brothers production was aborted in response to widespread controversy generated by the advance publicity. Prominent Jefferson scholars, including Dumas Malone, Merrill D. Peterson, and Virginia Dabney, along with Frederick E. Nolting of the Thomas Jefferson Memorial Foundation, registered strong opposition. "It will be a mockery of history," proclaimed Malone. Brodie, by contrast, saw no harm in the proposed miniseries, if it was faithful to Jefferson's genius. Thus Brodie and the members of the Jefferson establishment continued their adversarial relationship.[71]

PURSUING RICHARD NIXON

Despite all seeming distractions, Fawn Brodie's primary focus remained Richard Nixon, particularly after February 1979. It took some effort to resume work on a project she had characterized as "an obscenity" in the shock and anger that followed Bernard's death. But editor George Brockway's "good counsel" proved to be of great help.[72]

By April, work on the biography was moving forward, but not with the momentum Brodie had hoped. She continued to suffer from malaise and depression, which she fought constantly. Later that same month she traveled to New York to meet with Brockway and to interview two individuals with connections to Richard Nixon. The first was Roy Cohn, onetime aide to Sen. Joseph McCarthy. At the time of their meeting, Cohn was undergoing treatment in a New York hospital. Afterward Brodie reported to Brockway that he had a sinister look and "seemed to be covered with oil or grease . . . and I had the feeling that he had recently been fished out of the East River, like a[n] old slimy eel." "But that is being . . . nasty," she hastened to add, and conceded that Cohn had actually given her "a fairly decent interview . . . indicating an active dislike for Nixon which might mean a good quote or two."[73]

Brodie's second interview was with Dr. David Abrahamsen, a practicing psychoanalyst and author of several books, including a 1976 work, *Nixon vs. Nixon: An Emotional Tragedy*, in which he studied Nixon's inner life and the forces that drove the ex-president toward self-destructive behavior. As she had done in previous interviews with psychoanalysts Joelyn West and Arnold A. Hutschnecker, Brodie questioned Abrahamsen concerning Nixon's sexuality, specifically his alleged homosexual tendencies. Abrahamsen disclosed "no real evidence of overt homosexuality in Nixon" but detected what he termed "a homosexual bonding" between Nixon and Rebozo. Turning to other aspects of Nixon's sexuality, Abrahamsen asserted that Nixon and Rebozo "shared girls" but did not say how he knew; he also told Brodie he thought Nixon "had a problem with impotence."[74]

In June, Brodie reported to Brockway that the book was progressing, that she hoped to get Nixon out of the vice-presidency by the end of the summer, when she planned to send Brockway thirteen chapters for evaluation. But, progress on the manuscript was slowed by an unexpected but welcome family development. In mid-July 1979, Bruce, Janet, and little Jedediah Brodie arrived in Pacific Palisades. Eager to relocate to southern California, Bruce and Janet purchased a condominium in nearby Culver City, but when they were unable to move in immediately, they took up temporary residence with Fawn. The sudden presence of her younger son's family helped to alleviate Fawn's loneliness in the wake of Bernard's death. She relished the role of "doting grandmother,"

246 FAWN MCKAY BRODIE

embracing this role with redoubled enthusiasm following the birth of Bruce and Janet's second child shortly after the family's arrival in California. Nathaniel Brodie was born on August 27. "I have a new grandson," Fawn proudly announced. "He is already smiling at me when I call him 'Natty Bumppo.'"[75]

Meanwhile, Brodie described to Brockway what she envisioned as the general shape of the final biography. She expected her study of Nixon ultimately to total two volumes, although her immediate goal was to complete the first, which would conclude with the assassination of John Kennedy, an event she believed profoundly altered Nixon's life. In this way she planned to emphasize "the themes of death and assassination," which she saw as crucial. Such a dramatic ending would also spark reader interest in the second volume. She hoped to finish the first volume within a year. Research and writing for the second would be possible only after release of the long-awaited Nixon tapes.[76]

In August 1979, Brodie reported to Brockway that she had completed the first draft totaling 525 pages. Upon rereading the draft, she was astonished at how different it was from what she had originally envisioned. The material had shaped the writing far more than she had expected. She had planned to concentrate on Nixon's emotional life and do a rather spare, but well-documented, psychobiography. Instead, she found she had told everything in detail, including much about the men who shaped his life.[77]

Through the balance of the year, Brodie wrote and rewrote. She was frustrated by difficulties posed in dealing with the Nixon-Castro story in a chapter entitled "The Assassination Track." It took far too long to complete, and yet she considered it one of the book's most important chapters. With the turn of the year, Brodie was planning a two-week journey to Peru in pursuit of firsthand information relative to Richard Nixon's 1958 South American visit. During that turbulent, violence-ridden tour, Nixon had found himself in physical danger in Lima, where a crowd of angry students and political extremists spat on him, threw rocks at him, and smashed the windows of the automobile in which he was riding. Nixon had stood up to the mob, even further infuriating the rioters through deliberate provocative gestures, and the violent encounter became a major international incident. Nixon's actions in Lima were of particular interest to Brodie, and she wanted to gather carefully documented information of the incident. But she spoke no Spanish. Turning to Barbara Ward-Korsch, a friend and neighbor who was fluent in Spanish, Brodie invited her to accompany her as personal interpreter. Ward-Korsch readily accepted the invitation.[78]

The two women spent about a week doing research in Lima, visiting libraries to study back issues of local newspapers covering the 1958 incident. They also sought out journalists and citizens who could offer firsthand information. Among the most noteworthy of these was Enrique Zeleri, editor of the Lima daily newspaper *Caretas.* Zeleri told Brodie that the attack on Nixon should have come as no surprise. He was a natural target because of his right-wing sympathies. In general, the information gathered in Lima did not yield many surprises, but it did provide rich anecdotes. More important, it supported Brodie's basic interpretation of Nixon's pattern of behavior. "Nixon had learned in Latin America that to stand up to stoning was good political fortune," she would write in the biography. "It was also proof to the [local] populace that 'the Yankee had balls.' The opportunities for encouraging repetition he found irresistible."[79]

The work for which they came finished, Brodie and Ward-Korsch took an additional week to visit various historic sites in Lima, as well as in Cuzco and Machu Picchu. The latter two places, located high on the western Andes, were once centers of the ancient Incan civilization. In Cuzco, the women visited a Catholic convent, where Brodie became agitated over the self-flagellation practices of the nuns. She found the general conditions of the convent alarming, a clear affront to her feminist sensitivities and to her concept of justice. These feelings she openly expressed to the Catholic personnel conducting her tour.[80]

Also in Peru, Brodie observed the conspicuous activities of another religious denomination, the Latter-day Saints. Much to her surprise, she found that the Mormons had established a formidable presence in that nation through a combination of active proselytizing and the establishment of schools. She reacted with a combination of admiration and dismay, remarking that the Mormons were both tremendously effective and tremendously powerful. While impressed with Mormon efforts, she admitted that she wished they were not so effective.[81]

Concurrent with work on the Nixon biography, Brodie took significant time to develop and present lectures at numerous colleges and universities and to various professional groups throughout the United States.

Speaking to such audiences was nothing new for the author, who had long sought opportunities to discuss her research. She had started doing this occasionally in the late 1960s, but following her 1976 retirement from UCLA, she began to lecture with increasing frequency. She maintained a hectic schedule, giving as many as three, four, or even five presentations a month. To help in the scheduling, she enlisted the services of a Los Angeles-based speaker's bureau.[82]

Much as these lectures slowed Brodie's work on Richard Nixon, they actually complemented that work-in-progress, for she often drew lecture material directly from data newly collected for the biography, which gave her opportunities to analyze and to draw conclusions for what was becoming an increasingly complex study.[83]

Such lectures provided other benefits. On more than one occasion, Fawn found opportunities for research and/or for interviews with Nixon acquaintances living in the various places she visited. Also important were the honoraria received, which ranged from a few hundred dollars to a few thousand dollars. This additional revenue was particularly welcome following her retirement from UCLA. And, Brodie noted wryly, the lectures got her out of Los Angeles, a good thing in and of itself.[84]

As Brodie pushed ahead with the biography, she confronted a steady stream of newly published books on Richard Nixon and Watergate. Among the most prominent were Bob Woodward and Carl Bernstein's *All the President's Men* and its sequel, *The Final Days*; Dan Rather and Gary Paul Gates's *The Palace Guard*; and Theodore H. White's *Breach of Faith*. Also beginning to appear in the late 1970s were recollections and memoirs by individuals who had worked closely with the ex-president, H. Robert Haldeman and Joseph Dimona's *The Ends of Power*, William Safire's *Before the Fall*, Raymond Price's *With Nixon*, and John Ehrlichman's *The Company*. A novel, *The Company* had as its main character a President Monckton, clearly a caricature of the fallen president. While such a proliferation of books on the very topic on which she was working might have seemed intimidating, Brodie appeared unaffected. She read each "with optimism" and praised them all generously "for what they might contribute to her knowledge and insight."[85]

Concurrently, Richard Nixon weighed in with two books of his own— *RN, the Memoirs of Richard Nixon*, published in 1978, and *The Real War*, which appeared two years later. Brodie evaluated each through reviews in the *Chicago Sun-Times*. She proclaimed *RN* incomplete, since it utterly failed to deal with the childhood influences that shaped the future president's personality. She dismissed the work as "authentic Nixon," clear evidence of the disgraced ex-president's "capacity to hide behind a self-righteous facade, and to deny both his lying and his hatred." She was equally critical of *The Real War*, Nixon's call for a hard line against the Soviet Union. She asserted that in this book the ex-president was repudiating his own earlier policy of detente—most evident in U.S.– Soviet relations during Nixon's tenure in the White House. She characterized Nixon's current hard-line position as reflective of the eternally divided man and an indication that "the real war" Nixon was so concerned about was really the war within himself.[86]

CONFRONTING CANCER AND COMPLETING THE BIOGRAPHY

Brodie took time from her research and writing in July 1980 to attend a family reunion at the home of her brother, Thomas, in southwestern Wyoming. In attendance, along with Fawn and her brother, were her three sisters—Flora, Barbara, and Louise. It was a memorable occasion, this gathering of the immediate family to celebrate Flora's sixty-seventh birthday. And the setting in which the siblings gathered was a beautiful one. Thomas had built a spacious home on the western slopes of the Grand Tetons, just outside the hamlet of Alta, Wyoming. The setting caused Fawn to recall the many fishing trips over Teton Pass she had taken as a youth with her father. The gathering conjured other memories as well, specifically the childhood home in Huntsville, where the McKays had gathered for previous family reunions over the years.[87]

Fawn and Barbara actually stopped off in Huntsville on their drive back to Salt Lake following the reunion. There they visited the white, two-story, fourteen-room home with its white picket fence and Lombardy poplars. The McKay sisters found it all still well maintained though it had long since been abandoned as a family residence and was now used only for occasional family gatherings. On this day they found the house empty and locked. They tried every door and window, seeking entry. Unsuccessful, they had to satisfy themselves with peering in the windows and reminiscing. "Mrs. Grundy," the old outhouse, was still intact, located down the long stone walkway in the back of the house, but completely hidden now by vines and brush and long since replaced by indoor plumbing.

From the old house Fawn and Barbara walked to the Huntsville town square just two blocks away. The town park was overgrown with pine trees that had taken over everything except the ballpark. There were other changes. The old red brick, three-story schoolhouse had been replaced by a one-story modern building, and right next door the beautiful old white Mormon chapel with its bell tower was also gone. So too the old dance hall, the center of the town's social life during Fawn's formative years. But other than that, Huntsville and the surrounding valley looked very much as they had years earlier.[88]

The McKay family reunion of 1980 was noteworthy for another reason. While hiking around the Teton Pass area near her brother's home, Fawn noticed that she felt unusually tired—an uncharacteristic condition, given her regimen of daily walks in the Santa Monica Mountains. Then, in the month after her return to California, she became ill. She initially attributed the illness to influenza, but when her condition worsened and she developed a persistent cough, she suspected a case of viral pneumonia.[89]

In mid-September, following a hospital checkup, Fawn received the shattering news that she had lung cancer. Her condition was particularly grave: the carcinoma had invaded not only her lungs but had spread into the lymph glands in her neck and into her bones. In telling George Brockway of her condition in late September, Brodie was frank: "I have not been promised a long life," she wrote, "unless God is more compassionate than I have been led in recent years to believe."[90]

She then reflected on what her condition might mean to her work on Nixon. She was very mindful "of the irony of the fact that one important theme in my book is the importance in Nixon's life of 'Death as an ally.'" Now, with some arrogance and anger, she observed, "If [Nixon] loses his best biographer to death before I can write volume two, the terrible pact he must sometime have made with the devil still holds." Nixon's first two biographers, she noted, had committed suicide. To a family friend she remarked, "I had fully expected to outlive Nixon. Maybe I still will. But the bastard has the odds."[91]

While informing Brockway of her gloomy prognosis, Brodie reported significant progress on her manuscript. She had finished the last chapter "in a burst of creative energy that almost masked my acute discomfort." Initially entitled "The Nixon Character," this chapter had been extremely difficult to write. She had not known exactly what to say about the nature of the man. Then, suddenly having to confront her own mortality, it came clear. With dark humor, she quoted Samuel Johnson to Brockway: "It marvelously clarifies a man's mind to know that he is to be hanged in a fortnight."[92]

Brodie faced chemotherapy with both anxiety and hope. Though it would be some weeks before it could be determined if the chemotherapy was working, she was optimistic. She had never smoked, and her lungs "till now" had been healthy. "I may react badly to the chemotherapy," she said, but "God willing, I will not." She looked toward remission and recovery.[93]

As it turned out, the initial effects of the chemotherapy were "vicious." A rigorous procedure, it utilized five drugs, including platinum. "It just about did me in," Brodie confessed, but it seemed to be attacking the cancer. Her cough was gone, her lungs improved, and her back pain was reduced. But reaction to the platinum sent Fawn's blood pressure crashing and left her totally debilitated. She was frank in assessing the long-range prognosis; she knew the statistics were not in her favor for this kind of carcinoma.[94]

Still, she remained hopeful. Although hers was a swift-moving cancer, a clear, large-cell carcinoma, it was also sensitive to chemotherapy, and she was getting a full bombardment. She counted on being strong enough to finish the Nixon book. After that, she would consider "every extra day . . . manna from heaven." Her optimism grew: In late October, she was counting on a decent remission and a chance not only to finish the Nixon biography, but to see it in print, along with reviews.[95]

She continued to push ahead with the manuscript, making necessary revisions and refinements in response to suggestions made by George Brockway, who provided strong moral support. He gave her a pep talk, telling her of the similar situation faced by Norman Cousins, whom Brockway knew and whose works W. W. Norton had published. Diagnosed with cancer and given a gloomy prognosis, Cousins had "willed" himself well on two different occasions, had actually "laughed himself well." While conceding that Nixon wasn't "a laughing matter," Brockway told Brodie, "You are artist enough and scholar enough and workman enough to do what has to be done, not just with this book but with its sequel and with the happier books that will follow." He admitted that Brodie would find her bout with cancer "discouraging and frustrating and even sickening [but] in the meantime let's concentrate on making the [Nixon] book the great book it promises to be." "You have written four fine books and part of a fifth," he told her. "At least two of them are arguably great books. You won't stop now."[96]

Brodie also received support and advice from her psychoanalyst friends Maimon Leavitt and Gerald Aronson, whose suggestions she greatly valued. In the course of her work on Jefferson and Nixon, Brodie had developed a close personal bond with both men and with their wives, Peggy Leavitt and Jan Aronson. Now that relationship helped fill a void left by the limited contact she had with psychoanalyst Ralph ("Romi") Greenson, her close friend for many years. Both the Brodies, but particularly Bernard, had become increasingly distant from Greenson since the early 1970s. While the animosities that initially estranged Greenson and the Brodies lessened in later years, the relationship was never fully restored, and Greenson's own declining health had further limited Fawn's contact with him. Thus her friendship with the Leavitts and the Aronsons replaced, in many ways, the once-warm camaraderie with Romi and Hildi Greenson.[97]

By late October 1980 Brodie's physical condition appeared to be improved. The worst of the chemotherapy had run its course. Fawn noticed improvement in her lungs and diminished back pain. She used relaxation techniques for controlling pain, and she turned to a diet of health foods. Slowly she was moving the manuscript forward. But just one month later, she began radiation treatments, which had the effect of further reducing her energy. She also dealt with a new concern, psychologically rather than physically oriented—namely, her lifelong fear of fire. The fall of 1980 brought an unusual number of brushfires to the Los Angeles basin, several of which raged near Brodie's Pacific Palisades home. "The fires are really getting to me," she confessed to Brockway. "I have often said [that] if God wanted to destroy Los Angeles he'd give us an earthquake during a Santana [sic] wind." The fires, the ever-present threat of the "big earthquake," and the slow progress of the manuscript roused all of Brodie's anxieties.[98]

As she numbered her concerns, Brodie had to include a recent political development—the election of Ronald Reagan as president in November 1980. She had the same disdain for the former California governor as she did for Richard Nixon. "It was inevitable, I guess, that America would one day put a movie star in the White House," she lamented. What depressed her most of all, she said, was "all the Nixon men he's taking with him."

All through her ordeal, Brodie was remarkably open in sharing details of her ongoing struggle with cancer, even with those outside her immediate family and circle of close friends. "I have been fighting invasive cancer for several months," she told columnist and book review editor Art Seidenbaum of the *Los Angeles Times*, adding that "chemotherapy and radiation have certainly helped, but they rob one of practically all one's energy. . . . But I am expecting a decent remission and a joyful Christmas. Everything points that way," she concluded on an optimistic note.[100]

At the same time, realist that she was, Brodie prepared for the worst. She placed her financial affairs in order, allowing for the maximum benefit of her immediate family. She sought and received advice from George Brockway in establishing a trust for the payment of royalties to her children. She consulted with both her lawyer and her accountant regarding her varied investments and other assets. Her actions reflected not just the current state of her health, but also her long-standing concern for the financial well-being of the immediate family. Such concerns were deeply rooted in the childhood memories of her birth family's precarious financial situation. She was anxious to maximize for her children as much as possible her current financial assets, which were considerable. Her Pacific Palisades home alone was assessed at $450,000 to $500,000. And she looked for ways to minimize the anticipated inheritance taxes. For example, she immediately gave her two young grandsons each a cash gift of six thousand dollars. She also transferred to her three children the retirement benefits that both she and Bernard had accumulated from their years of teaching at the University of California, Los Angeles.[101]

As Fawn struggled with her illness and with the manuscript, she received significant help and encouragement from the children, who all lived nearby. Pam was still living in Bernard's old study just above the Brodie's main house, Dick resided just a block up the hill in Pacific

Palisades, and Bruce was just twenty minutes away in nearby Culver City. In addition to providing their mother much needed moral support, all three, along with daughter-in-law Janet, helped in making the final, necessary revisions on the Nixon manuscript. Fawn characterized the children as "uncommonly sensitive critics." Bruce carefully read and critiqued the entire manuscript, aiding in significant revisions of particular sections. Dick, according to his mother, eliminated a lot of commas and improved a lot of sentences. Like his father, he reportedly had a good ear for style. Brodie acknowledged the help of all four: "To Richard, Bruce, Pamela, and Janet, my children and daughter-in-law— expert editors all," the dedication page reads.[102]

By early December, Brodie was pushing ahead with the necessary revisions of her manuscript, despite experiencing misery and debility. She expected to send the completed manuscript to Brockway in late December or early January 1981. "Do you have any idea when [the manuscript] will be published?" she asked her editor. "Summer? Fall? Late Spring?" Indicating a sense of urgency, she confessed that the "one terrible thing about this illness is that one becomes so totally preoccupied with one's self and there are times when I fall into depression." But then there were the times she felt optimistic about recovery. She described a new cancer technique in which one's blood was taken out, heated, and returned, warm, to circulate in the body. Although this procedure was "respectable," Brodie indicated that she would stick with more conventional techniques for the time being.[103]

Despite all measures, Fawn's condition continued to worsen. She grew weaker and found it increasingly difficult to care for herself. But she resisted hospitalization. She was too worried about completing all the necessary revisions on her manuscript. She owed Brockway one more chapter after sending him the next-to-last one on December 9.[104] Her resistance to hospitalization also came from her horror of dependency, a fear rooted in past family trauma. She was haunted by the difficulties experienced by her own mother, years earlier, in caring first for her own ailing mother and then for her invalid husband over a period of some ten years. She knew it had all contributed to Fawn Brimhall's psychological problems and subsequent suicide. Thus she maintained her independence even as she grew weaker and weaker. She wanted no one to care for her, not even her daughter.

After completing her final manuscript revisions and mailing them off to Norton in mid-December, Fawn finally acknowledged that she could no longer manage on her own and agreed to go into St. John's Hospital in Santa Monica. Once there, she seemed to relax, ready to enjoy the time she had left. Pam stayed with her on a continuous basis, sleeping on a cot in the same room. "She actually wanted me there," Pam recalled, finding it most unusual that her mother would abandon her fiercely independent behavior. Fawn allowed Pam to look after her needs, and the two women passed hours in that room talking and reminiscing. "She was reasonably comfortable in the hospital," Pam recalled. "I never knew her to be so relaxed as she was when she was dying."[105]

FAWN'S FINAL CONTROVERSY—AND HER BELIEFS

As she neared death, Fawn Brodie found herself embroiled in one final controversy. By the end of December the cancer had spread to her brain and to her bones, causing them to break, and also causing intense, sometimes unbearable pain. To relieve this pain, Fawn's doctors sought, with increasing difficulty, to find an adequate drug. While she was in this condition, she received a visit from her brother, Thomas McKay, who had come to California to see his ailing sister and to attend the wedding of a niece, Leslie Jensen, daughter of older sister Flora. When her brother walked into the hospital room, Fawn suddenly blurted out, "Oh Tommy, Tommy, give me a blessing." McKay was surprised at his sister's request, given both her long-standing estrangement from the church—of which he had remained a devout member—and her relatively distant relationship with him. Nevertheless, he accepted Fawn's request as a "spontaneous reaction," and after talking with her at some length, Thomas gave Fawn the blessing. It was the only way he knew to console his dying sister.[106]

Within days, Fawn felt the need to issue a public statement clarifying her motives in making the request of her brother. Dated 31 December 1980 and addressed to "To Whom It May Concern," the statement explained that in the same way their father "had communicated blessings over the years as a kind of family patriarch," so too Fawn wanted a blessing from her brother. Grateful as she was for having received that blessing, Fawn did not want anyone to misinterpret the incident. "Any exaggeration . . . that I was asking to be taken back into the [Mormon] church at that moment I strictly repudiate and would for all time," she said.[107]

The contents of Fawn Brodie's formal statement, combined with the recollections of various family members, suggest at least three possible explanations for her extraordinary request. First, at the time of her brother's visit, Fawn was not completely lucid. Her son Bruce considered her "brain-damaged" at that point. Pam, who spent the most time with her mother during this period, recalled that Fawn was heavily drugged at the time of Thomas McKay's visit and that the particular drugs being prescribed at the time caused periods of hallucinations. Pam suggested that her mother's request came during such a period. It was later, when Fawn became lucid once more, that she realized that what had happened might be misinterpreted and she determined to write a disclaimer. "Since I was ill at the time," Fawn said in her statement, "I may have misunderstood his [Thomas's] answer [as given through the blessing]." But she was adamant on the issue: "I do not want to be misunderstood," she said.[108]

A second possible motive for Fawn's spontaneous outburst, also suggested by son Bruce, is that his mother was anxious to reconcile with her brother, with whom she had not been particularly close, especially in later years. According to Bruce, in this process of reconciliation, Fawn essentially gave her brother "a gift of saying, 'Do your Mormon thing. Give me your blessing. Be the [family] patriarch and do this. I will give that gift to you, accepting you in that role.'" But almost as soon as she had received the blessing, Fawn feared misinterpretation—and hence the statement, which was the last thing to appear under her signature. The document itself suggests reconciliation as a motive: "I was grateful at being taken into the family," Fawn said, "though I never felt I was out of the family. But my delight in asking for an opportunity for a blessing at that moment indicated simply the intensity of an old hunger."[109]

A third, somewhat less evident, motive for Fawn's request has been suggested by two other family members, Thomas McKay himself and Flora McKay Crawford, who agreed with her brother's conjecture. Thomas called Fawn's request a spontaneous reaction, made in the knowledge that she was close to death and miserable with pain. Within

this context, his ailing sister's desire for a blessing went back to her days
as a youth when, suffering from illnesses that did not always respond to
conventional cures, Fawn would receive faith-healing blessings—common
practice among Latter-day Saints—from her father and/or other Mormon
brethren. According to Thomas, Fawn "still had this basic Mormon
teaching in her thinking." To him, her behavior seemed natural. She was
acutely ill, and she made her request of him in a desperate situation.[110]

• • •

Whatever the reason (or reasons) for Fawn Brodie's plea for a blessing,
the incident raises a fundamental question: What was the basic nature of
Brodie's religious beliefs? Without question, she maintained a disdain,
sometimes bordering on hatred, for Latter-day Saint dogma and
practices, and for the Mormon Church as an institution. She expressed
her views often, openly, and unequivocally to various family members,
friends, and professional colleagues. Specifically, she viewed the Mormon
Church as a repressive institution. But while Brodie may have hated
Mormonism, she couldn't shake it. It dogged her to the end of her life—
as evident in the last meeting with her brother.[111]

While clearly repelled by Mormonism per se, Brodie was, at the same
time, paradoxically attracted to certain things Mormon. She maintained
a lifelong interest in many aspects of Mormon history and culture, topics
on which she continued to write, speak, and publish long after *No Man
Knows My History* had appeared and long after her dramatic excommunication from the church. Moreover, she admired certain values and
behavior that received special emphasis within the Mormon community:
a strong emphasis on family, on community involvement, and on mean-
ingful, productive hard work. She embraced such values and based her
adult life on them.

Such personal traits notwithstanding, Brodie remained unambiguous
in her distaste for Mormon institutions and dogma. Nor did she reserve
her animosity for Mormonism. Indeed, she looked upon all forms of
organized religion with similar disdain. "She did not like religion in any
shape or form," her daughter-in-law recalled. In particular, she considered the Roman Catholic Church just as narrow, restrictive, and
oppressive as the Mormon Church. She went further, rejecting and
discounting the basic tenets of Christianity itself, including belief in Jesus

as a savior. In writing a fellow historian, Monsignor Jerome Stoffel, Brodie confessed that "abandoning religion altogether has been a wholly liberating experience."[112]

Brodie frequently referred to Thomas Jefferson's maxim, "The earth belongs to the living," but at the same time, she was reluctant to discuss her beliefs concerning the supernatural. In this reticence, Fawn stood in contrast to her husband, who throughout his life made clear his atheism. According to her daughter, Fawn was not so clear in her position and was much less willing to discuss her beliefs, or disbeliefs. "I didn't see any signs of a belief in God," Pamela said, "but I don't remember her actually saying there isn't any. I think 'agnostic' would be a more accurate term [to describe her beliefs]."[113]

From Bruce's perspective, his mother "probably would have [been] called an agnostic in the early part of her adulthood and an atheist by the end." But she "was the type of person who maybe momentarily would get religion" in a crisis situation—for instance, "if a rattlesnake jumped out in front of her." Such behavior was "like a reflex," according to Bruce, an "instantaneous looking towards the heavens, but it was purely reflexive [and] never really involved enough to say maybe there is a God."[114]

It might be argued such a "reflex" motivated Fawn's request for a final blessing, though Bruce Brodie himself vigorously discounted that possibility.[115] Whatever the case, it is clear that Fawn's encounter with her brother generated one last controversy in a lifetime full of contention.

• • •

On the evening of Saturday, 10 January 1981, Fawn McKay Brodie died peacefully in her sleep. In accordance with her final wishes her body was cremated and the ashes spread over the Santa Monica Mountains near the Pacific Palisades home she loved and where she had spent the last thirty years of her life. She was sixty-five years old.

Epilogue

CONTROVERSY AND LEGACY

Fawn Brodie's death received notice in both the national press and the electronic media. It was announced on various television news shows—including the *Today* show, on which Brodie had been interviewed following publication of *Thomas Jefferson: An Intimate History*. The Associated Press announcement of Brodie's death, as printed in newspapers throughout the United States, generated confusion in stating that, following the publication of *No Man Knows My History,* Brodie "requested and was eventually granted excommunication by the Mormon Church." Fawn's family, both in Utah and in California, quickly reacted to the misstatement. In a subsequent AP news story, Brodie's younger sister, Barbara McKay Smith of Provo, Utah, denied that her sister had requested excommunication, noting that Fawn had simply chosen not to attend her June 1946 ecclesiastical trial.[1]

The AP error did not appear in newspaper obituaries announcing Brodie's death in Utah. Indeed, the *Salt Lake Tribune,* the *Ogden Standard-Examiner,* and the *Deseret News* never mentioned Brodie's excommunication. The same was true of a follow-up editorial tribute in the *Ogden Standard-Examiner,* which stated simply that Brodie had "caused a tremendous stir in LDS church circles with many leaders of the faith bitterly criticizing [her]."[2]

Other tributes offered in California and Utah were more accurate and less reticent in discussing the details of Brodie's excommonication. They also evaluated the deceased author within the context of her larger legacy. This was true, as well, of a memorial service for Fawn Brodie held on 17 January 1981, at the UCLA Faculty Center and attended by two hundred individuals, including family, friends, and former colleagues. The seven speakers included three former colleagues in the UCLA history department—Hans Rogger, Stanley Wolpert, and Peter Loewenberg. Also speaking were close friends and neighbors Polly Plesset and Lamont Johnson, psychoanalyst friend Mike Leavitt, and psychohistorian Elizabeth Marvick, another friend. All lauded Fawn Brodie as a wife, mother, neighbor, and hostess, and they praised her professional accomplishments as a writer, teacher, and crusader for causes she believed in.[3]

Through the pages of the *Utah Historical Quarterly*, Everett L. Cooley, director of special collections at the University of Utah and close friend in later years, pointed to the ironic fact that Brodie, while "Utah's best known and most respected author," remained "in her native state . . . a 'prophet without honor.'" He lauded "her pioneering efforts in writing critical biography." Sterling M. McMurrin, liberal Mormon philosopher and onetime U.S. commissioner of education, paid tribute to Brodie in *Dialogue: A Journal of Mormon Thought*, characterizing her as "the most widely known and read of all Mormon writers, a historian of distinction" whose work attracted international attention and acclaim. Pointing specifically to her impact on Mormon studies, McMurrin credited Brodie for helping to usher in what he termed "a new climate of liberation." "Because of *No Man Knows My History*, Mormon history, in general, moved toward more openness, objectivity and honesty," McMurrin said. Through the liberal Mormon magazine, *Sunstone*, Latter-day Saint historian-biographer Richard S. Van Wagoner called Brodie "the best-known Mormon rebel of all time"—but also "a very warm human being" and a "remarkably free-thinking woman of unflinching courage." Van Wagoner echoed McMurrin in calling Brodie's biography of Joseph Smith a "major impetus in the quest for a less apologetic, more objective Mormon history."[4]

• • •

Fawn Brodie's biography of Richard Nixon was nine months away from publication at the time of the author's death. She had intended to deal with Richard Nixon's life and activities up through Watergate and his resignation from the presidency. But when she realized her time was limited and knew she would not live to have access to his tapes and papers, she ended her study with Nixon's prepresidential years. Consequently, when *Richard Nixon: The Shaping of His Character* finally appeared in September 1981, there was some sense of incompleteness to the book. Nevertheless, it generated the controversy expected of it. In the words of Prof. Ingrid Winther Scobie, Brodie's *Richard Nixon* "climaxed a series of controversial psychobiographies written over the author's long career."[5]

Most controversial was the biography's interpretive focus, as suggested by its subtitle. Brodie developed several themes in explaining Nixon's "warped" personality. The first was what she saw as his tendency toward excessive, almost pathological, lying, his lack of any "emotional investment in the truth." A second major theme was that of death—in particular, fratricide, or the death of brothers. The deaths of two sets of brothers worked to Nixon's personal advantage. The deaths of his own brothers, first Arthur and then Harold, brought young Nixon some advantages but at the same time caused the inevitable survivor's guilt. Later, the deaths of the Kennedy brothers, first John and then Robert, helped facilitate his election to the presidency in 1968. For Nixon, Brodie maintained, "the shortest distance between two points [was] four corpses."[6]

A third, and a related, theme—Nixon's ability to survive and persevere—was, in Brodie's words, "the most consistent, the most remarkable, of all aspects of Nixon's life." A fourth theme, Nixon's warped capacity for love, was reflected in what Brodie saw as his unhappy marriage. According to her, Nixon's inability to love had its origins in his difficult relationships as a youth with both parents—an angry, brutal father and a "castrating mother," who quietly but persistently pointed out all her son's shortcomings while encouraging repressive behavior.[7]

A fifth theme involved Nixon's "delight in punishment." According to Brodie, this was manifested in his handling of the Alger Hiss case, which hardened his conviction that broad-scale attack was the certain way to victory. This tendency to punish was the by-product of a "deep, dark rage" and a "terrible temper." All five of these themes were interwoven with a sixth—Brodie's focus on her subject's failure to acquire a sense of his own identity. This so-called identity crisis caused Nixon to create a "grandiose fantasy life for himself."[8]

"Visit the Ruins with Fawn Brodie," a political cartoon drawn by *Deseret News* cartoonist Calvin Grondahl and published in the *Sunstone Review* in conjunction with a 1981 review of Brodie's *Richard Nixon: The Shaping of His Character*. Courtesy Calvin Grondahl and the Sunstone Foundation.

Given the radical claims of Brodie's *Nixon*, it is not surprising that the reviews were mixed. Lloyd Shearer, in a very favorable review in *Parade* magazine, found it "a compelling, revealing scholarly biography," Brodie's "magnum opus." *Publishers Weekly* praised the book as "assiduous [in] research and . . . stylish . . . [in] writing." John J. Fitzpatrick in the *Journal of American History* characterized the biography as "the best available account of Nixon's personal life and character," noting that other scholars would be indebted to Brodie for her research and for raising important questions about Nixon's life."[9]

Other reviewers were more critical. Robert Lekachman, writing in *The Nation*, conceded that Brodie's arguments seemed "plausible enough, though hardly novel, and open to criticism." "Similar circumstances," he pointed out, "evoke very different human responses. Hordes of boys grow up sadly in families with violent fathers and castrating mothers. They don't all turn into Richard Nixons." Writing in a similar vein in *The New Republic*, Godfrey Hodgson, an expert on the American presidency, criticized Brodie's analysis as "somehow just a bit too pat." He questioned her basic psychoanalytic approach and her motives. "Psychoanalysis . . . was developed as a tool of therapy," he cautioned. "In historical biography . . . we are in danger of having the insights of psychotherapy used as a tool for character destruction, certainly for libel, potentially for revenge."[10]

Jack Chatfield, a professor of history at Trinity College writing in *National Review*, characterized Brodie's work as "so segmented that it really becomes two books instead of one." He found the first half "a compassionate, sensitive, and moving account" of Nixon's early life, noting that the author seemed "impelled not so much by hostility as by a powerful sense of kinship in her portrayal of [Nixon's]. . .tormented" childhood. By contrast, the latter half of the biography clearly reflected Brodie's ideological and personal hostility toward her subject. Nixon's conduct of the Vietnam War, Chatfield asserted, "becomes for Mrs. Brodie the conclusive evidence of his all-consuming moral depravity." "There are two Nixons," Chatfield said. "And there are two Fawn Brodies as well."[11]

Peter Loewenberg, Brodie's close friend, former UCLA colleague, and fellow psychohistorian, also expressed mixed feelings concerning the biography's basic approach. On the one hand, he called it a work "of great power and persuasiveness" in evaluating the character of the president. But then he took issue: "Her emphasis on the theme of Nixon the liar from boyhood to maturity," Loewenberg wrote, "from parental home to the White House, is essentially static and while powerful is unbalanced in its neglect of Nixon's many ego strengths and adaptations in a long political career."[12]

Most critical was political scientist J. Philipp Rosenberg: "The real problem with this book is that the author's dislike for Nixon shows through her claim of objectivity, particularly in her use of 'loaded terms.' It is too bad that Brodie lets her feelings interfere with her objectivity," he wrote, then concluded: "After finishing the Nixon book, I have an urge to demand that psychobiographers be barred from writing about people they dislike. While this would create a huge gap in the literature, it would do wonders for the reputation of psychobiography."[13]

Perhaps reflecting the mixed reviews, Brodie's *Richard Nixon: The Shaping of His Character* was a commercial disappointment. In contrast to Brodie's pervious work, *Thomas Jefferson: An Intimate History*, which had sold briskly, Richard Nixon sold only some twenty-three thousand copies— far short of its first print run. It was, in fact, remaindered; the excess copies were picked up, rebound as paperbacks, and marketed by Harvard University Press in 1983.[14]

Undoubtedly contributing to disappointing sales was the fact that Brodie's *Richard Nixon* was merely one in a deluge of books on the thirty-seventh president published during the late 1970s and early 1980s. Soon after Brodie's biography came the publication of memoirs written by key Nixon aides, including Henry Kissinger, John Ehrlichman, and John Dean, all providing personal, often critical insights into the ex-president's actions, behavior, and attitudes.[15]

Moreover, Brodie's harsh assessment of Richard Nixon ran counter to the emergence in the 1980s of a "revisionist" evaluation of the ex-president. Nixon himself was central to the process of rehabilitating his image. By the time of his death in April 1994, the former president was viewed in a much more positive light by scholars and by the general public alike. Such revisionism was evident in the multivolume biographies by Stephen Ambrose and Roger Morris, both of whom conceded Nixon's mistakes and flawed personality but highlighted their subject's positive attributes and accomplishments. Godfrey Hodgson summarized the nature of the revisionist view: "A new consensus is forming," he wrote in the *New York Times Book Review*. "Richard Nixon, it suggests, was a deeply flawed individual, but an able President; too savage for his own good in the partisan wars of domestic politics, but, in spite of everything, in the front rank of Presidents for his understanding and management of foreign policy."[16]

While characterizing Richard Nixon's behavior and actions as less than ideal, some revisionists viewed them as normal, given the context of the larger American society. This view was in direct contradiction to Fawn Brodie's fundamental assertion that Nixon represented a deviant departure from the norm of American society. Such revisionist scholarship, however, was less than universal, even during the eighties. In 1984 columnist Anthony Lewis, echoing Fawn Brodie, denounced ongoing efforts to rehabilitate Richard Nixon, noting Nixon's "endless offenses, petty and grand, against decency."[17]

In fact, the "traditional" critical assessment of Richard Nixon's life and career, articulated in Fawn Brodie's biography, reemerged in the mid-1990s. Foremost in promoting this view was Stanley I. Kutler. In reviewing Tom Wicker's *One of Us: Richard and the American Dream,* Kutler, in a manner reminiscent of Brodie, rejected Wicker's central assertion that the ex-president reflected American society in his behavior: "'One of Us,' as Wicker contends? No, he was supposed to be better. He was after all, the president."[18]

In other ways, Fawn Brodie's *Richard Nixon* affected and indeed altered the way in which the man was viewed. Nixon scholar Roger Morris, himself a revisionist, conceded that Brodie's work was "far and away the most impressive intellectual spadework on the subject of Nixon's childhood and youth." In his own study, Morris admitted that he "had drawn gratefully" on Brodie's oral history archives, "albeit with rather different results."[19]

Similarly, Brodie's vivid, detailed portrait of Richard Nixon's troubled formative years clearly influenced and inspired Oliver Stone in writing the screenplay for his highly controversial 1995 movie *Nixon.* In crafting the film, Stone also drew on Brodie's assertion that Nixon was obsessed with the CIA's 1961 failed invasion of Cuba at the Bay of Pigs. Nixon actually blamed himself, at least in part, she said, for this failure. And Stone also incorporated Brodie's view "that Nixon suffered from some kind of 'survivor's guilt'" over the deaths of John and Robert Kennedy, whom he "envied and resented." Stone, in fact, acknowledged his debt to Brodie, singling out her biography for providing "a deeper understanding of what [Nixon] was thinking and feeling, what kind of a human being he was." Stone praised Brodie for her willingness "to push into the shadow areas—into the psychiatric areas, the relationship to mother and father and siblings—in order to understand why Nixon was so tortured."[20]

• • •

Thus Fawn Brodie's *Richard Nixon* served as a significant point of departure for subsequent analyses, scholarly and otherwise, of the thirty-seventh president. This was also the case with Brodie's four other biographies. Her portrait of Mormonism's founder in *No Man Knows My History* helped set the agenda for the so-called new Mormon history, particularly as it involved studies of Mormon origins and developments within the early Latter-day Saint movement.[21] "In many ways it was a seminal study that served as a transition point" between "the old and the New Mormon history," Mormon studies scholar Roger D. Launius noted, with "the 'old' generally viewed as polemical while the 'new' was considered less concerned with questions of religious truth and more interested in understanding why events unfolded the way they did." Launius concluded that "it is a measure of the success of [Brodie's] biography of Smith that it is still considered fifty years later the standard work on the subject and the starting point for all analyses of Mormonism." Brodie's *No Man Knows My History* continues by default to be the closest thing to a definitive biography on Joseph Smith.[22]

Similarly, Brodie's second biography, *Thaddeus Stevens: Scourge of the South*, while less controversial, represented a major benchmark in the so-called revisionist view of American Reconstruction history, facilitating the movement of scholarship away from the earlier, dominant "Dunning school," which had promoted a highly unfavorable view of Reconstruction. *Thaddeus Stevens* also broke ground in the way it examined not only the subject's "intimate life" but also the impact of Stevens's clubfoot, probing the critical question of what physical crippling could do to a man's psyche.[23]

Brodie's third major work, *The Devil Drives: A Life of Sir Richard Burton*, was perhaps the least controversial of all of the author's biographies, though it dealt with a subject who was highly controversial in and of himself. *The Devil Drives* continues to be acknowledged as the "best life . . . to date" of the flamboyant British explorer, despite the appearance of several subsequent biographies.[24]

Thomas Jefferson: An Intimate History, by far Brodie's most popular biography and perhaps her most controversial, sent shock waves throughout the community of Jefferson scholars, particularly within the Jefferson establishment based at Monticello, Virginia. The resulting storm sparked animated debate and discussion, particularly involving the central issues of slavery, race, gender, and class. These varied issues are the primary focus of the "new social history" that has come to dominate the larger field of American history. The debate at the center of Brodie's *Thomas Jefferson*—namely, the precise nature of Jefferson's relationship with his black slave, Sally Hemings—continues unabated to the present.[25]

Evidence of Brodie's influence is also found in the 1995 movie *Jefferson in Paris,* produced by Merchant-Ivory, with Nick Nolte in the title role. In the words of one reviewer, the filmmakers took "their lead from Fawn M. Brodie's controversial best-seller." The film, the reviewer said, did not "rake Jefferson over the coals for his racial hypocrisies"; rather, it "cast a cool objective eye on both his moral lapses and his intellectual virtues," much as Fawn Brodie had done. Nevertheless, the larger controversy continued, dividing not only historians but also members of Thomas Jefferson's own family—his white descendants and the black descendants of Sally Hemings. In 1998, DNA tests confirmed a direct lineal relationship between Eston Hemings, Sally's youngest son, and Thomas Jefferson, thus vindicating the assertions made by Brodie a quarter century earlier.[26]

Taken together, all five of Brodie's biographies, written over a period of some forty-five years, exemplify the craft of modern biography. That is, each was carefully researched and written in an effort to present the varied, multifaceted aspects of the subject's life and career. Brodie herself claimed to be a detective "of sorts." "In each of my books there was an important mystery to be solved," she once said. All of the men she wrote about—Joseph Smith, Thaddeus Stevens, Richard Burton, Thomas Jefferson, and Richard Nixon—were complex and enigmatic. "Show me a character whose life arouses my curiosity," she noted, "and my flesh begins crawling with suspense. I simply cannot stop until I piece together all the baffling bits of evidence and solve the puzzle."[27]

Other important patterns were evident in the subjects Brodie selected. Her son Bruce claimed that there "was an element of love and envy in her feelings towards the men she was writing about." Subconsciously she appeared to be saying, "If I had been a man, I would have been a man like this." This was clearly the case with both Richard Burton and Thomas Jefferson, whereas the author was much more ambivalent about Joseph

Smith and Thaddeus Stevens. The exception was, of course, Richard Nixon, "whom she detested as much as she loved Burton and Jefferson."[28]

Her particular interest in Richard Nixon conformed to yet another pattern, a preoccupation with truth and lying, a theme that manifested itself as an unbroken pattern across all five of her biographies. In Joseph Smith, Brodie "wrote about a man who called himself a prophet but whom she believed to be an imposter." With Thaddeus Stevens, the issue of truth lay in the precise nature of the relationship between Stevens and his black housekeeper, rumored to be pregnant with his child at the time of her mysterious death. In her treatment of Richard Burton, Brodie dealt with the Englishman's reputation as "an outrageous liar." With Thomas Jefferson, the tension, of course, centered in the man's alleged illicit relationships, first with Maria Cosway and then Sally Hemings. And in her final book, Brodie dealt with the man she called a pathological liar.[29]

Brodie's intense, almost obsessive interest in her varied biographical subjects appears to reflect characteristics fundamental to her psychological makeup. She felt "compelled" to do research and writing, even though she found it incredibly hard to do. "Everything I've ever done is easier than research or writing," she once said, then added, "Now you might wonder why I keep driving myself, a compulsive woman racing around frantically, tracking down trivia to build a biographical mosaic. Why do I do it? Because I am unhappy when I'm not doing it."[30]

Indeed, throughout her life Brodie was given to moods of depression. She was "inclined to fall into moments of bleak despair," she told one newspaper reporter in 1974, noting, "There's a melancholy that always comes through in pictures of me."[31] Such moods were a major factor—along with problems in sexuality—that had sent her into psychoanalysis in the 1950s, with the treatment continuing into the 1960s. But her research and writing were also therapy for her depression.

Fawn Brodie was driven by one other factor. What distinguished Fawn, according to her daughter, Pam, "was not her intelligence, but her enormous discipline and dedication to her work—a dedication that was unrelated to . . . any need or expectation of financial reward." Fawn's focus throughout her life was to make as much time as possible for her research and writing. She rarely participated in any form of recreation, and when she did it was always instigated by her husband, Bernard. Pam attributed her mother's drive to the fact that she was a fundamentally insecure person, a condition whose roots lay in her youth. "As a child she was valued not (as most girls are) for her disposition, obedience, charm, or looks," Pamela Brodie explained, "but for (as boys often are) her accomplishments."[32]

Bruce Brodie, in fact, theorized that somewhere deep in his mother's psyche was the feeling that she "should have been a man." He saw this reflected in the "love and envy" she felt toward her biographical subjects. Whatever the case, Fawn Brodie felt she had to work, to achieve notable accomplishments, to be of value as a person. "It wasn't until after she sent off the completed Nixon manuscript and lay dying that she learned to . . . value life for the living, instead of for the working," her daughter recalled with some melancholy. But by then it was "rather late."[33]

Notes

PREFACE

1. Digby Diehl, "Woman of the Year," Leon Edel, as quoted by Robert Dallack in "My Search for Lyndon Johnson," 84; James Atlas, "Choosing a Life."

2. Shirley E. Stephenson, "Biography of Fawn McKay Brodie," 10.

3. Newell G. Bringhurst, *Saints, Slaves, and Blacks.* The parallels and interactions between Fawn M. Brodie and this writer relative to the controversy surrounding the issue of blacks within the Mormon Church are discussed in Newell G. Bringhurst's "Fawn M. Brodie as a Critic of Mormonism's Policy toward Blacks."

4. Frank E. Vandiver, "Biography as an Agent of Humanism," 60.

5. Paul Murray Kendall, *The Art of Biography*, 2.

INTRODUCTION

1. Thomas Carlyle as quoted in Marc Pachter, "The Biographer Himself," 11; Mary Rhiel and David Suchoff, "Introduction: The Seduction of Biography," 2.

2. Kendall, *Art of Biography*, 114; Pachter, "Biographer Himself," 13.

3. Fern Marja Eckman, "Women in the News"; Arnold Hano, "Conversation with Fawn Brodie."

4. Stephenson, "Biography of Fawn Brodie," 25, 19.

5. Kendall, *Art of Biography*, 115; Stephen B. Oates, "Prologue," ix; Alan C. Elms, *Uncovering Lives*, 18.

6. Rhiel and Suchoff, "Introduction," 1–3.

7. Stephenson, "Biography of Fawn Brodie," 14–15, 8.

CHAPTER 1

1. Stephenson, "Biography of Fawn Brodie," 1–2; Eckman, "Women in the News"; Fawn M. Brodie (hereafter FMB), "The Protracted Life of Mrs. Gundy," 1.

2. Eckman, "Women in the News"; Stephenson, "Biography of Fawn Brodie," 1–2; Bruce Brodie, "Monologue on Fawn M. Brodie," 2.

3. Flora McKay Crawford, "Flora on Fawn"; Flora McKay Crawford, interview by Shirley E. Stephenson, 5 June 1986; Flora McKay Crawford, interview by author, 29 September 1988.

4. Jeanette McKay Morrell, *Highlights in the Life of President David O. McKay*, 6–8, 10.

5. Hugh Garner, interview by author, 20 September 1988.

6. Morrell, *Highlights*, 10; Llewelyn R. McKay, *Home Memories of President David O. McKay*, 3.

7. Morrell, *Highlights*, 12–13. According to family legend, Jennette was once nearly kidnapped by a young Indian who broke in and startled her with the announcement, "You be my squaw!" Fortunately, the timely intervention of her father-in-law, William McKay, saved the day.

8. FMB, "Inflation Idyl," 113; Morrell, *Highlights*, 23–26. The general prosperity of this period has been described by Dean L. May, "Towards a Dependent Commonwealth," 225–28. Flora McKay Crawford, Fawn Brodie's older sister, has suggested that the David McKay family finances were further helped by a generous inheritance from Jennette's brother, a Welsh miner who had prospected for gold in the eastern hills around Huntsville. Crawford interview by Stephenson, 5 June 1986.

9. Morrell, *Highlights*, 25; LaVerna Burnett Newey, *Remember My Valley*, 133–34; *Improvement Era*, vol. 21, 186.

10. Newey, *Remember My Valley*, 113; FMB, "Protracted Life of Mrs. Grundy," 2.

11. Newey, *Remember My Valley*, 111–13; Crawford, interview by Stephenson, 5 June 1986.

12. Thomas E. McKay's personality has been described by various family members to the author in written accounts and in oral interviews. See especially, Barbara McKay Smith, "Fawn McKay Brodie"; Pamela Brodie, interview by author, 8 January 1988; Thomas Brimhall McKay, interview by author, 24 July 1987.

13. Clifford E. Young, "Elder Thomas E. McKay," 226. For a discussion of the various activities of David O. McKay, see Morrell's *Highlights*. Also see Newell G. Bringhurst, "The Private versus the Public David O. McKay."

14. The dominance of the sisters was emphasized by Barbara McKay Smith in an interview by the author (21 July 1986) and in the author's interview with Flora McKay Crawford (29 September 1988). FMB, "Protracted Life of Mrs. Grundy," 2–4.

15. It appears that the David O. McKay Ogden residence on the corner of Madison and 21st Street was originally a part of the David McKay estate and was a second family residence in addition to the home in Huntsville. See *Salt Lake Tribune*, 7 January 1905, which makes reference to the death of Jennette Evans McKay in the "family residence" at 2071 Madison, Ogden. FMB, "Protracted Life of Mrs. Grundy," 2–4.

16. Young, "Elder Thomas E. McKay," 226; Thomas McKay interview, 24 July 1987.

17. Crawford interview, 29 September 1988; Smith, "Fawn McKay Brodie." The details of the courtship were recalled by Fawn B. McKay in her "Remarks," 4. Young, "Elder Thomas E. McKay," 226.

18. Raymond Brimhall Holbrook and Esther Hamilton Holbrook, *Tall Pine Tree*, 1–5, 7–21. In an oral interview with the author, Golden H. Brimhall (4 September 1988), told of Brimhall's marrying Myers without benefit of divorce. However, Holbrook and Holbrook in *Tall Pine Tree*, 5, assert that George Washington Brimhall was formally divorced from Lucretia, quoting him: "Lucretia had obtained a bill of devorcement from me by law, not withstanding my solicitations to her to join me in the valleys of the mountains." Genealogical records found in Family History Center, Salt Lake City: Sylvanus Brimhall, Family Group Record, 4, and George Washington Brimhall, Family Group Record, 1–4. Brimhall's *Workers of Utah*, originally published during the late nineteenth or early twentieth century, was allegedly suppressed because of its frankness but was reprinted in 1950, largely due to the efforts of grandson Dean R. Brimhall.

19. Much of the biographical information on George H. Brimhall is drawn from Richard S. Van Wagoner and Steven C. Walker, "George H. Brimhall," 24–28, in *A Book of Mormons*, and from Gary James Bergera and Ronald Priddis, *Brigham Young University*, 13–14; Brimhall interview, 4 September 1988, 9–11.

20. Brimhall interview, 39–40; Van Wagoner and Walker, "Brimhall," 25; Crawford interview, 29 September 1988. Further complicating Flora's family situation was that Brimhall apparently took a third plural wife, Alice Louise Reynolds—a well-known member of the faculty at Brigham Young Academy whose father was once private secretary to Brigham Young—an assertion made by granddaughter Barbara McKay Smith in an interview by author, 21 July 1986, and by Flora M. Crawford in a 29 September 1988 interview. However, Brimhall's sole surviving son, Golden H. Brimhall (4 September 1988, 11), asserted that his father never actually married Alice Louise Reynolds but "had an affair with her . . . in later years." Granddaughter Barbara McKay Smith rejected this notion, asserting that George H. Brimhall would "never carry on an affair with a woman

unless he was married to her" and adding that, according to family tradition, her grandfather traveled to southern California with Alice Louise Reynolds in the early twentieth century, purportedly to attend an educators' convention but primarily to cross the border to Mexico secretly so that they could be married (Barbara M. Smith to author, 9 August 1992). Another granddaughter, Flora McKay Crawford, agreed with Smith that George H. Brimhall and Alice Louise Reynolds traveled to Mexico to be married secretly (Crawford interview, 29 September 1988). For a biographical sketch of Alice Louise Reynolds, see Van Wagoner and Walker, *A Book of Mormons*, 224–27.

21. For discussion of the manifesto and its effects, see Thomas G. Alexander, *Mormonism in Transition*, and Alexander's more recent *Things in Heaven and Earth*.

22. Stephenson, "Biography of Fawn Brodie," 4; Thomas McKay interview, 24 July 1987. It should be noted, however, that in contrast to his grandchildren's perceptions, a somewhat different characterization of George H. Brimhall has been drawn by Bergera and Priddis in *Brigham Young University*, where Brimhall is described as "a devout Mormon," "orthodox" in his views of such matters as science and evolution. Free-spirited or orthodox, Brimhall gave evidence of mental instability. In quoting one former faculty member, Bergera and Priddis comment on Brimhall's "emotional response to many problems," suggesting that such behavior represented a "real educational danger" (13–14, 377). Walter Buss, interview by author, 21 September 1988; Barrie McKay, interview by author, 16 September 1988; Pamela Brodie to author, 22 January 1998.

23. Brimhall interview, 4 September 1988; Bergera and Priddis, *Brigham Young University*, 135–50; Van Wagoner and Walker, *A Book of Mormons*, 26–27; Pamela Brodie interview, 8 January 1988; Crawford interview, 29 September 1988; Thomas McKay interview, 24 July 1987.

24. Thomas McKay interview, 24 July 1987; *Deseret News*, 6 October 1960.

25. Fawn and Thomas McKay left immediately for their honeymoon following their 11 September 1912 marriage ceremony in the Salt Lake temple. Curiously, there was no wedding reception, despite the fact that both bride and groom came from prominent families. See the *Provo Herald*, 13 September 1912, and 7 September 1912, and the *Evening Standard* (Ogden), 16 September 1912. Thomas E. McKay recalled his doubts about his wife's fitting into her new family in "Remarks," 2; Edward R. McKay, interview by author, 23 July 1987; Joseph R. Morrell interview by author, 8 January 1988.

26. FMB, "Inflation Idyl," 113–14, vividly describes this whole episode.

27. Ibid., 114–15. There is some debate over who was primarily responsible for this unfortunate speculative venture. Brodie suggested that all four brothers jointly made the decision, whereas sister Flora McKay Crawford maintained that the oldest brother, David O. McKay, was the main promoter, coercing Thomas E. into going along. Crawford interview, 29 September 1988. However, Thomas B., Fawn's brother, suggested that the two older brothers, Thomas E. and David O., made the decision jointly (Thomas McKay interview, 24 July 1987).

28. Specific problems with the McKay's farmland have been described by Thomas B. McKay interview, 1 May 1989; Everett Doman, interview by author, 9 September 1988; Edward McKay interview, 23 July 1987. General problems with agriculture in Huntsville have been discussed by Howard R. Hunter, ed., *Beneath Ben Lomond's Peak*, 246–47; and more general problems with Utah agriculture are covered in Leonard J. Arrington and Thomas G. Alexander, *Dependent Commonwealth*, 63–70. FMB, "Inflation Idyl," 115.

29. FMB, "Inflation Idyll," 115–16.

30. FMB, "Protracted Life of Mrs. Grundy," 4.

31. Ibid., 7.

32. For a good overview of the varied church activities of David O. McKay, see Morrell, *Highlights*, in particular 299–303. The term "Golden Tongue" was noted by Jarvis Thurston, interview by author, 16 May 1989.

33. David Morrell, interview by author, 12 September 1988; Stephenson, "Biography of Fawn Brodie," 3.

34. *Deseret News*, 16 April 1947, 19 March 1955; *Salt Lake Tribune*, 15 April 1947, 19 March 1955.

35. FMB, "Protracted Life of Mrs. Grundy," 4; FMB to Dean Brimhall, 4 November 1959, original in Dean R. Brimhall Papers. Unless otherwise noted, all correspondence from FMB to Brimhall is found in the Dean R. Brimhall Papers.

36. Crawford interview, 29 September 1988; Joseph Morrell interview, 8 January 1988.

37. FMB, "Protracted Life of Mrs. Grundy," 3; Smith interview, 21 July 1986.

38. FMB, "Protracted Life of Mrs. Grundy," 5.

39. Ibid., 6.

40. Stephenson, "Biography of Fawn Brodie," 1, 3–4.

41. Keith Jensen, interview by author, 20 August 1988; Gay Doman, interview by author, 10 September 1988; Barrie McKay interview, 16 September 1988.

42. Crawford interview, 29 September 1988.

43. Quinn McKay, interview by author, 23 September 1988; Barrie McKay interview, 16 September 1988; Crawford interview by Stephenson, 5 June 1986; Monroe McKay, interview by author, 21 July 1986.

44. Brimhall interview, 4 September 1988; Smith interview, 21 July 1986; Crawford, "Flora on Fawn," 4.

45. Crawford, "Flora on Fawn," 1.

46. Crawford interview by Stephenson, 5 June 1986; Crawford, "Flora on Fawn," 1.

47. Crawford, "Flora on Fawn," 1; Crawford interview by Stephenson, 5 June 1986; FMB, "Libraries in My Life," 13.

48. Crawford, "Flora on Fawn," 1.

49. Ibid., 2. Flora felt she "was given this privilege [of advancement to fourth grade] because [of Fawn's advancement and because] in those days 'twins' were never separated." Crawford interview by Stephenson, 5 June 1986.

50. Edward McKay interview, 23 July 1987.

51. Thurston interview, 16 May 1989; Jean Jensen Mackay, interview by author, 26 January 1989; Elizabeth Jensen Shafter, interview by author, 6 September 1988; FMB, "Inflation Idyl," 115.

52. Crawford interview, 29 September 1988.

53. Thomas McKay likely secured his appointment through (1) his service in the state legislature, (2) the influence of his brother David O. McKay, (3) his church connections, or (4) a combination of the above. Information about the size and significance of the utilities comes from Frank Herman Jonas, "Utah: Sagebrush Democracy," 17, 38.

54. Crawford, "Flora on Fawn," 2.

55. Jeanette Morrell, interview by author, 22 September 1988.

56. Fawn McKay, "Just a Minute, Mother," 627.

57. Marshall Berges, "Fawn and Bernard Brodie."

58. Crawford interview by Stephenson, 5 June 1986; Crawford interview, 29 September 1988; Crawford, "Flora on Fawn," 3.

59. Crawford, "Flora on Fawn," 2.

60. Smith interview, 21 July 1986.

61. Crawford interview by Stephenson, 5 June 1986; Crawford interview, 29 September 1988.

62. Crawford interview by Stephenson, 5 June 1986; FMB, "Libraries in My Life," 13.

63. Crawford interview, 29 September 1988; Crawford interview by Stephenson, 5 June 1986.

64. Crawford, "Flora on Fawn," 4; Crawford interview, 29 September 1988.

65. Thomas McKay interview, 24 July 1987; Pamela Brodie to author, 22 January 1998; Crawford interview by Stephenson, 5 June 1986.

66. Newey, *Remember My Valley*, 241.

67. Quinn McKay interview, 23 September 1988; Gunn McKay, interview by author, 26 July 1987; Crawford, "Flora on Fawn," 2.

68. Thurston interview, 16 May 1989.

69. Gay Doman to Barbara McKay Smith, n.d.; copy in possession of Smith; Thurston interview, 16 May 1989.

70. Crawford, "Flora on Fawn," 3; Jensen interview, 20 August 1988; Thurston interview, 16 May 1989.

71. Jensen interview, 20 August 1988; Thomas McKay interview, 24 July 1987; Melvin Engstrom, interview by author, 7 August 1992; Crawford interview, 29 September 1988; Monroe McKay interview, 21 July 1986.

72. Thurston interview, 16 May 1989; Crawford interview by Stephenson, 5 June 1986; Gay Doman interview, 10 September 1988.

73. Crawford interview, 29 September 1988; Everett Doman interview, 9 September 1988; Smith interview, 21 July 1986.

74. Crawford interview by Stephenson, 5 June 1986.

75. Gay Doman interview, 10 September 1988; Louise McKay Card, interview by author, 31 July 1986.

76. Barbara McKay Smith, telephone conversation with author, 28 December 1997; Gay Doman interview, 10 September 1988.

77. Smith, "Fawn McKay Brodie"; Eckman, "Women in the News"; Smith interview, 21 July 1986.

78. FMB, "Inflation Idyl," 116.

79. Crawford interview by Stephenson, 5 June 1986.

80. Smith, "Fawn McKay Brodie," 5; FMB, "Protracted Life of Mrs. Grundy," 2.

81. Pamela Brodie to author, 22 January 1998.

82. Gay Doman interview, 10 September 1988; Crawford interview by Stephenson, 5 June 1986.

83. FMB, "Protracted Life of Mrs. Grundy," 1–12.

84. Thomas McKay interview, 24 July 1987.

85. Crawford interview, 29 September 1988.

86. Ibid.

87. Ibid.

88. Ibid; Crawford interview by Stephenson, 5 June 1986.

89. Shafter interview, 6 September 1988.

90. Ibid; Quinn McKay interview, 23 September 1988; Monroe McKay interview, 21 July 1986.

91. Smith, "Fawn McKay Brodie," 11; Mackay interview, 26 January 1989; FMB to Elizabeth Jensen Shafter, 16 October 1980; Crawford interview, 29 September 1988.

92. Mackay interview, 26 January 1989.

93. Jensen interview, 20 August 1988; Crawford interview by Stephenson, 5 June 1986.

94. Shafter interview, 6 September 1988.

95. Crawford interview, 29 September 1988.

96. Crawford, "Flora on Fawn," 2; FMB, "Commencement Address, Immaculate Heart College," 10 June 1972, typescript copy in FMB Papers, Bx 69, Fd 6.

97. Clarisse H. Hall, *Curricula at Weber State College*, gives an overview of the growth and development of the school.

98. FMB, "Inflation Idyl," 120; FMB, "It All Happened Very Quietly," 86; Crawford interview by Stephenson, 5 June 1986.

99. *Acorn* (Weber College Yearbook), 1931, 57; Fawn McKay, Weber College Course Transcript, 1930–32.

100. Richard L. Bushman's *Joseph Smith and the Beginnings of Mormonism* (1984) represents the most scholarly recent attempt to present Joseph Smith and the origins of the *Book of Mormon* from the perspective of a believing, practicing Latter-day Saint. This perspective is, of course, rejected in Brodie's own *No Man Knows My History*.

101. Everett Doman interview, 9 September 1988; Crawford interview, 29 September 1988.

102. Everett Doman interview, 9 September 1988; *Acorn*, 1931, 18.

103. "Story Given by Miss Fawn McKay," 16 December 1930, unpublished typescript in Weber State University Archives.

104. FMB to Ernest H. Linford, 15 November 1967, original in Ernest H. Linford Papers, Special Collections, University of Utah Library.

105. *Acorn*, 1931, 84. On this part of the tour the young women debated teams from Southwestern College (Winfield, Kansas), Pittsburg State (Pittsburg, Kansas), William Jewel College (Liberty, Missouri), Missouri State Teachers College (Maryville), the University of Missouri, McKendree College (Lebanon, Illinois), Blackburn College (Carlinville, Illinois), and Purdue University.

106. *Acorn*, 1931, 84. The actual bloodstains left on the floor of the Carthage jail by Joseph Smith's assassination are no longer shown, or even visible, to visitors as they were at the time of Fawn's visit.

107. *Acorn*, 1931, 84; FMB to Dale L. Morgan, 7 February 1946, original in Dale L. Morgan Papers. (Unless otherwise indicated, all correspondence cited from FMB to Dale Morgan can be found in the Dale L. Morgan Papers). For two good scholarly discussions of the emergence of the Reorganized Church and of Joseph Smith III, see Paul M. Edwards, *Our Legacy of Faith*, and Roger D. Launius, *Joseph Smith III*.

108. FMB to Morgan, 7 February 1946. Fawn and her siblings grew up knowing of Mormon polygamy in terms of its early practice among Utah's Latter-day Saints, but she was apparently unaware of Smith's involvement with the practice within the early Mormon movement. Barbara McKay Smith, telephone conversation with author, 28 December 1997.

109. *Acorn*, 1931, 84; Jetta Barker to Aaron Tracy, 4 March 1931, as copied by Lyle Bachman et al. eds., in "A Short History of Weber College Activities," original in Weber State University Archives.

110. As cited in Dilworth Jensen's journal entry, 5 March 1931, from typescript provided author by Patricia Jensen; *Acorn*, 1931, 84. The Nebraska debates were held at Nebraska Wesleyan University in Lincoln and at a small Presbyterian college in Hastings.

111. Fawn McKay to Aaron Tracy, 2 March 1931, as copied by Bachman et al. in "Short History of Weber College Activities"; Stephenson, "Biography of Fawn Brodie," 3; Jetta Barker to Aaron Tracy, 4 March 1931.

112. *Acorn*, 1931, 76, 79; Lyle Bachman, "Election of Student Officers," as copied by Bachman et al. in "Short History of Weber College Activities"; Thurston interview, 16 May 1989. Jarvis Thurston was the *Acorn*'s editor that year.

113. FMB to Elizabeth Jensen Shafter, 16 October 1980.

114. Fawn McKay, Weber College Course Transcript; Crawford, "Flora on Fawn," 3.

115. FMB, "It All Happened Very Quietly," 86.

116. Stephenson, "Biography of Fawn Brodie," 2; FMB, "It All Happened Very Quietly," 86; Eckman, "Women in the News."

117. FMB to Morgan, 12 March 1946; Crawford interview by Stephenson, 5 June 1986.

118. Stephenson, "Biography of Fawn Brodie, 3.

CHAPTER 2

1. Stephenson, "Biography of Fawn Brodie," 3.

2. Crawford interview by Stephenson, 5 June 1986; Crawford interview 29 September 1988.

3. Bergera and Priddis, *Brigham Young University*, 13–15; Thomas McKay interview 24 July 1987; Crawford interview by Stephenson, 5 June 1986.

4. Stephenson, "Biography of Fawn Brodie," 13.

5. FMB, "It All Happened Very Quietly," 85.

6. Ralph V. Chamberlin, *University of Utah*, 391, 414–15; FMB, "It All Happened Very Quietly," 86.

7. FMB, "It All Happened Very Quietly," 86.

8. Jeanette Morrell interview, 22 September 1988; Smith interview, 25 July 1987.

9. "Biography of Dean R. Brimhall," 5–6, in Dean R. Brimhall Papers; *Deseret News*, 8–9 April 1980.

10. FMB to Morgan, late 1944 (September or October?), 20 January 1945.

11. Brimhall interview, 4 September 1988; diary entry quoted by FMB to Morgan, 22 December 1945; Garner interview, 20 September 1988; Thomas McKay interview, 24 July 1987.

12. Brimhall interview, 4 September 1988; FMB to Morgan, 20 January 1945; Pamela Brodie to author, 22 January 1998; Garner interview, 20 September 1988.

13. Thomas McKay interview, 24 July 1987; FMB, "It All Happened Very Quietly," 92.

14. FMB, "It All Happened Very Quietly," 86.

15. Ibid., 91–92.

16. Crawford interview, 29 September 1988. Flora already had the training needed to teach elementary school by virtue of her two years at Weber College. But Fawn did not want to teach on the elementary level, intending instead to qualify herself to teach on the secondary level. So it was that even though Flora did not need two additional years at the university, she went to Salt Lake City at the urging of her parents to look after Fawn, who was still relatively young.

17. FMB, "It All Happened Very Quietly," 92–93.

18. Ibid., 86.

19. FMB, "Remembering," 2–3, a manuscript draft of the essay published in revised form as "It All Happened Very Quietly," original in FMB Papers, Bx 66,

Fd 10. The account of Brodie's encounter with her roommate was omitted from the essay as published in *Remembering: The University of Utah.*

20. Crawford interview, 29 September 1988; FMB to Morgan, 22 December 1945. While Brodie indicated in her letter to Morgan that this initial confrontation with the writings of Birney occurred while she was at University of Chicago, the nature and tone of her comments, combined with her sister's recollections, would seem to suggest the University of Utah as the more likely place.

21. Alice Smith McKay, "A Psychological Examination," 67.

22. Ibid., 68; Joseph Morrell interview, 8 January 1988.

23. FMB to Elizabeth Jensen Shafter, 16 October 1980; Crawford, "Flora on Fawn," 3.

24. FMB, "It All Happened Very Quietly," 92; Berges, "A Talk with Fawn Brodie," 8; Fawn McKay, "Experiment," 24–27.

25. FMB, "It All Happened Very Quietly," 95; Fawn McKay, Official Grade Transcript, University of Utah, 1932–34.

26. FMB, "It All Happened Very Quietly," 95.

27. Crawford interview, 29 September 1988; Jeanette Morrell interview, 22 September 1988.

28. Jeanette Morrell, letter to Barbara McKay Smith, n.d., copy in possession of author; Jeanette Morrell interview, 22 September 1988.

29. Crawford interview, 29 September 1988.

30. Shafter interview, 6 September 1988; Mackay interview, 26 January 1989.

31. Jensen interview, 20 August 1988; Crawford interview, 29 September 1988.

32. Crawford interview, 29 September 1988.

33. Ibid.

34. FMB to Elizabeth Jensen Shafter, 16 October 1980; Thomas McKay interview, 24 July 1987. For an interesting personal recollection of the Mormon Chicago movement, see Russel B. Swensen, "Mormons at the University of Chicago Divinity School," 37–47.

35. Barrie McKay interview, 16 September 1988; Pamela Brodie interview, 8 January 1988.

36. FMB to Elizabeth Jensen Shafter, 16 October 1980; Pamela Brodie interview, 8 January 1988; Shafter interview, 6 September 1988; Jensen interview, 20 August 1988; Mackay interview, 26 January 1989.

37. Stephenson, "Biography of Fawn Brodie," 3.

38. Bruce Brodie, "Monologue," 5; William H. McNeill, *Hutchins' University.* For two good overviews of the history of the University of Chicago, see McNeill, *Hutchins' University,* and Edward Shils, *Remembering the University of Chicago.* For treatments of the life and career of Robert Hutchins, see Mary Ann Dzuback, *Robert M. Hutchins,* and Harry S. Ashmore, *Unseasonable Truths.*

39. Bruce Brodie, "Monologue," 5; Stephenson, "Biography of Fawn Brodie," 3; Marvin Hill to author, 12 February 1988; John K. Edmunds, interview by

Gordon Irving, in James Moyle Oral History Program, February 1980 to May 79, copy in Archives, Church of Jesus Christ of Latter-day Saints.

40. Vernon Larson in telephone conversation with author, 15 December 1988; General Minutes, University Ward, Chicago South Stake, roll 2, 26 January 1936, 21 March 1936, 20 October 1935, 1 December 1935, all in Archives, Church of Jesus Christ of Latter-day Saints.

41. Stephenson, "Biography of Fawn Brodie," 11.

42. Bruce Brodie, "Monologue," 5; Berges, "Fawn and Bernard Brodie."

43. Leonard Brody, interview by author, 31 October 1988. The original and indeed prevalent spelling of Bernard's family name is "Brody."

44. Brody interview, 31 October 1988. Bernard Brodie, however, remembers his mother's reaction to his graduation in much less positive terms, according to Pamela Brodie, letter to author, 22 January 1998.

45. Brody interview, 31 October 1988.

46. Brody to author, 22 July 1991, original in possession of author.

47. Ibid.; Brody interview, Bringhurst, 31 October 1988. According to Brody, the name "Brodie" is almost never Jewish, while "Brody" is almost universally Jewish.

48. Pamela Brodie to author, 22 January 1998; Brody to author, 22 July 1991.

49. Pamela Brodie interview, 8 January 1988; Pamela Brodie to author 22 January 1998; Bruce Brodie, "Monologue," 5. Bernard was an accomplished horseman despite growing up in the urban environment of Chicago. He had joined a cavalry unit of the Illinois National Guard, headquartered near Grant Park, to pursue his love of riding. Brody interview, 31 October 1988.

50. Thomas McKay interview, 24 July 1987.

51. Crawford interview, 29 September 1988; Barrie McKay interview, 16 September 1988; Pamela Brodie interview, 6 January 1989; Edmunds interview, 79. David O.'s role in counseling his niece was in keeping with his position as the dominant figure within the extended McKay family, a position now enhanced by his elevation in the Mormon Church hierarchy in 1934 to the office of second counselor within the elite First Presidency.

52. Pamela Brodie interview, 6 January 1989.

53. Crawford interview, 29 September 1988; Pamela Brodie to author, 22 January 1998.

54. Pamela Brodie to author, 22 January 1998; Mackay interview, 26 January 1989.

55. Pamela Brodie interview, 6 January 1989.

56. Monroe McKay interview, 21 July 1986. In a somewhat less passionate fashion, Fawn recalled years later to Nephi Jenson that her own "study of the anthropology of the American Indians convinced me that they were of Mongoloid rather than Hebraic origin." FMB to Nephi Jensen, 15 February 1946, copy in possession of author.

57. Bruce Brodie, "Monologue," 5; Pamela Brodie to author, 22 January 1998. Bernard's younger brother, Leonard, asserted that his mother did not

attend because Bernard invited only her, snubbing him and his brothers. Brody interview, 31 October 1988.

58. Pamela Brodie interview, 6 January 1989. Fawn's assertion to the contrary, it appears that she was involved with the Chicago University ward on at least two subsequent occasions. See General Minutes, University Ward, Chicago South Stake, roll 2, 22 and 29 November 1936.

59. FMB, "Libraries in My Life," 13–14.

60. Ibid., 13–14.

61. For a brief discussion of the Church Security Program, see James B. Allen and Glen M. Leonard, *Story of the Latter-day Saints,* first edition, 519–21. For a description of Dean Brimhall's critique of the Church Security Program, see John Heinerman and Anson Shupe, *Mormon Corporate Empire,* 181–87.

62. FMB to Dean Brimhall, 13 April 1937. Fawn added, in regard to the church's profit, "Of course the Church probably isn't really making money, but at any rate it is clear that the people themselves are financing every bit of the plan & paying extra tithing beside. No Church capital is being endangered."

63. Martha Emery (FMB), "Mormon Security," 182–83.

64. Ibid.

65. Bruce Brodie, "Monologue," 6; Thomas McKay interview, 24 July 1987; Smith interview, 21 July 1986; Card interview, 31 July 1986; Barrie McKay interview, 16 September 1988; Shafter interview, 6 September 1988; Mackay interview, 26 January 1989.

66. Pamela Brodie interview, 6 January 1989.

67. Crawford interview by Stephenson, 5 June 1986; Card interview, 31 July 1986; Shafter interview, 6 September 1988; Mackay interview, 26 January 1989.

68. Bruce Brodie, "Monologue," 9–10; Crawford interview by Stephenson, 5 June 1986; Crawford interview, 29 September 1988.

69. Card interview, 31 July 1986; Shafter interview, 6 September 1988.

70. Thurston interview, 16 May 1989. The standard account on Bernard De Voto is Wallace Stegner's *The Uneasy Chair.* A good overview of Mormondom's so-called lost generation is Edward A. Geary, "Mormondoms's Lost Generation."

71. Thurston interview, 16 May 1989.

72. The important role played by David O. in McKay's appointment was mentioned by several family members and individuals acquainted with the family, but the information is particularly attributable to Flora McKay Crawford in an interview with the author, 29 September 1988. Jonas, in "Utah: Sagebrush Democracy," 27–29, briefly discusses the changing political environment in Utah that caused Thomas McKay to lose his position with the utilities commission.

73. FMB, "Inflation Idyl," 120–21.

74. Thomas McKay interview, 24 July 1987. Brimhall's associations with the New Deal are noted in "Register of the Papers of Dean R. Brimhall," 9, in Dean Brimhall Papers.

CHAPTER 3

1. FMB to Nephi Jensen, n.d.; Stephenson, "Biography of Fawn Brodie," 6, 7.

2. FMB, "Libraries In My Life," 14.

3. Ibid.

4. FMB to Dean Brimhall, 14 June 1939.

5. Thomas McKay interview, 24 July 1987.

6. Ibid.

7. FMB to Dean Brimhall, 14 June 1939.

8. Fred Kaplan, *Wizards of Armageddon*, 11–16, gives the best overview of Bernard Brodie's early academic career and scholarly activities while at the University of Chicago.

9. According to Douglas F. Tobler, "The Jews, the Mormons, and the Holocaust," 75. The 12,000 German Mormons, however, represented only a tiny fraction of the total Mormon Church membership of 670,000 in 1930. See *Deseret News Church Almanac*, 1991–1992, 335.

10. Tobler, "Jews, Mormons, and the Holocaust," 77, 63.

11. Thomas McKay interview, 24 July 1987; FMB to Dean Brimhall, 14 June 1939.

12. FMB to Dean Brimhall, 14 June 1939.

13. David O. McKay to Thomas B. McKay, 4 September 1939, original in Thomas B. McKay Papers; Young, "Elder Thomas E. McKay," 224–26; *Deseret News*, 15 January 1958.

14. FMB to Dean Brimhall, 26 March 1940; FMB to Morgan, 1 April 1994, original in Madeline McQuown Papers. In describing her mother's prior religious beliefs, Brodie noted, "She was a moderately devout Mormon always until she went to Europe."

15. Bruce Brodie, "Monologue," 7.

16. Kaplan, *Wizards of Armageddon*, 16–17.

17. Bruce Brodie, "Monologue," 7.

18. S. F. Bryant, Review, 202; F. E. Hirsch, Review, 390; W. D. Puleston, Review, 13; Kaplan, *Wizards of Armageddon*, 17.

19. Kaplan, *Wizards of Armageddon*, 18. For reviews, see Carol Thompson, *Current History*, 163; D. W. Mitchell, *Nation*, 455; Garrett Mattingly, 9.

20. FMB, *Our Far Eastern Record*; William Mulder, "Citation Honoring Fawn McKay Brodie on Her Election as an Honorary Alumna Member of Phi Beta Kappa," June 1978, in FMB Papers, Bx 1, Fd. 7; *Los Angeles Times*, 14 June 1942.

21. *Salt Lake Tribune*, 30 May 1943; FMB, *Peace Aims and Postwar Planning*, vi.

22. Crawford interview by Stephenson, 5 June 1986.

23. FMB to Dean Brimhall, 18 June, 3 November 1942. Brodie's allusion to "a blanket stretched across the room" refers to the fact that Joseph Smith dictated the contents of the "golden plates" to a scribe who sat on the other side of the room, behind a blanket and unable to see the plates for himself.

24. FMB to Thomas E. and Fawn B. McKay, 18 May 1943, original in FMB Papers, Bx 2, Fd 1.

25. FMB to Alfred A. Knopf, 14 February 1943, original in Knopf Papers. In outlining the nature of the biography at this point, Brodie noted, "Of the period covering the Mormon 'wars' in Missouri during the 1830s, I have written a first draft. But the final four-year period during which Joseph Smith built Nauvoo, Illinois, making of it at the same moment a holy shrine and a political cauldron, remains to be studied as well as written. I hope to have the book finished in time for publication in 1944, since it is the centennial of his death."

26. Ibid.

27. M. Rugoff, Biography Fellowship Evaluation, 17 March 1943, original in Knopf Papers. It should be noted that favorable opinion rendered by Alfred A. Knopf was not unanimous. In contrast to M. Rugoff's opinion, a second Knopf reader, H. Strauss, submitted a very negative evaluation, stating, "I don't like her present project," and expressing his belief that her "book would encounter very substantial sales obstacles." This reader was, moreover, critical of her writing: "I cannot call [it] the least bit exciting. She never made me want to read on in the extensive sample section." "The book," the reader said, "remains for me a bit on the dull side."

28. E. Gordon Bill to Bernard Brodie, n.d., as quoted in Kaplan, *Wizards of Armageddon*, 18.

29. Kaplan, *Wizards of Armageddon*, 18–19.

30. FMB to Thomas E. and Fawn B. McKay, 18 May, 24 May 1943, originals in FMB Papers, Bx 2, Fd 1.

31. *Deseret News*, 7 April 1941; FMB to Thomas E. and Fawn B. McKay, 18 May 1943.

32. "Fawn Brodie, Donald W. Mitchell Receive Alfred A. Knopf Literary Fellowships for 1943," press release, 28 May 1943, original in Knopf Papers.

33. *Washington Post*, 22 May 1943; *Salt Lake Tribune*, 30 May 1943; *Ogden Standard-Examiner*, 23 May 1943.

34. FMB to Thomas E. and Fawn B. McKay, 24 May 1943. *Washington Post*, 22 May 1943.

35. Brodie, "Libraries in My Life," 14–15.

36. FMB, KUTV interview, Salt Lake City 8 March 1978; Pamela Brodie to author, 22 January 1998.

37. FMB to Morgan, 9 September 1943. According to Brodie, the restrictive policy of the Mormon Church Historical Department was implemented in reaction to the recent publication of R. English's "The Mormons Move Over," an essay dealing with the Mormons in a somewhat critical light.

38. FMB to Morgan, 9 September 1943. The existence of the Joseph Smith diary had been disclosed to Brodie by M. Wilford Poulson, professor of psychology at Brigham Young University. FMB, "Libraries in My Life," 15.

39. FMB to Morgan, 9 September 1943.

40. Ibid. In a later account, Brodie described her "rather difficult interview with my uncle, David O. McKay, who told me at first that he would rather I would not use the library at all, and who later the next day sent me a note telling me I could use it. Seeing his anxiety, I decided then not to use it further, I wrote him a letter telling him I would not. I never returned." Brodie, "Libraries in my Life," 15.

41. FMB to Morgan, 9 September 1943.

42. Ibid.

43. FMB, "Libraries in My Life," 14–15.

44. FMB to Morgan, 9 September 1943.

45. The best overview of the life and activities of Dale L. Morgan is John Phillip Walker, ed., *Dale Morgan on Early Mormonism.* Also see Gary F. Novak's review-essay of this work under the title, "'The Most Convenient Form of Error.'"

46. FMB to Claire Noall, 6 May, 25 May 1944, 5 February 1945, originals in Claire Noall Papers.

47. FMB, *No Man Knows My History,* xi.

48. Memo from Dale Morgan, n.d., original in Morgan Papers.

49. For a brief description of the activities of Vesta Crawford, who was counted among the members of Mormondom's so-called lost generation, see Allene Jensen, "Utah Writers of the Twentieth Century," master's of science thesis, University of Utah, 1977, 27. FMB to Claire Noall, 8 April, 7 and 22 June 1944, originals in Claire Noall Papers. Although completing significant research on Emma Smith, Crawford never actually wrote her projected book-length study. Materials relative to this research are contained in the Vesta Crawford Papers, Special Collections, Marriott Library, University of Utah.

50. FMB to Claire Noall, 14 October 1943, original in Claire Noall Papers. Two brief descriptions of the life and career of Claire Noall are contained in obituaries carried in the *Salt Lake Tribune,* 3 September 1971, and the *Deseret News,* 3 September 1971.

51. FMB to Claire Noall, 13 and 31 December 1943, 17 January 1944, originals in Claire Noall Papers.

52. FMB to Claire Noall, 5 February 1944, original in Claire Noall Papers.

53. Levi S. Peterson, in *Juanita Brooks,* discusses the various aspects of this Utah writer's life and career. Juanita Brooks to Dale L. Morgan, 7 October 1943, as quoted in Peterson, 141; FMB to Claire Noall, 8 April 1944, original in Claire Noall Papers.

54. See "Martin Wilford Poulson," in *Utah's Distinguished Personalities,* 173, and Peterson, *Juanita Brooks,* 65, 266–67.

55. FMB to Morgan, 7 December 1943; Samuel W. Taylor, *Rocky Mountain Empire;* FMB to Morgan, 22 March 1944.

56. FMB to Morgan, 26 September, 26 October, 5 December 1944; Wilford Poulson to FMB, 5 January 1945, original in FMB Papers, Bx 9, Fd 12.

57. FMB to Morgan, 19 November 1943.

58. Ibid; FMB to Morgan, 18 December 1943.

59. FMB to Morgan, 7 and 18 December 1943, 22 March 1944.

60. FMB to Morgan, 19 November 1943.

61. FMB to Morgan, 22 March 1944. A 20 March 1944 article in *Time* magazine drew Brodie's attention to this incident. The historical background concerning the incident and the whole Mormon fundamentalist movement is discussed in Richard S. Van Wagoner, *Mormon Polygamy*.

62. FMB to Morgan, 26 April 1944.

63. FMB to Morgan, 1 April 1944, original in Madeline McQuown Papers.

64. FMB to Morgan, 26 April, 6 May 1944.

65. FMB to Morgan, 31 May 1944.

66. FMB to Morgan, 7 June 1944.

67. FMB to Morgan, 13 July 1944.

68. Ibid.

69. FMB to Morgan, 4 August 1944.

70. Morgan to FMB, 28 August 1944, original in FMB Papers, Bx 7, Fd. 4.

71. Ibid.

72. FMB to Morgan, 2 and 26 September 1944.

73. FMB to Morgan, 26 October 1944.

74. Wilson Follett to Alfred A. Knopf, 6 December 1944, original in Knopf Papers.

75. Milo M. Quaife, "Report on Fawn M. Brodie Narrative," 3 April 1945, original in Knopf Papers.

76. Wilson Follett to Alfred A. Knopf, Memo, 16 January 1945, original in Knopf Papers; FMB to Morgan, 20 January 1945; FMB to Claire Noall, ca. January 1945, original in Morgan Papers. In the original, "ca. January 1944" is indicated by the archivist who processed the Morgan Papers, but internal evidence and other documentary materials suggest that the 1944 date is incorrect. FMB to Morgan, ca. late 1944. The dedication in *No Man Knows My History* reads, "To the memory of my cousin Lieutenant McKeen Eccles Brimhall killed in France September 20, 1944."

77. FMB to Morgan, 17 February 1945.

78. FMB to Morgan, 24 March, 9 August 1945.

79. Kaplan, *Wizards of Armageddon*, 19–21.

80. Ibid., 9–10; Gregg Herken, *Counsels of War*, 2–3; Lawrence Freedman, *Evolution of Nuclear Strategy*, 29–30.

81. Bernard Brodie, ed., *Absolute Weapon*, 73; Kaplan, *Wizards of Armageddon*, 18.

82. FMB to Morgan, 9 August 1945.

83. FMB to Morgan, 22 August 1945.

84. FMB to Morgan, 24 September 1945.

85. FMB to Morgan, 5 December 1944.

86. FMB to Morgan, 22 October, 27 November 1945.

87. FMB to Morgan, 10 December 1945.

88. FMB to Morgan, 19 January, 12 March 1946.

89. FMB to Morgan, 19 January 1946.

90. FMB to Morgan, 24 September 1945; Israel A. Smith to S. A. Burgess, 19 September 1945, original in RLDS Archives.

91. FMB to Morgan, 24 September 1945; Israel A. Smith to Alfred A. Knopf, 18 October 1945, copy of original in FMB Papers, Bx 9, Fd 15.

92. FMB to Morgan, 22 October, 24 September 1945.

93. *Saints' Herald*, 1 and 8 December 1945.

94. FMB to Morgan, 22 October, 24 September 1945. It is not clear if Alfred A. Knopf took the initiative in sending McKay a copy of the galleys in an effort to generate increased publicity or if Knopf sent the galleys in response to McKay's own request.

95. Morgan to Lydia Clawson Hoopes, 29 January 1946; Morgan to FMB, 7 March 1946, both copies in Morgan Papers; Crawford interview by Stephenson, 5 June 1986; Smith interview, 21 July 1986; Card interview, 31 July 1986; FMB to Dean Brimhall, 4 November 1959; Thomas McKay interview, 24 July 1987.

96. Dean Brimhall to Preston Nibley, 26 May 1946, copy in Brimhall Papers; Thomas McKay interview, 1 May 1989.

97. J. M. Cummings to FMB, 5 November 1945, original in FMB Papers, Bx 9, Fd 14; FMB to Morgan, 15 November 1945. There is no evidence of a written response from Brodie to Cummings within any of the various materials examined by the author.

98. Beatrice Johnson to Dale Morgan, 7 October 1946, original in Morgan Papers. Morgan to FMB, 2 March 1947, original in FMB Papers; FMB to Dean Brimhall, 8 March 1947. A short newspaper description of Ernest McKay's activities is found in "Kaysville Class to Hear Current Book Discussed," typescript in FMB Papers.

99. In that same article, however, Brayer criticized her for "coloring episodes in such a manner as to leave her open to criticism." *Mississippi Valley Historical Review*, March 1946, 601–3; *New York Times*, 9 January 1946; *Newsweek*, 26 November 1945; *Time*, 28 January 1946.

100. The *Cleveland Plain Dealer* (25 November 1945) called the book "a scholarly work of accurate detail and painstaking research," praising it as "the life of Joseph Smith to which all future historians and biographers must refer." The *Chicago Sun* (25 November 1945) called it "a rare combination of sound scholarship and lively, readable narrative," giving the reader "a believable picture of one of America's most interesting characters." *American Historical Review*, July 1946, 725–26; *New York History*, April 1946.

101. FMB to Morgan, 12 May 1946; *New York Times Book Review*, 25 November 1945. Fisher was best known for *Children of God: An American Epic*, a fictionalized account of the rise and progress of Mormonism, published in 1939. For an excellent overview of Fisher's life and work, see Leonard J. Arrington and John Haupt, "Mormon Heritage of Vardis Fisher." Fisher's most telling criticism was that the

biography was "almost more a novel than a biography because she rarely hesitates to give the content of a mind or to explain motives which at best can only be surmised." He then predicted, "It is this reviewer's notion that [Brodie] will turn novelist in her next book, and that she should."

102. FMB to Morgan, 27 November 1945; FMB to Thomas E. and Fawn B. McKay, 7 December 1945, original in FMB Papers, Bx 2, Fd 1. In defending herself against Fisher, Brodie asserted that in her biography "there is not a single line of dialogue that didn't come directly out of a primary source book or manuscript, in every case I indicated the source in the footnotes. If I so much as changed a comma, I felt guilty about it."

103. *New York Herald-Tribune*, 16 December 1945. For De Voto's "paranoid thesis," see Bernard De Voto, "Centennial of Mormonism," and De Voto, *Year of Decision: 1846*.

104. FMB to Thomas E. and Fawn B. McKay, 17 December 1945, original in FMB Papers; FMB to Morgan, 18 December 1945.

105. *Saturday Review of Literature*, 24 November 1945, 7–8. Regarding the assignment of the review, Brodie had written Morgan on 15 November 1945, "I had assumed that it is against reviewing policy to send a book to someone mentioned in the acknowledgments, but I guess either that is wrong, or else they didn't bother to read that page." But she confessed her pleasure at being "so lucky in the reviewer."

106. FMB to Morgan, 30 December 1945; Clip Boutell, "Authors Are Like People"; John K. Hutchens, "People Who Read and Write." In this latter source, Brodie admitted that by the time she had examined two-thirds of her research materials she had "arrived at her thesis that until a certain point in his career Smith was an impostor."

107. FMB to Morgan, 12 March, 12 May 1946, 30 December 1945. By May 1946 the sales of Brodie's book totaled some four hundred copies, according to Fred Scrivan, an Ogden bookseller. Total book sales for all of Utah numbered "about" nine hundred by March 1946, according to a report given by Knopf to Brodie (FMB to Morgan, 12 March 1946). Such sales, while significant, were considerably less than rumored sale of five thousand copies in Ogden in one day alone (Morgan to FMB, 7 March 1946, original in FMB Papers, Bx 7, Fd 7).

108. FMB to Morgan, 10 December 1945.

109. As printed in the *Deseret News*, Church Section, 23 February 1946. A somewhat different version of this story appears in typescript under the title "The Thoroughbred." It was brought to the author's attention by Barbara M. Smith. According to McKay's son, his strong feelings against his niece and her book included resentment, disappointment, and betrayal. Brodie had "culled her information from the garbage cans of the Church," David O. McKay said. Edward McKay interview, 23 July 1987.

110. FMB to Morgan, 12 March 1946.

111. *Improvement Era*, March 1946.

112. *Deseret News*, 8 April 1946; FMB to Morgan, 12 May 1946.

113. *Deseret News*, 11 May 1946; *Appraisal of the So-Called Brodie Book*. The article—and the tract—was written by a church committee of which Apostle Albert E. Bowen was apparently the principal author.

114. Hugh Nibley, *No, Ma'am, That's Not History*, 21, 7–8.

115. FMB to Morgan, 27 May 1946; FMB to Thomas E. and Fawn B. McKay, 27 May 1946, original in FMB Papers. Also attacking Brodie and her work with the apparent approval of Mormon Church leaders were Milton R. Hunter, a member of the church's First Quorum of the Seventy, who reviewed *No Man Knows My History* in the *Pacific Historical Review*, 226–28; and, somewhat later, Francis W. Kirkham through his *A New Witness for Christ in America*, 359–94. In a specific, if private, response to Bowen's charge in *Appraisal* that her harsh treatment of Smith was encouraged if not prompted by her Jewish husband's bias against Mormonism, Brodie asserted that her biography "would have been a harsher indictment of Joseph Smith had it not been for [Bernard's] influence" in that he "kept urging me to look at the man's genius, to explain his successes, and to make sure that the reader understood why so many people loved and believed him. If there is real compassion for Joseph Smith in the book," Brodie said, "and I believe there is, it is more the result of the influence of my husband than anyone else." FMB to Revere Hansen, 29 January 1979, copy in FMB Papers, Bx 9, Fd 9.

116. FMB, "Polygamy Shocks the Mormons," 399–405.

117. William H. Reeder to FMB, 23 May 1946, copy in FMB Papers, Bx 1, Fd 6. That Brodie was directed to a local church court in Cambridge and not summoned directly to Mormon Church headquarters in Salt Lake City might appear puzzling, particularly given compelling evidence that orders to excommunicate the errant author originated at the highest levels of the Mormon Church. But the handling of Brodie's excommunication proceedings within the confines of the New England Mission was in keeping with general church practice, which mandated that disciplinary actions involving individual members be handled by church authorities on the local level. The conclusion that the process originated at much higher levels was reached by the author on the basis of oral interviews with various family members and with G. Richard Palmer, present in the New England Mission as a young missionary, who described conditions leading up to the formal excommunication of Brodie in 1946. One family member suggested that the formal excommunication of Brodie, while orchestrated from church headquarters in Salt Lake, was handled within the confines of the New England Mission in order to mask the involvement of David O. McKay in the matter. G. Richard Palmer, interview by author, 27 April 1989; Garner interview, 20 September 1988.

118. FMB to Morgan, 27 May 1946; Palmer interview, 27 April 1989; Manuscript History, New England Mission, 1 June 1946, original in Historical Department, Church of Jesus Christ of Latter-day Saints; William H. Reeder to FMB, 19

June 1946, original in FMB Papers, Bx 1, Fd 6. It is probable that had Mormon Church officials, particularly William H. Reeder, been aware of Brodie's condition, they would have been willing to postpone her court hearing. The letter of summons stated that if there was any good reason Brodie could not be present, she should notify the individuals delivering the summons, something Brodie failed to do.

119. FMB to Dean Brimhall, 18 June 1946, original in FMB Papers,

120. FMB to Morgan, 27 May 1946.

121. FMB to Morgan, 27 May 1946; FMB to Thomas E. and Fawn B. McKay, 2 June 1946, original in FMB Papers, Bx 2, Fd 1. Crawford interview, 29 September 1988; Thomas McKay interview, 24 July 1987.

122. FMB to Morgan, 27 May 1946. Stegner, *Conversations with Wallace Stegner* (109–10); (Thomas McKay interview, 24 July 1987; Crawford interview, 29 September 1988; Smith interview, 21 July 1986). FMB to Thomas E. and Fawn B. McKay, 27 May 1946, original in FMB Papers, Bx 2, Fd 1. Brodie also tried to reassure her parents after they received details of her own emotional reaction from Dean Brimhall: "I hope Dean didn't give you an exaggerated picture of my own attitude. It was just that I could see so clearly what it might mean for you and Daddy." FMB to Thomas E. and Fawn B. McKay, 2 June 1946, original in FMB Papers, Box 2, Fd 1.

123. FMB to Morgan, 7 February, 12 March 1946.

124. FMB to Morgan, 12 May, 7 February 1946.

125. FMB to Morgan, 19 January 1946. During this pregnancy, Fawn took DES—a drug then commonly used to prevent miscarriages. Pamela Brodie interview, 6 January 1989. According to her sister Flora, Fawn's nervousness may have contributed to her difficulties during pregnancies. Certainly the tensions surrounding reception of *No Man Knows My History* would have contributed to her anxieties. (Crawford interview, 29 September 1988). FMB to Morgan, 13 July 1946.

126. FMB to Morgan, 13 July 1946; Morgan to FMB, 7 January 1946, original in FMB Papers, Bx 7, Fd 7. On a personal level, Morgan cautioned Brodie that, as he saw it, she was "still in . . . a mood or rebellion," a mood that reflected "a sense of emotional insecurity which may require several more years to overcome."

127. FMB to Morgan, 19 January 1946.

CHAPTER 4

1. Stephenson, "Biography of Fawn Brodie," 14–15.

2. Berges, "Fawn and Bernard Brodie"; Stephenson, "Biography of Fawn Brodie," 14–15.

3. *Los Angeles Times*, 21 March 1975.

4. FMB, *No Man Knows My History*, 173–74, 423–25. For a discussion of Brodie's active concern throughout the course of her life about the status of blacks within the Mormon Church, see Bringhurst, "Fawn M. Brodie as a Critic of Mormonism's Policy toward Blacks."

5. Berges, "Fawn and Bernard Brodie"; Stephenson, "Biography of Fawn Brodie," 19.

6. Stephenson, "Biography of Fawn Brodie," 14.

7. For two good historical overviews of the changing role of American women during and after World War II, see Lois W. Banner, *Women in Modern America*, 182–244, and William H. Chafe, *American Woman*, 135–225.

8. Stephenson, "Biography of Fawn Brodie," 46.

9. Ibid., 47–48; FMB to Morgan, 3 September 1946.

10. FMB to Morgan, 25 July 1946.

11. FMB to Morgan, 3 September 1946; FMB to Juanita Brooks, 1 October 1946, original in Juanita Brooks Papers; FMB to Morgan, 2 December 1946.

12. FMB to Morgan, 21 January 1947, 2 December 1946.

13. FMB to Morgan, 21 January, 8 February, 14 March 1947.

14. FMB to Morgan, 14 March, 12 and 28 April 1947.

15. FMB, *No Man Knows My History*, 30–31, 427–29; FMB to Morgan, 14 and 31 March 1947.

16. FMB, "Libraries in My Life," 15. For a fuller, detailed account of Brodie's successful 1947 quest for the Purple account, see FMB to Morgan, 31 March 1947, original in Madeline McQuown Papers. The fact of an 1826 trial was corroborated by other materials, including a second eyewitness account of the trial written just five years after the event and discovered by Dale Morgan, who with Stanley Ivins "put the pieces of mosaic history together." See FMB, "Libraries in My Life," 15, 18. Brodie later stated that had the document she went in search of proved a forgery she would have had to make major revisions in one of the chapters in her biography. (FMB, "Libraries in My Life," 18). Kirkham, *New Witness for Christ*, 458–94.

17. FMB to Morgan, 23 January, 8 February 1947; FMB, "'This Is the Place.'"

18. FMB, "'This Is the Place.'"

19. FMB to Morgan, 23 July 1947.

20. FMB to Morgan, 14 March 1947.

21. FMB to Morgan, 23 August 1947.

22. FMB to Morgan, 6 January, 4 March, 17 April, 28 May 1948.

23. FMB to Morgan, 17 April, 4 March 1948.

24. FMB to Morgan, 17 April, 26 May, 23 August 1948.

25. FMB to Morgan, 28 September, 26 May 1948.

26. FMB to Morgan, 28 September 1948.

27. "Brodies of Hilltop House," 20–22.

28. FMB to Claire Noall, 5 October 1948, original in Noall Papers; FMB to Morgan, 20 December 1948.

29. FMB to Claire Noall, 5 October 1948, original in Claire Noall Papers; FMB to Morgan, 17 February, 1 April 1949.

30. FMB to Morgan, 17 February 1949.

31. FMB to Morgan, 1 April 1949.

32. FMB to Morgan, 17 February 1949. In her remarks concerning the relationship between inertia and the "female mind," Brodie was agreeing with—and reiterating the observations made on this matter by—Henry Adams in his autobiographical *The Education of Henry Adams*.

33. FMB to Morgan, 15 and 30 June 1949. According to her sister Flora, Fawn's condition became life-threatening after she was given the wrong type of blood during her hospitalization. Crawford interview, 29 September 1988.

34. FMB to Morgan, 30 June, 13 September 1949; FMB to Dean Brimhall, 24 October 1949. Fawn also confessed similar feelings to Dale Morgan: "I can't pretend to complete objectivity now, but at least I am mercifully relieved of the guilt feelings that have disturbed me in the past. That was one positive gain in an otherwise disastrous visit." FMB to Morgan, 13 September 1949.

35. FMB to Morgan, 30 June 1949.

36. Ibid., 13 September 1949.

37. Alfred A. Knopf to FMB, 14 November 1949, original in Knopf Papers.

38. FMB to Knopf, 21 November 1949, copy in Knopf Papers.

39. Knopf to FMB, 23 November 1949, copy in Knopf Papers.

40. FMB to Morgan, 19 December 1949, 22 February, 20 July 1950.

41. FMB to Morgan, 22 February, 11 April 1950.

42. FMB to Morgan, 14 March 1950; FMB to Dean Brimhall, 22 March 1950; FMB to Morgan, 11 April 1950.

43. FMB to Morgan, 11 April, 14 March 1950.

44. FMB to Morgan, 18 October 1950. The baby's name was derived from the eighteenth-century novel by Samuel Richardson, *Pamela, or Virtue Rewarded*. Fawn noted that she "was by no means sure whose virtue was being rewarded, probably not my own, but certainly someone's was and reward, believe me, is a mild word for what I was feeling then and have felt ever since."

45. FMB to Morgan, 11 April 1950; Kaplan, *Wizards of Armageddon*, 37–45.

46. Kaplan, *Wizards of Armageddon*, 40, 47–48; FMB to Morgan, 11 April 1950.

47. FMB to Morgan, 29 December 1950. The memories that took shape in the Bethany house centered largely for Fawn on her two little sons. She had periodically written her uncle Dean Brimhall of the boys' development. Dick, she told him, was competitive in all things, "always matching his performance against that of the other children," while Bruce had no concern for such things. On the other hand, Bruce was far more utilitarian and practical than Dick. For Christmas 1950 their great-uncle had given the boys five silver dollars each. In writing Brimhall a thank-you note for his generous gift, Fawn reported that Dick looked upon the coins "as a wonderful addition to his . . . collection, but definitely not as something to spend," whereas Bruce was "already thinking of

something to buy." The boys also reacted differently to the birth of their sister. Dick expressed "one hundred percent enthusiasm," but Bruce had mixed feelings. The first night after Fawn and the baby came home, "he sat on the couch and said solemnly three times in succession: 'I hate my dear, darling sister.'" FMB to Dean Brimhall, 28 June, 29 December 1950; FMB to Morgan, 19 October 1950.

48. FMB to Morgan, 28 July 1950, 21 February 1951. Fawn's deep dissatisfaction with the Brodies' temporary living quarters was evident in comments made to Dale Morgan in inviting him over for dinner. She was not sure what kind of a meal she could prepare in the "closet kitchen," she wrote, "but if you are willing to take the uncomfortable chairs along with it, we would be happy to see you." On another occasion, she expressed regrets at missing him when he dropped by unexpectedly on a weekend, explaining that she and the rest of the family were so desperate to get out of their apartment that they routinely left every Saturday and Sunday, not returning until late in the day. FMB to Morgan, 21 February, 23 April 1951.

49. FMB to Morgan, 23 April 1951. Fawn took some satisfaction from her uncle's first official act as president, when he demoted his longtime adversary in the church hierarchy, J. Reuben Clark, whom Brodie herself loathed, from first to second counselor. McKay covered his true motives with a less-than-convincing public explanation in keeping with his reputation for "kindliness and saintliness," but to Brodie it only exposed McKay's domineering dark side. She had long seen her uncle as nothing more than a tyrant.

50. Dale L. Morgan to Juanita Brooks, 23 June 1951, copy in Morgan Papers; Bernard Brodie to Truman Landon, 25 June 1951, copy in Bernard Brodie Papers, Bx 3, Landon Correspondence folder.

51. Herken, *Counsels of War*, 31–32.

52. Bruce L. R. Smith, *The RAND Corporation*, 104.

53. FMB to Bernard Brodie, 3 December 1951, original in Bernard Brodie Papers, Bx 3, Landon Correspondence folder.

54. Bernard Brodie to Truman Landon, 17 August 1951, copy in Bernard Brodie Papers, Bx 3, Landon Correspondence folder; FMB to Morgan, 12 July 1951.

55. Knopf to FMB, 5 June 1951; FMB to Knopf, 22 June 1951, both in Knopf Papers.

56. FMB to Knopf, 22 June 1951; Knopf to FMB, 27 June 1951, both in Knopf Papers.

57. Bernard Brodie to Truman Landon, 17 August, 25 June 1951, copies of both in Bernard Brodie Papers, Bx 3, Landon Correspondence folder.

58. FMB to Morgan, 12 August, 19 December 1951.

59. FMB to Morgan, 15 March 1952.

60. Ibid.

61. FMB to Dean Brimhall, 11 June, 3 July 1952.

62. Bruce Brodie, "Monologue," 8–9; FMB to Dean Brimhall, 25 November 1952.

63. FMB to Dean Brimhall, 3 July 1952; FMB to Morgan, 15 March 1952, 7 June 1953.

64. FMB, "New Writers and Mormonism," 17.

65. Ibid., 18–19.

66. FMB to Morgan, 7 June 1953.

67. Ibid.; FMB to Knopf, 25 October 1953; Knopf to FMB, 27 October 1953, both in Knopf Papers.

68. FMB to Dean Brimhall, 1 February 1954; FMB to Morgan, 1 February, 22 November 1954.

69. FMB to Morgan, 22 November 1954.

70. Ibid.

71. Ibid.

72. FMB to Dean Brimhall, 4 January 1955.

73. FMB to Dean Brimhall, 25 November 1952. At one point, Bernard Brodie opined, in private, that he feared Eisenhower was senile. Alexander George, interview by author, 3 January 1989.

74. FMB to Dean Brimhall, 13 January 1953, 4 February 1955; Bernard Brodie to Max Ascoli, 29 September 1954, copy in Bernard Brodie Papers, Bx 4, Fd 15. It should be noted the Bernard Brodie was much more restrained in his public criticisms of the American political leaders. See, for example, his *Strategy in the Missile Age*.

75. FMB, *Thaddeus Stevens*, v.

76. Ibid.; FMB to Morgan, December, 20 April 1955. Strangely enough, letters between Brodie and Knopf during this time are not to be found in either the Knopf Papers or the FMB Papers.

77. FMB to Morgan, December, 20 April 1955; Bernard Brodie to Herbert S. Bailey, 8 February 1955; Bailey to Bernard Brodie, 12 February 1955, both in Bernard Brodie Papers, Bx 1, Fd 8.

78. Stephenson, "Biography of Fawn Brodie," 19; Kaplan, *Wizards of Armageddon*, 222–23.

79. FMB to Dean Brimhall, 30 February 1955; FMB, *Thaddeus Stevens*, 14; Hildi Greenson, interview by author, 2 November 1988. Greenson, born in New York City in 1910, was a contemporary of Bernard Brodie. Like Bernard, he descended from Jewish immigrant parentage. Also like Bernard, he had changed his name as a young man—from Romeo Samuel Greenschpoon to Ralph R. Greenson. Educated at Columbia University and at the University of Berne, Switzerland, in medicine, Greenson ultimately became interested in psychiatry, particularly Freudian analysis. During World War II he was chief of neuropsychiatric service at the Army Air Force Convalescent Hospital at Fort Logan, Colorado. His wartime experiences served as the basis for the best-selling novel, and later the movie, *Captain Newman, M.D.*, written by his close friend, Leo Rosten. After the war,

Greenson, along with his wife Hildi and their two children, moved to Los Angeles. Through his charismatic personality and some important personal and family connections, he established himself as one of southern California's foremost psychiatrists, numbering among his patients prominent entertainers such as Frank Sinatra and Marilyn Monroe. See Donald Spoto, *Marilyn Monroe*, 421–29, and Kitty Kelley's *His Way*, 208, 217–18, 226, 410, where Greenson's interactions with Monroe and Sinatra, undoubtedly the most famous of his patients, are discussed.

80. Spoto, *Marilyn Monroe*, 423–24; Pamela Brodie to author, 22 January 1998; Greenson interview, 2 November 1988; Crawford interview, 29 September 1989. Years later, Fielding was destined to achieve fame as the psychiatrist of Daniel Ellsberg, whose office was broken into by operatives working on behalf of the then-president Richard Nixon. Greenson interview, 2 November 1988.

81. Pamela Brodie interview, 8 January 1988.

82. FMB to Morgan, 7 June 1953.

83. FMB to Morgan, 29 July 1953; Young, "Elder Thomas E. McKay," 224–26, 271; FMB to Morgan, 30 April 1954. Also amusing to Fawn was the fact that the editors of the *Improvement Era* doctored the photograph. Fawn's sisters Flora and Louise were wearing sleeveless blouses on the day they were photographed. In other words, they were not wearing Mormon temple garments. In the published photo, however, their shoulders were covered up. Ironically, Fawn was wearing a blouse with sleeves. Pamela Brodie to author, 22 January 1998.

85. FMB to Morgan, 30 April 1954, 20 April 1955.

86. FMB to Dean Brimhall, July 1956.

87. FMB to Dean Brimhall, 23 August 1956.

88. FMB to Dean Brimhall, 12 October 1956.

89. FMB, interview conducted by Judy Hallet in 1977, typescript of complete unedited interview in FMB Papers, Bx 70, Fd 6.

90. FMB to Dean Brimhall, July 1956.

91. FMB to Dean Brimhall, 12 October, 23 August 1956.

92. FMB to Dean Brimhall, 15 January 1957.

93. Crawford interview, 29 September 1989.

94. FMB to Dean Brimhall, 15 January 1957, 23 August 1956.

95. FMB to Dean Brimhall, 15 January, 20 May 1957.

96. FMB to Dean Brimhall, 2 January 1958; *Salt Lake Tribune*, 15 January 1958; *Deseret News*, 15 and 18 January 1958.

97. FMB to Dean Brimhall, 3 February 1958.

98. FMB to Morgan, 20 April 1955; FMB to Dean Brimhall, 20 December 1955.

99. Crawford interview, 29 September 1989; FMB to Morgan, December 1956; Thomas McKay interview, 24 July 1987; FMB to Dean Brimhall, 16 September 1958, 11 August, 1 September 1959.

100. FMB to Morgan, 10 December 1959; FMB to Dean Brimhall, 2 January 1958.

101. FMB to Morgan, 25 May 1955; Pamela Brodie to author, 22 January 1998; Crawford interview, 29 September 1989.

102. FMB to Morgan, 20 April 1955, December 1958; Crawford interview, 29 September 1989; Pamela Brodie interview, 6 January 1989.

103. FMB interview by Judy Hallet; Pamela Brodie interview, 6 January 1989; Pamela Brodie to author, 22 January 1998.

104. Pamela Brodie to author, 22 January 1998.

105. Ibid.

106. FMB to Dean Brimhall, 4 April 1956; Pamela Brodie to author, 22 January 1998.

107. FMB interview by Judy Hallet.

108. FMB to Dean Brimhall, 12 October 1956; Bruce Brodie, "Monologue," 13; FMB to Juliette George, 13 March 1957, copy in possession of author; FMB, *Thaddeus Stevens*, 14.

109. Bruce Brodie interview, 10 October 1987. The history of the manuscript at Princeton comes from the recollections of Herbert S. Bailey to Bernard Brodie, 22 February 1973 (in Bernard Brodie papers). The author was unable to secure direct information from the Princeton University Press relative to Brodie's interaction with the publisher in the mid-1950s, since Princeton does not keep files for rejected manuscripts dating back that far. (Mary E. Rude to author, 3 January 1989). Also, a careful examination of the materials in Fawn Brodie's own papers failed to turn up any information concerning the author's interaction with Princeton University Press.

110. FMB to Dean Brimhall, 16 September 1958, 27 September 1959, 29 January 1960.

111. FMB to Dean Brimhall, 1 September 1959; FMB to Morgan, 29 April 1960.

112. *Washington Post*, 25 October 1959; *Springfield (Mass.) Republican*, 25 October 1959; *Baltimore Sun*, 25 October 1959.

113. *New York Herald Tribune*, 1 November 1959; *New York Times*, 22 November 1959.

114. Allan Nevins to FMB, 27 January 1960, copy in Dean R. Brimhall Papers; FMB to Dean Brimhall, 29 January 1960.

115. *Nashville (Tenn.) Banner*, 13 November 1959; *Louisville Courier-Journal*, 22 November 1959. Also see reviews in *Roanoke (Va.) Times*, 24 November 1959, and *Atlanta Journal-Constitution*, 21 February 1959.

116. *Lancaster (Pa.) News*, 10 January 1960.

117. *American Historical Review*, January 1960, 391.

118. *Salt Lake Tribune*, 10 January 1960.

119. FMB to Dean Brimhall, 29 January 1960.

120. Bernard Brodie to Peter J. Caws, 17 September 1965, copy in Bernard Brodie Papers, Bx 3. The letter describes the nature of the fellowship. FMB to Morgan, 29 April 1960; Bruce Brodie, "Monologue," 9.

CHAPTER 5

1. Stephenson, "Biography of Fawn Brodie," 16.

2. *Los Angeles Times,* 21 March 1975; FMB, *The Devil Drives,* 15.

3. FMB, *The Devil Drives,* 15; Stephenson, "Biography of Fawn Brodie," 46; Berges, "Fawn and Bernard Brodie."

4. Stephenson, "Biography of Fawn Brodie," 17.

5. Ibid.

6. Pamela Brodie to author, 22 January 1998; Stephenson, "Biography of Fawn Brodie," 17; Bruce Brodie, "Monologue," 12.

7. Bernard Brodie's increasing disatisfaction with conditions at RAND was noted by a number of his former associates—in particular, his former supervisor, Hans Speier, in an interview by the author, 23 January 1989; Charles Hitch, interview by author, 3 March 1989; and Roman Kolkowicz, interview by author, 12 December 1988. Other family reactions are known from Pamela Brodie interview, 6 January 1989, and FMB to Dean Brimhall, 21 July 1960.

8. Pamela Brodie interview, 6 January 1989; FMB to Dean Brimhall, 7 June 1960.

9. FMB to Dean Brimhall, 21 July 1960. At this point, Dean and Lila were living apart. She continued on in Salt Lake City, a member of the faculty at the University of Utah.

10. Ibid., FMB to Dean Brimhall, 5 October 1960; Pamela Brodie interview, 6 January 1989.

11. Pamela Brodie interview, 6 January 1989; FMB to Dean Brimhall, 5 October 1960.

12. Crawford interview, 29 September 1989; Gunn McKay interview, 26 July 1987.

13. *Salt Lake Tribune,* 7 October 1960; *Deseret News,* 6 October 1960.

14. FMB to Dean Brimhall, 6 October 1960.

15. Ibid.

16. FMB to Dean Brimhall, 5 November 1960.

17. FMB to Dean Brimhall, 6 July 1960 [sic], 5 November 1960. The date on the 6 July 1960 letter is obviously incorrect in light of its contents; specifically, its references to her mother's recent death and the Brodies' activities during the Christmas holidays. Thus it appears that this letter was written sometime in early 1961, probably January.

18. FMB to Dean Brimhall, 5 November 1960, 29 May 1961.

19. FMB to Dean Brimhall, 11 September 1961; FMB to Morgan, 19 October 1961.

20. FMB to Dean Brimhall, 12 August, 23 August 1961.

21. FMB to Dean Brimhall, 11 September, 23 August 1961.

22. FMB to Dean Brimhall, 11 September 1961; Horst Mendershausen, interview by author, 1 November 1988.

23. RAND personnel who served as McNamara's consultants included William Kaufmann, Thomas Schelling, Henry Rowen, Charles J. Hitch, Paul Nitze, Alain Enthoven, and Daniel Ellsberg. For a good discussion of the role and activities of these individuals and the influence and interaction of RAND vis-à-vis the Kennedy administration, see Herken, *Counsels of War*, 134–204. A thorough examination by the author of the Bernard Brodie papers failed to turn up any correspondence between Bernard Brodie and John F. Kennedy, but Brodie noted Kennedy's personal comments in his recollections to Colin S. Gray, n.d., in Bernard Brodie Papers, Bx 8, Fd 17.

24. Herken, *Counsels of War*, 147; Kolkowicz interview, 12 December 1988; Hitch interview, 3 March 1989; Bernard Brodie to Colin S. Gray, n.d., copy in Bernard Brodie Papers, Bx 8, Fd 17.

25. Robert Dahl to Bernard Brodie, 9 January 1961; Bernard Brodie to Robert Dahl, 16 January 1961, Bx 1, Fd D, originals in Bernard Brodie Papers.

26. FMB to Morgan, 19 October 1961.

27. Knopf to FMB, 8 August 1961, copy in Knopf Papers; FMB to Dean Brimhall, 11 September 1961; FMB to Knopf, 19 September 1961, original in Knopf Papers.

28. FMB to Morgan, 19 October 1961; *New York Times*, 5 August 1962.

29. *New York Times*, 23 September 1962; FMB to Dean Brimhall, 27 September 1962.

30. FMB to Dean Brimhall, 10 November 1961.

31. FMB to Morgan, 16 February 1962; FMB to Dean Brimhall, 19 October 1961; FMB to William A. Koshland, 31 January 1962, original in Knopf Papers.

32. FMB to Knopf, 11 July 1962; Knopf to FMB, 16 July 1962, both in Knopf Papers.

33. FMB to Knopf, 25 July 1962, original in Knopf Papers.

34. FMB to Dean Brimhall, 20 August 1962; FMB to Juanita Brooks, 3 February 1963, original in Juanita Brooks Papers.

35. Byron Farwell, *Burton*; Knopf to FMB, 22 August 1963; FMB to Knopf, 28 August 1963; Knopf to FMB, 29 August 1963, all in Knopf Papers.

36. FMB to Morgan, 31 May 1963.

37. FMB to Morgan, December 1963; FMB to Dean Brimhall, 24 October 1963; Brodie, "Libraries in My Life," 19; Quentin Keynes, interview by author, 11 April 1991.

38. Keynes interview, 11 April 1991.

39. FMB to Dean Brimhall, 23 September 1963; FMB to George Brockway, 15 March 1964, copy in FMB Papers, Bx 6, Fd 2; FMB to Dean Brimhall, 24 October 1963.

40. FMB to Dean Brimhall, 21 February 1964; FMB to Brockway, 15 March 1964, copy in FMB Papers; FMB to Mian Muhammad Sadullah, 14 March 1964, copy in FMB Papers.

41. FMB to Dean Brimhall, 21 February, 31 March, 9 September 1964.

42. Bernard Brodie, "What Price Conventional Capabilities?" 25–29, 32–33; Kaplan, *Wizards of Armageddon*, 194.

43. Pamela Brodie interview, 6 January 1989.

44. FMB to Morgan, 6 July 1964; FMB, "Parks and Politics," 40.

45. FMB to Morgan, 6 July 1964; FMB, "Parks and Politics," 40.

46. FMB, "Parks and Politics," 40.

47. Neighbor and friend Barbara Ward-Korsch told the author that Fawn "fought . . . harder than anybody" in the neighborhood to preserve the Santa Monica Mountains. Barbara Ward-Korsch, interview by author, 25 January 1989. Brodie's remarks to the developer are quoted from Lamont Johnson, "Tribute," given at the memorial service for FMB, 17 January 1981, copy of typescript in FMB Papers. But Pamela Brodie dismissed this account as "a Lamont Johnson invention," noting that it did not sound like her mother at all. Pamela Brodie to author, 22 January 1998.

48. FMB to Morgan, 6 July 1964.

49. FMB to Morgan, 9 September, December 1964.

50. FMB, "Parks and Politics," 40; FMB to Dean Brimhall, 26 February, 19 April 1965. For one perspective on the political dynamics leading to creation of the Santa Monica Mountains National Recreation Area, see John Jacobs, "Park Barrel," 16–20.

51. FMB, *No Man Knows My History*, 173, 365, 423–25.

52. For two views of Romney's emergence and its impact on the issue of race within the Mormon Church, see Dennis L. Lythgoe, "1968 Presidential Decline of George Romney," 214–40, and the author's *Saints, Slaves, and Blacks*, 186–87.

53. FMB to Dean Brimhall, 28 April 1962.

54. *New York Times*, 7 June 1963; *Newsweek*, 17 June 1963; FMB to Morgan, 13 June 1963.

55. FMB to Dean Brimhall, 21 February 1964, 19 April 1965.

56. FMB to Dean Brimhall, 19 April 1965; FMB to Morgan, December 1965.

57. FMB to Dean Brimhall, 1 August, 8 September 1965, 21 April 1966.

58. FMB, *The Devil Drives*, 11.

59. Stephenson, "Biography of Fawn Brodie," 21.

60. George Brockway to FMB, 30 June 1966, original in FMB Papers, Bx 6, Fd 2.

61. Ibid.

62. Ibid.

63. FMB to Brockway, 4 July 1966, copy in FMB Papers, Bx 6, Fd 2.

64. FMB to Dean Brimhall, 16 August 1966; John Bright-Holmes to FMB, 25 July 1966, original in FMB Papers, Bx 6, Fd 6.

65. FMB to Brockway, 28 October 1966, copy in FMB Papers, Bx 6, Fd 6; FMB to Bright-Holmes, 17 November 1966, copy in FMB Papers, Bx 6, Fd 6; FMB to Morgan, 3 January 1967. This last letter was misdated by Brodie "3 January 1966," an obvious error, given the matters discussed in the letter.

66. Brockway to FMB, 18 October 1966; FMB to Brockway, 13 May 1967, both letters in FMB Papers, Bx 6, Fd 2; *History Book Club Review*, August 1967, 3.

67. Thomas Lask, Review, *New York Times*, 27 May 1967; J. H. Plumb, Review, ibid., 18 June 1967; Josh Greenfield, Review, *Washington Post*, 28 May 1967; Orville Prescott, Review, *Saturday Review*, 8 July 1967. Also see positive reviews in *Washington Star*, 4 June 1967, and *Wall Street Journal*, 12 June 1967.

68. *Salt Lake Tribune*, 24 June 1967; *Utah Alumnus*, n.d.

69. Philip Toynbee, Review, *Observer* (London), 19 November 1967; Paul Zimmerman, Review, *Newsweek*, 12 June 1967; Harry Stone, Review, *Los Angeles Times*, 4 June 1967. Reviews in the United Kingdom, some critical of Brodie's use— or misuse—of psychology, included those in the *Times (London) Literary Supplement*, 11 January 1958; Robert Nye, Review, the *Scotsman* (Edinburgh), 30 December 1967; and Penelope Maslin, Review, *Cardiff Western Mail*, 2 December 1967.

70. *Geographical Journal*, June 1968.

71. Bright-Holmes to FMB, 16 May 1963, copy in FMB Papers, Bx 6, Fd 6.

72. Brockway to FMB, 4 May 1965, original in FMB Papers, Bx 6, Fd. 2; Current quotation from Brodie, Thaddeus Stevens, front cover, 1966 paperback ed.

73. FMB, "A Lincoln Who Never Was"; FMB, "Who Won the Civil War Anyway?"; FMB, "Lincoln and Thaddeus Stevens"; FMB, "Who Defends the Abolitionist?"; FMB, "Abolitionists and Historians"; FMB, "Thaddeus Stevens." In December 1965, Brodie was further acknowledged within the historical community when she chaired a session focusing on the abolitionist movement at the American History Association's annual meeting in San Francisco. FMB to Dean Brimhall, 15 November 1965.

74. Everett L. Cooley to Utah Historical Society Board Members, 8 August 1967; Cooley, "Introduction to Presentation of Fellow Award to Fawn M. Brodie," 23 September 1967; FMB to Cooley, 27 August 1967; all in Utah State Historical Society Archives. In being given this award, Brodie joined the distinguished company of Dale Morgan, Juanita Brooks, Wallace Stegner, LeRoy Hafen, and Leonard J. Arrington, all previous recipients. Cooley to FMB, 23 August 1967, copy in Utah State Historical Society Archives.

75. FMB, Acceptance Speech for Fellow Award, 23 September 1967, typescript in Utah State Historical Society Archives.

76. Stephenson, "Biography of Fawn Brodie," 30; Joseph P. Lash, *Eleanor and Franklin and Eleanor: The Years Alone*. It is worth noting that both volumes of Lash's biography were ultimately published by W. W. Norton.

77. FMB to Morgan, 14 August 1967. For an extensive discussion of the dynamics of the relationship between Morgan and McQuown, see Craig L. Foster, "Madeline McQuown, Dale Morgan, and the Great Unfinished Brigham Young Biography."

78. Morgan to FMB, 21 August 1967, original in FMB Papers, Bx 7, Fd 14; FMB to Morgan, 14 August 1967.

79. Wesley P. Walters, "New Light on Mormon Origins." The fact that Brodie had communicated directly with Walters is indicated in FMB to Morgan, 13 November 1967. F. L. Stewart, *Exploding the Myth*; FMB to Morgan, 13 November 1967. Brodie indicated to Morgan that Stewart had telephoned her from Salt Lake City a year earlier, asking to see and discuss with Brodie her Joseph Smith research. But according to Brodie's recollections, Stewart "was so obviously hostile that I ducked the whole idea . . . . I knew from other sources that actually she intended an attack on me. So I simply told her to search the sources and point out what errors she could find, and I would cheerfully try to eliminate them in the next edition."

80. Leonard J. Arrington, *Great Basin Kingdom*; Arrington, "Scholarly Studies of Mormonism"; FMB to Dean Brimhall, 18 November 1967; Klaus J. Hansen, *Quest for Empire*; FMB to Morgan, 25 November 1967.

81. FMB to Morgan, 25 November 1967. For an overview of California's political environment during this period, see John H. Culver and John C. Syer, *Power and Politics in California*.

82. FMB to Dean Brimhall, 16 August 1966.

83. FMB to Dean Brimhall, 16 January 1967.

84. FMB, "Ronald Reagan Plays Surgeon." A line the Reagan character utters in *Kings Row*, "Where's the rest of me?" became the title of Reagan's autobiography, and throughout the article Brodie played with the amputation analogy. "Today the man who admits searching for twenty-five years for an amputated portion of his psyche is hacking away with zeal at California's school budgets, welfare programs, and parks," she wrote. In this clinical analysis she showed her disdain for the conservative governor and her deep fascination for Freudian psychology.

85. FMB, "Inside Our Mental Hospitals"; FMB to Dean Brimhall, 9 February 1968; FMB to Morgan, 9 February 1968. Brodie's intentions to write Reagan's life are indicated in the recollections of George Brockway, her editor at Norton, as related some years later to Andrew Rolle. Brockway to Rolle, 16 February 1987, copy in possession of author.

86. Gary B. Nash, interview by author, 30 November 1988.

87. Peter Loewenberg, interview by author, 12 December 1988; Eugen Weber, interview by author, 23 January 1989; Peter Reill, interview by author, 3 November 1988.

88. Although she had taught two other disciplines on a college level—English at Weber College in 1934–35 and journalism at Crane College in 1938—these stints were not considered adequate academic background for appointment at UCLA. The concerns reflected by various history department members were recalled by Gary Nash in an interview with the author, 30 November 1988. Those who supported the appointment included not only Drs. Woloch and Loewenberg but also Eugen Weber, chair of the department, who was taken with her personality and her scholarship, having found *The Devil Drives* "wonderful."

Other faculty described Brodie as warm, gracious, and interested in people—and a promising member of the department. Weber interview, 23 January 1989; Norris Hundley, interview by author, 3 November 1988; Reille, interview, 3 November 1988.

89. Bill Fitzgerald, interview by author, 27 July 1991. Brodie's insecurities were related by various individuals, including her daughter, Pamela Brodie, in an interview, 8 January 1988.

90. Fitzgerald interview, 27 July 1991.

91. Bernard Brodie, *Escalation and the Nuclear Option*; Kaplan, *Wizards of Armageddon*, 320; Herken, *Counsels of War*, 210.

92. Herken, *Counsels of War*, 218; Konrad Kellen, interview by author, 30 November 1988.

93. Joan Goldhamer, interview by author, 29 November 1988; Irving Bernstein, interview by author, 2 November 1988; Kellen interview, 30 November 1988; Kolkowicz interview, 12 December 1988; Pamela Brodie to author, 22 January 1998.

94. FMB to Dean Brimhall, 12 November, 7 December 1965, 16 August 1966; FMB to Morgan, 18 October, 30 August 1967; Bernard Brodie to Klaus Knorr, 8 April 1966, copy in Bernard Brodie Papers.

95. FMB to Morgan, 30 August 1967; Pamela Brodie to author, 22 January 1998; FMB to Morgan, 30 August 1967.

96. Goldhamer interview, 29 November 1988.

CHAPTER 6

1. Clifford Egan, "How Not to Write a Biography," 129–30; FMB to Joseph Horach, 14 April 1979, copy in FMB papers, Bx25, Fd 22.

2. Stephenson, "Biography of Fawn Brodie," 17–18, 31; *Los Angeles Times*, 21 March 1975; FMB to George Brockway, ca. December 1974, original in Norton Archives.

3. *Los Angeles Times*, 20 February 1977, 21 March 1975; Stephenson, "Biography of Fawn Brodie," 40–41.

4. *Los Angeles Times*, 21 March 1975.

5. Ibid., 20 February 1977.

6. A perceptive discussion of these and other reasons for the popularity of Brodie's *Thomas Jefferson* can be found in Harry W. Fritz's "Sex and Identity in Early America," paper presented at the Western Social Science Association meeting, Tempe, Arizona, 30 April 1976.

7. Kolkowicz interview, 12 December 1988; Kellen Interview, 30 November 1988; Bernstein interview, 2 November 1988; Loewenberg interview, 2 November 1988.

8. *New York Post*, 27 April 1974; Hano, "Conversation with Fawn Brodie," 4.

9. George Brockway to FMB, 16 November 1967, original in FMB Papers, Bx 6, Fd. 2; FMB to Morgan, 24 January 1968; John James to FMB, 27 March 1968, original in Utah State Historical Society Archives; Stephenson, "Biography of Fawn Brodie," 24. Even though McQuown researched and collected materials for a book-length biography over a period of some thirty years, by the time of her death in 1975 she had managed to draft only six chapters, taking the life of Brigham Young up to the early Nauvoo period. See Madeline R. McQuown Papers, Bx 8, Fds 1–8. For an in-depth discussion of McQuown's work on this project relative to her complex relationship with Dale Morgan, see Foster, "Madeline McQuown, Dale Morgan, and the Great Unfinished Brigham Young Biography."

10. Stewart Udall, Letter to the Editors; FMB to Dean Brimhall, 22 August 1967; Stewart Udall to FMB, n.d., in FMB Papers, Bx 4, Fd 21. It appears that this letter was written in early 1965 in light of the fact that Brodie wrote Brimahll commenting on having just received it. See FMB to Dean Brimhall, 26 February 1965.

11. FMB to Morgan, 12 December 1967. John Gee, in an unpublished paper, "Suppression of the Joseph Smith Papyri," delivered at the 1994 meeting of the Mormon History Association in Park City, Utah, discusses the ebb and flow of Brodie's interest in this issue during the 1950s and 1960s.

12. FMB to Morgan, 12 December 1967.

13. FMB to Morgan, 9 February 1968. For a discussion of, and responses to, the findings of these Egyptologists, see John A. Wilson, Richard A. Parker, Richard P. Howard, et al., "The Joseph Smith Egyptian papyri," a series of articles published in *Dialogue*, and Klaus Baer, "The Breathing Permit of Hor."

14. The controversy surrounding the Mormon-black issue as it stood in the late 1960s and early 1970s is explored in the author's *Saints, Slaves, and Blacks*, 176–203. Also see Armand L. Mauss, "The Fading of the Pharaohs' Curse," and Lester L. Bush, "Mormonism's Negro Doctrine."

15. FMB to Cooley, 16 November 1970, original in FMB Papers, Bx 4, Fd 6; FMB to Morgan, 17 December 1970.

16. FMB, *Can We Manipulate the Past?* 10–13. Smith's enlightened stand was further evident in the Mormon leader's ordination of Elijah Abel, whom Brodie characterized as Smith's "black friend." This act represented "a decisive repudiation of the 'scriptural precedent' of the Book of Abraham" that blacks were "cursed as pertaining to the priesthood."

17. Ibid., 13, 14.

18. Ibid., 13–14.

19. "Church 'Misreads' Past to Justify Doctrine, Author Charges," *Salt Lake Tribune*, 4 October 1970; FMB to Morgan, 17 December 1970; Cooley to FMB, 19 October 1970, original in FMB Papers, Bx 4, Fd15.

20. The only direct Mormon reaction came from Marvin S. Hill, who was at that time engaged in historical research for a projected biography of Joseph

Smith, a work Hill himself did not write. Ultimately, his sister, Donna Hill, wrote the book and published it under the title, *Joseph Smith: The First Mormon.* See Marvin S. Hill, "The Manipulation of History."

21. FMB to Cooley, 6 June 1970, original in FMB Papers, Bx 4, Fd 6; FMB to Morgan, 11 May 1970; Stephenson, "Biography of Fawn Brodie," 7, 8.

22. Stephenson, "Biography of Fawn Brodie," 9; Willian Fitzgerald, class notes for course in American Political Biography, copy in possession of author.

23. FMB to Dean Brimhall, 8 May 1968. Brodie's abiding interest in Mormonism produced at least five works from her hand between 1968 and 1972. These included not only *Can We Manipulate the Past?* but two other published works and two unpublished essays. Brodie's two published essays were "Sir Richard F. Burton: Exceptional Observer of the Mormon Scene," which appeared in the *Utah Historical Quarterly* in the fall of 1970, and "Inflation Idyl: A Family Farm in Huntsville," which came out in the same journal in the spring of 1972. One of the unpublished essays was entitled "The Mormon Intellectual," written in response to a request by the *Western Review* in early 1968. For reasons that are not clear, it was never published. See Irma Saffold to FMB, 11 January 1968, original in FMB Papers, Bx 69. Brodie also wrote a semifictional essay entitled "The Protracted Life of Mrs. Grundy," recalling the dynamics of McKay family life in Huntsville during her formative years.

24. Ann Kerr, interview by author, 8 July 1989.

25. FMB, "Big Daddy vs. Mr. Clean." Born in a small rural Texas community, Unruh was the youngest of five children. His father was an illiterate Mennonite sharecropper. The "seriousness and piety" of his Mennonite heritage and Presbyterian upbringing were extremely important in shaping Unruh's character, values, and attitudes, according to Brodie.

26. Ibid.; FMB to Dean Brimhall, 8 May 1968.

27. Winthrop D. Jordan, *White over Black.* See, in particular, 430–81. Interestingly, Jordan's actual speculation on a possible Jefferson-Hemings liaison is the focus of a mere five pages (465–69) in the book. Jordan concludes, "The question of Jefferson's miscegenation, it should be stressed, . . . is of limited interest and usefulness even if it could be satisfactorily answered" (468). Janet Ferrell Brodie, interview by author, 20 October 1988.

28. Pearl N. Graham, "Thomas Jefferson and Sally Hemings"; FMB to Pearl Graham, 28 May 1968, copy in FMB Papers, Bx 19, Fd22; FMB to Mrs. Charles Smith, 14 March 1969, copy in FMB Papers, Bx 19, Fd 22.

29. Stephenson, "Biography of Fawn Brodie," 41.

30. Dumas Malone to FMB, 26 February, 14 March 1969, originals in FMB Papers, Bx 24, Fd 5.

31. Merrill D. Peterson to FMB, 8 February 1969, original in FMB Papers, Bx 24, Fd 5.

32. FMB to James A. Bear, 14 March 1969, copy in FMB Papers, Bx 19, Fd 27; FMB to Dean Brimhall, 20 February 1969.

33. FMB to Edgar F. Shannon, Jr., 23 June 1969, copy in FMB Papers, Bx 70, Fd 1. Brodie's address was published as "The Political Hero in America" in the *Virginia Quarterly Review.*

34. FMB, "Political Hero."

35. FMB to Herbert Bailey, 22 October 1969, copy in FMB Papers, Bx 6, Fd 9.

36. FMB to Brockway, 26 October 1969, original in Norton Archives.

37. Brockway's swiftness in responding was undoubtedly due, in large measure, to the fact that Brodie was also discussing her proposed biography with Knopf, who had offered her a contract and a ten thousand dollar advance. Brodie had taken care to keep Norton informed of her negotiations with Knopf, thereby placing Norton in the position of having to make a better offer. FMB to Asbel Green, 26 October, 15 November 1969, copies in FMB Papers, Bx 6 Fd 1; Brockway to FMB, 6 November 1969; FMB to Brockway, 15 November 1969, both in Norton Archives.

38. Brockway to FMB, 15 November 1969, copy in Norton Archives; FMB to Dean Brimhall, 31 January 1970. FMB to Morgan, ca. late 1969, 6 February 1970.

39. Harold Coolidge to FMB, 14 December 1970, original in FMB Papers, Bx24, Fd 6.

40. FMB to Brockway, 8 January 1971, original in Norton Archives.

41. Brodie's OAH presentation was published the following year under the title "The Great Jefferson Taboo" in *American Heritage*, and with footnotes—a departure from that magazine's general format. The editors explained, "Although *American Heritage* rarely prints all the scholarly apparatus supporting a story, in this inevitably controversial case we have included Mrs. Brodie's notes."

42. FMB to Brockway, 6 August 1971, original in Norton Archives. Brodie, in commenting on Peterson's negative response, observed, "But it did give me a sample of the kind of review he would likely give the book, and he could do a lot of damage, if he should turn out to be the reviewer for the *New York Times*, for example." Brockway, however, had a ready answer for her concerns: "You mention the blast by Merrill Peterson. When the times comes to send out review copies it will be useful for us to have a list of potential blasters so that we can forewarn the review editors against them. They don't always respect warning but they usually do." (Brockway to FMB, 12 August 1971, copy in Norton Archives.) Jordan's favorable reaction is not too surprising. In his *White over Black*, according to Brodie, Jordan was "the first white historian in our time to describe dispassionately evidence for the Sally Hemings liaison, as well as the case against it." FMB, "Great Jefferson Taboo," 50.

43. FMB to Dean Brimhall, 8 May 1968, 15 May 1969; Lamont Johnson, interview by author, 28 November 1988; Keynes interview, 11 April 1991; FMB to Brockway, 15 November 1969, original in Norton Archives.

44. FMB to Brockway, 23 March 1971, 28 February 1970, both in Norton Archives; Keynes interview, 11 April 1991. As indicated in letter from Richard

Burton to FMB, 10 September 1967, FMB Papers, Bx 15, Fd 17. Unfortunately no copy of Brodie's letter to Burton has been located.

45. FMB to Brockway, 6 August 1971, original in Norton Archives.

46. FMB to Brockway, 14 January 1972, original in Norton Archives.

47. Ibid.

48. Johnson interview, 28 November 1988.

49. FMB to Morgan, 24 January 1968.

50. FMB to Morgan, 9 February 1968.

51. FMB to Morgan, December 1968.

52. Janet Brodie interview, 20 October 1988; Stephenson, "Biography of Fawn Brodie," 44; Mauricio Mazon, interview by author, 8 March 1992.

53. Janet Brodie interview, 20 October 1988; Stephenson, "Biography of Fawn Brodie," 44; Mazon interview, 8 March 1992. The fact that Fawn Brodie's hands would "tremble" in class was related to Janet Brodie, Fawn's daughter-in-law, by former student Judith Anderson. In addition to Anderson's observations, a colleague in the history department noted that Brodie's hands would shake during history department faculty meetings. Afof Marsot, interview by author, 7 July 1989.

54. Janet Brodie interview, 20 October 1988; FMB to Dean Brimhall, 24 March 1971; Richard Weiss interview, by author, 29 November 1988.

55. Weber, Change in Employment Status, 19 January 1968, original in FMB Papers, Bx 55, Fd 1; FMB to Charles E. Young, 16 July 1971, original in FMB Papers, Bx 55, Fd 4; *Guidepost* (UCLA student evaluation of faculty), 1974, UCLA Reference Library.

56. Stanley Wolpert, interview by author, 29 November 1988; Dalleck interview, 29 November 1988; Loewenberg interview, 12 December 1988; Mazon interview, 8 March 1992; Hundley interview, 3 November 1988; Nash interview, 30 November 1988.

57. FMB to Charles E. Young, 16 July 1971, original in FMB Papers, Bx 55, Fd 4; Reill interview, 3 November 1988.

58. Jeffrey Symcox, interview by author, 13 December 1988; Nash interview, 30 November 1988.

59. FMB to Charles E. Young, 16 July 1971, copy in FMB Papers, Bx 55, Fd 4; Kolkowicz interview, 12 December 1988; Loewenberg interview, 12 December 1988.

60. Loewenberg to Robert Wohl, 30 March 1971, copy in FMB Papers, Bx 55, Fd 4; FMB to Charles E. Young, 16 July, 10 September 1971; Charles E. Young to FMB, 30 September 1971, all in FMB Papers, Bx 55, Fd 4.

61. FMB to Morgan, ca. December 1968, 17 December 1970; FMB to Richard M. Brodie, n.d., original in FMB Papers, Bx 2, Fd 6; FMB to Dean Brimhall, 1 and 11 September 1970; FMB to Alexander and Juliette George, ca. December 1970, copy in possession of author.

62. FMB to Dean Brimhall, 20 August 1970.

63. FMB to Dean Brimhall, 29 March 1969, 2 December 1968.

64. FMB to Dean Brimhall, 29 March, 15 May 1969.

65. FMB to Dean Brimhall, 15 August, 15 May 1969.

66. FMB to Dean Brimhall, 15 August 1969; FMB to Morgan, ca. December 1969.

67. FMB to Dean Brimhall, 31 January 1970; Eckman, "Women in the News"; FMB to Dean Brimhall, 20 August 1970.

68. FMB to Morgan, 11 May 1970; Kolkowicz interview, 12 December 1988. Roman Kolkowicz and Konrad Kellan (30 November 1988), both close family friends, spoke of Bernard's opposition to the wedding—and the reasons behind his opposition—in interviews with the author.

69. FMB to Dean Brimhall, 5 September 1970.

70. Eckman, "Women in the News."

71. Cooley to FMB, 11 December 1970, original in FMB Papers, Bx 4, Fd 6; FMB to Morgan, 30 January 1971.

72. FMB to Dean Brimhall, 8 February 1971.

73. FMB to Dean Brimhall, 11 October, 12 November, 16 December 1971.

74. FMB to Lila Brimhall, 19 May 1972, original in Brimhall Papers. Brodie wrote a tribute to Dean Brimhall shortly before his death. Entitled "The Brimhall Saga" and published in *American West* magazine, it described Brimhall's contributions as the foremost authority on Indian art in Utah's canyonlands. His extraordinary archaeological findings of Indian pictographs, Brodie noted, opened a treasure chest of great scientific worth. FMB, "Brimhall Saga," parts I and II.

75. FMB to Alfred L. Bush, 17 January 1972, original in FMB Papers, Bx 4, Fd 4; FMB to Brockway, 20 April, 30 November, 20 July 1972, all in Norton Archives.

76. FMB to Brockway, 14 January, 12 December 1972, both in Norton Archives. As for who among the "Jefferson establishment" might be approached, she stated:

> The only one who would be sympathetic would be James A. Bear, Jr., head of the Jefferson Memorial Foundation at Monticello. He might be willing to have a look at [it] providing his contribution was kept strictly anonymous. He would pick up errors, for no one knows the family letters better than he. His letters to me have been extremely guarded; his conversation was most friendly, however, when I met him at Monticello, and he put me on the track of important material. He said frankly, however, that he had to live with the Jefferson heirs.

77. Brockway to FMB, 26 December 1972, copy in Norton Archives.

78. FMB to Robert McBride, 26 January 1973; FMB to Bernice Frances, 28 January 1973, copies in FMB Papers, Bx 24, Fd 8; Janet Brodie to FMB, September 1972, original in Fawn M. Brodie Papers, Bx 19, Fd 8; FMB to James H. Rodabaugh, 12 February 1973, copy in FMB Papers, Bx 19, Fd 25.

79. FMB to Brockway, 31 January, 26 February 1973, originals in Norton Archives. In describing "the three analysts" reading the manuscript she noted that her "husband feels strongly that the more obvious psychoanalytic theorizing might detract from what I have written, and I am inclined to agree with him." FMB to Brockway, 26 February 1973, original in Norton Archives. Erikson's work on Thomas Jefferson was published under the title, *Dimensions of a New Identity: Jefferson Lectures 1973.*

80. FMB to Brockway, 4 March 1973; Brockway to FMB, 12 March 1973, both in Norton Archives. Brockway told Brodie that his recommendation that she limit her psychological analyses had been reenforced by remarks made to him by Erik Erikson after Erikson had read Brodie's manuscript. Brockway continued:

> He [Erikson] is always bothered by the extreme claims made for psychohistory and most anxious that the discipline keep as low a profile as possible. The Bullitt-Freud book on Wilson he thought as disaster, and the recent books on Nixon and the Kennedys disgraceful. He has, and urgently wants me to assure you, no such feelings about your work. At the same time he does, as I said, feel it politic to reduce the opportunities for sniping by unsympathetic reviewers.

81. Brockway to FMB, 22 March 1973; Thelma Sargent to Brockway, 12 April 1973, both in Norton Archives.

82. Thelma Sargent to Brockway, 12 April 1973, original in Norton Archives.

83. Brockway to FMB, 12 April 1973; FMB to Brockway, 22 April 1973, both in Norton Archives.

84. Norman S. Fiering to Brockway, ca. March 1973; Brockway to FMB 22 March 1973, both in Norton Archives.

85. FMB to Brockway, 31 March 1973, original in Norton Archives. Brockway took it upon himself to respond to Fiering on behalf of Brodie: "There are several fallacies in the [Adair argument]. . . . Mrs. Brodie has both negative evidence concerning Peter Carr's role and positive evidence concerning Jefferson's." (Brockway to Norman S. Fiering, 29 March 1973, original in Norton Archives). As for Adair's essay, it was never published in *Willaim and Mary Quarterly* but was published in a volume entitled *Fame and the Founding Fathers.*

86. FMB to Brockway, 31 March 1973, original in Norton Archives.

87. FMB to Brockway, 30 March 1973, original in Norton Archives.

88. Brockway to "LC" (publicity department), 5 April 1973, original in Norton Archives.

89. Brockway to FMB, 11 June 1973; Mary E. Ryan to FMB, 15 June 1973; Brockway to FMB. 26 July, 1 August 1973, all in Norton Archives. Book-of-the-Month Club apparently selected Brodie's biography because of its relevance to the approaching American bicentennial and because the club had earlier selected Gore Vidal's equally controversial novel *Burr* for its fall collection. Since Jefferson was portrayed in Vidal's novel as a villain—as a contrast to his "hero," Aaron Burr, the controversial vice-president and Jefferson's rival, the Book-of-

the-Month Club reportedly felt obligated to allow its readers exposure to Brodie's relatively empathic treatment of Thomas Jefferson. (Brockway to FMB, 7 May 1973, original in Norton Archives). It appears, moreover, that Brockway personally lobbied on behalf of Brodie's biography. For in this same letter, he mentioned to Brodie that he had had "lunch with the traffic manager of the Book-of-the-Month Club, who expressed great interest in the book."

90. FMB to Brockway, 24 September 1973; Brockway to FMB, 5 October 1973, both in Norton Archives.

91. FMB to Brockway, 15 October 1973; Brockway to FMB, 19 November 1973, both in Norton Archives.

92. Gilbert Highet to Evan Thomas, 28 November 1973; Brockway to FMB, 4 December 1973; FMB to Brockway, 8 December 1973; Brockway to FMB, 11 December 1973, all in Norton Archives.

93. Brockway to Christopher Stafford, 1 April 1974; Brockway to FMB, 10 July, 21 August 1974; Norton royalty statement to FMB, 21 August 1974; FMB to Brockway, ca. December 1974, all in Norton Archives.

94. FMB to Everett Cooley, 2 April 1973, original in FMB Papers, Bx 4, Fd 6; New York Post, 27 April 1974; Washington Post, 5 May 1974; Garrick Utley to FMB, 6 August 1974, original in FMB Papers, Bx 19, Fd 8; Fredrick G. Dutton to FMB, 12 April 1974, original in FMB Papers, Bx 24, Fd 10.

95. New York Times, 7, 8, and 28 April 1974. For two somewhat different appraisals of the varied overall reaction to Brodie's biography, see Jerry Knudson, "Jefferson the Father of Slave Children? One View of the Book Reviewers," and Louis Midgley, "The Brodie Connection: Thomas Jefferson and Joseph Smith."

96. Washington Post, 25 March, 7 July 1974; New York Review of Books, 18 April 1974.

97. Ray Allen Billington, Opinion Card for W. W. Norton Publicity, n.d.; Page Smith, Opinion Card for W. W. Norton Publicity, n.d.; Justin Kaplan, Opinion Card for W. W. Norton Publicity, n.d.; Wallace Stegner, Opinion Card for W. W. Norton Publicity, n.d., all in FMB Papers, Bx 23, Fd 19; Wallace Stegner as quoted in William Hogan, "The Boys from Utah."

98. Lois Banner, American Historical Review; Paul Boller, Southwest Review; Winthrop Jordan, William and Mary Quarterly.

99. T. Henry Williams, Reviews in American History; Bruce Mazlish, Journal of American History.

100. Malone, Peterson, and Boyd quoted in Virginius Dabney, "Facts and Founding Fathers," 171, 172; Time, 17 February 1975.

101. Egan, "How Not to Write a Biography," 129–30.

102. FMB to Brockway, 17 July 1973, 8 February 1974, both in Norton Archives; FMB to National Endowment for the Humanities, copy in FMB Papers, Bx 6, Fd 9.

103. FMB to National Endowment for the Humanities, in FMB Papers, Bx 6, Fd 9.

104. Johnson Interview, 28 November 1988.

105. FMB to Paul Crandall, 10 March 1973, copy in FMB Papers, Bx 1, Fd 8; FMB to Brockway, 20 and 22 March 1974, originals in Norton Archives.

106. Pamela Brodie interview, 6 January 1989; FMB to Brockway, 11 October 1974, original in Norton Archives; Kolkowica interview, 12 December 1988.

107. Bernard Brodie, *War and Politics.* In presenting this thesis, Bernard utilized concepts developed in the nineteenth century by the great German military strategist, Carl von Clausewitz—whom Bernard greatly admired and with whom he strongly identified, both on a personal and an intellectual level.

108. Janet Brodie interview, 20 October 1988; Kaplan, *Wizards of Armageddon,* 337–42; Bruce Brodie interview, 10 October 1987.

109. Bruce Brodie interview, 10 October 1987; Loewenberg interview, 12 December 1988; Nash interview, 30 November 1988.

110. Weiss interview, 29 November 1988; Wolpert, speech given at memorial service for FMB, 17 January 1981, copy of typescript in possession of author; Bruce Brodie, "Monologue," 12.

111. FMB to Alexander and Juliette George, 29 March 1974.

CHAPTER 7

1. FMB, KUTV (Salt Lake City) interview, 8 March 1978.

2. *Los Angeles Herald Examiner,* 7 December 1980; Berges, "Fawn and Bernard Brodie."

3. Fitzgerald interview, 27 July 1991; *Los Angeles Times,* 21 November 1973.

4. Mike and Peggy Leavitt, interview by author, 2 November 1988; Pamela Brodie interview, 8 January 1988. However, Fawn Brodie's daughter-in-law, Janet Brodie, discounts the time spent watching television as a major motivating factor for the Nixon biography, finding the explanation too simplistic. Janet Brodie interview, 20 October 1988.

5. Bruce Brodie, "Monologue," 14. Janet Brodie interview, 20 October 1988; Monroe McKay interview, 21 July 1986.

6. Mazon interview, 8 March 1992. Brodie's vigorous pursuit of evidence concerning Nixon's relationship with Rebozo is reflected in her research materials, specifically one large box of materials with sixteen folders on Bebe Rebozo. See FMB papers, Bx 39, Fd 1–16. See also FMB, *Richard Nixon,* 340–44, 468–77, 501, for her carefully crafted discussion of the nature of the Nixon-Rebozo relationship.

7. *Los Angeles Herald Examiner,* 7 December 1980; Elizabeth Marvick, speech given at memorial services for FMB, 17 January 1981, typscript in FMB Papers.

8. Dalleck interview, 29 November 1988; Victor Wolfenstein, interview by author, 25 January 1989; Symcox interview, 13 December 1988; Mazon interview, 8 March 1992; Leavitt interview, 2 November 1988.

9. Ward-Korsch interview, 25 January 1989; Loewenberg interview, June 1986. Brodie's direct anger toward Nixon relative to his conduct of the Vietnam War was evident in a letter from FMB to Richard Nixon, 9 May 1970, original in FMB Papers, Bx 4.

10. FMB, Research Notes on Richard Nixon, FMB Papers, Bx 35, Fd 12.

11. FMB, Research Notes on Richard Nixon, FMB Papers, Bx 35, Fd 13; Berges, "Fawn and Bernard Brodie"; Janet Brodie interview, 20 October 1988.

12. Everett L. Cooley to FMB, 28 May 1974; Helen Z. Papanikolas, 19 May 1974; Obert C. Tanner to FMB, 13 May 1974, all in FMB Papers, Bx 4, Fds 6, 17, and 11, respectively. Cooley had one cautionary note: "I frankly do not know how available these [Mormon Church] sources would be to you. The name Fawn Brodie still throws a lot of people into a fit—even though they have never read your book or even Hugh Nibley's attack on it."

13. Hundley interview, 3 November 1988; FMB to Cooley, 5 June 1974, original in FMB Papers, Bx 4, Fd 6; Sam Weller, interview by author, 21 September 1988.

14. Nash interview, 30 November 1988; Stephenson, "Biography of Fawn Brodie," 45–46.

15. Brockway to FMB, 20 May 1974, original in FMB Papers, Bx 6, Fd 4; FMB to Brockway, 23 August 1974, 28 January, 13 February 1975, originals in Norton Archives; Janet Brodie interview, 20 October 1988. The Bantam paperback remains in print in 1999.

16. Frederick G. Dutton to FMB, 22 July 1975, original in FMB Papers, Bx 70, Fd 12. FMB to Brockway, 25 July 1975, original in Norton Archives; Brockway to FMB, 29 July 1975, original in FMB Papers, Bx 6, Fd 4.

17. *Washington Post*, 28 August 1975.

18. Stephenson, "Biography of Fawn Brodie," 31–32.

19. FMB to Calvin A. Behle, 24 September 1975, original in FMB Papers, Bx 70, Fd 3; FMB to Brockway, Christmas 1975, original in Norton Archives.

20. FMB to Brockway, 25 July, 17 November 1975, originals in Norton Archives; E. M. Halliday to FMB, 1 April 1976, original in FMB Papers, Bx 19, Fd 30; FMB to Gloria Roberts, 12 August 1975; FMB to Margaret Jefferson, n.d.; FMB to Jean J. Stand, n.d.; FMB to Julia Jefferson Westerinen and Jean Jefferson Stand, 11 September, 10 October 1975; Julia Jefferson Westerinen to FMB, 11 October 1975; FMB to Julia Jefferson Westerinen, 19 October 1975, all in FMB Papers, Bx19, Fd 13; FMB to Brockway, 20 October 1976, original in Norton Archives.

21. FMB to Cooley, 2 April 1974; Cooley to FMB, 15 March 1974, both in FMB Papers, Bx 4, Fd 6.

22. *Salt Lake Tribune*, 19 October 1974.

23. FMB to Brockway, 14 August 1974, original in Norton Archives, FMB, Application for Sabbatical Leave, 15 February 1974, copy in FMB Papers, Bx 55, Fd 1.

24. FMB to Brockway, 11 October 1974, original in Norton Archives.

25. Ibid.; Pamela Brodie interview, 6 January 1989; Brockway to FMB, 16 October, 11 November 1974, both originals in FMB Papers, Bx 6, Fd 4.

26. FMB to Brockway, 3 November 1974, 23 January, 24 April 1975, all originals in Norton Archives.

27. Berges, "Fawn and Bernard Brodie." For a complete list of those she interviewed, see Brodie, *Richard Nixon*, 561–62.

28. FMB, Research notes of oral interview with Dr. "Jolly" West, 4 March 1975, FMB Papers, Bx 43, Fd 19.

29. FMB, Research notes of oral interview with Dr. Arnold A. Hutschnecker, 7 November 1976, FMB Papers, Bx 42, Fd 12.

30. FMB, Research notes of oral interview with Dr. Arnold A. Hutschnecker, 12 October 1977, FMB Papers, Bx 42, Fd 12.

31. FMB to Arnold Hutschnecker, 24 June 1977, copy in FMB Papers, Bx 42, Fd 12; FMB to Richard M. Nixon, 17 January 1978, copy in FMB Papers, Bx 51, Fd 9.

32. FMB to Henry A. Kissinger, 4 January, 10 February 1978; Henry Kissinger to FMB, 6 March 1978, all in FMB Papers, Bx 51, Fd 8.

33. FMB to James Reston, 3 December 1976, 15 June 1977, James Reston to FMB, 29 May 1977, all in FMB Papers, Bx 43, Fd 14; FMB to Jim Bishop, 15 April 1976, copy in FMB Papers, Bx 19, Fd 30; FMB to Irving Wallace, 22 March 1975, n.d., Irving Wallace to FMB, 22 March, 29 March 1975; FMB to Bob Woodward, 22 April 1980, Bob Woodward to FMB, 12 May 1980, all in FMB Papers, Bx 4, Fd 23; Wallace Stegner to FMB, 28 April 1978, original in FMB Papers, Bx 4, Fd 19; FMB to Wallace Stegner, 31 March 1975, 19 April 1978, 14 April 1979, copies in author's possession; FMB to Standfield Turner, 4 January 1978, copy in FMB Papers, Bx 51, Fd 9; FMB to James Reston, 15 June 1977, copy in FMB Papers, Bx 43, Fd 14.

34. FMB to Brockway, 13 August 1977, original in Norton Archives.

35. FMB to Brockway, 4 October 1977, original in Norton Archives.

36. Brockway to FMB, 11 October 1977, original in FMB Papers, Bx 6, Fd 5; FMB to Asbel Green, 4 October 1977, Asbel Green to FMB, 1 November 1977, both copies in FMB Papers, Bx 6, Fd 1; FMB to Brockway, 23 November 1977, original in Norton Archives.

37. FMB to Reed Brockbank, 30 July 1977, copy in FMB Papers, Bx 70, Fd 5; W. Turrentine Jackson to FMB, 29 November 1976, original in FMB Papers, Bx 70, Fd 4; W. Turrentine Jackson to author, 10 February 1989; Alfred A. Bush, interview by author, October 1989.

38. FMB to Juliette and Alexander George, 29 March 1974; FMB to Brockway, 20 June 1975, original in Norton Archives.

39. FMB to Brockway, 27 July 1975, 15 September 1976, both in Norton Archives; Loewenberg interview, 12 December 1988.

40. FMB to Brockway, 15 September 1976, original in Norton Archives; Nash interview, 30 November 1988.

41. Bruce Brodie, "Monologue," 9; Wolpert interview, 29 November 1988; Gerald and Jan Aronson, interview by author, 2 November 1988; Loewenberg interview, 12 December 1988; Kerr interview, 8 July 1989.

42. FMB to Brockway, 18 October 1977, original in Norton Archives; Pamela Brodie interview, 6 January 1989; Kolkowitz interview, 12 December 1988; John Gallman to Bernard Brodie, 6 Januay 1977, original in Bernard Brodie Papers, Bx 9, Fd 10; FMB to Nancy and Charles Hitch, Christmas 1976, copy in possession of author.

43. FMB to Brockway, 2 November, 8 December 1977, originals in Norton Archives.

44. FMB to Brockway, 8 December 1977, 7 January 1978, originals in Norton Archives.

45. FMB to Brockway, 11 April, 16 January, 21 April, 17 May 1978, all in Norton Archives.

46. FMB to Brockway, 17 July 1978, original in Norton Archives.

47. FMB to Brockway, 17 August 1978, original in Norton Archives.

48. FMB to Brockway, 1 December 1978, original in Norton Archives; FMB to Alexander and Juliette George, 7 December 1978, copy in possession of author; Gerald and Jan Aronson interview, 2 November 1988.

49. FMB to Alexander and Juliette George, 7 December 1978.

50. Bruce Brodie, "Monologue," 10; Crawford interview, 29 September 1988; Bush interview, October 1989; FMB to Jan Shipps, 8 January 1979, copy in University of Utah Special Collections, MS 336; FMB to Wallace Stegner, 14 April 1979, copy in possession of author; FMB to Alexander and Juliette George, 8 December 1979, copy in possession of author.

51. FMB to Brockway, 1 December 1978, original in Norton Archives; FMB to Allen Weinstein, 7 December 1978, copy in FMB Papers, Bx 51, Fd 4; FMB to Jan Shipps, 8 January 1979; FMB to Brockway, 1 December 1978, original in Norton Archives.

52. Crawford interview, 29 September 1988; FMB to Nancy Hitch, 15 March 1977, copy in possession of author.

53. FMB to Nancy Hitch, 15 March 1977; Charles Hitch interview, 3 March 1989; FMB to Charles and Nancy Hitch, 8 May 1978, copy in possession of author; Gerald and Jan Aronson interview, 2 November 1988.

54. Kolkowitz interview, 12 December 1988; Gerald and Jan Aronson interview, 2 November 1988.

55. FMB to Charles and Nancy Hitch, 8 May 1979.

56. Originally published in *Los Angeles Times*, 13 December 1976, reprinted as "Amy's School Can Look Back Proudly," in *Student Outlook*, 4 January 1977, and as "The Hero of Amy's School," in *NRTA Journal*, March-April 1977; FMB to

Amy Carter, 14 December 1976; Rosalynn Carter to FMB, 9 January 1977, both in FMB Papers, Bx 4, Fd 5.

57. FMB, "Hidden Presidents."

58. Kenneth P. O'Donnell to Lewis H. Lapham, 19 April 1977; Angie Santoro to FMB, 22 April 1977; FMB to Angie Santoro, 26 April 1977, copies in FMB Papers, Bx 65, Fd 15.

59. FMB to Jan Shipps, 16 September 1978, original in University of Utah Special Collections, MS 336.

60. FMB to Wallace Stegner, 19 April 1978, copy in possession of author. FMB to Carol Stavrakakis, 14 April 1978, copy in FMB Papers, Bx 70, Fd 6.

61. *Ogden Standard-Examiner*, 20 October 1978.

62. Stephenson, "Fawn McKay Brodie," 99–116.

63. Typescript of FMB interview, KUTV, 8 March 1978; Judy Hallet to FMB, 20 May 1977, containing complete typescript of television interview, copies in FMB Papers, Bx 70, Fd 6. About this same time Brodie found herself at the center of another controversy involving her past and present status relative to Mormonism. For years, there had been persistent rumors that she had rejoined the Mormon Church, thereby recanting what she had written in *No Man Knows My History*. Acting on these rumors, noted anti-Mormon writer and publisher Sandra Tanner wrote Brodie in June 1977, inquiring as to her present relationship with the church. In a carefully written, cryptic note, Brodie responded, "I have not returned to the Mormon Church." Sandra Tanner to FMB, 29 June 1977; FMB to Sandra Tanner, 6 July 1978, both in FMB Papers, Bx 10, Fd 7. For a good historical overview and discussion of the Tanners and their activities, see Lawrence Foster, "Apostate Believers," 343–65.

64. FMB, "Libraries in My Life."

65. *Salt Lake Tribune*, 17 March 1979; FMB to Arthur Deck, *Salt Lake Tribune*, 17 March 1979, copy in FMB Papers, Bx 6, Fd 9; FMB to Wallace Stegner, 14 April 1979, copy in possession of author. Brodie expressed similar concerns about sharing her personal side to Everett L. Cooley. FMB to Cooley, 23 March 1979, copy in FMB Papers, Bx 4, Fd 6.

66. *Los Angeles Times*, 24 November 1978.

67. Quoted in Richard S. Van Wagoner, "Fawn Brodie," 37. For a discussion of the Sonia Johnson case, see Alice Allred Pottmayer, "Sonia Johnson," 366–89. Also see Sonia Johnson's own account, From Housewife to Heretic.

68. FMB to Jane Fonda, 1 February 1977; Jane Fonda to FMB, February 1977, both in FMB Papers, Bx 4, Fd 10. In her reply, Jane Fonda did offer some encouragement, giving Brodie her father's address and suggesting she "write to him directly" but without "mentioning my involvement." She also encouraged Brodie to write producer David Rintells, who had written the script for Darrow (from which Brodie had gotten the idea for her own proposal). Brodie did subsequently write Henry Fonda with essentially the same proposal as that originally submitted to his daughter, suggesting him in the role of Jefferson but not

mentioning the role(s) she envisioned for Jane Fonda. FMB to Henry Fonda, 26 February 1977, copy in FMB Papers, Bx 4, Fd 10. There is, however, no evidence of any response on the part of Henry Fonda.

69. Barbara Chase-Riboud, *Sally Hemings*; William K. Robertson, "Sally Hemings Is Focus of Novel."

70. Robert A. Lawrence to FMB, 13 March 1979, original in FMB Papers, Bx 25, Fd 22; FMB to Brockway, 2 May 1979, original in Norton Archives; FMB to Joseph Horacek, 14 April 1979, copy in FMB Papers, Bx 25, Fd 22; FMB to Roberta Pryor, 22 February 1979, copy in FMB Papers, Bx 6, Fd 7; Agreement between FMB and Art Stolnitz, Warner Bros. Television, 9 October 1979, copy in FMB Papers, Bx 6, Fd 7.

71. "Historians Protest TV Mini-Series," *San Diego Union*, 12 February 1979; Charitey Simmons, "Thomas Jefferson"; Blaine Harden, "Revival of 'Rumor' Disturbs Jefferson Scholars."

72. FMB to Roberta Pryor, 22 February 1979, copy in FMB Papers, Bx 6, Fd 7; FMB to Brockway, 26 February 1979, original in Norton Archives.

73. FMB to Brockway, 16 April, 2 May 1979, originals in Norton Archives.

74. David Abrahamsen, *Nixon vs. Nixon*; FMB to David Abrahamsen, 4 April 1979, and Notes on FMB interview of David Abrahamsen, 25 April 1979, both in FMB Papers, Bx 42, Fd 1.

75. FMB to Brockway, 17 June, 30 July 1979, originals in Norton Archives; Janet Brodie interview, 20 October 1988; FMB to Brockway, 2 September 1979, original in Norton Archives.

76. FMB to Brockway, 30 July, 18 August 1979, originals in Norton Archives.

77. FMB to Brockway, 18 August 1979, original in Norton Archives.

78. FMB to Brockway, 30 January 1980, original in Norton Archives; Ward-Korsch interview, 25 January 1989. Like Brodie, Ward-Korsch had recently lost a husband to cancer.

79. Ward-Korsch interview, 25 January 1989; FMB, *Richard Nixon*, 542, 376.

80. Ward-Korsch interview, 25 January 1989; FMB to Brockway, 16 March 1980, original in Norton Archives.

81. Ward-Korsch interview, 25 January 1989.

82. The agency that handled Brodie was the Ruth Alben Speakers Service. See FMB to Ruth Alben Speakers Service, 3 April 1977, in FMB Papers, Bx 70, Fd 5. Also see correspondence between Brodie and various colleges, universities, and professional organizations throughout this period, as contained in FMB Papers, Bx 70.

83. FMB to Brockway, 16 March 1980, original in Norton Archives.

84. Ibid.

85. Elizabeth Marvick, speech given at memorial service for FMB, 17 January 1981. Bob Woodward and Carl Bernstein, *All The President's Men*; Woodward and Bernstein, *Final Days*; Dan Rather and Gary Paul Gates, *Palace Guard*; Theodore H. White, *Breach of Faith*; H. Robert Haldeman and Joseph

Dimona, *Ends of Power*; Willaim Safire, *Before the Fall*; Raymond Price, *With Nixon*; John Ehrlichman, *The Company*. Among the other journalist accounts listed and apparently utilized in Brodie's own biography are Herbert Block, *Herblock Special Report*; Jimmy Breslin, *How the Good Guys Finally Won*; David Halberstram, *Powers That Be*; Frank Mankiewicz, *Perfectly Clear*; and Daniel Schorr, *Clearing the Air*.

86. Richard M. Nixon, *RN: The Memoirs of Richard Nixon*; Nixon, *The Real War*; *Chicago Sun-Times*, 25 June 1978, 18 May 1980.

87. FMB to Cooley, 9 July 1980, original in FMB Papers, Bx 4, Fd 6.

88. Smith, "Fawn McKay Brodie."

89. Crawford interview, 29 September 1988; FMB to Elizabeth Jensen Shafter, 16 October 1980.

90. FMB to Brockway, 30 September 1980, original in Norton Archives.

91. Ibid.; FMB to Bernard Liptz, 1 October 1980, original in FMB Papers, Bx 6, Fd 8. The two biographers who, according to Brodie, committed suicide were Richard Gardner, whose manuscript "Richard Nixon, Fighting Quaker" was never published, and Bela Kornitzer, author of *The Real Nixon*.

92. FMB to Brockway, 30 September 1980, original in Norton Archives.

93. Ibid.

94. FMB to Elizabeth Jensen Shafter, 16 October 1980.

95. FMB to David Dealey, 13 October 1980, copy in FMB Papers, Bx 6, Fd 8; FMB to Elizabeth Jensen Shafter, 16 October 1980; FMB to Alexander and Juliette George, 30 October 1980.

96. Brockway to FMB, 7 October 1980, original in FMB Papers, Bx 6, Fd 5.

97. Leavitt interview, 2 November 1988; Aronson interview, 2 November 1988; Greenson interview, 2 November 1988. The professional advice of Leavitt and Aronson is acknowledged in FMB, *Richard Nixon*, 13.

98. FMB to Brockway, 22 October, 25 November 1980, both in Norton Archives; FMB to Cooley, 3 December 1980, original in FMB Papers, Bx 4, Fd 6.

99. Polly Plesset, in memorial service for FMB, 17 January 1981, typescript in FMB Papers.

100. FMB to Art Seidenbaum, November 1980. See Art Seidenbaum, "Endpapers."

101. Brockway to FMB, 7 October 1980, original in FMB Papers, Bx 6, Fd 5; FMB to Bernard Liptz, 1 October 1980; FMB to David Dealey, 13 October 1980, both in FMB Papers, Bx 6, Fd 8; Janet Brodie interview, 20 October 1988; Helene Kolkowicz, To Whom It May Concern, 1 December 1980; FMB to David Dealey, 13 October 1980, in FMB Papers, Bx 6, Fd 8, and FMB to Donna Haasarud, 1 November 1980, both in FMB Papers, Bx 6, Fd 8.

102. FMB to Brockway, 30 September, 22 October 1980, originals in Norton Archives; Bruce Brodie interview, 10 October 1987; FMB to Brockway, 25 November 1980, original in Norton Archives; acknowledgments in Brodie's *Richard Nixon*, 13, and on dedication page.

103. FMB to Brockway, 3 December 1980, original in Norton Archives; FMB to Cooley, 3 December 1980, original in FMB Papers, Bx 4, fd 6.

104. FMB to Brockway, 9 December 1980, original in Norton Archives.

105. Pamela Brodie interview, 6 January 1989.

106. Ibid.; Thomas B. McKay interview, 24 July 1987. The distance between brother and sister was carefully noted by both Janet Brodie (20 October 1988) and Bruce Brodie (10 October 1987) in interviews by the author. The precise nature of the blessing was not recorded. Thomas McKay declined to elaborate on the words he used. "What I said was between me and Fawn," McKay told the author in an interview on 24 July 1987. Further discussion of this incident took place in an interview conducted by the author on 1 May 1989.

107. FMB, To Whom It May Concern, 31 December 1980 (signed by Brodie on 1 January 1981), original in FMB Papers, Bx 1.

108. Bruce Brodie interview, 10 October 1987; Pamela Brodie interview, 6 January 1989; FMB, To Whom It May Concern, 31 Decmeber 1980.

109. Bruce Brodie interview, 10 October 1987; FMB, To Whom It May Concern, 31 December 1980.

110. Thomas B. McKay interview, 24 July 1987; Crawford Interview, 29 September 1988.

111. Janet Brodie interview, 20 October 1988.

112. Janet Brodie interview, 20 October 1988; Ward-Korsch interview, 25 January 1989; FMB to Jerome Stoffel, 18 October 1967, original in FMB Papers, Bx 9, Fd 3.

113. Janet Brodie interview, 20 October 1988; Pamela Brodie interview, 6 January 1989.

114. Bruce Brodie interview, 10 October 1987.

115. Ibid. Bruce Brodie reiterated this same point in a 30 November 1988 letter to the author.

EPILOGUE

1. See, for example, "Fawn McKay Brodie Dies; Known for Biographies of Jefferson, Mormon Leader," *Washington Post,* 13 January 1981; "Relatives of Fawn Brodie Dispute Statement on Excommunication," *New York Times,* 30 January 1981.

2. "Fawn M. Brodie, 65, Dies in California," *Salt Lake Tribune,* 12 January 1981; "Ogden-born author Fawn Brodie dead," *Odgen Standard-Examiner,* 12 January 1981; "Biographer Fawn M. Brodie dies," *Deseret News,* 12–13 January 1981; "Controversial Author Fawn Brodie," *Ogden Standard-Examiner,* 13 January 1981.

3. As noted in overview by George D. Smith, "Fawn McKay Brodie—A Personal View," typescript in FMB Papers. For complete typescript of the seven

speeches, see "Memorial Services for Fawn M. Brodie, 17 January 1981," FMB Papers.

4. Everett Cooley, "In Memoriam," 204–8; Sterling McMurrin, "A New Climate of Liberation," 73–76; Van Wagoner, "Fawn Brodie," 32–37.

5. Ingrid Winther Scobie, Review of Richard Nixon, 474–75.

6. FMB, *Richard Nixon*, 504, 28–29.

7. Ibid., 29.

8. Ibid., 232, 24, 25.

9. Lloyd Shearer, "Richard Nixon," 10; *Publishers Weekly*, 28 September 1981; John J. Fitzpatrick, "Review of Fawn M. Brodie," 506.

10. Robert Lekachman, "Original Sin," 385–87; Godfrey Hodgson, "The Liar on the Couch," 25–27.

11. Jack Chatfield, "No, Ma'am, That's Not History," 50–51.

12. Peter Loewenberg, "Nixon, Hitler, and Power," 28–29.

13. J. Philipp Rosenberg, Review of FMB's *Richard Nixon*, 512–14. Other reviews, including those from Brodie's former home state of Utah, were mixed. Writing in the *Salt Lake Tribune*, columnist Jack Goodman noted that as a psychobiographer Brodie was "at her worst when probing . . . Nixon's strained relations with his wife, or when relating the gossip concerning his relationship with his best friend . . . Bebe Rebozo." He concluded that Brodie's "book is not the definitive biography of a complex (and accomplishing) human being." Davis Bitton, onetime Latter-day Saint assistant church historian, was bothered by Brodie's repeated use of speculative statements, noting that "such words and phrases as 'perhaps,' 'may have,' 'may explain' [and] 'we don't know if' should not be mistaken for solid evidence." Jack Goodman, "Fawn M. Brodie Psycho-analyzes Nixon"; Davis Bitton, Review of FMB's *Richard Nixon*, 1, 30–31.

14. Jeannie Luciano to Johnathan Matson, 22 November 1982, copy in possession of author.

15. Henry A. Kissinger, *Years of Upheaval*; John Ehrlichman, *Witness to Power*; John Dean, *Lost Honor*. The recent release of H. R. Haldeman's *The Secret Diaries* (1995) supplements his earlier *The Ends of Power* in providing essential insights from the perspective of Nixon's onetime chief of staff, the man who was closest to him.

16. Stephen E. Ambrose, *Nixon: The Education of a Politician, Nixon: The Triumph of a Politician,* and *Nixon: Ruin and Recovery*; Roger Morris, *Richard Milhous Nixon*. Morris's other volumes in his projected multivolume biography are forthcoming. Godfrey Hodgson, "Staying Power," 1, 14–15. Liberal news-paper columnist Tom Wicker in *One of Us: Richard Nixon and the American Dream* and scholar-writer Herbert S. Parmet in *Richard Nixon and His America* both sought to place Nixon's entire life in a comprehensive cultural and political context, each arguing that the thirty-seventh president was more enlightened and closely attuned to what contemporary Americans wanted than previously acknowledged. Even more contrary to Fawn Brodie's interpretation was Prof.

Joan Hoff. In her *Nixon Reconsidered*, Hoff refuted the so-called traditionalist liberal paradigm in downplaying the Watergate scandal while emphasizing what she characterized as Nixon's outstanding record of accomplishments, particularly in domestic affairs. Tom Wicker, *One of Us*; Herbert Parmet, *Richard Nixon and His America*; Joan Hoff, *Nixon Reconsidered*.

17. Anthony Lewis, "Still Nixon."

18. Stanley I. Kutler, "In Praise of Nixon." Kutler's *Abuse of Power: The New Nixon Tapes* (1997) presented a far more powerful indictment of the resigned president than the public revelations that forced Nixon from office in 1974. In excerpts from the tapes as published in Kutler's work, Nixon demanded breakins, condoned and encouraged hush-money payments, and sought to orchestrate IRS investigations of his enemies. Kutler, *Abuse of Power*.

19. Morris, *Richard Milhous Nixon*, xii–xiii.

20. Eric Hamburg's *Nixon: An Oliver Stone Film* contains the complete screenplay of the movie as written by Stephen J. Rivele, Christopher Wilkinson, and Oliver Stone. According to sources consulted, the script contains numerous references to Brodie's *Richard Nixon*. "Whose Obsession It It, Anyway?" *Newsweek*, 11 December 1995; "A Conversation between Mark Carnes and Oliver Stone," in *Past Imperfect*, ed. Mark Carnes, 306–7.

21. Brodie's pervasive influence was the focus of discussion when a group of scholars participated in a Fawn Brodie symposium held on 9 August 1995 at the University of Utah. Papers from this gathering have since appeared in a published volume, Newell G. Bringhurst, ed., *Reconsidering "No Man Knows My History."*

22. Roger D. Launius, "From Old to Knew Mormon History," 195–96. For a discussion of the staying power of Brodie's work, see Newell G. Bringhurst, "Applause, Attack, and Ambivalence."

23. Stephenson, "Biography of Fawn Brodie," 19.

24. Jim Casada, noted Richard Burton scholar, in Alan Jutzi, ed., *In Search of Sir Richard Burton*, 136.

25. For a good overview of the controversy as it has evolved, see Annette Gordon-Reed's *Thomas Jefferson and Sally Hemings*, where Gordon-Reed gives a great deal of attention to Fawn Brodie and her role relative to this issue.

26. David Anson, "Jefferson's Dangerous Liaisons." See also Allen Brinkley's discussion in that same issue, "When Thomas Met Sally." For a more scholarly discussion of the impact of Brodie's *Thomas Jefferson* after some twenty years, see Scot A. French and Edward L. Ayers, "The Strange Career of Thomas Jefferson," 418–64. Barbara Murray, in "Clearing the Heirs," reported that the question of Jefferson's paternity could be settled through the scientific means of DNA mapping, testing both blacks and whites who claim to be Jefferson's heirs to see if they are cousins.

27. Diehl, "Woman of the Year"; Eckman, "Women in the News"; Berges, "Fawn and Bernard Brodie."

28. Bruce Brodie, "Monologue," 12.

29. Ibid., 12–14.

30. Berges, "Fawn and Bernard Brodie."

31. Eckman, "Women in the News."

32. Pamela Brodie to author, 22 January 1998.

33. Bruce Brodie, "Monologue," 11–12; Pamela Brodie to author, 22 January 1998.

Works by
Fawn McKay Brodie

(IN CHRONOLOGICAL ORDER)

"Just a Minute, Mother" (as Fawn McKay). *Juvenile Instructor* 60 (November 1925): 627.

"Experiment" (as Fawn McKay). *University (of Utah) Pen*, spring 1934: 24–27.

"Mormon Security" (as Martha Emery). *Nation* 146 (12 February 1938): 182–83.

Our Far Eastern Record: A Reference Digest on American Policy. Vol. II. New York: American Council Institute of Pacific Relations, 1942.

Peace Aims and Postwar Planning: A Bibliography. Boston: World Peace Foundation, 1942.

No Man Knows My History: The Life of Joseph Smith. New York: Knopf, 1945. 2d ed., 1971.

"Polygamy Shocks the Mormons." *American Mercury* 62 (April 1946): 399–405.

"'This Is the Place'—And It Became Utah." *New York Times Magazine*, 20 June 1947.

"New Writers and Mormonism." *Frontier Magazine*, December 1952: 17–19.

"A Lincoln Who Never Was." *Reporter* 20 (25 June 1959): 25–27.

Thaddeus Stevens: Scourge of the South. New York: Norton, 1959.

With Bernard Brodie. *From Crossbow to H-Bomb.* New York: Dell Books, 1962. Rev. ed. Bloomington: University of Indiana Press, 1973.

"Lincoln and Thaddeus Stevens." In *Lincoln: A Contemporary Portrait*, edited by Allan Nevins and Irving Stone. New York: Doubleday, 1962.

"Who Won the Civil War Anyway?" *New York Times Book Review*, 5 August 1962.

Richard Burton's *The City of the Saints and Across the Rocky Mountains to California.* Edited by Fawn Brodie. New York: Knopf, 1963.

Frederick Hawkins Piercy's *Route from Liverpool to the Great Salt Lake Valley.* Edited by Fawn Brodie. Cambridge, Mass.: Harvard University Press, 1963.

"Thaddeus Stevens, the Tyrant Father." In *Psychological Studies of Famous Americans: The Civil War Era*, edited by Norman Kiell. New York: Twayne, 1964, 180–89.

"Parks and Politics in Los Angeles," *Reporter* 26 (11 February 1965): 40–43.

"Abolitionists and Historians." *Dissent* 12 (summer 1965): 348–60.

"Who Defends the Abolitionists?" In *The Antislavery Vanguard: New Essays on the Abolitionists*, edited by Martin Duberman. Princeton, N.J.: Princeton University Press, 1965.

"Ronald Reagan Plays Surgeon." *Reporter* 28 (April 1967): 12–16.

The Devil Drives: A Life of Sir Richard Burton. New York: Norton, 1967.

"Inside Our Mental Hospitals: How Did We Get Here Anyway?" *Los Angeles Times West Magazine*, 4 February 1968, 12.

"Big Daddy vs. Mr. Clean." *New York Times Magazine*, 21 April 1968, 31.

"The Mormon Intellectual." ca. 1968. Typescript in Fawn McKay Brodie Papers, Box 69, Special Collections Division, Marriott Library, University of Utah, Salt Lake City.

"The Political Hero in America: His Fate and His Future." *Virginia Quarterly Review* 46 (1970): 46–60.

Can We Manipulate the Past? Salt Lake City: University of Utah Press, 1970.

"Sir Richard F. Burton: Exceptional Observer of the Mormon Scene." *Utah Historical Quarterly* 40 (fall 1970): 295–311.

"The Brimhall Saga: Some Remarkable Discoveries in the Cliffs of Utah." Part I: "The Man." *American West* 8 (July 1971): 4–9, 62.

"The Brimhall Saga." Part II: "The Discoveries." *American West* 8 (September 1971): 18–23, 63.

"Jefferson Biographers and the Psychology of Canonization." *Journal of Interdisciplinary History* 2 (1971): 155–71.

"Inflation Idyl: A Family Farm in Huntsville." *Utah Historical Quarterly* 40 (spring 1972): 112–21.

"The Great Jefferson Taboo." *American Heritage,* June 1972, 49–57, 97–100.

"President Nixon's Distortion of History." *Los Angeles Times*, 21 November 1973.

Thomas Jefferson: An Intimate History. New York: Norton, 1974.

"Thomas Jefferson's Unknown Grandchildren: A Study in Historical Silences." *American Heritage*, October 1976, 29–33, 95–99.

"The Hero of Amy's School." *Los Angeles Times*, 13 December 1976. Reprinted in *NRTA Journal*, March-April 1977, 55.

"Amy's School Can Look Back Proudly." *Student Outlook*, 4 January 1977.

"Hidden Presidents." *Harper's*, April 1977, 61–76.

"The Libraries in My Life." *Utah Libraries: Journal of the Utah Library Association* 22 (spring 1979): 13–22.

"It All Happened Very Quietly." In *The University of Utah: Remembering*, edited by Elizabeth Haglund. Salt Lake City: University of Utah Press, 1981.

Richard Nixon: The Shaping of His Character. New York: Norton, 1981. Reissued as paperback. Cambridge, Mass.: Harvard University Press, 1983.

"The Protracted Life of Mrs. Grundy," n.d. Typescript in possession of Barbara McKay Smith.

Selected Bibliography

UNPUBLISHED SOURCES

Anderson, Judith Icke. "Fawn McKay Brodie, a Teacher and Biographer," ca. 1982. Privately held.

———. "Fawn McKay Brodie: The Early Years," ca. 1983. Privately held.

Bachman, Lyle, et al. "A Short History of Weber College Activities 1930–1931." Archives, Weber State University, Ogden Utah.

Brimhall, Dean R. Papers. Correspondence to and from Fawn M. Brodie, 1937–74. Special Collections Division, Marriott Library, University of Utah, Salt Lake City.

Bringhurst, Newell G. "Bernard Brodie and RAND: A Western Intellectual Faces the Cold War—An Overview of His Interpersonal Relationships." Paper presented at 1991 meeting of the Western History Association, Austin, Texas. Original in possession of author.

Brodie, Bernard. Papers. Correspondence and other manuscript materials illuminating activities and relationships within the Brodie family, 1910–78. Special Collections Division, University Research Library, University of California, Los Angeles.

Brodie, Bruce R. "Monologue on Fawn M. Brodie." Original typescript in Fawn M. Brodie Papers, Bx 1, Fd 10.

———. Personal letter to author, 30 November 1988.

Brodie, Fawn McKay. Papers. Materials related to varied aspects of both her public and private life, 1915–81. Special Collections Division, Marriott Library, University of Utah, Salt Lake City.

————. Church records and other materials illuminating Brodie's involvement with the Mormon Church, 1915–60. Archives, Church of Jesus Christ of Latter-day Saints, Salt Lake City.

————. Correspondence between Fawn M. Brodie and W. W. Norton & Co. relative to writing and publication of book manuscripts, 1962–81. W. W. Norton & Co. Archives. New York.

————. Varied manuscript materials, including letters to and from Fawn M. Brodie as contained in Juanita Brooks Papers and various other items in the society's general archives. Utah State Historical Society Archives, Salt Lake City.

————. Varied manuscript materials related to Brodie's activities while a student 1930–32. Weber State University Archives, Ogden, Utah.

————. "The Mormon Intellectual," ca. 1968. Original typescript in Fawn M. Brodie Papers, Bx 69.

————. "The Protracted Life of Mrs. Grundy," n.d. Original typescript in possession of Barbara McKay Smith.

————. Personal letter to Nephi Jensen, 15 February 1946. Copy provided author by Barbara McKay Smith.

Brodie, Pamela. Personal letter to author, 22 January 1998.

Brody, Leonard. Personal letter to author, 22 July 1991.

Crawford, Flora McKay. "Flora on Fawn" 1982. Copy of typescript in possession of author.

Doman, Gay. Personal letter to Barbara McKay Smith, n.d. Copy provided author by Barbara McKay Smith.

Family History Center, Church of Jesus Christ of Latter-day Saints, Genealogical records relative to Brodie's immediate and extended family. Salt Lake City.

Fitzgerald, William. Class notes from American Political Biography, as taught by Fawn M. Brodie at University of California, Los Angeles, March 1972. Copies provided author by William Fitzgerald.

Fritz, Harry W. "Sex and Identity in Early America: Fawn Brodie's Thomas Jefferson." Paper presented at meeting of the Western Social Science Association, Tempe, Ariz. 30 April 1976. Copy provided author by Harry W. Fritz.

Gee, John. "The Suppression of the Joseph Smith Papyri." Paper delivered at the 1994 annual meeting of the Mormon History Association in Park City, Utah. Copy provided author by Louis Midgley.

George, Alexander and Juliette. Unpublished correspondence to and from Fawn M. Brodie. Privately held.

Hill, Marvin. Personal letter to author, 12 February 1988.

Hitch, Charles J. Unpublished correspondence to and from Fawn M. Brodie. Privately held.

Jackson, W. Turrentine. Personal letter to author, 10 February 1989.

Jackson, W. Turrentine. Unpublished correspondence to and from Fawn M. Brodie. Privately held.

James Moyle Oral History Program, February 1980 to May 1982. John K. Edmunds interview by Gordon Irving. Archives, Church of Jesus Christ of Latter-day Saints.

Jensen, Allene A. "Utah Writers of the Twentieth Century: A Reference Tool." Master's thesis, University of Utah, 1977.

Jensen, Dilworth. Journal entry, 5 March 1931. Provided to author by his daughter Patricia Jensen.

Knopf, Alfred A., Co. Papers. Correspondence between Fawn M. Brodie and Alfred A. Knopf Co. relative to writing and publication of various book manuscripts, 1942–77. Harry Ransom Humanities Research Center, University of Texas, Austin.

Larson, Vernon. Telephone conversation with author, 15 December 1988. Typescript in possession of author.

Linford, Ernest H. Papers. Correspondence between Fawn M. Brodie and Linford. Special Collections Division, Marriott Library, University of Utah, Salt Lake City.

McKay, Alice Smith. "A Psychological Examination of a Few Prophecies of the Early Founders of Mormonism." Master's thesis, University of Utah, 1930.

McKay, Thomas E. Papers. Materials related to varied aspects of both his public and private life, 1900–58. Special Collections, Harold B. Lee Library, Brigham Young University, Provo, Utah.

McQuown, Madeline. Papers. Correspondence between Fawn M. Brodie and Dale L. Morgan during the late 1940s. Special Collections Division, Marriott Library, University of Utah, Salt Lake City.

Morgan, Dale L. Papers. Correspondences to and from Fawn Brodie and other related materials, 1943–70. Bancroft Library, University of California, Berkeley.

Morrell, Jeanette. Personal letter to Barbara McKay Smith, n.d. Copy provided author by Barbara McKay Smith.

Noall, Claire. Papers. Copies of correspondence between Noall and Fawn M. Brodie, 1944–48. Special Collections Division, Marriott Library, University of Utah, Salt Lake City.

Rolle, Andrew. Personal letter from George P. Brockway, 16 February 1987. Copy provided author by Andrew Rolle.

Shafter, Elizabeth Jensen. Unpublished correspondence from Fawn M. Brodie. Privately held.

Shipps, Jan. Unpublished correspondence to and from Fawn M. Brodie. Privately held.

Smith, Barbara McKay. "Fawn McKay Brodie." Speech given to Alice Louise Reynolds Forum, Brigham Young University, Provo, Utah, 1982. Original typescript in possession of author.

———. Unpublished correspondence to and from Fawn M. Brodie. Privately held.

Smith, Israel A. Correspondence with S. A. Burgess, September 1945, relative to
    Fawn Brodie's *No Man Knows My History*. Archives, Reorganized Church of
    Jesus Christ of Latter Day Saints, Independence, Missouri.
Stegner, Wallace. Unpublished correspondence to and from Fawn M. Brodie.
    Privately held.
Stephenson, Shirley E. "Biography of Fawn McKay Brodie." Based on an inter-
    view, 30 November 1975. Oral History Collection, Fullerton State University,
    Fullerton, Calif.

BOOKS AND ARTICLES

Abrahamsen, David. *Nixon vs. Nixon: An Emotional Tragedy*. New York: Farrar,
    Straus, & Giroux, 1976.
Acorn. 1931. Weber College Yearbook.
Adair, Douglas. *Fame and Founding Fathers*. Edited by H. Trevor Colbourn. New
    York: Norton, 1974.
Alexander, Thomas G. *Mormonism in Transition: A History of the Latter-day Saints,
    1890–1930*. Urbana: University of Illinois Press, 1986.
————. *Things in Heaven and Earth: The Life and Times of Wilford Woodruff, A
    Mormon Prophet*. Salt Lake City: Signature Books, 1991.
Allen, James B., and Glen M. Leonard. *The Story of the Latter-day Saints*. Salt Lake
    City: Deseret Book Co., 1976.
Ambrose, Stephen E. *Nixon: The Education of a Politician, 1913–1962*. New York:
    Simon & Schuster, 1987.
————. *Nixon: The Triumph of a Politician, 1962–1972*. New York: Simon &
    Schuster, 1989.
————. *Nixon: Ruin and Recovery*. New York: Simon & Schuster, 1991.
Anson, David. "Jefferson's Dangerous Liaison." *Newsweek*, 3 April 1995.
Appraisal of the So-Called Brodie Book. Salt Lake City: Deseret Book Co., 1946.
Arrington, Leonard J. *Great Basin Kingdom: An Economic History of the Latter-day
    Saints*. Cambridge, Mass.: Harvard University Press, 1958.
————. "Scholarly Studies of Mormonism in the Twentieth Century." *Dialogue:
    Journal of Mormon Thought* 1 (spring 1966): 24–25.
Arrington, Leonard J., and Thomas G. Alexander. *A Dependent Commonwealth:
    Utah's Economy from Statehood to the Great Depression*. Provo, Utah: Brigham
    Young University Press, 1974.
Arrington, Leonard J., and Davis Bitton. *Mormons and Their Historians*. Salt Lake
    City: University of Utah Press, 1988.
Arrington, Leonard J., and John Haupt. "The Mormon Heritage of Vardis
    Fisher." *Brigham Young University Studies* 18 (fall 1977): 27–47.
Ashmore, Harry S. *Unseasonable Truths: The Life of Robert Maynard Hutchins*.
    Boston: Little, Brown, 1990.

Atlas, James. "Choosing a Life." *New York Times Book Review,* 13 January 1991.

Baer, Klaus. "The Breathing Permit of Hor: A Translation of the Apparent Source of the Book of Abraham." *Dialogue: Journal of Mormon Thought* 3 (autumn 1968): 109–34.

Banner, Lois. Review of Fawn M. Brodie's *Thomas Jefferson: An Intimate History. American Historical Review* 80 (December 1975): 1390.

————. *Women in Modern America: A Brief History.* 2d ed. New York: Harcourt Brace Jovanovich, 1984.

Bergera, Gary James, and Ronald Priddis. *Brigham Young University: A House of Faith.* Salt Lake City: Signature Books, 1985.

Bitton, Davis. Review of Fawn M. Brodie's *Richard Nixon: The Shaping of His Personality. Sunstone Review* 1 (November/December 1981): 1, 30–31.

Bolitho, Hector. Review of Fawn M. Brodie's *The Devil Drives: A Life of Sir Richard Burton. Washington Star,* 4 June 1967.

Boller, Paul F. Review of Fawn M. Brodie's *Thomas Jefferson: An Intimate History. Southwest Review* 59 (summer 1974): 321–24.

Boutell, Clip. "Authors Are Like People." *New York Post,* 10 January 1946.

Brayer, Herbert O. Review of Fawn M. Brodie's *No Man Knows My History. Mississippi Valley Historical Review,* March 1946, 601–3.

Bringhurst, Newell G. *Saints, Slaves, and Blacks: The Changing Place of Black People within Mormonism.* Westport, Conn." Greenwood, 1981.

————. "Fawn Brodie and Her Quest for Independence." *Dialogue: Journal of Mormon Thought* 22 (summer 1989): 79–95.

————. "Applause, Attack, and Ambivalence—Varied Responses to Fawn M. Brodie's *No Man Knows My History.*" *Utah Historical Quarterly* 57 (1989): 46–63. Reprinted in *Reconstructing No Man Knows My History: Fawn M. Brodie and Joseph Smith in Retrospect,* edited by Newell G. Bringhurst, 39–59. Logan: Utah State University Press, 1996.

————. "Fawn M. Brodie—Her Biographies as Autobiography." *Pacific Historical Review* 59 (May 1990): 203–30.

————. "Fawn M. Brodie, 'Mormondom's Lost Generation,' and *No Man Knows My History.*" *Journal of Mormon History* 16 (1990): 11–13.

————. "Fawn M. Brodie as a Critic of Mormonism's Policy toward Blacks—A Historiographical Reassessment." *John Whitmer Historical Association Journal* 11 (1991): 34–46.

————. "Fawn Brodie's Richard Nixon—The Making of a Controversial Biography." *California History* 70 (winter 1991–92): 378–91.

————. " 'The Renegade' and the 'Reorganites': Fawn Brodie and Her Varied Encounters with the Reorganized Church of Jesus Christ of Latter-day Saints." *John Whitmer Historical Association Journal* 12 (1992): 16–30.

————. "Fawn Brodie's *Thomas Jefferson:* The Making of a Popular and Controversial Biography." *Pacific Historical Reveiw* 62 (November 1993): 433–54.

————. "Fawn McKay Brodie: Dissident Historian and Quintessential Critic of Mormondom." In *Differing Visions: Dissenters in Mormon History*, edited by Roger Launius and Linda Thatcher, 279–300. Urbana: University of Illinois Press, 1994.

————. "Juanita Brooks and Fawn Brodie—Sisters in Mormon Dissent." *Dialogue: Journal of Mormon Thought* 27 (summer 1994): 105–27.

————. "Fawn M. Brodie and Deborah Laake: Two Perspectives on Mormon Feminist Dissent." *John Whitmer Historical Association Journal* 17 (1997): 95–112.

————. "The Private versus the Public David O. McKay: Profile of a Complex Personality." *Dialogue: Journal of Mormon Thought* 31 (fall 1998): 11–32.

————, ed. *Reconsidering No Man Knows My History: Fawn M. Brodie and Joseph Smith in Retrospect*. Logan: Utah State University Press, 1996.

Brinkley, Allen. "When Thomas Met Sally." *Newsweek*, 3 April 1995.

Brodie, Bernard. *Sea Power in the Machine Age*. Princeton, N.J.: Princeton University Press, 1941.

————. *A Layman's Guide to Naval Strategy*. Princeton, N.J.: Princeton University Press, 1942.

————. *Strategy in the Missile Age*. Princeton, N.J.: Princeton University Press, 1959.

————. "What Price Conventional Capabilities in Europe?" *Reporter* 28 (May 1963): 2529; 32–33.

————. *Escalation and the Nuclear Option*. Princeton, N.J.: Princeton University Press, 1966.

————. *War and Politics*. New York: Macmillan, 1973.

————, ed. *The Absolute Weapon: Atomic Power and World Order*. New York: Harcourt, Brace, 1946.

Brodie, Bernard, and Fawn M. Brodie. *From Crossbow to H-Bomb*. New York: Dell Books, 1962. Rev. and enlarged ed. Bloomington: University of Indiana Press, 1973.

"The Brodies of Hilltop House." *Your House and Home*, 1950, 20–22.

Bryant, S. F. Review. *Annual of the American Academy* 218 (November 1941): 202.

Berges, Marshall. "Fawn and Bernard Brodie." *Los Angeles Times Home Magazine*, 20 February 1977.

Burnett, James. Review of Fawn M. Brodie's *No Man Knows My History*. *New York History*, April 1946.

Bush, Lester L. "Mormonism's Negro Doctrine: An Historical Overview." *Dialogue: Journal of Mormon Thought* 8 (spring 1973): 11–68.

Bushman, Richard L. *Joseph Smith and the Beginnings of Mormonism*. Urbana: University of Illinois Press, 1984.

Carnes, Mark, ed. *Past Imperfect: History According to the Movies*. New York: Henry Holt, 1996.

Chafe, William H. *The American Woman: Her Changing Social, Economic, and Political Role, 1920–1970*. New York: Oxford University Press, 1972.

Chamberlin, Ralph V. *The University of Utah: A History of Its First Hundred Years*. Salt Lake City: University of Utah Press, 1960.

Chamberlin, William Henry. Review of Fawn M. Brodie's *The Devil Drives: A Life of Sir Richard Burton. Wall Street Journal,* 12 June 1967.

Chase-Riboud, Barbara. *Sally Hemings.* New York: Viking, 1979.

Chatfield, Jack. "No, Ma'am, That's Not History." *National Review,* 22 January 1982, 50–51.

Cooley, Everett L. "In Memoriam: Fawn McKay Brodie, 1915–1981." *Utah Historical Quarterly* 49 (spring 1981): 204–8.

Cooper, John Milton. Review of Fawn M. Brodie's *Thomas Jefferson: An Intimate History. Wisconsin: Magazine of History* (autumn 1974): 63–64.

Culver, John H., and John C. Syer. *Power and Politics in California.* 2d ed. New York: Wiley, 1984.

Current, Richard N. Review of Fawn M. Brodie's *Thaddeus Stevens: Scourge of the South. American Historical Review* 65 (January 1960): 391.

Dabney, Virginius. "Facts and Founding Fathers." In *Representative American Speeches, 1974–1975,* edited by Waldo W. Brandon. New York: Wilson, 1975.

Dallack, Robert. "My Search for Lyndon Johnson." *American Heritage* 42 (September 1991), 84–88.

Davis, David Brion. Review of Fawn M. Brodie's *Thaddeus Stevens: Scourge of the South. Pennsylvania History,* July 1960, 333–34.

Deseret News Church Almanac, 1991–1992.

De Voto, Bernard. "The Centennial of Mormonism." *American Mercury* 19 (1930).

———. Review of Fawn M. Brodie's *No Man Knows My History. New York Herald-Tribune,* 16 December 1945.

———. *The Year of Decision: 1846.* Boston: Little, Brown, 1946.

Diehl, Digby. "Woman of the Year: Humanizer of History." *Los Angeles Times,* 21 March 1975.

Donald, David. Review of Fawn M. Brodie's *Thaddeus Stevens: Scourge of the South. New York Herald Tribune,* 1 November 1959.

Dzuback, Mary Ann. *Robert M. Huchins: Portrait of an Educator.* Chicago: University of Chicago Press, 1991.

Eckman, Fern Marja. "Women in the News: Fawn M. Brodie, Jefferson's Secret." *New York Post,* 27 April 1974.

Edwards, Paul M. *Our Legacy of Faith: A Brief History of the Reorganized Church of Jesus Christ of Latter Day Saints.* Independence, Mo.: Herald House, 1991.

Egan, Clifford. "How Not to Write a Biography: A Critical Look at Fawn Brodie's Thomas Jefferson." *Social Science Journal* 16 (1977): 129–30.

Elms, Alan C. *Uncovering Lives: The Uneasy Alliance of Biography and Psychology.* New York: Oxford University Press, 1994.

English, R. "The Mormons Move Over." *Colliers,* 12 December 1942, 86–87.

Erikson, Erik E. *Dimensions of a New Identity: Jefferson Lectures 1973.* New York: Norton, 1974.

"Evaluation of Fawn M. Brodie as a Teacher." *Guidepost.* UCLA student evaluation of faculty (1974). Copy in UCLA Reference Library.

Farwell, Byron. *Burton.* London: Longmanns, 1963.

Fisher, Vardis. Review of Fawn M. Brodie's *No Man Knows My History. New York Times,* 25 November 1945.

Fitzpatrick, John J. Review of Fawn M. Brodie's *Richard Nixon: The Shaping of His Personality. Journal of American History* 69 (September 1982): 506.

Foster, Craig L. "Madeline McQuown, Dale Morgan, and the Great Unfinished Brigham Young Biography." *Dialogue: Journal of Mormon Thought* 31 (summer 1998): 111–23.

Foster, Lawrence. "Apostate Believers: Jerald and Sandra Tanner's Encounter with Mormon History." In *Differing Visions: Dissenters in Mormon History,* edited by Roger D. Launius and Linda Thatcher. Urbana: University of Illinois Press, 1994.

Freedman, Lawrence. *The Evolution of Nuclear Strategy.* New York: St. Martin's, 1981.

French, Scot A., and Edward L. Ayers. "The Strange Career of Thomas Jefferson: Race and Slavery in American Memory, 1743–1993." In *Jefferson Legacies,* edited by Peter S. Onuf. Charlottesville: University of Virginia Press, 1993.

Gabriel, Ralph H. Review of Fawn M. Brodie's *No Man Knows My History. American Historical Review* 51 (July 1946): 725–26.

Geary, Edward A. "Mormondom's Lost Generation: The Novelists of the 1940s." *Brigham University Studies* 18 (fall 1977): 89–99.

Goodman, Jack. Review of Fawn M. Brodie's *Richard Nixon: The Shaping of His Personality. Salt Lake Tribune,* 18 October 1981.

Gordon-Reed, Annette. *Thomas Jefferson and Sally Hemings: An American Controversy.* Charlottesville: University of Virginia Press, 1997.

Graham, Pearl N. "Thomas Jefferson and Sally Hemings." *Journal of Negro History* 44 (1961): 89–103.

Greenfield, Josh. Review of Fawn M. Brodie's *The Devil Drives: A Life of Sir Richard Burton. Washington Post,* 28 May 1967.

Hall, Clarisse H. *The Development of the Curricula at Weber State College, 1889–1993.* Ogden, Utah: Weber State College, 1969.

Hamburg, Eric, ed. *Nixon: An Oliver Stone Film.* New York: Hyperion, 1995.

Hano, Arnold. "A Conversation with Fawn M. Brodie," *Book-of-the-Month Club News,* spring 1974.

Hansen, Klaus J. *Quest for Empire: The Political Kingdom of God and the Council of Fifty in Mormon History.* Lansing: Michigan State University Press, 1967.

Harden, Blaine. "Revival of 'Rumor' Disturbs Jefferson Scholars." *Washington Post,* 13 February 1979.

Heinerman, John, and Anson Shupe. *The Mormon Corporate Empire.* Boston: Beacon Press, 1985.

Herken, Gregg. *Counsels of War.* New York: Knopf, 1985.

Hill, Donna. *Joseph Smith: The First Mormon.* New York: Doubleday, 1977.

Hill, Marvin S. "The Manipulation of History." *Dialogue: Journal of Mormon Thought* 5 (autumn 1970): 96–99.

Hirsch, F. E. "Review." *Library Journal* 66 (1 May 1941): 390.

"Historians Protest TV Mini-Series." *San Diego Union,* 12 February 1979.

———. "Staying Power." Review of Tom Wicker's *One of Us: Richard Nixon and the American Dream. New York Times Book Review,* 10 March 1991.

Hodgson, Godfrey. "The Liar on the Couch." Review of Fawn M. Brodie's *Richard Nixon: The Shaping of His Character. New Republic* 185 (9 September 1981): 25–27.

Hoff, Joan. *Nixon Reconsidered.* New York: Basic Books, 1994.

Hogan, William. "The Boys from Utah." *San Francisco Chronicle,* 25 February 1974.

Holbrook, Raymond Brimhall, and Esther Hamilton Holbrook. *The Tall Pine Tree: The Life and Work of George H. Brimhall.* Salt Lake City: By the authors, 1988.

Hooker, Richard. Review of Fawn M. Brodie's *Thaddeus Stevens: Scourge of the South. Springfield (Mass.) Republican,* 25 October 1959.

Hudson, Roy. Review of Fawn M. Brodie's *The Devil Drives: A Life of Sir Richard Burton. Salt Lake Tribune,* 25 June 1967.

Hunter, Howard R., ed. *Beneath Ben Lomond's Peak: A History of Weber County 1824–1900.* Salt Lake City: Deseret Book Co., 1945.

Hunter, Milton R. Review of Fawn M. Brodie's *No Man Knows My History. Pacific Historical Review* 15 (June 1946): 226–28.

Hutchens, John K. "People Who Read and Write." *New York Times,* 20 January 1946.

Jacobs, John. "Park Barrel." *California Journal,* January 1996, 16–20.

Johnson, Sonia. *From Housewife to Heretic.* Garden City, N.Y.: Doubleday, 1981.

Jonas, Frank Herman. "Utah: Sagebrush Democracy." In *Rocky Mountain Politics,* edited by Thomas C. Donnelly. Albuquerque: University of New Mexico Press, 1940.

Jordan, Winthrop. Review of Fawn M. Brodie's *Thomas Jefferson: An Intimate History. William and Mary Quarterly* 32, 3d series (July 1975): 512.

———. *White over Black: American Attitudes toward the Negro 1550–1812.* Chapel Hill: University of North Carolina Press, 1968.

Jutzi, Alan H., ed. *In Search of Sir Richard Burton: Papers from a Huntington Library Symposium.* San Marino, Calif.: Huntington Library, 1993.

Kammen, Michael. Review of Fawn M. Brodie's *Thomas Jefferson: An Intimate History. Washington Post,* 7 July 1974.

Kaplan, Fred. *The Wizards of Armageddon.* New York: Simon & Schuster, 1983.

Kazin, Alfred. Review of Fawn M. Brodie's *Thomas Jefferson: An Intimate History. New York Times,* 7 April 1974.

Kelley, Kitty. *His Way: The Unauthorized Biography of Frank Sinatra.* New York: Bantam Books, 1986.

Kendall, Paul Murray. *The Art of Biography.* New York: Norton, 1965.

Kirkendall, Richard S. Review of Fawn M. Brodie's *Richard Nixon: The Shaping of His Personality. American Historical Review* 87 (October 1982): 512–14.

Kirkham, Francis W. *A New Witness for Christ in America.* Independence, Mo.: Herald House, 1947.

Knudson, Jerry. "Jefferson the Father of Slave Children?" *Journalism History* 3 (summer 1976): 56–50.

Kutler, Stanley I. *The Wars of Watergate: The Last Crisis of Richard Nixon.* New York: Knopf, 1990.

———. *Abuse of Power: The New Nixon Tapes.* New York: Free Press, 1997.

Lash, Joseph P. *Eleanor and Franklin: The Story of Their Relationship.* New York: Norton, 1971.

———. *Eleanor: The Years Alone.* New York: Norton, 1972.

Lask, Thomas. Review of Fawn M. Brodie's *The Devil Drives: A Life of Sir Richard Burton. New York Times,* 27 May 1967.

Launius, Roger D. *Joseph Smith III: Pragmatic Prophet.* Urbana: University of Illinoiis Press, 1988.

Lehmann-Haupt, Christopher. Review of Fawn M. Brodie's *Thomas Jefferson: An Intimate History. New York Times,* 8 April 1974.

Lekachman, Robert, "Original Sin." Review of Fawn M. Brodie's *Richard Nixon: The Shaping of his Character. Nation,* 17 September 1981, 385–87.

Lewis, Anthony. "Still Nixon." *New York Times,* 1 August 1984.

Linford, Ernest L. Review of Fawn M. Brodie's *Thaddeus Stevens: Scourge of the South. Salt Lake Tribune,* 10 January 1960.

———. Review of Fawn M. Brodie's *The Devil Drives: A Life of Sir Richard Burton. Salt Lake Tribune,* 24 June 1967.

Loewenberg, Peter. "An Interdisciplinary Psychoanalytic Study Group on Political Leadership in Los Angeles." *Journal of History of Behavioral Sciences,* July 1969, 271–72.

———. "Nixon, Hitler, and Power: An Ego Psychological Study." *Psycholanalytic Inquiry* 6 (1986): 28–29.

Lythgoe, Dennis L. "The 1968 Presidential Decline of George Romney: Mormonism or Politics." *Brigham Young University Studies* 11 (spring 1971): 214–40.

Maslin, Penelope. Review of Fawn M. Brodie's *The Devil Drives: A Life of Sir Richard Burton. Cardiff Western Mail,* 2 December 1967.

Mattingly, Garrett. Review of Bernard Brodie's *Sea Power in the Machine Age. New York Times,* 4 October 1942.

Mauss, Armund L. "The Fading of the Pharaohs' Curse: The Decline and Fall of the Priesthood Ban against Blacks in the Mormon Church." *Dialogue: Journal of Mormon Thought* 14 (autumn 1981): 10–45.

May, Dean L. "Towards a Dependent Commonwealth." In *Utah's History,* edited by Richard D. Poll. Logan: Utah State University Press, 1989.

Mazlish, Bruce. Review of Fawn M. Brodie's *Thomas Jefferson: An Intimate History. Journal of American History* 61 (March 1975): 1090.

McKay, Fawn Brimhall. "Remarks to Brigham Young University Student Body." In *Standards for LDS Youth by Thomas E. McKay.* Brigham Young University Extension Division and Delta Phi, 9 January 1953.

McKay, Llewelyn R. *Home Memories of President David O. McKay.* Salt Lake City: Deseret Book Co., 1956.

McKay, Thomas E. "Remarks to Brigham Young University Student Body." In *Standards for LDS Youth by Thomas E. McKay.* Brigham Young University Extension Division and Delta Phi, 9 January 1953.

McMurrin, Sterling M. "A New Climate of Liberation: A Tribute to Fawn McKay Brodie, 1915–1981." *Dialogue: Journal of Mormon Thought* 14 (spring 1981): 73–76.

McMurtry, Larry. Review of Fawn M. Brodie's *Thomas Jefferson: An Intimate History. Washington Post,* 25 March 1974.

McNeill, William H. *Hutchins' University: A Memoir of the University of Chicago, 1929–1950.* Chicago: University of Chicago Press, 1991.

Midgley, Lewis. "The Brodie Connection: Thomas Jefferson and Joseph Smith." *Brigham Young University Studies* 20 (1979): 59–67.

Mitchell, D. W. Review of Bernard Brodie's *Sea Power in the Machine Age. Nation* 155 (31 October 1942): 455.

Morgan, Dale L. Review of Fawn M. Brodie's *No Man Knows My History. Saturday Review of Literature,* 24 November 1945, 7–8.

Morrell, Jeanette McKay. *Highlights in the Life of President David O. McKay.* Salt Lake City: Deseret Book Co., 1966.

Morris, Roger. *Richard Milhous Nixon: The Rise of an American Politician.* New York: Holt, 1990.

Murray, Barbara. "Clearing the Heirs." *U.S. News & World Report,* 22 December 197, 54–56.

Newey, LaVerna Burnett. *Remember My Valley: A History of Ogden Canyon, Huntsville, Liberty, and Eden, Utah, from 1825 to 1876.* Salt Lake City: Hawks Publishing, 1977.

Nibley, Hugh. *No, Ma'am, That's Not History.* Salt Lake City: Deseret Book Co., 1946.

Nixon, Richard M. *RN: The Memoirs of Richard Nixon.* New York: Grosset & Dunlap, 1978.

———. *The Real War.* New York: Warner Books, 1980.

Novak, Gary F. "'The Most Convenient Form of Error': Dale Morgan and Joseph Smith and the Book of Mormon." *FARMS Review of Books* 8 (1996): 122–67.

Nye, Robert. Review of Fawn M. Brodie's *The Devil Drives: A Life of Sir Richard F. Burton. Scotsman* (Edinburgh), 30 December 1967.

Oates, Stephen B. "Prologue." In *Biographies as High Adventure,* edited by Stephen B. Oates. Amherst: University of Massachusetts Press, 1986.

———, ed. *Biography as High Adventure.* Amherst: University of Massachusetts Press, 1986.

Oliver, Caroline. Review of Fawn M. Brodie's *The Devil Drives: A Life of Sir Richard F. Burton. Journal of African History* 9 (1968): 673–74.

Pachter, Marc. "The Biographer Himself: An Introduction." In *Telling Lives: The Biographer's Art,* edited by Marc Pachter. Washington, D.C.: New Republic Books, 1979.

Parmet, Herbert S. *Richard Nixon and His America.* Boston: Little, Brown, 1990.

Peterson, LaMar. Review of Fawn M. Brodie's *The Devil Drives: A Life of Sir Richard F. Burton. Utah Historical Quarterly* 35 (fall 1967): 353–54.

Peterson, Levi S. *Juanita Brooks: Mormon Woman Historian.* Salt Lake City: University of Utah Press, 1988.

Plumb, J. H. Review of Fawn M. Brodie's *The Devil Drives: A Life of Sir Richard Burton. New York Times,* 18 June 1967.

Pottmyer, Alice Allred. "Sonia Johnson: Mormonism's Feminist Heretic." In *Differing Visions: Dissenters in Mormon History,* edited by Roger D. Launius and Linda Thatcher. Urbana: University of Illinois Press, 1994.

Prescott, Orville. Review of Fawn M. Brodie's *No Man Knows My History. New York Times,* 9 January 1946.

———. Review of Fawn M. Brodie's *The Devil Drives: A Life of Sir Richard F. Burton. Saturday Review of Literature,* 8 July 1967, 27.

Puleston, W. D. Review of Bernard Brodie's *Sea Power in the Machine Age. Saturday Review of Literature,* July 1941, 13.

"Relatives of Fawn Brodie Dispute Statement on Excommunication." *New York Times,* 30 January 1981.

Rhiel, Mary, and David Suchoff. "Introduction: The Seduction of Biography." In *The Seductions of Biography,* edited by Mary Rhiel and David Suchoff. New York: Routledge, 1996.

Riddleberger, Patrick. Review of Fawn M. Brodie's *Thaddeus Stevens: Scourge of the South. Washington Post,* 25 October 1959.

Robertson, William K. "Sally Hemings Is Focus of Novel." *Salt Lake Tribune,* 22 July 1979.

Rosenberg, J. Philipp. Review of Fawn M. Brodie's *Richard Nixon: The Shaping of His Personality. Political Science Quarterly* 97 (fall 1982): 512–14.

Schearer, Lloyd. "Richard Nixon: Character Study." *Parade,* 1 March 1981.

Scobie, Ingrid Winther. Review of Fawn M. Brodie's *Richard Nixon: The Shaping of His Personality. Pacific Historical Review,* 52 (November 1983): 474–75.

Seidenbaum, Art. "Endpapers." *Los Angeles Times,* 25 January 1981.

Shils, Edward. *Remembering the University of Chicago: Teachers, Scientists, and Scholars.* Chicago: University of Chicago Press, 1991.

Simmons, Charity. "Thomas Jefferson: Intimate History, Public Debate." *Chicago Tribune,* 3 July 1979.

Smith, Bruce L. R. *The RAND Corporation: Case Study of a Nonprofit Advisory Corporation.* Cambridge, Mass.: Harvard University Press, 1966.

Sparks, David S. Review of Fawn M. Brodie's *Thaddeus Stevens: Scourge of the South. Baltimore Sun,* 25 October 1959.

Spoto, Donald. *Marilyn Monroe: The Biography.* New York: HarperCollins, 1993.

Stegner, Wallace. *The Uneasy Chair: A Biography of Bernard De Voto.* Garden City, N.Y.: Doubleday, 1974.

Stegner, Wallace and Richard Etulain. *Conversations with Wallace Stegner.* Salt Lake City: University of Utah Press, 1990.

Stephenson, Shirley E. "Fawn McKay Brodie: An Oral History Interview." *Dialogue: Journal of Mormon Thought* 14 (summer 1981): 99–116.

Stevenson, John W. Review of Fawn M. Brodie's *The Devil Drives: A Life of Sir Richard F. Burton. Roanoke (Va.) Times,* 13 August 1967.

Stewart, F. L. *Exploding the Myth about Joseph Smith the Mormon Prophet.* New York: House of Stewart, 1967.

Stone, Harry. Review of Fawn M. Brodie's *The Devil Drives: A Life of Sir Richard F. Burton. Los Angeles Times,* 4 June 1967.

Swensen, Russel B. "Mormons at the University of Chicago: A Personal Reminiscence." *Dialogue: Journal of Mormon Thought* 7 (summer 1972): 37–47.

Taylor, Samuel W. *Rocky Mountain Empire: The Latter-day Saints Today.* New York: Macmillan, 1978.

Thompson, Carol. Review of Bernard Brodie's *Sea Power in the Machine Age. Current History* 3 (October 1942): 163.

Tobler, Douglas F. "The Jews, the Mormons, and the Holocaust." *Journal of Mormon History* 18 (spring 1992): 59–92.

Toynbee, Philip. Review of Fawn M. Brodie's *The Devil Drives: A Life of Sir Richard F. Burton. Observer* (London), 19 November 1967.

Udall, Stewart. Letter to the Editors. *Dialogue: Journal of Mormon Thought* 2 (summer 1967): 5–7.

Vandiver, Frank E. "Biography as an Agent of Humanism." In *Biography as High Adventure,* edited by Stephen B. Oates. Amherst: University of Massachusetts Press, 1986.

Van Wagoner, Richard S. "Fawn Brodie: The Woman and Her History." *Sunstone Review* 7 (July-August 1982): 32–37.

————. *Mormon Polygamy: A History.* Salt Lake City: Signature Books, 1986.

Van Wagoner, Richard S., and Steven Walker. *A Book of Mormons.* Salt Lake City: Signature Books, 1982.

Walker, John Phillip. *Dale Morgan on Early Mormonism: Correspondence and a New History.* Salt Lake City: Signature Books, 1986.

Walters, Wesley P. "New Light on Mormon Origins from the Palmyra (N.Y.) Revival." *Evangelical Theological Society Bulletin* 10 (fall 1967): 227–44.

————. "New Light on Mormon Origins from the Palmyra Revival." *Dialogue: Journal of Mormon Thought* 4 (spring 1969): 60–81.

Waterfield, Gordon. Review of Fawn M. Brodie's *The Devil Drives: A Life of Sir Richard F. Burton. Geographical Journal,* June 1968.

"Whose Obsession It It, Anyway?" *Newsweek,* 11 Decmeber 1995.

Wicker, Tom. *One of Us: Richard Nixon and the American Dream.* New York: Random House, 1991.

Widtsoe, John A. Review of Fawn M. Brodie's *No Man Knows My History*. *Improvement Era*, March 1946.

Williams, T. Harry. Review of Fawn M. Brodie's *Thomas Jefferson: An Intimate History*. *Reviews in American History* 2 (December 1974): 523–29.

Wills, Garry. Review of Fawn M. Brodie's *Thomas Jefferson: An Intimate History*. *New York Review of Books*, 18 April 1974.

Wilson, John A., Richard A. Parker, Richard P. Howard, et al. "The Joseph Smith Egyptian Papyri: Translations and Interpretations." A series of articles published in *Dialogue: Journal of Mormon Thought* 3 (summer 1968): 67–105.

Woodward, C. Vann. Review of Fawn M. Brodie's *Thaddeus Stevens: Scourge of the South*. *New York Times*, 22 November 1959.

Young, Clifford E. "Elder Thomas E. McKay." *Improvement Era*, April 1954.

Zimmerman, Paul D. Review of Fawn M. Brodie's *The Devil Drives: A Life of Sir Richard F. Burton*. *Newsweek*, 12 June 1967.

NEWSPAPERS AND NEWSMAGAZINES

Atlanta Journal-Constitution, 21 February 1960.

Chicago Sun, 25 November 1945.

Chicago Sun-Times, 25 June 1978, 18 May 1980.

Cleveland (Ohio) Plain Dealer, 25 November 1945.

Deseret News (Salt Lake City), 7 April 1941; 23 February 1946; 8 April 1946; 11 May 1946; 16 April 1947; 19 March 1955; 15, 18 January 1958; 6 October 1960; 3 September 1971; 8–9 April 1980; 12–13 January 1981.

Evening Standard (Ogden, Utah), 16 September 1912.

Improvement Era 21, 186.

Lancaster (Pa.) News, 10 January 1960.

Los Angeles Herald Examiner, 7 December 1980.

Los Angeles Times, 14 June 1942, 21 March 1975, 20 February 1977, 24 November 1978, 25 January 1981.

Louisville Courier-Journal, 22 November 1959.

Nashville (Tenn.) Banner, 13 November 1959.

Newsweek, 25 November 1945, 17 June 1963.

New York Post, 27 April 1974.

New York Times, 9 January 1946, 23 September 1962, 7 June 1963, 28 April 1974, 30 January 1981.

Ogden Utah Standard-Examiner, 23 May 1943; 29 September 1975; 20 October 1978; 12, 13 January 1981.

Provo (Utah) Herald, 7, 13 September 1912.

Publishers Weekly, 29 September 1981.

Roanoke (Va.) Times, 24 November 1959.

Saints' Herald (Independence, Mo.), 1, 8 December 1945.

Salt Lake Tribune, 7 January 1905, 30 May 1943, 16 June 1946, 15 April 1947, 19 March 1955, 15 January 1958, 7 October 1960, 4 October 1970, 3 September 1971, 19 October 1974, 17 March 1979.

Time, 20 March 1944, 28 January 1946, 17 February 1975.

Times (London) Literary Supplement, 11 January 1958.

Washington Post, 22 May 1943, 5 May 1974, 28 August 1975, 13 January 1981.

INTERVIEWS*

Aronson, Gerald and Jan. Los Angeles, 2 November 1988.

Bernstein, Irving. Los Angeles, 2 November 1988.

Brimhall, Golden H. Ogden, Utah, 4 September 1988.

Brodie, Bruce R. Pacific Palisades, Calif., 10 October 1987.

Brodie, Janet Ferrell. Pacific Palisades, Calif., 20 October 1988.

Brodie, Pamela. Sacramento, Calif. 8 January 1988, 6 January 1989.

Brody, Leonard. Venice, Fla., 31 Ocrober 1988.

Bush, Alfred A. Tacoma Wash., October 1989.

Buss, Walter, Ogden, Utah, 21 September 1988.

Card, Louise McKay. Salt Lake City, 31 July 1986.

Crawford, Flora McKay. Sun City, Ariz., interview by Shirley E. Stephenson, June 1986. Copy of typescript in possession of author.

————. Sun City, Ariz., 29 September 1988.

Dalleck, Robert. Los Angeles, 29 November 1988.

Doman, Everett. Ogden, Utah, 9 September 1988.

Doman, Gay. Ogden, Utah, 9 September 1988.

Engstrom, Melvin. Salt Lake City, 7 August 1992.

Fitzgerald, Bill. Madison, Wisc., 27 July 1991.

Garner, Hugh. Salt Lake City, 20 September 1988.

George, Alexander. Palo Alto, Calif., 3 January 1989.

Goldhamer, Joan. Santa Monica, Calif., 29 November 1988.

Greenson, Hildi. Santa Monica, Calif., 2 November 1988.

Hitch, Charles J. Berkeley, Calif., 3 March 1989.

Hundley, Norris. Malibu, Calif., 3 November 1988.

Jensen, Keith. Huntsville, Utah, 20 August 1988.

Johnson, Lamont. Hollywood, Calif., 28 November 1988.

Kellen, Konrad. Pacific Palisades, Calif., 30 November 1988.

Kerr, Ann. Pacific Palisades, Calif., 8 July 1989.

Keynes, Quentin. Visalia, Calif., 11 April 1991.

Kolkowicz, Roman. Los Angeles, 12 December 1988.

Leavitt, Mike and Peggy. Los Angeles, 2 November 1988.

* Conducted by the author unless otherwise noted.

Loewenberg, Peter. Honolulu and Los Angeles, August 1988; 12 December 1988.

Mackay, Jean Jensen. San Clemente, Calif., 26 January 1989.

Marsot, Afaf. Los Angeles, 7 July 1989.

Mazon, Mauricio. Alhambra, Calif., 8 March 1992.

McKay, Barrie. Salt Lake City, 16 September 1988.

McKay, Edward R. Salt Lake City, 23 July 1987.

McKay, Gunn. Huntsville, Utah, 26 July 1986.

McKay, Monroe. Salt Lake City, 21 July 1986.

McKay, Quinn. Salt Lake City, 23 September 1988.

McKay, Thomas Brimhall. Alta, Wyo. And Logan, Utah, 24 July 1987, 30 September 1988, 1 May 1989.

Mendershausen, Horst. Santa Monica, Calif., 1 November 1988.

Morrell, David. Salt Lake City, 12 September 1988.

Morrell, Jeanette. Salt Lake City, 22 September 1988.

Morrell, Joseph R. San Francisco, 8 January 1988.

Nash, Gary B. Los Angeles, 30 November 1988.

Palmer, G. Richard. Ogden, Utah, 27 April 1989.

Reill, Peter, Los Angeles, 3 November 1988.

Shafter, Elizabeth Jensen. Ogden, Utah, 6 September 1988.

Smith, Barbary McKay. Provo, Utah, 21 July 1986; 25 July 1987; 9 August 1992.

Speier, Hans. Santa Monica, Calif., 23 January 1989.

Symcox, Jeffery. Los Angeles, 13 December 1988.

Thurston, Jarvis. St. Louis, Mo., 16 May 1989.

Ward-Korsch, Barbara. Pacific Palisades, Calif., 25 January 1989.

Weber, Eugen. Los Angeles, 23 January 1989.

Weiss, Richard. Los Angeles, 29 November 1988.

Weller, Sam. Salt Lake City, 21 September 1988.

Wolfenstein, Victor. Los Angeles, 25 January 1989.

Wolpert, Stanley. Los Angeles, 29 November 1988.

Index

Subentries are in chronological order.

Abel, Elijah, 303n.16
Abolitionists, 177, 300
Abrahamsen, David, 245
Absolute Weapon, The: Atomic Power and World Order (B. Brodie, 1946), 98
Adair, Douglass, 212, 308n.85
Adams, Abigail, 243
Adams, Henry, 292n.32
Adler, Mortimer, 57
Alexandria, Va., 130
Alta, Wyo., 249
Ambrose, Stephen, 264
Anderson, Dr., 143
Anderson, Jack, 231
Anti-intellectualism, 180; in Utah, 35, 104
Anti-Semitism, 74, 76, 235
Antislavery Vanguard: New Essays on the Abolitionists (ed. Duberman), 177
"Appraisal of the So-Called Brodie Book," 110
Arizona, 16, 33, 37, 143
Aronson, Gerald, 252
Aronson, Jan, 252
Arrington, Leonard J.: criticizes *No Man*, 179; becomes LDS church historian, 226; receives USHS Fellow Award, 300n.74

Bailey, Herbert S., 139, 151
Banner, Lois W., 218
Barker, Jetta, 39
Basel, Switzerland, 69, 73
Bear, James A., Jr., 194–95, 307n.76
Bennett, James Gorden, 100
Benson, Ezra Taft, 138
Bethany (Conn.) home: 114, 119, 123–25, 128, 158, 292n.47

Biography: heroic, 3; psychological, 3–4; popularity of, 4; biographer's approach to, 71, 267; FMB's books exemplify craft of, 267; "against" subject, 268
Birney, Hoffman, 51, 280n.20
Bishop, Jim, 232
Boller, Paul F., 218
Book of Abraham, The (LDS scripture): viewed by FMB as ahistorical, 188–91; used to support priesthood ban on blacks, 303n.16
Book of Mormon, The (LDS scripture): orthodox "historical" view of, 37, 41, 93; accepted as scripture by young FMB, 39; on origins of American Indians, 51; viewed by FMB as ahistorical, 63, 90, 106, 192; FMB's studies of lead to *No Man*, 71–72; connections between translation of and folk magic, 78, 283n.23; FMB accepts environmental influences on, 83–86. *See also* Smith, Joseph, Jr.
Boudinot, Elias, 72
Bowen, Albert E., 110, 289n.113
Boyd, Julian, 213, 219
Brayer, Herbert O., 104–105, 287n.99
Bright-Holmes, John, 174
Brimhall, Alice Reynolds. *See* Reynolds, Alice
Brimhall, Alsina Elizabeth Wilkins (first wife of FMB's grandfather), 13
Brimhall, Dean R. (FMB's uncle), 12–13, 22, 54, 65–67, 90, 158, 273n.18; FMB's close relationship with, 47–48; unorthodoxy of, 48; involved with New Deal, 70; FMB shares early findings on Joseph Smith with, 72, enthusiasm of for *No Man*, 103; comforts FMB at her excommunication, 113; correspondent of FMB, 136, 146, 151, 167, 172, 209, 292; searches for Indian

pictographs, 209–10; 307n.74; decline and death of, 209–10

Brimhall, Fay. *See* Cummings, Fay Brimhall

Brimhall, Flora Robertson (FMB's grandmother), 13–14, 145, 273n.20

Brimhall, Frances (FMB's cousin), 47

Brimhall, George H. (FMB's grandfather), 12, 36, 45; president of Brigham Young University, 13–14; reputed unorthodoxy of, 14, 274n.22; takes plural wives, 13, 273–74n.20; mentally unstable, 274n.274; commits suicide, 46

Brimhall, George Washington (FMB's great-grandfather), 12, 273n.18

Brimhall, Golden H. (FMB's uncle), 273n.20

Brimhall, Lila Eccles (FMB's aunt), 47, 67

Brimhall, Lucretia Metcalf (first wife of FMB's great-grandfather), 12, 273n.18

Brimhall, McKeen Eccles (FMB's cousin): FMB very close to, 48; killed in combat, 96, 286n.76; *No Man* dedicated to, 96, 286n.76

Brimhall, Rachel Ann Myers (FMB's great-grandmother), 12

Brockway, George P., 167, 188, 197–99, 228, 230, 236, 244, 301n.85, 305n.42, 308n.80; easy for FMB to work with on *Thaddeus Stevens,* 165; suggests changes in *Devil Drives,* 173; advises FMB against biography of Eleanor Roosevelt, 178; enthusiasm of for first draft of *Thomas Jefferson,* 196; editorial suggestions for *Thomas Jefferson,* 211–12; consults with FMB on best reviewers for *Thomas Jefferson,* 213–15; lobbies for FMB at Book-of-the-Month Club, 308–309n.89; discourages FMB from writing book on Jefferson's descendants, 229; enthusiasm of for first chapters of *Richard Nixon,* 233; gives FMB moral support as Bernard's health fails, 238; gives FMB moral support as she endures cancer, 250–51; advises FMB on final financial affairs, 253–54

Brodie, Bernard (FMB's husband), 59–60, 62, 67, 94, 204; character of, 61–62, 168; rejection of Jewish religion, 61, 281; studies international relations at Chicago, 73; at Princeton, 76; at Dartmouth, 77, 81, first books published, 77; joins U.S. Navy, 81; softens tone of *No Man,* 289n.115; at Yale, Institute of International Studies, 98; and nuclear bomb studies, 98, 120, 129, 140, 148, 183; appointed to National War College, 114; as gardener, 120, 148, 237; becomes consultant with Air Targets Division, U.S. Air Force, 129; reputation as military thinker, 129; resigns from Air Force, 131; accepts position at RAND, 131; enters therapy for insomnia, 140; as father, 148; love for classical music, 62, 148, 237; enjoys recreation, 268; as horseman, 62, 68, 148, 235, 281n.49; influence of on FMB's writing as chief critic and editor, 149, 151, 172, 238, 308n.79; receives Carnegie fellowship for

year in Paris, 153; returns to RAND a Francophile, 162; restrained in public criticisms of leaders, 294n.74; back problems of, 168, 220, 221; tensions at RAND, 168, 183; leaves RAND to accept position at UCLA, 183; has extramarital affair, 187; enraged at UCLA's treatment of FMB, 203; has difficulties accepting son-in-law, 207–208; works in special study, 221; "writer's block" and diminished visibility in 1960s, 221; completes last book, 221; feels jealousy for Thomas Jefferson, 222; advises FMB against debating Garry Wills, 227; tries to dissuade FMB from writing Nixon biography, 230; invited to participate in opening of Leonard Davis Institute of International Relations in Jerusalem, 234; quality of marriage to FMB, 235; retires from UCLA, 235; utilizes concepts of von Clausewitz, 235, 310n.107; diagnosed with cancer, 235–36; final days and death of, 237. *See also* RAND

Brodie, Bruce Robertson (FMB's son), 117, 119, 123, 163, 183, 256, 267, 269; birth of, 114; early character of, 147, 292–93; attends U.C. Berkeley, 168, 184; joins VISTA, 205; attends University of Chicago, 206; avoids Vietnam War draft, 206–207; marries Janet Ferrell, 207; does research in Illinois for FMB, 211; receives doctorate as clinical psychologist, 239; first job in Boston, 239; relocates in Culver City, Calif., 245; near FMB in her last illness, 254; helps edit FMB's Nixon biography, 254

Brodie, Esther (FMB's mother-in-law), 60, 64, 281–82n.57

Brodie, Fawn McKay:
  YOUTH: birth of, 7; character of, 23, 28, 43; religious background, 21, 29, 37, 40–43; religious doubts, 30; political background, 19, 22; early education, 22, 25, 27, 28, 36, 275n.49; "twins" with older sister Flora, 23, 275n.49, 279n.16; in grade school, 23, 25; genteel poverty of family, 24, 31–33; move to Salt Lake City, 25; in Junior High School, 25; return to Huntsville, 26; close bond with mother, 27, ambivalent relationship with father, 27, 93, 95, 103, 144, early publications, 25, 29, 39, 42, 53; begins Weber High School, 28; early storytelling, 31; sexuality of, 34
  COLLEGE CAREER: at Weber College, 36–39, 42; debate trip to Midwest, 39–42; at University of Utah, 45–54; religious doubts of, 45, 49–52, 54; political influences, 48–49; interest in psychology, 50; debate trip to California, 49; teaches at Weber College, 54; attends University of Chicago, 57; growing secularism of at Chicago, 58, 63–4; historical training at Chicago, 59; attends LDS ward, 282n.58; courtship with Bernard, 59–63; marriage to Bernard, 63–64

MARRIAGE: opposition of FMB's family to
marriage, 235; influence of Bernard on,
225; begins historical research on
Mormonism, 65; difficulties of in sexual
relations, 68; becomes liberal Democrat,
70; teaches journalism at Crane College,
71; lives in Princeton, N.J., 75; lives in
Hanover, N.H., 77; works for Committee
for International Studies, 77; publishes
pamphlets, 78; attends International
Peace Conference, 78

AS MOTHER: first child, Richard, born, 78;
attempts research for *No Man* in LDS
Archives, 84–85, 111; researches in RLDS
archives, 85; growing alienation from
LDS church, 91–93; suffers miscarriage,
96, 290n.125; in New Haven, Conn., 98;
adjustments after *No Man* completed, 99;
looks for new biography subjects, 100,
114; feminism of, 99; as mother, 101;
travels to New York to promote *No Man*,
107; excommunication of, 5, 112–13,
141, 259, 289–90nn.117,118; Brodies buy
home, 114; second child, Bruce, born,
114; domesticity of, 118–19, 126–28, 130,
137, 146; research trip to New York, 120;
moves into Bethany home, 124;
miscarriage while visiting Utah, followed
by depression, 126; rests in southern
California, 126; third child, Pam, born,
128–29; moves to Washington, D.C., 129;
in temporary apartment, 130, 293; moves
into "Hollen Hills" home, 130; vacations
in Santa Monica, 132

IN CALIFORNIA: moves to Pacific Palisades,
133; builds house, 134; liberal politics of,
138–39; enters therapy, 140; treated for
depression and sexual repression, 140,
268; enjoys Santa Monica Mountains,
148; to Paris with family, 153; reaction to
mother's death, 160; returns to
California, 161; endures nearby forest
fires, 164; travels to England, Greece,
Turkey, Egypt, 167; efforts to save Santa
Monica Mountains, 168, 299n.47; second
trip to England, 172; honored as fellow
of Utah State Historical Society, 177;
gives acceptance speech, 177–78; after
Burton biography, debates next project,
178; attacks Reagan, 179–81

UCLA ERA: begins as part-time lecturer at
UCLA, 181; UCLA teaching provides
stimulus for Jefferson biography, 185;
delivers speech in Utah on LDS position
on blacks, 188; researches Jefferson at
Charlottesville, 194–96; receives leave
from UCLA for Jefferson biography,
196–97; gives controversial speech on
Jefferson and Hemings in New Orleans,
198; involved in scripting Richard
Burton movie, 199; becomes full-time
teacher at UCLA, 200; political fight on

candidacy for full professorship,
201–202; promoted to full professorship,
205; has difficulties accepting son-in-law,
Jonathan, 207–208; observes thirty-fifth
wedding anniversary with Bernard, 208;
works on Indian pictographs with Dean
Brimhall, 209; obtains leave of absence
to complete Jefferson biography, 210;
frustrations of at UCLA, 211; publicity
trip for *Thomas Jefferson*, 216–17;
interviewed on *Today* show, 217; seeks TV
or movie treatment for *Thomas Jefferson*,
219–20; emotional involvement with
Jefferson, 222

FINAL YEARS: turns to Richard Nixon as
subject, 223, 229–30; UCLA teaching
provides stimulus for Nixon biography,
223; fascinated by House Judiciary
Committee hearings, 224; appears at
National Town Meeting at Kennedy
Center, 227; speaks for American Bar
Foundation, 228; continues research on
Jefferson and Hemings, 228; speaks at
University of Utah, 229; researches
Nixon in Whittier during UCLA
sabbatical, 230; resigns position at UCLA,
231; on speaking circuit, 248, 315n.82;
unsuccessfully attempts interviews with
Nixon and Kissinger, 232; receives
$75,000 advance for Nixon biography,
233; becomes grandmother, 234; speaks
at San Francisco Psychoanalytic Institute,
234; visits Israel, 234; fortieth wedding
anniversary, 234; difficulties and
strengths of marriage to Bernard, 235;
Bernard's cancer delays Nixon
biography, 236; dislike of for Nixon,
236–38, 241, 250, 253; grief of at
Bernard's death, 237–38; speaks at
University of Utah, 240; speaks in
Ogden, 240–41; interviewed on KUTV,
241; interest in LDS feminist issues, 48,
242–43; meets Sonia Johnson, 243;
approaches Jane Fonda for TV series on
Jefferson, 243; serves as consultant for
TV miniseries, 244; continues work on
Nixon biography, 244; as grandmother,
245–46; visits Peru, 247; critical of plight
of women in convent, 247; lectures
frequently, 248; attends family reunion in
Wyoming, 249; revisits Huntsville with
Barbara, 250; notices first symptoms of
cancer of lymph nodes, 250; undergoes
treatment, 251; endures fires near home,
252; arranges financial affairs for death,
253; difficulty of giving up
independence, 254; hospitalized, 255;
asks for health blessing from brother
Thomas, 255; false rumors about her
rejoining LDS church, 314n.63; issues
clarifying statement, 255–56; final
acceptance of life, 269; death of, 258;

ashes spread over Santa Monica Mountains, 258; reactions to death, 259; memorial service for, 260; tributes to in Mormon journals, 260

AS AUTHOR: major theme of, sexuality as illustrative of character, 68, 92, 224; major theme of, importance of childhood in formation of character, 224; major theme of, lying vs. truth-telling, 224, 268; revisionist tendencies, 5; views on own objectivity, 80, 292; motivations for writing biography, 100, 267; psychological focus of, 47, 111, 140, 202; "love and envy" toward biographical subjects, 267–68; lack of attraction for female subjects, 227; seen as ushering in more open and objective Mormon history, 260, 266; influence of, 266–67

CHARACTER: work ethic of, 149, 257, 268, work ethic derived from childhood insecurity, 269, 302n.89; compulsive nature of, 156, 268; ambivalence toward authoritarianism, 149; psychoanalytic aspects of thought, 160, 164, 195; fear of fire, 164, 252; friends linked to psychoanalysis, 172, 182, 252, 260; rejection of Christian faith, 258; attitude toward LDS religion, 206, 208, 257, disdain for most organized religion, 247, 257; ambivalence between religious heritage and desire for independence, 135; probable agnosticism, 258; hints of belief in God, 208, 250; and civil rights, 5, 117; liberal Democrat leanings of, 70, 149, 179, 193; as teacher, 182, 200–201, 302, 306; concern for education, 180–81; reticence concerning personal life, 242; feminism of, 242, 247; tendencies toward depression, 126, 140, 245, 268; rarely engaged in recreation, 268; personality of, 301–302n.88

BOOKS: See individual titles

ARTICLES AND TALKS: "Mormon Security" (1938), 66–67; "Polygamy Shocks the Mormons" (1946), 111–12; "'This Is the Place'—And It Became Utah" (1947), 121–22; "Denazification, Our First Experiment" (unpublished), 128; "New Writers and Mormonism" (1952), 134–35; "A Lincoln Who Never Was" (1959), 176; "Who Won the Civil War Anyway?" (1962), 163; "Lincoln and Thaddeus Stevens" (1962), 176; "Thaddeus Stevens, the Tyrant Father" (1964), 177; "Who Defends the Abolitionist?" (1965) 176–77; "Parks and Politics in Los Angeles" (1965), 170; Acceptance Speech for Fellow Award, Utah State Historical Society (1967), 177, 300n.73; "Ronald Reagan Plays Surgeon" (1967), 180; "Inside Our Mental Hospitals: How Did We Get Here

Anyway?" (1968), 181; "Big Daddy vs. Mr. Clean" (1968), 193; "The Mormon Intellectual" (1968), 304; Can We Manipulate the Past? (talk and pamphlet) (1970), 190–91; "The Political Hero in America—His Fate and His Future" (1970), 195; "Sir Richard F. Burton: Exceptional Observer of the Mormon Scene" (1970), 304n.23; "The Brimhall Saga: Some Remarkable Discoveries in the Cliffs of Utah" (1971), 307; "Inflation Idyl: A Family Farm in Huntsville" (1972), 304n.23; "The Great Jefferson Taboo," presented orally as "Thomas Jefferson and Miscegenation" (1972), 197, 305n.41; "President Nixon's Distortion of History" (1973), 224; "Jefferson Revisited: How Relevant" (discussion/debate), 227–28; "A Judgment on Nixon: The Historical Hazard" (1974), 229; "Thomas Jefferson the Lawyer" (1976), 228; "Thomas Jefferson's Unknown Grandchildren: A Study in Historical Silences" (1976), 229; "Nixon, the Child in the Man" (1977), 234; "The Hero of Amy's School" (1977), 239; "Hidden Presidents" (1977), 239; "Richard Nixon: Child to the Man" (1978), 241; review of RN: The Memoirs of Richard Nixon (1978), 248–49; "The Libraries in My Life" (1979), 241–42; review of Richard Nixon's The Real War (1980), 248–49; "The Protracted Life of Mrs. Grundy" (unpublished, n.d..), 304n.23

Brodie, Janet Ferrell (FMB's daughter-in-law), 207, 257; helps edit FMB's Nixon biography, 254

Brodie, Jedediah (FMB's grandson), 234, 245

Brodie, Leonard (FMB's brother-in-law), 60

Brodie, Morris (FMB's father-in-law), 60; secularism of, 60–61

Brodie, Nathaniel (FMB's grandson), 246

Brodie, Pamela Beatrice (later Kuntz) (FMB's daughter): birth of, 128–29, 132, 224, 292n.44; character of as pre-teen, 147–48; in Paris, 159; returns to California, 163; attends high school, 168; attends U.C. Berkeley, 184; marries Jonathan Kuntz, 207; divorce from Kuntz, 238; moves into Bernard's study, 238; enters environmental studies program at UCLA, 238; works for Sierra Club, 238; helps FMB during last illness, 253–54; helps edit FMB's Nixon biography, 254; thoughts of on FMB's insecurity, 269; stays with FMB in hospital, 255–56

Brodie, Richard ("Dick") McKay (FMB's son), 83, 94, 119, 123, 129, 136, 161, 183; birth of, 78–79; early character of, 292–93n.47; as toddler, 91; adventurous character of in high school, 147; in France, 158–59; attends University of Grenoble, 154, 159, 161; attends U.C. Berkeley, 163; indecision after graduation, 167; attends UCLA, 167; attends the Sorbonne, 184; attends University of Stockholm, 184, 205; lives in Los Angeles and Salt Lake City, 205; indecision as to career, 205; studies art history at UCLA, 238; difficult relationship with father, 238–39; reconciliation before father's death, 239; near FMB during her last illness, 253–54; helps edit FMB's Nixon biography, 254

Brooks, Juanita, 89, 135, 300n.74

Brossard, Edgar A., 92

Brown, Edmund G. (Pat), 170, 179, 193; interviewed by FMB, 231

Buell, Oliver, 96–97

Buell, Presendia Huntington (later Smith Kimball), 96–97

Burgess, S.A., 85

Burnett, James, 104

Burr, Aaron, 100, 212, 214, 308n.89

Burton, Isabel Arundell (wife of Richard F. Burton), 157, 166, 173

Burton, Richard F., 155, 267–68; compulsive nature of, 156; open sexuality of, 155–57; homosexual tendencies, 157, 167; idealized by wife, 157; reasons for FMB's interest in, 156–57; army career ruined by sexual writing, 167. *See also Devil Drives, The: A Life of Richard F. Burton*

Bushman, Richard, 277

Callender, James T., 198, 228

Cambridge, Mass., 112, 289n.117

Carr, Peter and Samuel, 212, 308n.85

Carter, Amy, 239

Carter, Rosalynn, 239

Carthage, Ill., 40–41, 93, 278n.106

Charlottesville, Va., 194

Chase, Daryl, 95

Chase-Riboud, Barbara, 243–44

Chatfied, Jack, 263

Church of Jesus Christ of Latter-day Saints (LDS Church), 189; typical Sunday meetings of, 19; typical rituals of, 21; in Nauvoo, Ill., 12, 40–41, 284n.25; "lost generation" of, 69, 282n.70, 285n.49; in Missouri, 284; and Naziism, 74, 130; availability of archives, 84–85, 226, 311n.12; in Ohio, 88; and relations with blacks (banned from priesthood), 117, 170–171, 188, 190–92, 303nn.14,16; ambivalence toward education, 121; authoritarianism of, 121; attitude toward writers, 135–36; policy change allows black males to receive priesthood, 240; patriarchal aspects of, 160; growth of, 226; opposes Equal Rights Amendment, 242; perceived as anti-women, 242; in Peru, 247

Church Security Program of LDS church (later, Church Welfare Program), 65–66, 282n.61

City of the Saints and Across the Rocky Mountains to California, The (Richard F. Burton, 1862) (ed. FMB, 1963), 155, 163–64; FMB finishes, 165

Clark, J. Reuben (in LDS First Presidency), 92, 146, 293n.49; attacks *No Man*, 108

Clayton, William, 86

Cohn, Roy, 245

Cooley, Everett L. (friend of FMB), 177, 226, 260

Coolidge, Calvin, 228

Coolidge, Harold, 197

Cosway, Maria (reputed mistress of Jefferson), 210, 212, 243, 268

Cousins, Norman, 251–52

Crane College: FMB teaches at, 71, 301n.88

Crawford, Flora McKay Jensen (FMB's sister): 8, 21, 256; "twins" with FMB, 23, 275n.49, 279; attends elementary and middle school with FMB, 25; oriented toward outdoor farm work, 27; does household chores with FMB, 32; lack of sexual inhibitions, 34; attends University of Utah to "look after" Fawn, 47, 279n.16; teaches elementary school, 54; becomes engaged to Leslie Jensen, 55; elopes, 56; visits to or from FMB, 132, 141–42, 249

Crawford, Vesta, 88, 285n.49

Culver City, Calif., 245, 254

Cummings, Fay Brimhall (FMB's aunt), 23, 47

Cummings, Julian (FMB's uncle), 47; criticizes *No Man*, 104

Current, Richard, 138, 152–53, 176

Dabney, Virginia, 244

Darrow, Mr., 314

Dawes, Charles G., 228

Dean, John, 226, 231, 264

Democratic Party, 19, 70, 149, 179, 193

Deseret News (LDS newspaper), 74, 95, 112, 146, 153, 191, 259

Devil Drives, The: A Life of Richard F. Burton (by FMB, 1967), 184, 301; genesis of, 155, 164–65; FMB's research for, 165, 166, 172; writing of, 167; psychoanalytic component of, 172–73, 175; reflects FMB's interest in sexuality, 6, 155; FMB sends manuscript of to Norton, 173; editorial process for, 173–74; publication of, 174; chosen for Literary Book Club, 174; positive reviews of, 175; critiqued for excessive psychoanalyzing, 175, 300n.69; movie script based on, 198–99; final impact of, 266

De Voto, Bernard (historian): leader of Mormondom's lost generation, 69; review of *No Man*, 106; discussed by FMB as leading Utah writer, 135; theorizes that Joseph Smith had "paranoid" personality, 139–40; Stegner writes biography of, 218

Dick, Thomas, 90

Donald, David, 152

Dulles, John Foster, 138

Eccles, David, 47

Eden, Utah, 10

Ehrlichman, John, 264

Eisenhower, Dwight B., 138, 294n.73

Ellsberg, Daniel, 162 , 295, 298n.23
English, R., 284n.37
Ericksen, E. E., 50
Erikson, Erik, 3–4, 211, 213, 308nn.79,80
Escalation and the Nuclear Option (B. Brodie, 1966), 183

Farwell, Byron, 165
Feminism, 118, 125, 186, 202
Fenichel, Hanna, 140
Fielding, Lewis J., 172, 295n.80
Fiering, Norman, 212, 308n.85
Finch, Robert, 231
Fisher, Vardis, 105, 135, 287–88n.101
Fitzpatrick, John J., 262
Follett, Wilson, 96
Fonda, Henry, 243, 314–15n.68
Fonda, Jane, 243, 314–15n.68
Fox, Margaret and Katherine, 119
Frankenheimer, John, 199
Frankfurt, Germany, 11
Franklin, Benjamin, 214
Freud, Sigmund, 3, 69
From Crossbow to H-Bomb (Bernard and Fawn Brodie, 1962), 154, 161; FMB finishes research on, 158; FMB writes, 159; revised and republished, 235
Fruita, Utah, 158
Fuller, Margret, 100
Fullerton, Calif., 241
Fundamentalism, Mormon (schismatic polygamists), 92, 111, 286n.61

Gabriel, Ralph H., 105
Galbraith, John, 203
Gettysburg, Penn., 149
Goldson, Joe, 183
Goodman, Jack, 318n.13
Graham, Pearl N., 194
Great Depression, 37, 40, 50–51, 65
Greeley, Horace, 100–101, 114
Green, Asbel, 234
Greenfeld, Josh, 175
Greenson, Hildi, 252, 295n.79
Greenson, Ralph ("Romi") R.: psychoanalyst friend of FMB, 294–95n.79; helps FMB analyze Stevens, 140–41; helps FMB analyze Burton, 172; FMB and Bernard become distant from, 252

Hamilton, Alexander, 212
Hanover, N.H., 77, 81, 92
Hansen, Klaus, 179
Hemings, Eston, 228, 267
Hemings, Madison, 228
Hemings, Sally: regarded by FMB as mistress of Jefferson, 5, 186, 194–95, 197–98, 211–12, 217, 228, 243, 267–68, 304n.27. *See also* Jefferson, Thomas
Highet, Gilbert, 215
Hill, Donna, 304n.20
Hill, Marvin S., 303n.20

Hiss, Alger, 236
Hodgson, Godfrey, 263–64
Hollen Hills (Va.) home, 130–31
Hooker, Richard, 151
Hoover, Herbert, 49
Hopkins, Harry, 65
Hopkins, John, 198–99
Huntsville, Utah, 7–9; old home and farm in, 15–20, 22–23, 26–30, 32–34, 37, 50, 68, 141, 145, 159, 161, 167, 187, 242, 249, 250, 275n.28, 304n.23; FMB's nostalgia for, 7, 249
Hutchins, Robert M., 56
Hutschnecker, Arnold, Dr., 231–32, 245

Independence, Mo., 41, 85
Ivins, Stanley, 291

Jackson, W. Turrentine, 234
Jefferson, Maria, 243
Jefferson, Martha Wayles Skelton, 5, 186
Jefferson, Polly, 243
Jefferson, Thomas, 5, 149, 240, 243, 267–68; authoritarian aspects of, 187; idealized, 195; possible sexual relationship with Sally Hemings, 186–87, 196–98; 211–12, 304n.27, 319n.26; as slaveholder, 186. *See also Thomas Jefferson: An Intimate History*
Jensen, Dilworth (FMB's boyfriend), 34–36; serves LDS mission, 42; attends University of Utah, 52; transfers to Utah State, 54; reaction to FMB's decision to attend Chicago, 57; reaction to FMB's engagement to Bernard, 62–63
Jensen, Leslie (FMB's brother-in-law), 35, 55–56. *See* Crawford, Flora
Jensen, Leslie (FMB's niece), 255
Jesperson, Edward, 23
Jobe, Ola Welch, 231
Johnson, Andrew, 122–23
Johnson, Lady Bird, 227
Johnson, Lamont, 220, 260
Johnson, Lyndon, 183, 187–88, 240
Johnson, Sonia, 242–43
Jordan, Winthrop D., 194, 198, 213–14, 218, 304n.27, 305n.42

Kahn, Herman, 131
Kammen, Michael, 217
Kaplan, Justin, 213–14, 218
Kaufmann, William W., 131, 162, 298n.23
Kazin, Alfred, 217
Kefauver, Estes, 149
Kellen, Konrad, 183
Kennedy, Jacqueline, 240
Kennedy, John F., 162, 187, 240, 246
Kennedy, Rose, 240
Keynes, Quentin, 166
Kimball, Spencer W., 242
King, Ernest J., Adm., 81
Kirkham, Francis, 120
Kissinger, Henry, 131, 141, 193, 232, 264

Knopf, Alfred A.: 179, 188, 210, 287, 305n.37;
    FMB applies for Knopf fellowship, 79; FMB
    wins fellowship, 80, 82; editorial process of
    for *No Man*, 96–97; concerned about being
    sued for *No Man*, 101; urges FMB to
    complete Stevens biography, 127, 132;
    readers for are critical of Stevens biography,
    136–37; rejects Stevens biography, 139; asks
    FMB to edit Burton's *City of the Saints*, 163;
    hopes to enlist FMB to write Burton
    biography, 165
Korean War, 129–31
Korngold, Ralph, 127–28, 152, 166
Kuntz, Jonathan, 207–208, 238
Kuntz, Pamela Beatrice Brodie. *See* Brodie,
    Pamela
Kutler, Stanley I., 265, 319n.18

Lash, Joseph, 178
Launius, Roger D., 266
Layman's Guide to Naval Strategy, A. (B. Brodie),
    77, 139
LDS Church. *See* Church of Jesus Christ of
    Latter-day Saints
Leavitt, Maimon (Mike), 172, 252, 260
Leavitt, Peggy, 252
Lehmann-Haupt, Christopher, 217
Leites, Nathan, 140, 172
Lekachman, Robert, 263
LeMay, Curtis, Gen., 131
Lewis, Anthony, 265
Lewis and Clark expedition, 212
Lightner, Mary Elizabeth Rollins (Smith Young),
    90
Lima, Peru, 246–47
Lincoln, Abraham, 116, 122, 149, 176, 230
Lincoln, Mary Todd, 100
Lincoln: A Contemporary Portrait (ed. Nevins and
    Stone), 176
Linford, Ernest, 153, 175
Loewenberg, Peter (friend of FMB), 182, 203,
    260, 263, 301n.88
Logan, Utah, 12, 54
Lund, A. William, 84
Lyman, Richard, 92

Malone, Dumas: FMB's meeting with, 194–96;
    FMB concerned about negative review from,
    213–14; negative reactions of to FMB's
    Thomas Jefferson, 219; opposes CBS miniseries
    on Jefferson and Hemings, 244
Marquand, Richard, 220
Marvick, Elizabeth, 260
McCarthy, Joseph, 137–38, 245
McCormick, "Bertie," 100
McKay, Alice Smith (FMB's cousin-in-law), 51–52
McKay, Annie (FMB's aunt), 11, 18, 19
McKay, Barbara (FMB's sister). *See* Smith,
    Barbara
McKay, David (FMB's grandfather), 8–10, 272n.8
McKay, David Oman (FMB's uncle), 9–10, 20,
    42, 62, 69, 171, 273, 282n.15; becomes

apostle, 17; speculative ventures of, 33,
    274n.27; view of by FMB, 293n.49; tries to
    dissuade FMB from marriage to Brodie, 62,
    281n.51; confronts FMB on her research at
    LDS church archives, 84–85, 242; reads *No
    Man*, 103; criticizes *No Man*, 108–109,
    288n.109; possible role in FMB's
    excommunication, 113, 289n.117; counsels
    FMB, 281n.51; becomes church president,
    130, 293n.49
McKay, Edward (FMB's cousin), 23
McKay, Elizabeth (FMB's aunt), 11, 18–19
McKay, Emma Ray (FMB's cousin), 47
McKay, Emma Ray Riggs (FMB's aunt), 12
McKay, Ernest (FMB's cousin), 104
McKay Family Corporation, 11–12, 17, 33
McKay, Fawn Brimhall (FMB's mother), 8,
    12–13, 15, 18, 26, 31, 33, 56, 62–63, 95, 125,
    158; marriage of, 12, 274; unorthodoxy of,
    20–21, 46; sexual dysfunctions of, 34, 36;
    changes while in Europe, 75, 283n.14;
    supports *No Man*, 103; visits FMB, 141;
    depression of, 143, 145, 236, 254; attempts
    suicide, 143; death of sister, 145; undergoes
    shock therapy, 145; seeming recovery of,
    146; second suicide attempt and death of,
    159; FMB's reaction to death of, 159–60
McKay, Flora. *See* Crawford, Flora McKay Jensen
McKay, Gunn, 159
McKay, Jennette Evans (FMB's grandmother),
    8–11, 272nn.7,8
McKay, Katherine. *See* Ricks, Katherine
McKay, Llewelyn (FMB's cousin), 51
McKay, Louise (FMB's sister), 31, 70, 75, 120,
    142, 145, 249
McKay, Morgan (FMB's uncle), 18
McKay, Thomas Brimhall (FMB's brother), 30,
    72, 74, 103, 142, 145, 249; gives FMB
    deathbed blessing, 255–57, 317n.106
McKay, Thomas Evans (FMB's father), 7–8,
    10–11, 47, 50, 58, 67, 84, 92, 125, 274n.27;
    character of, 11, 187; president of Swiss-
    Austrian mission, 12, 69, 73–75; marriage of,
    12, 16, 274n.25; orthodoxy of, 20, 30; LDS
    stake president, 21, 43; financial struggles of,
    16, 24, 26, 33, 37, 43; political offices, 22, 24,
    37, 69, 276n.53; tries to stop FMB's
    marriage, 62; becomes assistant to Council
    of Twelve (LDS General Authority), 82,
    282n.72; endures heart attack, 93; reaction
    to *No Man*, 95, 103, 241; second heart attack,
    126; visits FMB, 141; deteriorating health,
    142; demands on wife, 143; defends FMB,
    144; death of, 146
McKay, William (FMB's uncle), 18
McKay, William (FMB's great-grandfather), 8,
    272n.7
McMurrin, Sterling M., 260
McMurtry, Larry, 217
McNamara, Robert S., 162, 183, 298n.23
McQuown, Madeline, 178–79, 188, 226, 303n.9
Mercer, Lucy, 211

Milton, George Fort, 127
Moench, Louis, Dr., 143
Monson, Leland, 39, 58
Monticello, Va., 187, 220, 307n.76
Moorehead, Alan, 173
Morgan, Dale: mentor of FMB, 86–87, 130, 135,
  140, 293, 300n.74; researches Joseph Smith's
  1826 trial, 291n.16; discourages FMB from
  writing Brigham Young biography, 178–79,
  188; as FMB's correspondent, 122–23, 129,
  146, 163, 166, 169, 171, 208; death of,
  208–10
Mormonism. *See* Church of Jesus Christ of
  Latter-day Saints (LDS Church)
Morrell, Jeanette (FMB's cousin), 47
Morrell, Jeannette McKay (FMB's aunt), 8, 11,
  18, 19
Morrell, Joseph R. (FMB's uncle), 8; rejects *No
  Man,* 104
Morris, Roger, 264–65
Mountain Meadows Massacre, The (Brooks), 89,
  135
Muddy River, Nev., 13

Nauvoo, Ill., 12, 40–41, 284n.25
Neff, S. B., 50
Nevins, Allan, 152, 176
New Haven, Conn., 98–100, 112, 119
Nibley, Hugh: attacks *No Man,* 110, 311; studies
  Book of Abraham, 189
Nixon, Richard: 187, 193, 206, 240, 267–68;
  Quaker background of, 223, 233; influence
  of father and mother on, 224, 230, 261;
  influence of deaths of brothers on, 261, 265;
  possible homosexual tendencies, 224, 231–33,
  245; sexual life of, 245; political survival of,
  261; ego strengths of, 263; marriage of seen
  as unhealthy, 261; role in Alger Hiss case,
  236, 261; reliance on attack for political
  gain, 261; dirty tricks used by, 319n.18; role
  in Watergate scandal, 223–24; and Cuba, 265;
  role in bombing Vietnam, 223, 233; seen as
  exhibiting patterns of lying and deception,
  223–24, 233, 241, 261, 268; similarities and
  contrasts to FMB, 223; and Bebe Rebozo,
  224, 231–32, 310n.6; similarities to Joseph
  Smith, 224; treated for stress, 231; rage of,
  233; life changed by Kennedy assassination,
  246, 261; and Castro, 246; visit to Peru, 246;
  courage of, 247; hard line on Communism,
  249; detente with Soviet Union, 249;
  "revisionist" positive view of, 264–65,
  318–19n.16; reemergence of "traditional"
  negative view of, 265, 319n.18. *See also
  Richard Nixon: The Shaping of His Character*
Noall, Claire, 88, 125
Nolte, Nick, 267
Nolting, Frederick E., 244
No Ma'am, That's Not History (Nibley), 110–11,
  311n.12
No Man Knows My History (by FMB, 1945), 5,
  121, 125, 164–65, 178, 208, 257, 259, 277;

genesis of, 71; influence of Bernard Brodie
  on, 73, 289n.115; exhibits a compassion for
  Joseph Smith, 289n.115; first draft of, 78;
  Knopf readers comment on, 80, 284n.27;
  receives Knopf fellowship, 79–80; research
  for, 83–86, 91, 242; and FMB's difficult
  relationship with father, 84, 93, 95; critiqued
  by Dale Morgan, 87–88, 91; critiqued by
  Poulson, 90–91; final revision process, 93–94;
  Morgan's final critique, 94–95; represents
  FMB's rebellion, 290; limited psychoanalytic
  tendencies in, 224; submission to Knopf, 96;
  finalizing proofs of, 97; FMB's emotional
  commitment to, 101, 115; attacked by RLDS
  Church, 101–102; ambivalent reactions to
  from FMB's family, 103, 241; positive and
  negative reviews of, 104–107, 287n.100;
  meticulous quotations in, 288n.102; initial
  sales of, 108, 288n.107; official LDS church
  response to, 103, 107–11; FMB
  excommunicated as result of, 112; FMB's
  feelings of guilt for writing, 116; FMB loses
  guilt for writing, 126; addresses race
  relations in Mormonism, 170, 188; British
  edition of, 176; revised edition of, 192;
  controversial nature of, 213; influence of, 91.
  See also Smith, Joseph, Jr.
Nyswander, Dorothy, Dr., 50

O'Donnell, Kenneth P., 240
Ogden, Utah, 8, 11–12, 15, 21, 26, 28–29, 32,
  34–37, 42–43, 46, 50, 54–56, 108, 240,
  273n.15
Our Far Eastern Record (FMB, 1941), 78

Pacific Palisades, Calif., 133–34, 148, 150, 168,
  184, 207–208, 227, 234, 252–54
Palmer, G. Richard, 289n.117
Papanikolas, Helen Z., 226
Peace Aims and Postwar Planning: A Bibliography
  (FMB, 1942), 78
Peterson, Merrill, 195–96, 198, 213–14, 219, 244,
  305n.42
Piercy, Frederick Hawkins, 163
Plesset, Polly, 260
Polygamy, LDS practice of, 10–11, 41–42, 51,
  83–84, 91–92, 111; in Brimhall family, 13–15,
  273n.20; FMB researches Joseph Smith as
  polygamist, 86, 88–89; seen by FMB as
  disguised promiscuity, 89; taboo topic in
  modern Moronism, 179. *See also*
  fundamentalism; Smith, Joseph, Jr.
Poulson, M. Wilford, 90, 124, 284n.38
Prescott, Orville, 105
Princeton, N.J., 75–76
Provo, Utah, 13, 15, 45, 108
"Psychological Examination of a Few Prophecies
  of the Early Founders of Mormonism, A"
  (Alice Smith McKay), 51–52
*Psychological Studies of Famous Americans: The Civil
  War Era,* 177
Purple, W. D., 121, 291

Quaife, Milo M., 96

Race relations, between blacks and whites in
    America, 116–17, 186; FMB's interest in LDS
    position on, 170–71, 188, 190, 291n.4; in
    Civil War era, 164. *See also* Church of Jesus
    Christ of Latter-day Saints; *Thaddeus Stevens:
    Scourge of the South; Thomas Jefferson: An
    Intimate History*
Ralling, Christopher, 200
RAND (strategic think-tank), 131, 133, 140, 141,
    148–49, 158, 162, 167–68, 183
Reagan, Ronald, 179–81, 192–93, 253, 301n.84,
    FMB considers writing biography of, 301n.85
Rebozo, Bebe, 224, 231–32, 245, 310n.6,
    318n.13
Reconstruction era, 5, 116, 122–23, 128, 152,
    176, 202
Reeder, William H., 112, 290n.118
Rees, Alfred C., 74
Reorganized Church of Jesus Christ of Latter
    Day Saints (RLDS Church), 41, 85; rejects
    connection of Joseph Smith and polygamy,
    86, 93, 101, response to *No Man,* 101–102
Republican Party, 22, 49, 169–71, 179–80, 193;
    radical republicanism, 122–23, 139. *See also*
    Nixon, Richard; Reagan, Ronald; Stevens,
    Thaddeus
Reston, James, 232
Reynolds, Alice Louise (plural wife of George H.
    Brimhall), 273–74n.20
Richard Nixon: The Shaping of His Character (FMB,
    1981): genesis of, 223, 229; writing of
    difficult, 223; reflects FMB's and Bernard's
    health problems, 6; psychoanalytic themes
    in, 224; theme of lying and truth in, 223–24,
    261; theme of death/fratricide, 261; research
    for in Whittier, 230–31; research for at Cal.
    State Fullerton, 231; writing of begins, 233;
    Bernard's cancer delays work on, 236;
    envisioned as two volumes, 246; first draft of
    completed, 246; FMB diagnosed with cancer
    during writing of, 250; ending of, 261;
    revisions during editing process, 251; FMB's
    children help finish editing of, 254; final
    chapters and revisions of sent to Norton,
    254–55; posthumous publication of, 223, 261;
    reviews of, 262; seen as perceptive view of
    Nixon's character, 263, 265; seen as using
    psychological analysis for expressing hostility,
    263–64; criticisms of, 318n.13; limited
    commercial success of, 264; paperback
    edition of, 264; influence of on filmmaker
    Oliver Stone, 265. *See also* Nixon, Richard
Richards, Willard, 86
Ricks, Joel (FMB's uncle), 104
Ricks, Katherine McKay (FMB's aunt), 11, 18–19
Riddleberger, Patrick, 151
Rintells, David, 314n.68
Rogger, Hans, 260
Romney, George, 170–71, 193
Roosevelt, Eleanor, 117, 178, 227

Roosevelt, Franklin, 65, 73, 187, 211
Rosenberg, J. Philipp, 264
Routes from Liverpool to Great Salt Lake Valley
    (Piercy, 1855, ed. FMB, 1963), 163–64
Rugoff, M., 80, 284n.27

Sadullah, Mian Muhammad, 167
Sally Hemings (Chase-Riboud), 243–44
Saloutos, Theodore, 203
Salt Lake City, Utah, 8, 12, 18, 22, 24–26, 45–54,
    76, 84–85, 107–108, 110, 143–44, 146, 155,
    240
Santa Monica, Calif., 131–33, 255. See RAND
Santa Monica Mountains, Calif., 148; FMB fights
    to save, 168–70, 258, 299n.47
Sargent, Thelma, 211–12
Schlesinger, Arthur, Jr., 39
Scobie, Ingrid Winther, 261
Sea Power in the Machine Age (B. Brodie, 1941),
    77, 139
Seidenbaum, Art, 253
Shearer, Lloyd, 262
Shipps, Jan, 237
Slavery, 164. *See also* Jefferson, Thomas;
    Hemings, Sally
Smith, Barbara McKay (FMB's sister), 26, 31, 70,
    75, 142, 145, 249, 259, 273n.20
Smith, Datus, 79
Smith, Emma Hale (wife of Joseph Smith, Jr.),
    88, 93, 100–101
Smith, Ethan, 72, 86
Smith, Frederick M., 85
Smith, George Albert, 110, 130
Smith, Israel, 85–86, 101–102
Smith, Joseph Fielding, 84, 171
Smith, Joseph, Jr., 92, 100, 125, 165, 179, 213,
    267; charisma of, 95, 289n.115;
    "enlightened" attitude toward blacks,
    190–91, 303n.16; first vision of, 106;
    idealized by Mormons, 82, 86, 112; as
    money-digger, folk magic practitioner, 72,
    78, 120, 291n.16; as translator of the Book of
    Mormon, 283n.23; paranoid theory of, 140;
    practices polygamy, 41, 51, 83, 88–91, 93–94,
    111, 179, 278n.108; practices polyandry, 89;
    exposed by William Law, 226; regarded by
    FMB as conscious fraud, 5, 106, 119, 192,
    225, 268, 288n.106; regarded by FMB as
    similar to Richard Nixon, 225–26. *See also*
    Book of Mormon; *No Man Knows My History*
Smoot, Reed, 40
Spanish Fork, Utah, 13
Sparks, David S., 152
St. George, Utah, 89
Stanley, Henry, 165
Stegner, Wallace, 135, 218, 300n.74
Stephenson, Shirley, 241
Stevens, Thaddeus, 116–17, 128, 177, 267; as
    liberal reformer, 138; as revolutionary, 123;
    psychological impact of club foot of, 117,
    266; story of murdering a black woman, 149.
    See also Thaddeus Stevens: Scourge of the South

Stevenson, Adlai E., 138
Stewart, F. L., 179, 301n.79
Stoffel, Jerome, Monsignor, 258
Stone, Irving, 176
Stone, Oliver, 265
Strang, James J., 90
Strategy in the Missile Age (B. Brodie, 1959), 162
Strauss, H., 284n.27

Tanner, Sandra, 314n.63
Taylor, Samuel W., 90
Teller, Edward, 141
Thaddeus Stevens: Scourge of the South (FMB, 1959), 5, 165, 177, 184; genesis of, 116, 122; deals with racial issues, 116, 170; psychoanalysis in, 117, 140, 266; difficulty of researching, 125; distractions from, 127, 132; research for at Library of Congress, 130; writing of, 136; negative response from Knopf readers for, 136; Knopf rejects, 139; research for in Gettysburg, 149; submitted to Princeton, 151; submitted to W.W. Norton, 151; George Brockway editor for, 165; publication of, 151; limited sales of, 151; positive reviews of, 151–52; reviewed in newspapers, 152; paperback edition of, 176; seen as key revisionist book on Reconstruction, 266
Thomas Jefferson: An Intimate History (FMB, 1974), 259; genesis of, 185–87; research on begins, 194; research for at Charlottesville, 194; deals with race relations with blacks, 186; analyzes Jefferson's sexual relations, 5; psychological nature of, 3, 224; reacts against "cover up" by traditional scholars, 195; first three chapters completed, 196; advance from W.W. Norton, 196; research trip to New York for, 210, FMB sends most of manuscript to Brockway, 210; Brockway's first evaluations of, 210–201; critiques from husband and pyschoanalyst friends, 211, 308n.80; sends final manuscript to W.W. Norton, 211; final editing for, 211–12, controversial nature of, 213, FMB receives proofs for, 214; chosen for Book-of-the-Month Club, 214; publication of, 215; popularity of, 4, 185, 215, 219; FMB's publicity trip to the East for, 215; positive reviews of, 217; critiqued for "psychologizing," 218–19; paperback edition of, 227; influences TV series, 243–44; seen as representative of "new social history," 267; impact of on movie *Jefferson in Paris*, 267
Thurston, Jarvis, 68
Tracy, Aaron, 39, 54, 58

UCLA. *See* University of California at Los Angeles

Udall, Stuart, 188
University of Chicago, 56–65, 70–73, 280. *See also* Brodie, Bernard; Brodie, Fawn McKay
University of Utah (Salt Lake City), 11, 25, 45–54, 86
University of California at Los Angeles (UCLA), 167, 238. *See also* Brodie, Bernard; Brodie, Fawn McKay
Unruh, Jesse, 192–94, 304

Vandenberg, Hoyt, Gen., 129
Van Wagoner, Richard, 260
Vietnam War, 183, 206–207, 221, 263
View of the Hebrews (E. Smith), 86
Viner, Jacob, 73
Voorhis, Jerry, 231

Walters, Wesley P., 179, 301n.79
War and Politics (B. Brodie, 1973), 221, 235
Ward-Korsch, Barbara, 247, 299n.47
Washington, D.C., 81, 83, 86–87, 92, 129–30, 132, 194, 215, 227, 239
Waterfield, Gordon, 175
Wayles, John, 197
Weber, Eugen, 202, 301n.88
Weber State University (formerly College), 34, 36–38, 42, 54–56, 58
West, Joelyn, Dr., 231, 245
Wexler, Milton, 140
White over Black: American Attitudes toward the Negro 1550–1812 (Jordan), 194, 218, 304n.27, 305n.42
Wicker, Tom, 265, 318n.16
Widtsoe, John A., 109
Williams, T. Harry, 219
Wills, Barry, 217
Wills, Garry, 227–28
Wohl, Robert, 203, 205
Wohlstetter, Albert, 131; B. Brodie's tensions with, 162–63
Woloch, Isser, 182, 301n.88
Wolpert, Stanley, 203, 260
Woodward, Bob, 223, 232, 248
Woodward, C. Vann, 152
Wright, Louis B., 174
Wright, Quincy, 73
Wyth, George, 197

Yorty, Sam, 169–70
Young, Brigham, 49, 92, 171, 273n.20; FMB considers writing biography of, 178, 188, 226–27
Young, Charles E., 203, 205

Zeleri, Enrique, 247
Zimmerman, Paul D., 175